THE LEGACY OF WINDFIELDS FARM

THE LEGACY OF WINDFIELDS FARM

TURQUOISE AND GOLD, BRED IN THE PURPLE

COLIN NOLTE &
MICHAEL ARMSTRONG

BARIUS
BOOKS

ISBN 978-1-9991685-0-6 (paperback)
ISBN 978-1-9991685-1-3 (ebook)

Barius Books

Produced by Page Two
www.pagetwo.com

Cover design by Jen Lum
Cover photo by Colin Nolte
Interior design by Taysia Louie

mfdarmstrong.wordpress.com
thoroughbredancestry.com

CONTENTS

INTRODUCTION

THOROUGHBRED RACING IS one of the oldest sports in the world and still one of the most popular, followed in all corners of the globe. Racing has grand traditions that have endured for centuries, and more than any other sport it relies on its own rich and colourful history. The pedigree of a racehorse is a snapshot of the past. Meticulous records of every Thoroughbred's ancestry have been charted and preserved for more than three centuries. The breed's name, "Thoroughbred," reflects the strict criteria of breeding one pedigreed Thorough-bred, registered in the stud book, to another. This keeps the breed pure and closed to other horse breeds.

The idea is that through this carefully tracked and planned breeding, the champions of yesterday will produce champions in future generations—but this doesn't always happen. The inexact science of genetics plays an important role. "Breed the best to the best and hope for the best" is an axiom of Thoroughbred breeding. Over the years, certain stallions and broodmares have been exceptionally reliable, producing offspring who either won races or consistently passed on desirable qualities to their own sons and daughters. These stallions and mares then become keenly sought by breeders and owners of racehorses.

Windfields Farm has been a paramount contributor to this ongoing success. Horses from Windfields have had a profound effect, shaping the breed from the middle of the twentieth century to the present day. The farm's great contribution to international horse racing is a Canadian success story, ranking among this country's highest achievements in sport and business. The irony is that the exciting details of this story remain unknown to most Canadians.

Established in 1936 by Edward Plunket "E.P." Taylor on his property in Willowdale, Ontario, Windfields Farm expanded from these humble roots to a large property in the northern portion of Oshawa, Ontario, and ultimately encompassed a sprawling acreage in the Chesapeake Bay area of Maryland.

The first stakes winner bred by E.P. Taylor was also named Windfields. The horse Windfields became one of the foundation sires for the breeding operation, which over time was able to breed and buy stallions and mares who became some of the greatest influences on future generations. The result was the farm attained worldwide fame, with consistent success in the biggest races on the planet. The Epsom Derby, Kentucky Derby, Irish Derby and many more of the most prestigious races have been won by horses bred by Windfields Farm. These same races are now dominated by horses whose breeding bears the mark of generations stemming from Windfields. In many cases multiple Windfields breeding crosses are found in the pedigrees of today's champions.

In the breeding shed, the families of most of the top broodmares and many of the greatest stallions have their roots firmly within the pantheon of the breeding program initiated and nurtured first by E.P. Taylor and then by his son, Charles. Many key advisors and astute horsepeople associated with the Taylor family or in the employ of Windfields Farm have also put their stamp on successful stallion–mare combinations. These breeding foundations are still prevalent today. The equine families have flourished.

E.P. Taylor was a visionary, a man ahead of his time. His ideas and programs revolutionized Thoroughbred breeding. His love of horses and racing led him to continually invest in land for his farms and horses for his breeding and racing stock. As a result, he will always be famous for his beloved Windfields Farm.

Taylor always learned from the past in order to move forward. When he became involved in racing, he was instrumental in improving the sport's status in Ontario using methods similar to those he had used to remodel the brewery business, as we will see in Chapter One.

Another of Taylor's characteristics is summed up in his frequently quoted statement: "When I get an idea, I try to find the best people I can to implement the idea, so I can move on to the next idea. I always found that with anything you do, you could always find someone who can do it better than yourself. That is the secret to success, I think." This was his modus operandi in business and on his farm, which was a business unto itself. He surrounded himself with such highly capable people as Joe Thomas, Gil Darlington, Peter Poole, Bernard McCormack, George Blackwell, Dr. Rolph de Gannes, Joe Hickey, Andre Blaettler, Gordon J. "Pete" McCann, Macdonald "Mac" Benson, Harry Green, John Neville, Ben Miller and many more, all astute and savvy horsepeople who knew their craft very well. He put the ideas forward; these people executed them.

This is not to say that Windfields Farm was a dictatorship, with Taylor determining what was to be done. Far from it. He always consulted his team members and valued their input and opinions. His view was that if you are going to hire the best, consult with the best and respect their experience and intelligence. E.P. Taylor was no fool.

The steady stream of stakes winners and champions from the breeding and foal-raising program of Windfields Farm set new records, raising the bar for other serious breeders and raising the standard by which Thoroughbred breeding farms are evaluated. E.P. Taylor became the first person in Thoroughbred history to be credited as the breeder of record of more than three hundred individual stakes winners. The farm's slogan during the heyday of the yearling sales boom in the 1980s was "The World's No. 1 Source of Stakes Winners." A well-earned and accurate description of the farm's production.

Of course there were disappointments as well as grand successes. Horses are flight animals. They are born to, and love to, run. Horses, especially Thoroughbreds, can be unpredictable and can get themselves into dire situations in racing or on a farm through no fault of their own. Accidents happen. When a horse is injured or becomes seriously ill, every possible method to save the horse is considered and attempted. At times, the injury or illness is too severe for treatment.

Windfields Farm was not immune to the loss of a beloved friend.

The stories of near catastrophe that involved many of the breed-shaping horses in the annals of Windfields Farm are important, as they determined the course not only of Windfields but also of Thoroughbred racing and breeding worldwide for decades after. Tragedy or hardship at the farms in Oshawa and Maryland only served to solidify the unshakable determination of Taylor and the entire staff at Windfields.

Taylor was always ready for a challenge. Early in his horse-breeding career, he was constantly told by fellow Thoroughbred breeders that it was impossible to breed world-class racehorses in Canada due to the severe winter climate. Taylor set out not only to prove that it could be done, but also to establish Canada as a viable and prolific country in the game. Successes in his own program and in the programs of many other Canadian Thoroughbred enthusiasts have markedly proved his point.

Today, Canadian owners and breeders boast many champions around the world, bred by establishments that have their roots in Windfields Farm. This was important to the proud Canadian E.P. Taylor, and he took great satisfaction in the accomplishments of his fellow countrymen.

As the breeder and owner of Northern Dancer, the greatest stallion of the twentieth century, Taylor and Windfields Farm gave the world today's most desired and influential male sire lines. The descendants from this one stallion read like a roll of honour for every breeding jurisdiction of the Thoroughbred industry. However, Northern Dancer is only the tip of the Windfields pyramid. There are many far-reaching breeding influences from other Thoroughbred lines, male and female, descending from the Windfields program. These families have had considerable influence on shaping the breed into the twenty-first century.

In this book, we tell the stories of the great racehorses, the predominant broodmare families and the key people who shaped the destiny of what is perhaps the most successful Canadian sports endeavour in history. Recollections from many of the key contributors to Windfields' success give a unique perspective on how important decisions were made pertaining to specific stallion and mare pairings, purchases of stallions and yearlings, and the ground-breaking advances Taylor initiated in equine care and development. This book is an ode to the people and horses who shaped the fortunes of Windfields Farm and thus the fortunes of Thoroughbred racing worldwide.

Here is the exciting story of the legend and legacy that is Windfields Farm.

{ 1 }

A MAN OF FORESIGHT

I N 1901, THE Dominion of Canada celebrated its thirty-fourth birthday as well as the ascension to the throne of King Edward VII. Queen Victoria, who was the British Empire's longest-serving monarch to that time, passed away on January 22, and her son ushered in the Edwardian era of the twentieth century. Edward VII was a keen patron of Thoroughbred racing and had won the cherished Derby Stakes at Epsom twice when he was the Prince of Wales. When his horse Minoru won the Derby in 1909, Edward became the only reigning monarch to date to win the race.

On January 29, one week after the changing of the monarchy, Major Plunket Taylor and his wife, Florence Magee-Taylor, celebrated the birth of their first child in Ottawa. The proud new parents named their son Edward Plunket Taylor. Little did anyone know at the time that young "Eddie" was destined to become one of the leading businessmen in Canadian history and the leading breeder of Thoroughbred racehorses in the world. He also became the saviour of Canadian racing through his expansive breeding and racing operation, Windfields Farm. With his savvy, forward-thinking business practices, he remodelled the Canadian racing landscape as chairman of the Ontario Jockey Club. So how did this future racing saviour acquire the wealth and business acumen to achieve such success in "the Sport of Kings"?

Growing up in Ottawa, young Eddie was an energetic child. He loved to tinker with things and learn how they worked. He was bright, but school was not his main interest. Sports and the new technologies of the time interested him more. He also had an entrepreneurial spirit, which he would use later in his life to great success. In his own words, he lived a standard childhood. His brother Fred arrived in 1906.

When Britain declared war on Germany in 1914, Canada joined the rest of the British Commonwealth in the "war to end all wars." Major Taylor, at age fifty-two, was called back to military duty to serve his king and country. Once he was established in his posting in England, Plunket Taylor sent for his family. They arrived in Hampstead, England, in 1916. Also on the voyage, the first for Eddie, was his grandfather, Charles Magee. The seventy-five-year-old Magee was a successful businessman in Ottawa and had holdings in a diverse array of companies. Magee stayed in England only a week before he returned to Canada.

When patriotic Eddie tried to enlist in the British Army, his father, now Lieutenant Colonel Taylor, would have none of it. He sent his son back to Canada to live with Magee.

By this time, Eddie Taylor was a strapping six-foot teenager with plenty of drive. While he was living with his grandfather, Eddie began to take a greater interest in the workings of business. He had a good mentor in Magee, who held investments in banking, a trust company, a railway and a brewery. Magee noticed his grandson's potential and guided the impressionable sixteen-year-old in the world of finance.

Unfortunately, Charles Magee passed away the year after Eddie's return to Canada. The loss of his grandfather saddened young Eddie, but the older man had given him a foundation in business and left him with the tools he would use in his future career.

Edward Taylor took his first job, as an apprentice toolmaker, the summer after his grandfather died. After graduating from high school, he was accepted at McGill University in Montreal and began studies in engineering there in the fall of 1918, shortly after his father, mother and brother returned from England. While attending McGill, Edward invented a more efficient two-sided toaster and sold the patent, which financed his education. From this bit of ingenuity, the seeds were planted for Edward Plunket Taylor to begin his rise to entrepreneurial and financial success.

During his McGill days, Edward also discovered Thoroughbred horse racing, a life-changing experience that became a passion. He frequently attended Blue Bonnets racetrack in Montreal. Taylor did not grow up around horses, but when the racing bug bit him, it bit hard. As with everything he was interested in, he learned as much as he could about the thrilling action of racing and the wagering that went along with it, immersing himself in both pursuits with zeal.

Edward graduated from McGill in 1922 with a Bachelor of Science degree in engineering, though he would never earn a paycheque as an engineer. After university, Taylor returned to live with his parents in Ottawa. Jobs were scarce in those days, so Edward ventured into his first business, purchasing a bus and creating the Yellow Line Bus Company. He sold the company a year later and used the profits to set up his Red Line Taxi Company. After establishing the company as a solid business, he sold this enterprise at a profit as well. This business is still in operation today and is known as the Blue Line Taxi Company.

During the mid-1920s, young Edward was busy. He joined the Princess Louise Dragoon Guards and learned how to ride horses. A natural athlete who had played on the football and hockey teams at McGill, he now took up golf as a hobby. He ventured into his father's profession and sold securities for the McLeod Young Weir firm, and he also gained a seat on the board of Brading Breweries, the brewery his late grandfather had shares in.

In 1926, Eddie Taylor met a spirited young lady named Winifred Duguid at the club where they both played golf. The two were instantly smitten, and Edward married the Lancashire-born Winifred on June 17, 1927, in Ottawa. Their union produced three children, Judith, Louise and Charles, and a lifetime of enjoyment from their shared interest in horses.

By now, Taylor was on his way as a successful securities salesman. After selling his taxi business, he could devote all his professional time to this endeavour, and things went so well that in 1928 Eddie and Winnie moved to Toronto. He flourished working for McLeod Young Weir, but it was his seat on the Brading Breweries board that opened up opportunities for him to become wealthy and successful beyond all expectations. His timing could not have been better.

The influence of the temperance movement, which campaigned to have the manufacture and consumption of alcohol banned, had become stronger during the years of the First World War. Because Canada was a young country, largely populated with first-generation immigrants from Europe, primarily from the British Isles, the idea of abstaining from alcoholic beverages was often seen as an affront to their normal way of life. But the temperance supporters were zealous, and between 1915 and 1921, most provinces imposed some form of prohibition, including Quebec and Ontario, the provinces with the largest manufacturing and distribution sectors. Quebec's prohibition lasted less than a year, but Ontario's lasted for nine. Finally, in 1926, the province re-elected a premier who had promised to lift the drinking ban, which he did in 1927.

The ever-alert Edward Taylor was aware of this and devised a plan for Brading to be ready to supply Canadians with the beer they would consume. In 1930, he took a leave of absence from his well-paying job at McLeod Young Weir and began to implement his plan of acquisitions and mergers to grow the brewing business. In a few short years, he had changed the face of the brewing industry in Ontario by buying struggling breweries and either closing them down or expanding their operations, depending on the viability of the plant. In doing this, Taylor developed a singularly strong and prosperous business. There were troubles along the way, as in any business dealings, but the resourceful and driven Taylor pressed on. He built Brading into the largest brewing company in Ontario, earning for himself the public nickname "Beer Baron." Brading eventually became known as Canadian Breweries Limited and encompassed such brands as Carling, Kuntz, Regal, Capital and O'Keefe. The manner in which Taylor expanded the company became a template for future business enterprises, including, in later years, his remodelling of racing in Canada.

His success in consolidating the brewing industry gave Taylor new wealth and a respected standing in the business community. By 1936, he and Winnie had purchased a parcel of land in Willowdale, just north of Toronto, where they established their residence. Winnie named the property "Windfields," due to the winds that blew across the property nearly constantly. Windfields was the Taylor family's home for many years and eventually spread to 250 acres of prime real estate.

In spite of his success, which might have been enough for other businessmen, E.P. Taylor could not, or would not, sit still. He branched out into all sorts of businesses, such as debentures, household products, land acquisitions for housing development, soft drinks, tractors and farm equipment, sawmills, and grocery chain stores. Among the companies he controlled were Canadian Food Products, Massey-Harris, Orange Crush, Standard Chemical, Dominion Stores, British Columbia Forest Products, Dominion Tar and Chemical, Standard Broadcasting, and Hollinger Mines. In the mid-1940s, he merged all his business holdings into the massive Argus Corporation. E.P. Taylor and his partners had a financial stake in so many consumer products that it was difficult for Canadians to buy a product that was not associated with Argus.

Later Taylor took his business acumen to other parts of the world. He brewed and sold beer in England, pioneered the concept of gated communities in exotic places, and built housing and estates in the Bahamas. In 1959, he founded the exclusive Lyford Cay gated community on New Providence Island in the Bahamas. To this day, members of the Lyford Cay Club include some of the world's wealthiest people.

Taylor was a cutting-edge sort and developed the concept of the community within a community. His idea for building houses in a planned area created the subdivisions we all take for granted today. A testament to his vision is the long-established Don Mills area in northeastern Toronto. His philanthropic projects included the Art Gallery of Ontario and the O'Keefe Centre for the Performing Arts.

"People don't understand that the principal motivation for me is not money," Taylor once said. "I enjoy doing something that is constructive. There are people who like to paint or garden. I like to create things."

E.P. Taylor became a powerful and well-respected man in the business community. He had contacts, and made friends, with many bankers and business moguls, as well as high-ranking politicians. These connections led Taylor to become a dollar-a-year man during the Second World War. Among his wartime appointments, Taylor was the vice chairman of the British Supply Council in North America (which bought wartime supplies for Britain) and Canadian chairman of the joint war aid committee. He was also executive assistant to C.D. Howe, federal minister of Munitions and Supply, essentially becoming Howe's right-hand man.

Taylor devoted himself to the present task, leaving decisions regarding his personal business dealings to trusted staff. He was instrumental in the dispersal of arms to the Allies and made a significant contribution to the war effort that has often gone unnoticed in the history books. Taylor was responsible for getting the needed ammunition into the hands of the front line soldiers for many of the important campaigns of the war. His savvy organizational skills were a key ingredient to achieve such success.

Taylor's responsibility as liaison to the British and American Armed Forces required him to travel to meet important people in the war effort in the United States and England. During a trip to England in December 1940, the ship he was passenger on, the *Western Prince*, was torpedoed and lost. Taylor, C.D. Howe and other survivors bobbed around the north Atlantic in lifeboats for eleven frigid hours until they were rescued by the crew of the *Baron Kinnaird* under Captain Dewar. Dewar was relieved of his command because he had disobeyed Admiralty orders that ships not alter course or stop to take on survivors for fear they would also be torpedoed. But if Taylor, Howe and all the others in the lifeboats had perished in the sinking of the *Western Prince*, what would Canada, and the world, look like today without their wartime contributions? And in the case of Taylor, what would the world of horse racing look like?

Let's Go Racing and Sell Beer

During the 1930s, after the shackles of prohibition were removed, another shackle of sorts came to light for the brewing business. Beer and alcohol could not be advertised in the newspapers and magazines of the day, or on what was then the new medium of radio. Ever resourceful, E.P. Taylor came up with an idea. One of his recent brewing acquisitions was the Cosgrave Brewery, and he was keen to promote this brand. Taylor's idea was to start a racing stable, which he would name the "Cosgrave Stable." If one of the stable's horses won a race, the resulting race chart in the newspapers would have this name under the owner heading. This was not advertising the beer, but it did put the Cosgrave name into the mind of the reader.

Ever since he attended the races in Montreal during his McGill days, Taylor had wanted to take his participation in the sport to a higher level. He was a frequent patron of the racing scene in Toronto and had made some friends and good contacts within the Ontario Jockey Club, the governing body for many of the racetracks in Ontario. Now he told his Jockey Club friends that he wanted to become involved in racing on an ownership level and needed to find someone who could make this possible and train his horses.

Someone gave E.P. Bert Alexandra's name, and the beer baron put a call out to the fellow. Alexandra had done well in racing and was thinking about retiring. But he was intrigued by this call from a man he knew nothing about, who told him he was looking to start a big racing stable and needed a trainer. So on April 25, 1936, Bert Alexandra drove to E.P. Taylor's office.

Alexandra was not one to do things by half measures. If he was to delay his retirement, he would have to be fully committed to his new client. The two met, and during the conversation, Taylor told Bert that he had $6,000 to invest. Bert considered this, then told E.P. that he would put off his retirement to acquire and train horses for him if E.P. agreed to one stipulation. Bert owned a racehorse named Madfest, and the stipulation was that Taylor had to buy the horse as he, Bert, did not want to own horses and train for someone else. Alexandra viewed this as a conflict of interest. Taylor agreed to buy Madfest and became a racehorse owner that day. With the deal consummated by a handshake, Taylor gave Alexandra the money. A few days later, the trainer set off for Pimlico racetrack in Baltimore in search of horses to stock the new Cosgrave Stable.

Even in E.P. Taylor's wildest dreams, he could never have imagined what would transpire in the next two weeks. Alexandra was a master at acquiring horses in the claiming ranks and winning with them. He arrived at Pimlico and quickly went to work, buying an eight-year-old gelding named Annimessic for $500. He needed to start the horse in a race in order to qualify to claim horses at the meet, so on May 1 he started the horse in a claiming race, and Annimessic won. The purse (winnings) was $1,000, which gave Bert more cash to work with.

The trainer sent his new boss a telegram, congratulating him on his first win. Taylor was puzzled. Alexandra had only been gone a few days; how could he have had a winner so soon? Taylor suspected his new employee might be a bit loony, so he called him in Maryland.

Bert proceeded to tell his new boss that his new horse had won the second race on the card that day. Even E.P. Taylor, a man who never let time stand in his way when accomplishing things, was stunned by the speed at which Bert Alexandra was stocking his new racing stable. Within the next ten days, Bert the "claiming king" acquired five more horses for the Cosgrave Stable.

Among the horses Alexandra acquired on behalf of his client were the colt Jack Patches and the filly Nandi. The former would be the first stakes winner campaigned by E.P. Taylor, while Nandi became a foundation mare for Taylor's future breeding farm. In fact, hers is one of the exalted names in Windfields history.

Alexandra brought the new Cosgrave Stable back to Toronto in time for the May 24 opening day of the spring meet at Woodbine. Every horse that Bert bought or claimed at Pimlico won during the seven-day meet—and three of them won twice. The stable was off to a fantastic start.

The highlight of the year came a few months later when Jack Patches won the Autumn Handicap. E.P. Taylor was hooked. There was no going back.

He was still very busy with the brewing business at this point, so he had Jimmy Cosgrave, former president of Cosgrave Brewery and now on the Brading Breweries board, oversee the stable. Jimmy did not have a financial stake in the stable that bore his family name, but he was an enthusiastic racing fan and gladly accepted this duty.

The Cosgrave Stable carried on for ten years, winning a very respectable 355 races. Taylor expanded the stable with purchases of yearlings, while Bert Alexandra claimed more horses, lost some to claims and generally continued to be a successful trainer.

In September 1936, Taylor bought a yearling filly by Osiris II, out of Belmona by King James, and named her Mona Bell. This filly was Taylor's first equine star, and he would experience the highs and lows of the racing game with her. Mona Bell won the Breeders' Stakes, the Maple Leaf Stakes and the Orpen Memorial. She was also second in the King's Plate to the popular Bunty Lawless. When these two raced against each other, they made great headlines and brought out the fans. To the great joy of those fans, it was announced that Mona Bell would be bred to Bunty Lawless after the 1939 season. However, Mona Bell broke her leg in a race at Stamford Park and could not be saved. She was buried in the infield at the track.

Four years later, Taylor purchased Mona Bell's full sister and named her Iribelle. We will hear more about her later in this volume.

Taylor was a regular purchaser of yearlings for many years. In 1938, he bought a yearling filly by Gino, out of Dark Fairy by Traumer. Given the name Fairy Imp, the filly won only two races, but when she was bred to Bunty Lawless, she produced E.P. Taylor's first King's Plate winner, Epic.

By the time Epic came into the world in 1946, E.P. Taylor had fulfilled his wartime obligations and returned to running his business empire. He had dabbled in breeding during the war, and now he committed fully to developing Thoroughbreds in Canada, establishing a breeding farm on his Willowdale property. But it was during the war years that Taylor bred the horse that would forever solidify his commitment to racing and breeding racehorses.

E.P. Taylor sent Nandi to Bunty Lawless in 1942 for a breeding liaison. The resulting foal, born the following spring, was a dark brown colt that looked like he could be a good one. Winnie wanted to name him after their estate, so the brown colt was known as Windfields. Windfields became the first stakes winner bred by E.P. Taylor.

As a two-year-old in 1945, Windfields broke the track record at Woodbine when he won the 5-furlong Victoria Stakes in 59 seconds flat. This performance came on the heels of his smashing debut, which he won by six lengths. He went on that season to win the Goodwood Plate and the Rosedale Purse. In the latter race, Windfields lowered his own track record but sustained a knee injury that curtailed his initial season.

Due to a quirk in the rules of the day, Windfields was ineligible to run in the King's Plate, Canada's most prestigious race for three-year-old Thoroughbreds. He had spent time racing outside Canada, and the prevailing rules prohibited Plate contenders from racing beyond Canadian borders before entering the race. So Bert Alexandra raced Windfields in the United States, with some degree of success. He finished second to Triple winner

Assault in the Dwyer Handicap, and beat Australian champion Shannon at Santa Anita. The 1946 King's Plate was won by another crack three-year-old named Kingarvie.

Kingarvie was bred and raced by Canadian auto pioneer Colonel R.S. "Sam" McLaughlin at his Parkwood Stables in Oshawa, Ontario. McLaughlin was one of the leading patrons on the Ontario circuit. He had previously won the Plate with Horometer and would own the following year's winner, Moldy. The press and the public developed a "who is best" rivalry between Windfields and Kingarvie during the spring and summer of 1946. Both Taylor and McLaughlin were sportsmen and agreed that the two horses should meet in the prestigious Breeders' Stakes to settle the issue.

The race did not go off without a unique story to tell. E.P. Taylor was getting an awful lot of flak from fans and the press, who were asking why Windfields did not come back to race in Canada. He had to talk his trainer, Bert Alexandra, into bringing the well-raced colt home from Belmont Park for the showdown with Kingarvie. The plan was to fly Windfields from New York to Toronto, but the ceiling in the cargo plane that the colt was to board was too low. Taylor had boldly announced that his star would be in the Breeders' Stakes, so with this latest setback, he found himself in a predicament.

There were only a handful of planes that were equipped to carry horses in those days. One of those was in California. Taylor called a friend, the president of American Airlines, and arranged for the plane to go to New York, pick up Windfields along with his groom Andy and trainer Bert, and then continue to Toronto in time for the race. The plane had four engines, and such an aircraft had never been flown into Toronto before.

C.D. Howe was also flying to Toronto in a four-engine plane, and he was designated to be the first passenger to do so. A crowd of reporters had gathered at Malton Airport in Toronto to greet

Howe and record the momentous landing. However, the plane carrying Windfields arrived before the one carrying Howe, and the reporters became confused when the passengers emerging were a horse, his groom and Bert Alexandra. C.D. Howe's plane touched down half an hour later. Windfields became the first horse to be flown into Canada, and he pushed his owner's former wartime boss off the front pages of the local newspapers.

The race was the next day, and despite the hasty travel plans for Windfields, the colt overcame everything, including a lacklustre start, to win the race by five lengths. Windfields was then flown back to New York, thus becoming the first Canadian horse to fly out of Canada.

By this time, Taylor had changed the name of his racing operation from Cosgrave Stable to Windfields Farm, and he had his own racing colours: turquoise tunic with gold polka dots on the sleeves, and a gold cap. The racemares in the Cosgrave Stable became the nucleus of the Windfields broodmare band. E.P. Taylor was investing on a greater scale in bloodstock, primarily in yearlings, and began expanding his breeding operation at Willowdale. He studied pedigrees and breeding methods, sought advice from successful friends he made in racing and hired the best horsemen he could.

In 1949, E.P. Taylor came very close to becoming a partner in a syndicate hoping to purchase Nasrullah, a racehorse in England who became one of the most important stallions of the twentieth century. The syndicate included fellow horsemen "Bull" Hancock, William Woodward and Harry Guggenheim. Taylor was acting as the lead, negotiating the deal with the horse's owner, Joseph McGrath, because Taylor had connections in English banking. The purchase was set to take place, with Nasrullah coming to stand at Hancock's Claiborne Farm in Kentucky, when Taylor was advised by McGrath's agent that the English pound was to be devalued on the next business day.

Since the deal was in that currency, McGrath was not inclined to complete the transaction. (Hancock was successful a year later and brought Nasrullah to Kentucky, but at three times the price from the previous year. Taylor was not involved in this transaction.)

The following year, E.P. Taylor became interested in purchasing a young stallion named Relic. The dark bay, almost black, horse was a son of War Relic, who in turn was a son of the legendary Man O' War. Relic was out of the Black Toney mare Bridal Colors and had won the Hopeful Stakes as a two-year-old and the Bahamas and Hibiscus Stakes at three. He came from the successful breeding program of Colonel E.R. Bradley's Idle Hour Stock Farm in Kentucky.

As Taylor was preparing to leave Toronto for Lexington to personally make the deal for Relic, he ran into his friend François Dupré, who asked if he could hitch a ride to Lexington as he was going there to discuss some business of his own. While en route, Dupré told Taylor that he was going to Kentucky to buy a stallion for Haras d'Ouilly, his stud in France. The stallion in question was none other than Relic.

With a bemused look, Taylor informed Dupré that the reason for his trip was also to buy Relic. Taylor then told his friend that he would defer to Dupré and would only make an offer for Relic if Dupré could not reach a purchase agreement. Dupré was successful in his negotiations and bought Relic for Haras d'Ouilly. Relic went on to sire thirty-two stakes winners, six of whom were champions, including the good stakes winner and sire Olden Times and the very good broodmare Relance. Relance is the dam of Epsom Derby winner Relko, Grand Prix de Paris winner Reliance, and King George VI and Queen Elizabeth Stakes winner Match. Olden Times raced and subsequently stood in the United States. He won many races that are now considered Grade One events, such as the Metropolitan Handicap and the San Antonio Handicap. He became a top-class sire in Kentucky.

Relic would no doubt have been a success in Canada, but Taylor never despaired about not acquiring the horse. Relic's success only confirmed to E.P. that he had a good eye for horses, and it gave him confidence in his own ability to judge a horse and to understand pedigrees. He continued to search for and purchase high-class breeding stock.

As if to make up for his miss on Relic, in 1951, Taylor's Bull Page became the first horse to be officially named Canadian Horse of the Year. Taylor had paid $35,000 for Bull Page in 1948, when he was a yearling. This son of leading sire Bull Lea, out of the Blue Larkspur mare Our Page, went on to establish himself as one of the four pillar stallions of the Windfields Farm breeding program.

E.P. Taylor's passion for racing was far reaching. He bought shares in the Ontario Jockey Club and gained a seat on the board of trustees. He persuaded some of his business friends to invest in horses and enjoy the pleasures that came with owning winning racehorses. Windfields Farm began producing a steady stream of stakes winners. His commitment to racing was now in full force, and when E.P. Taylor was in full force, there was no force that could stop him.

We Need to Establish an Industry

E.P. Taylor wanted to bring Canadian racing out of the backwater where it had been operating and usher in a new era of professional, world-class racing. He had been studying the economics of racing and concluded that the present system in Canada was doomed to fail. He was interested in top-level racing and wanted to breed stakes winners and champions. The current purse structure in Canada, and the bloodlines of most Canadian racehorses, did not encourage such ambitions.

To implement his plan, Taylor began by buying up shares of the Ontario Jockey Club until he had a majority share. Then he instituted a system based on the British racing format that emphasized stakes, handicaps and classic races. This system had been successfully used for over two centuries. He initiated the gradual removal of the eligibility and training restrictions for Canadian-bred horses competing in important races such as the King's/Queen's Plate, thus opening up those races to more horses worthy of entry.

At this point he took a look at the existing facilities and came to the conclusion that most of the tracks were rundown and dilapidated. He examined the charters that each track had. Five of the seven area tracks in southern Ontario were allowed only fourteen days of racing in each calendar year. This was definitely not enough to produce any sort of profit, let alone provide money for lucrative purses and track improvements. So E.P. Taylor, as chairman of the OJC, took a page from his brewery amalgamation plan and began to buy up the area tracks, and their charters, in order to consolidate racing in Ontario. He concluded that only two of the tracks were worth keeping: Woodbine in the eastern end of Toronto along Lake Ontario's shore, and Fort Erie, the beautiful track on the US border near Buffalo. The other tracks were known as "the leaky roof circuit," for good reason. Their stables were ramshackle, almost resembling shantytowns. The tracks were uneven, and the patrons' facilities were abysmal at best. Taylor's plan was to close down five of the tracks. Stamford Park, Dufferin, Thorncliffe, Long Branch and Hamilton were sold to land developers, and the resulting infusion of cash was used for the biggest phase in Taylor's remodelling scheme.

In 1952, he unveiled his plan to build a state-of-the-art racing plant on a tract of land in the Etobicoke region at the western end of Toronto. Many thought he was crazy to build such a place there, but E.P. Taylor was always thinking ahead. He could get more land in this location for the money he had and could expand the site to encompass all sorts of activities in the future. Furthermore, the extra land could house more stables and a bigger track. On a fact-finding trip to California, as his plane descended over Hollywood Park on its way into Los Angeles International Airport, Taylor noticed the parking lot at the racetrack was completely full. He inquired as to the acreage of Hollywood Park. When informed that the facility had just over 300 acres, he immediately contacted his team back home. Taylor instructed them to acquire an additional 300 acres for the racetrack in Etobicoke, raising the total to 720 acres. In his vision, the new facility would need the additional land in order to grow and avoid the restrictions he had seen at Hollywood Park.

The speed at which Taylor moved to make the changes was dizzying to most in the industry. Many of the board members just let him go, riding his coattails and watching with amazement as E.P. Taylor changed the face of racing in Canada almost overnight.

The biggest obstacle to Taylor's plan to make Ontario racing a viable investment was that it required a lot of cooperation from many people, especially from the provincial government. Taylor firmly believed that the taxes the government took from each dollar wagered were far too high. The racing industry needed a bigger take from the wagering dollars in order to offer better purse money and attract more owners and better horses. Taylor organized lobbyists and also personally lobbied the government to reduce the government take on wagering. This took time, but when the government eventually agreed to reduce its take from 12 percent of every dollar to 6 percent, Taylor's vision for racing became reality.

On June 12, 1956, Ontario's premier Leslie Frost cut the ribbon at the finish line of the sprawling New Woodbine Racetrack, and the modern era of racing in Canada began. The first race run at the new track was won by Landscape, ridden by Avelino Gomez and bred and owned by none other than E.P. Taylor.

The new track was a one-mile oval dirt course, with an inner grass course of seven furlongs. There was an additional grass course running parallel to, and outside, the dirt course backstretch, which went around the far turn, then crossed over the main dirt track and onto the inner grass course, thus giving New Woodbine the flexibility to run various distances of grass racing. It was a bold new concept in North America, and the course became the standard by which all the continent's tracks were judged.

The Queen's Plate moved to the track from Old Woodbine, along with other top-class races, while new races were inaugurated. Grass racing became very popular with horsemen and fans alike. (The track at Fort Erie had built a grass course as well, which was one of the reasons why Taylor decided to retain that track when he consolidated the industry.)

The stables and stalls for the horses at New Woodbine were plentiful and first class. There was an abundance of clean housing for the stable staff living there, with a large cafeteria serving hot meals all day, every day.

The amenities were also first-rate—providing something for every racing fan but also for families and businesspeople who might not have a knowledge of racing but wanted a fun day out. In the large five-level grandstand, various restaurants on each level overlooked the track, giving patrons a view of the races while they dined and entertained friends. The food at all restaurants and quick-service outlets was fresh and tasty. Lakes and fountains were placed in the infield to enhance the beautiful setting. And there was a scenic paddock and saddling area directly behind the grandstand, where everyone could have a close view of the stars of the show as they prepared for the next race.

Woodbine became the centrepiece of Canadian racing as soon as it opened and has remained so to this day. It gave Ontario a bona fide world-class facility, as well as two updated tracks in Old Woodbine (later renamed Greenwood) and Fort Erie. But what about the class of the stars of the show?

Well, while E.P. Taylor was changing the face of Canadian racing, he was also busy acquiring and breeding better horses to run at this new modern marvel. His bloodstock population soon became far too large to be easily managed. As was his way, Taylor the entrepreneur came up with a unique plan to remedy the situation.

In 1950, octogenarian Colonel Sam McLaughlin had decided to cease his racing and breeding activities. He approached his friend Eddie Taylor about acquiring his lovely farm Parkwood, situated just north of Oshawa. Taylor was not really looking to buy additional breeding space, but he asked the Colonel to give him a week and he would see what he could do. Taylor began to think that it might be a good idea to have a National Stud in Canada, like the one in England, where well-bred stallions could be housed and which local breeders could access easily.

Taylor made calls to every horseman he knew to see if the scheme could fly. His idea was that nine other breeders could have equal shares in this National Stud, and the property would carry on as a horse-breeding farm, thus keeping it going as Colonel Sam wished. Among the breeders interested was Taylor's French horseman friend François Dupré. Dupré was keen, but his wife was not interested in having a stake in Canadian racing, so Dupré backed out.

Then, when Taylor did the math to see if the scheme was financially viable, he came to the conclusion that a National Stud could not make money for some time. He informed the consortium he had put together of his findings and released them all from their commitments. E.P. Taylor would go it alone and purchase the farm and all the horses from the retiring Colonel Sam. He held an auction to sell off most of the stock, retaining a few stallions and mares, then set about restocking the farm with his own horses.

Parkwood was a beautiful setting and came complete with housing for employees, various barns for mares and foals, training and breaking facilities, and a large indoor arena that also contained a stallion barn. The original tract of land in the purchase consisted of 450 acres. Taylor bought additional land adjacent to the farm over several years, eventually expanding it to 1,450 acres.

As the farm grew, Taylor had a new stallion barn constructed, as well as more modern housing for staff and several additional barns. The new barns accommodated the increased population after the yearling division was moved from the Willowdale farm in 1969 to centralize the entire operation. At peak times during the breeding season, over six hundred horses of all ages could be found on the property.

Taylor hired Gil Darlington to run the operation. Darlington had been running his own Trafalgar Farm until he decided to take Taylor up on his offer and became the farm manager of the newly named National Stud. At Trafalgar, he stood a stallion named Chop Chop, a grandson of Triple Crown winner Gallant Fox, whom he had leased from American owners. Later, E.P. Taylor purchased Chop Chop outright and moved him to the National Stud.

As Taylor developed the new stud, his horses were winning all of the important races on the Ontario circuit. After winning his first King's Plate with Epic in 1949, E.P. Taylor dominated the big race during the 1950s. He bred the first four Plate winners of the decade, making it five in a row with Epic. After a two-year lull, he bred three of the next four to close out the decade. His seven winners were, in order, McGill, Major Factor, Epigram, Canadiana, Canadian Champ, Lyford Cay and New Providence.

By now, Taylor was becoming unpopular with racing fans, who were tired of his stable winning all the time. Taylor hit upon an ingenious plan to trim his horse population and disperse some of his better-bred yearlings to other horsemen. He would hold a sale where every yearling he had was offered at a pre-set price. Once half the colts and half the fillies were sold, the sale was over. If multiple buyers were looking to buy the same horse, their names went into his cashmere cap, and the lucky winner would be drawn from the headgear. By putting all his yearlings on the block, he could not be accused of selling only the inferior horses. And though many fast and successful horses were sold, a great many remained to run in the Windfields colours.

This distribution system put well-bred Thoroughbreds into the hands of other good stables and went a long way to establish a viable and competitive Canadian racing industry. Many significant stakes winners and champions trace back to the program initiated by Taylor. As well, fillies purchased at the sales became outstanding broodmares and made major contributions to the breeding programs of such horsemen as Bill Beasley, Conn Smythe and Jean-Louis Lévesque. The result was that the sales program successfully levelled the playing field in Canadian racing.

While he didn't always lead the list of earnings by owners, E.P. Taylor would lead all Canadian breeders for longer than anyone else before or since. By seeding his first-rate stock throughout the Canadian racing scene, he ensured there were horses capable of competing with those who remained with the Windfields racing stable. Of the seven Plate winners mentioned above, three of them, McGill, Canadian Champ and Epigram, raced for owners other than the Taylors. And other breeders in the Dominion eventually caught up with him as well, predominantly thanks to descendants of horses purchased from the Windfields sales, which improved the overall quality in Canadian breeding. Many of these breeders brought in new blood to breed to their Windfields stock. Canadian-breds were becoming not only classier but also more divergent. It wasn't long before Canadian-bred horses were establishing themselves as legitimate competitors in many of the most prestigious races on the planet.

In little more than two decades, E.P. Taylor had developed a way to get better horses to other stables, orchestrated the building of a world-class racing facility, successfully lobbied for more money in racing coffers and created a market for racing to flourish in Canada. Many of the horses sold at his sales did very well on the track for their new owners. Buyers could see a chance to make their racing endeavour financially feasible. Confidence to invest in racing was at a new high, and it was all down to the vision and hard work of E.P. Taylor.

{ 2 }

MAPLE LEAF PRIDE

THE TRANSFER OF the Oshawa property signalled a seismic shift in fortunes not only for E.P. Taylor, but for Canadian racing and breeding in general. Colonel Sam McLaughlin had bred many stakes winners and champions on the farm, and stood some very successful stallions along the way, including Osiris II and Fairaris. Taylor's first racing star, Mona Bell, was a daughter of Osiris II, and he had privately purchased that one's full sister, Iribelle, from her breeder, Dr. T.H. Callahan. Osiris II died in 1947, having led the Canadian sire list four times.

Sam McLaughlin made his name as the pioneer of horse-power of a modern ilk. He established McLaughlin Motor Car Company in Oshawa and later became the founding president of General Motors of Canada when he merged his company with the large General Motors Corporation, thus establishing

Oshawa as the country's centre for automotive manufacturing. The sprawling assembly plants in the area have been in existence in one form or another for over a hundred years, and they have been the main source of jobs and business for both the city and the surrounding area.

Revered as the founder of the Canadian automotive industry, Colonel Sam is also seen as the founding father of Oshawa. His grand estate, Parkwood, is a National Historic Site and the shining jewel of Oshawa. With its lavish, well-maintained gardens, the property is open for tours throughout the year and has played host to countless local weddings. The grandeur of its architecture has drawn film crews, and Parkwood has been used many times for authentic period settings in historical movies and TV shows.

Parkwood Stables

Under the ownership of Colonel Sam's Woodlands Investments Ltd., the farm property, a few miles north of McLaughlin's home along Simcoe Street, was named Parkwood Stables to honour his beautiful Parkwood estate. The large arena on the farm and Barn Two were originally built on the Parkwood estate site and later dismantled, to be brought from the estate brick by brick and reconstructed in the heart of the farm. Colonel Sam then built a stallion barn that was connected to the arena. These structures are still standing and intact today.

A large main stable was built no more than a hundred feet from the arena. Under Taylor's ownership, this barn became known as Barn Six and was the main foaling barn, where many of the legendary horses bred by Windfields entered the world. This barn is also still standing today.

Colonel Sam spared no expense in building his horse paradise. The arena was well lit, well ventilated and large, 200 by 85 feet, so any number of equestrian activities could take place simultaneously in the event of inclement weather. The lounge overlooking the riding area was luxurious, with a fireplace and leather furniture. There were dressing rooms complete with baths, and tack rooms for storing all horse and rider needs. The entire lounge/preparation area was adorned with ribbons and hardware won by McLaughlin family members. Fifteen hundred ribbons and more than four hundred trophies and plates were on display. The paddocks were spacious and full of lush grass and gently sloping terrain. Every stall in the stables had ample room for its occupant.

McLaughlin bred and raised hunters and jumpers as well as Thoroughbreds on the property. He also raised cattle on the farm. Raising cattle and rotating the herd around different fields and paddocks helped to reduce parasites in the grass, which could affect the general health of the horses. E.P. Taylor continued this practice after he bought the farm, raising an Angus show herd for many years.

Colonel Sam's colours of bright gold, blue and red were a frequent sight in the winner's circle at Ontario racetracks, and Parkwood Stables had been home to several top Canadian Thoroughbreds. The aforementioned King's Plate winners Horometer, Kingarvie and Moldy were bred there. Horometer was a legendary Canadian champion and an inaugural inductee to the Canadian Racing Hall of Fame. A perfect five-for-five juvenile season enhanced Horometer's reputation among turf fans. The undefeated gelding captured the 1934 King's Plate as the $\frac{1}{20}$ overwhelming favourite, shattering the track record by a full second. Horometer lost only one race, by a nose, in his career. Kingarvie and Moldy were back-to-back winners of the King's Plate in 1946 and 1947, and both were sired by Parkwood stallion Teddy Wrack.

McLaughlin was not afraid to spend money on quality Thoroughbreds. He imported a British-bred chestnut yearling colt named Fairaris, who won several stakes races in the United States for the stable, including the Peter Pan Stakes. The well-bred son of Fair Trial, out of Nunnery by Friar Marcus, retired to stud at Parkwood and later became the property of E.P. Taylor when he bought Colonel Sam's farm and breeding stock.

Though the farm was already widely known in Canada as a place where quality Thoroughbreds were born and raised, after Taylor's purchase and subsequent expansion and capital investment, this equine haven became hallowed ground in the Sport of Kings on a global scale.

National Stud Begins

E.P. Taylor still envisioned the farm as a likely spot to create a National Stud similar to the one in England. Since he had decided to go it alone, Taylor needed to acquire additional stallions and mares with the pedigrees he considered capable of improving the breed in Canada. This would take time and considerable investment, not to mention full commitment.

Soon after, the farm welcomed client mares for year-round boarding, along with foaling and weaning services. A fee was set that would allow the farm to break even financially, and many area breeders took advantage of the expertise Windfields offered at the National Stud. Most of Taylor's own broodmares were relocated from Willowdale, and in a short time the farm was running at full capacity.

Beginning with the 1951 breeding season, E.P. Taylor stood stallions at both the Windfields Willowdale farm and the National Stud in Oshawa. Illuminable, Windfields and Admirals Mate stood in Willowdale. Tournoi, Fenelon, Firethorn, Fairaris and Teddy Wrack stood in Oshawa. The following season, Bull Page joined the stallion ranks at Willowdale, while Illuminable transferred to the National Stud. Admirals Mate was returned to his owner, E.G. Burton.

Stallions went back and forth between the two farms, which were only thirty miles apart, until the 1958 breeding season, when the entire Windfields stallion roster and broodmare band moved to Oshawa. E.P. Taylor had acquired additional acreage adjacent to the original land tract and built barns, paddocks and staff housing to accommodate the increase in population. The Willowdale farm became the yearling division, where Taylor conducted his pre-priced sales.

The new National Stud continued the tradition set by Sam McLaughlin, raising quality foals for racing. No detail was too small to be considered when it came to the preparation and care of the horses. Everything was state of the art and continued to evolve to maintain currency throughout the history of the farm. Challenges that came were dealt with swiftly. The farm was a well-maintained and efficiently operated enterprise.

Early Important Personnel

As the operation continued to expand and become more successful, Taylor hired additional staff and key personnel to run various portions of the racing and breeding sections. In 1955, he hired the man who would become his most trusted and essential contributor to the success of Windfields, Joe Thomas.

Thomas was born in Pocatello, Idaho, in 1924, although he was raised in Los Angeles. He did not grow up around horses but developed a powerful interest in the sport when the bug bit him at the age of ten. He and his family would listen to the racing broadcasts on the radio, and young Joe would try to handicap each race. When Joe was in his late teens, he got hands-on experience at the grassroots level, walking hots and rubbing horses for trainer Bob Roberts on the Southern California circuit. His fascination with racing led him to a wonderful career.

He later got a job with trainer John Clark and, through him, learned the ropes of assessing conformation and pedigrees. Joe went to Lexington with Clark in 1950 and immediately took a side job writing for the *Lexington Herald*. His work there got him additional writing work with the *Daily Racing Form* (DRF). While at the DRF, Joe suggested to management that the journal could increase revenue by soliciting advertising. The idea was a smash and DRF management increased Joe's workload and pay.

By 1955, Joe Thomas found he was at his desk more than he was around the horses and the track. He yearned for more direct involvement. Through friends, he met Warner Jones, a prominent breeder in Kentucky. Jones knew E.P. Taylor well and also knew that Taylor was looking for someone capable of overseeing his racing and breeding operation. Warner Jones, having met Joe, figured that Thomas and Taylor would be a perfect match.

Joe Thomas was introduced to E.P. Taylor at a Lexington dinner party Jones was throwing. The two hit it off immediately, just as Warner Jones expected, and Taylor hired Joe later that year, to begin early in 1956. This was a classic case of being in the right place at the right time. Joe's principal duties as outlined by E.P. Taylor were the following:

- maintain records for racing and breeding
- maintain records for purchases and sales of yearlings
- organize the annual yearling sale
- arrange promotion and advertising of stallions and farms
- work with trainers at the track to organize horse racing entries
- ensure all Jockey Club payments were submitted on time and up to date
- work closely with E.P. at all racing and sales functions

Taylor gave Thomas a one-year contract to see if he could handle such an extensive portfolio, which most people would find overwhelming. Joe Thomas not only thrived in his new job, but also became one of racing's most beloved and admired men.

Gil Darlington, as the farm manager, also hired astute and capable people for the National Stud. Dr. Howard Aldous became the resident veterinarian until he left to pursue human medicine in British Columbia in 1973. A tall man of around six foot six, Aldous was a constant and very visible presence on the farm until his departure. He was well respected in the industry for his ability with horses and his affable, easygoing nature.

Peter Poole was one of the first hires when the National Stud opened in 1951. Poole worked as Darlington's principal assistant, learning all facets of operating such a large and constantly evolving farm. Peter became the farm manager in July 1968, when Gil Darlington died, and remained in the role until his retirement in 1986.

Andre Blaettler came to Windfields from Switzerland in 1951. He left to work for three years at Conklin Farm in Brantford, Ontario, as farm manager, but returned to Windfields to become the yearling division manager on Darlington's invitation. Andre's leadership became integral to Windfields' global importance when it came to raising quality foals, as well as to the subsequent success at the yearling sales. Andre remained with Windfields until his retirement in 1988.

Harry Green worked up the ranks to become the head stallion groom, an important job that can be dangerous due to the unpredictability of many high-strung stallions. Harry had a gift for gaining the trust and friendship of such horses. His talent and sociable personality made him another of the highly respected horsemen at Windfields.

Upward Mobility

Acquiring better bloodlines for the National Stud meant careful selection of bloodstock, which required an exhausting amount of time. We have already seen that Taylor was unsuccessful in acquiring Man o' War's grandson Relic for stud duty, or syndicating Nearco's son Nasrullah. He decided he needed to spread his net wider and dig deeper to find the right mix of stallions, broodmares and yearlings. He attended the major sales in Kentucky, flew to the British Isles to attend the big sales there, and worked the phones and telegraphs in search of affordable bloodstock that could improve what he already had. He purchased mares and stallions from England, France, Ireland and the United States, the countries in which the best of the breed were being produced.

This is not to say that every horse in Canada was inferior, but there weren't many that could be considered worth developing for future improvement. Beyond a few stallions he could acquire a breeding right to in the United States, Taylor bred only to the best available stallions in Ontario. Before he acquired Parkwood, the best local stallions were Bunty Lawless, Fairaris, Osiris II, Boswell and Teddy Wrack. Taylor's own stallion Windfields began his influential stud career in 1950. However, this was not enough to see his vision come to fruition.

E.P.'s enthusiastic commitment to racing and breeding led him to contact the British Bloodstock Agency in 1952. He was put in touch with highly regarded bloodstock expert George Blackwell. During their initial conversation, Taylor instructed Blackwell to find him the best mare available in the upcoming sales in Europe. Blackwell identified eight-year-old Lady Angela, a daughter of the great Hyperion, leading sire in England and Ireland six times, as the best and most promising mare to go up for auction. She was due to be entered in the December sales in Newmarket.

Lady Angela was to be sold in foal to Nearco. Nearco and Hyperion were widely considered the supreme stallions of the day, and each had sired many champions and first-class stakes winners. These two also were proving to be sires of sons who became exceptional sires, and daughters who became outstanding broodmares.

Taylor saw a glorious chance to get a foal with the two most productive bloodlines in the world. However, many breeders viewed this union with trepidation. The Hyperion–Nearco cross had been tried many times with somewhat limited success. But Blackwell was quick to note that Lady Angela was out of the Abbot's Trace mare Sister Sarah, who had previously produced Lady Sybil by Nearco. Lady Sybil, from her sire's first crop, was the champion two-year-old filly of 1942. She was also the highest-weighted juvenile, male or female, on the experimental free handicap for the year (an annual ranking of the top two-year-olds to race during the year). So the family of Lady Angela had proven to have a successful alliance with Nearco.

E.P. Taylor wasn't satisfied with having only one foal from this union. He had one request before the purchase. Taylor wanted Lady Angela to have her foal in England and then be bred back to Nearco. Once she was certified in foal, she would be sent to Canada. This took a lot of negotiation, and Taylor had to dig deep into his pockets to attain his request. There was also the stud fee to be paid for the return engagement to Nearco. A deal was reached with Martin Benson, who owned both Lady Angela and Nearco, and Blackwell purchased the mare on Taylor's behalf for 10,500 guineas. Lady Angela produced a chestnut colt in 1953, and after a successful reunion with Nearco, she was shipped to Canada.

Blackwell also advised Taylor to buy Abondance, a mare sired by Maurepas, at the same time as he purchased Lady Angela. Abondance was in foal to a French stallion named Menetrier, and she delivered a dark brown filly at the National Stud in 1953. The filly was named Orchestra, and as she developed, Darlington and Taylor thought her to be vastly superior to most of the other youngsters on the farm. Menetrier was standing at Haras d'Ouilly, the stud belonging to Taylor's friend François Dupré, who had purchased Relic. When Eddie inquired if the stallion was available, Dupré said he was, and the two came to an agreement. Menetrier was shipped to Canada, and both father and daughter played a huge role in the rapidly improving ability of Windfields-bred horses.

E.P. Taylor added other well-pedigreed stallions, such as the well-bred French horse Tournoi, a son of three-time leading sire Tourbillon. Epic, the first Queen's Plate winner bred by Windfields, stood for a few years. Canadian champion Queen's Own, bred by Taylor, and Chain Reaction, bred by Gil Darlington, also spent time as stallions at the National Stud, along with Navy Page, a son of Triple Crown winner War Admiral, and British-bred Espalier, a son of Borealis.

Not every stallion succeeded, and some were out-and-out flops. But the fact that E.P. Taylor was willing to import, breed and generally try to improve the quality of Canadian Thoroughbreds demonstrated his commitment.

Taylor also augmented the nucleus of broodmares in the Windfields colony with additional international purchases. He bought Flaring Top, a daughter of Menow, out of Flaming Top by Omaha, from Bull Hancock at the 1948 Summer Yearling Sale in Keeneland, for $8,500. Six years later, Taylor bought another yearling filly from Hancock, this time by the sensational sire Nasrullah, and named her Ivy.

From Europe came the likes of Queen's Statute, Lachine, Stalina, Mythical II and Fair Colleen. Taylor found a gem of a mare locally in the form of the Teddy Wrack daughter Reply. He purchased Solar Display from Kentucky breeder John A. Bell. Also from Kentucky came Heliostrings, a $20,000 purchase as a yearling. This was a significant sum considering that the filly was a twin (horses rarely have twins, and when they do, the babies tend to be runts, if they survive at all).

In 1956, Blackwell purchased on E.P. Taylor's behalf a yearling grey son of the stallion Grey Sovereign, himself a son of

Nasrullah. The yearling was shipped to Canada and raced under the name Grey Monarch for Windfields. Grey Monarch was the epitome of durability, starting in eighty-three races over a five-year career, and winning thirteen, seven of which were top stakes races. He later stood as a stallion for a few years at the National Stud.

At the same time, Blackwell also secured the dam of Grey Monarch from breeder Dr. F.A. Smorfitt. The mare's name was White Lodge, and she was in foal to Mossborough, a well-bred stakes-winning son of Nearco. White Lodge remained in England and produced a bay colt in 1957, then was bred to Epsom Derby winner Never Say Die. This breeding did not take, but Taylor instructed Blackwell to try the mating again. This time White Lodge became pregnant. Once she was certified in foal, she was sent to the National Stud in Oshawa. The Mossborough colt was sold as a yearling by Windfields and named Whiteborough by his new owner, for whom the horse made seventy-six starts. Whiteborough won several stakes races, including the Valedictory Stakes twice. The Never Say Die colt was also sold as a yearling and named King Gorm by the purchaser, Lanson Farm. King Gorm raced five years, making ninety-three starts and winning the Prince of Wales Stakes, Canadian Maturity and five other important stakes races.

In 1958, Taylor purchased another bellwether filly, Natalma, who would later play a huge role in Windfields' fortunes. Possessing world-class bloodlines on both sides of her pedigree, Natalma infused considerable class in the broodmare band once her racing career ended. Little did the Windfields brass know when they purchased Natalma just how important she would become.

These mares and many more will be covered in depth in later chapters.

Leading Breeder

In 1952, E.P. Taylor became the leading breeder in Canada for the first time. For the next four decades, he dominated the breeders' charts like no one before or since. By the 1960s, he had upped the ante and was dominating the entire North American continent. He stayed at the top from 1960 to 1984, winning more than half the titles over that quarter century, and finishing lower than second only once, when he ended the year in third place.

The success of the breeding program at the National Stud in Oshawa was unparalleled in history. Winning horses were raced by clients who had purchased the colts and fillies from Windfields' annual yearling sales. The Windfields racing stable also campaigned many big winners during this era, mainly homebreds not purchased at the annual sale, with a few yearling purchases scattered in.

The fact that Windfields was winning with horses who had been offered at the sale but had been overlooked by buyers went unnoticed by certain members of the press and public on the day Canebora won the 1963 Queen's Plate. Canebora was the twelfth Plate winner bred by Taylor in fifteen years, and this was the eighth time Taylor accepted the trophy and royal purple bag of fifty guineas personally as the winning owner. He received a loud chorus of boos when he went to claim his prize. Many of the fans had been spurred on by a small faction of negative press writers. E.P. Taylor took it all with a smile and did not display any upset, maintaining his dignity. Secretly it did hurt him, however.

The next year, Northern Dancer won the Queen's Plate following his electrifying victories in the Kentucky Derby and Preakness Stakes. A mere twelve months after Taylor was booed unmercifully, he was enthusiastically cheered as breeder and owner of the beloved Northern Dancer. At the post-race celebration, Taylor was approached by sportswriter Dick Beddoes, whose *Globe and Mail* column had been one of the main sites for Taylor bashing. Beddoes said, "They are cheering you today, Mr. Taylor. That hasn't happened for a while."

E.P. responded with a smile and said, "That was when they used to read your column."

Beddoes smiled. Taylor then added, "Touché." (There will be much more about Northern Dancer's racing and breeding career later in this book.)

Taylor-bred horses were winning not only the Queen's Plate, but also the year-end awards in various divisions. The stallions who called the National Stud home dominated the leading sire lists in Canada. Prices for yearlings from proven stakes-winning mares and their families were rising. The wave of improved Canadian breeding continued to build each year as other Canadian breeders purchased yearlings from Windfields, then raised, raced and bred that stock. A golden age was coming to fruition before the eyes of racing fans.

The farm went from strength to strength. The success of Northern Dancer inspired a flood of inquiries to Gil Darlington from breeders in Ontario and the United States regarding Nearctic's stud services. When Northern Dancer was retired to the farm, the inquiries increased. This new interest from American breeders spilled over to other stallions currently on the farm. This began the exciting chapter in the farm's history of foreign owners and breeders coveting the yearlings up for sale.

Windfields was now firmly on the map in the world of Thoroughbred breeding. Through his efforts to improve Canadian breeding, E.P. Taylor came in contact with the high rollers in the business. These people became his good friends, and it did not take long for Taylor to become a respected member of racing society. In 1958, he had been the first Canadian elected as a member of the Jockey Club of America, and by the 1960s, he was regularly approached when a highly regarded horse was to be retired to stud. He became involved in the syndication of many elite stallions, such as Buckpasser, Dr. Fager, Damascus, Ribot, Sir Ivor and more.

The success of Taylor and his horses was no accident. Many years of hard work and creative equine care went into the standard Windfields daily routine. The farm grew its own hay and dried the harvests in well-ventilated steel barns. Pastures were analyzed every year for parasites and, as mentioned, a herd of Angus cattle was rotated through the pastures to combat affected fields. The farm had conducted studies on different grass types with an eye to eliminating parasites, but it found that there was no magical solution to the problem all horse-breeding farms face; hence the cows, which eliminated the parasitic cycles. A special pellet crunch feed was developed for the growing yearlings on the Canadian farm and, later, the American farm. Windfields was the first major farm to extensively implement palpation of mares to ready them for breeding. Every aspect of the breeding and raising of horses was recorded. No detail was left unanalyzed in the operation, and no expense was spared for the horses' health and well-being.

A Lofty Position

All the pieces for continued success were in place. However, there were also changes beginning in 1967. Nearctic was syndicated and relocated to Woodstock Farm in Maryland, though Windfields retained majority ownership in the stallion. The following year, Northern Dancer was also syndicated and relocated to Windfields' new breeding centre in Cecil County, Maryland. He would now stand at stud across the street from his sire. The National Stud was renamed Windfields Farm. And, tragically, Gil Darlington passed away.

Darlington had known E.P. Taylor from the early years of Taylor's foray into breeding, when he brought his mares to the quality stallions at Gil's Trafalgar Farm. Gil had overseen the Oshawa farm from the beginning. He was the one who hired competent and talented horsemen to take care of the horses, and the farm's success was the embodiment of his excellent organizational skills and innate horsemanship. Gil was the main man.

Although the death of Gil Darlington was a great loss, his assistant, Peter Poole, seamlessly took over the helm. Poole had begun working on the farm as soon as E.P. Taylor purchased the property from Colonel Sam McLaughlin. He worked his way through the ranks in various divisions until becoming Darlington's principal assistant. Darlington knew talent when he saw it, and he educated Poole in the intricacies of breeding farm management.

Poole's ascension to the position of manager came just as Windfields entered the era of worldwide success. Darlington's nurturing got the farm to this point, but his protege, Poole, steered the farm during the heyday years, working tirelessly with Joe Thomas and the crack team already in place.

It was also in 1968 that E.P. Taylor abandoned his private yearling sales and entered Windfields' entire yearling crop in the Canadian Thoroughbred Horse Society (CTHS) sales at Woodbine. This decision caused an uproar from many of the local consignors, who thought that buyers would be swooning over the Windfields yearlings on offer and ignoring the other yearlings. What they failed to realize was that with the addition of the Windfields yearlings, prospective buyers from around the world would be attending. What had been a local, rather parochial, yearly sale was now a prime destination for racehorse owners with deeper pockets. The result was new record prices for horses sold at Canadian public auction. Many of those records were set by the cream of the Windfields crop, but the fears of other local breeders were set aside when they saw an upswing in revenue for their yearlings due to the attendance of the wealthier buyers.

Three of the youngsters in the initial public consignment of Windfields yearlings went on to worldwide fame. All three are now members of the Canadian Racing Hall of Fame.

A full brother to Viceregal, the leading two-year-old of 1968, went unsold with a $100,000 reserve. The strapping chestnut son of Northern Dancer was retained by Windfields for racing and was named Vice Regent. After a brief and unlucky racing career in which he displayed exceptional talent but did not win a stakes race, Vice Regent was retired and became a wonderful stallion at the Oshawa farm.

A bay filly by New Providence, out of Shining Sun, entered the sale with no reserve. She was bought by Charles Taylor when the bidding stalled. He named her South Ocean, and she went on to win the Canadian Oaks, defeating champion Fanfreluche. Later, she was the dam of champions Storm Bird in Europe and Northernette in North America. Both were sired by Northern Dancer.

The third big name to emerge from the 1968 yearling sale was an impressive bay colt sired by Northern Dancer, out of Canadian champion Flaming Page. The colt, a son of two Queen's Plate winners, became the record-breaking sales topper. Racing in Europe as Nijinsky, the Taylor-bred became the first winner of the British Triple Crown in thirty-five years. Nijinsky blew the lid off the notion that superior horses could not be bred in Canada.

Nijinsky, Vice Regent and Storm Bird each became outstanding sires, important branches of the fabled Northern Dancer sire line that dominates breeding to this day.

The emergence of Windfields-bred horses on the world stage, beginning with the success of Nijinsky, set the scene for the incredible string of champions and breeding successes to come from the Oshawa nursery. No longer was the farm a haven only for Canadian racing participants. The world had come to Canada, and Windfields kept delivering the goods.

In time, the demand for Windfields yearlings led to the farm sending consignments to the elite sales in Kentucky and

Saratoga. After the yearling division was moved from Willow-dale to Oshawa in 1969, visitors from around the world came to the farm to view them each year. Andre Blaettler, the man in charge of the yearlings, would escort the eminent bloodstock agents and big-spending owners around the paddocks so they could see the horses in action. These visitors would have the Windfields yearling catalogue in hand and make note of the colts and fillies they had an interest in.

During the busy time of prepping and selling yearlings, Andre's staff would swell to thirty-six handlers. These extra employees, primarily students with a background in horses, came from around the world or just down the road in Oshawa or Toronto. They were in addition to the sixteen to eighteen full-time staff entrusted with the yearlings' well-being. Despite the busy nature of the operation, the farm always had a serene and peaceful feeling, which was important when it came to han-dling highly strung Thoroughbreds and safely bringing them to maturity.

By now, Windfields had gained a devoted following among average racing fans. The farm published periodic newsletters and annual stallion handbooks documenting the accomplish-ments achieved by Windfields' racing and breeding divisions. The stallion brochures gave breeders and fans insight about the individual horses as well as their pedigrees, and included descrip-tions of their merits and achievements. These publications were mailed to anyone who signed up to be on the mailing list.

Changing of the Guard

Continuity at Windfields Farm in Oshawa was provided by Peter Poole and Andre Blaettler, but other long-time staff members were leaving and new people joining the operation. Alan Kerr and Bruce Clazie were two men who came to Windfields in the late 1960s and early 1970s and made significant contributions to the continued success of the farm. Alan became responsible for the stallions, while Bruce served in many capacities and eventually headed the broodmare division.

When Dr. Howard Aldous left veterinary medicine in 1972 and went back to school in British Columbia to study human medicine, Peter Poole hired Dr. Rolph de Gannes, a native of Trinidad and Tobago, to replace him. Dr. de Gannes received his veterinary training at Guelph University, where he met his wife, Sheila, before moving back to his homeland. He practised veterinary medicine and trained Thoroughbreds in Trinidad, but he visited Canada often and had made several friends and contacts in the horse business.

In 1980, an English rider by the name of John Neville arrived at Oshawa. Having previously worked for Ian Balding at Kingsclere in Newmarket, John had been associated with some elite horses, the most notable being the marvellous Mill Reef. John also had a front-row seat at Epsom for the 1977 Derby when Hot Grove, a horse he worked in training, finished a neck behind a Windfields-bred, The Minstrel, following a stirring stretch duel for Derby glory. John began with the yearling division in the breaking and training area. He helped trainer Mac Benson at Woodbine and assisted in Barn Six during foaling season. Eventually, he came under the leadership of Andre Blaettler in the yearling division and took over the helm of this important section when Andre retired in 1988.

Bobby Pearson was another English-born ex-jockey who immigrated to Canada after he was hired to work at Windfields. Bobby came into contact with E.P. Taylor in England when he was working for Ron Smythe, who trained Taylor's small stable based at Epsom. Taylor, noticing the young man had excellent work habits and good horsemanship, offered him employment in Canada. Bobby accepted and brought his young family over in 1967 to live in one of the cottage-style houses on the farm reserved for farm employees.

In 1979, a young Irish lad, son of a successful turf writer, was looking to establish himself in the Thoroughbred world. Bernard McCormack came to America and eventually found a job at Windfields Farm in Chesapeake City. He worked there for ten months before accepting a transfer to the Ontario farm. Here he worked up through the ranks to become Peter Poole's assistant, taking over the post of farm manager in 1986 when Peter retired. Bernard was the main man in charge of Windfields' breeding and foal raising after the death of Joe Thomas, the retirement of Peter Poole and the closing of the Maryland farm. He oversaw the continued importance of Vice Regent and the addition of successful stallions Ascot Knight, Silver Deputy, Regal Classic, Dom Alaric and more. His leadership also steered the farm in new directions as a consignor for other Canadian breeders to the elite yearling sales, providing this service to many breeders of high-class stakes winners.

The biggest change in leadership for the Oshawa farm came late in 1980. E.P. Taylor suffered a debilitating stroke that left him incapacitated. His son, Charles, had been taking on more duties in the years before his father's illness, and he subsequently took control of the entire operation. With the guidance of Joe Thomas, George Blackwell, Peter Poole and Maryland manager Joe Hickey, Charles immersed himself in the task at hand. He put aside his successful writing career, though not entirely, and helmed the family equine empire.

The passing of the baton of responsibility was one of the key ingredients for the continued success of the farm. This, along with the outstanding equine families first developed by E.P. Taylor and his advisors, the breakthrough developments in equine care and research, and the total commitment of all involved, solidified the importance Windfields Farm had attained in Thoroughbred breeding.

{ 3 }

THE FOUR PILLARS

IN THE HISTORY of every successful Thoroughbred breeding farm, there are seminal stallions that play an important role. In the case of Windfields Farm, four stallions made significant contributions to the long-term success not only of Windfields but also of other breeders and owners who bought Windfields-bred yearlings at the big sales, even long after those "Four Pillars" were gone. The four stallions were Chop Chop, Menetrier, Bull Page and Windfields.

E.P. Taylor used the top existing Canadian bloodlines, notably Bunty Lawless and Fairaris, and augmented that blood with astute bloodstock purchases. He made contacts with people in the industry who had connections to top-class stallions and mares. By studying breeding patterns and bloodlines, and investing intelligently in yearlings and mares for breeding stock,

E.P. Taylor launched his breed-development plan. He imported quality bloodlines from England, France, Ireland and the United States. Not every purchase panned out—that would be impossible—but his success rate was astonishing. The result was generation-by-generation improvement in class and racing ability with each successive crop. The upwardly improving Canadian Thoroughbred came a long way in a short time.

Chop Chop, Menetrier, Bull Page and Windfields sired some exceptional daughters that in turn produced stakes-winning families. Later well-bred stallions standing under the farm's banner then had a nucleus of excellent younger broodmares, thus creating the foundations for future world-class stakes winners. The stallions Victoria Park (by Chop Chop) and New Providence (by Bull Page) carried on this trend for improved quality, siring many exceptional daughters when their turns at stud arrived.

Chop Chop

The oldest of the Four Pillars was Chop Chop. Bred by Charles Thierot in 1940 in Kentucky, Chop Chop won four of his eleven races, finished second four times and third twice. His most important wins came in the Endurance Handicap and the Empire City Handicap. In the latter, he set a track record of 1:57 ⅕ at the old Jamaica Park track, defeating champion handicap horse Princequillo in the process. In his only out-of-the-money finish, Chop Chop lost his rider at the starting gate in a race at Aqueduct. The bay horse was a good, honest competitor on the track.

Chop Chop's sire was Flares, a full brother to US Triple Crown winner Omaha. Flares's sire was Triple Crown winner Gallant Fox. Chop Chop came from a solid tail male line (that is, the male ancestral line, working back through the sire, grandsire, etc.), which descended from the great Teddy through his accomplished son Sir Gallahad iii, Gallant Fox and on to Flares. Gallant Fox and his sons Omaha and Flares were all bred by turf legend William Woodward, owner of the famous Belair Stud in Maryland. Flares raced for Woodward in England. Among Flares's eight stakes wins were the prestigious Ascot Gold Cup and the Champion Stakes.

Chop Chop began his stud career in Kentucky, without any support. Bull Hancock, the astute horseman and owner of fabled Claiborne Farm in Kentucky, spoke to Gil Darlington about the stallion. Hancock pointed out to Darlington that Chop Chop's bloodlines were out of style in Kentucky but would make an excellent cross for the Canadian market. Hancock was convinced that the stallion would be a success in Canada. He proved to be a prophet.

Gil Darlington leased Chop Chop in 1947 to stand at his Trafalgar Farm in Ontario, where he was patronized by Windfields Farm, among other Canadian breeders. When Darlington accepted E.P. Taylor's offer to manage his new National Stud in Oshawa, Chop Chop was returned to his owners.

One of the first important stakes winners sired by Chop Chop was Chain Reaction, bred in 1950 by Darlington. Chain Reaction won two Canadian classic races, the Prince of Wales and Breeders' Stakes. He went on to add to his resumé the Canadian Derby, the Durham Cup in track record time, Canadian Maturity, Connaught Cup, King Edward Gold Cup and Dominion Day Handicap, also in record time.

From this same Chop Chop foal crop came the E.P. Taylor–bred Canadiana, who was out of Iribelle, the full sister to Taylor's first major stakes winner, Mona Bell. The superstar filly Canadiana began her Hall of Fame career with important wins as a two-year-old in the Coronation Futurity, Cup and Saucer Stakes and Princess Elizabeth Stakes. The first two mentioned races are the premier stakes events for two-year-olds in Canada, while the Princess Elizabeth Stakes is the top stakes race for Canadian juvenile fillies. Canadiana swept them all.

The following year, Canadiana won the Queen's Plate. After this important victory, she became a major stakes winner in the United States, with wins in the Test Stakes and Vagrancy Handicap, as well as winning other Canadian stakes races like the Jacques Cartier Stakes and the Highlander Handicap.

The early success of Canadiana was the catalyst for Taylor to purchase Chop Chop and stand him at the National Stud in Oshawa, which put the stallion back under Darlington's management.

Chop Chop went from success to success at Windfields. He was now getting better mares, including the best that Windfields had on the farm, and he took full advantage of this. He sired three more Queen's Plate winners, Lyford Cay, Victoria Park and Blue Light, all bred by Windfields. The first two raced in Windfields colours, but Blue Light was purchased from the Windfields yearling sales in 1959 by Colonel K.R. Marshall and raced carrying his colours. After their racing careers, Lyford Cay did not turn out to be a good sire, but Victoria Park did. In fact, Victoria Park became one of the pivotal horses in Windfields history.

And Chop Chop became an important sire in Canada. Many of his daughters contributed to the outstanding tail female lines that came out of the Windfields breeding program (the tail female line is the bottom line on a pedigree, starting with the horse's dam and flowing back through a series of mares to the foundation mare). Ciboulette, Allegro, Shining Sun, Chorus Beauty and Canadiana all contributed worthy stakes winners and important stakes-producing daughters who continued an upwardly improving series of bloodlines. Ciboulette stands tall as the dam of the great Fanfreluche.

The success of Chop Chop as a sire was not lost on the punters at Canadian racetracks. "I have heard of many people who bet on horses, that if there is a son or daughter of Chop Chop in the race, they will put their money on that horse," said Joe Thomas back in 1963. He added, "While this may not seem like a sound system, it does make sense. The offspring of Chop Chop are generally fast, sound animals that can run over a variety of distances and track conditions. You always get a run for your money."

Chop Chop was not an attractive horse. It was said of him that "Chop Chop would finish third in a two-horse beauty contest." Many of his get, or offspring, did not win beauty contests either, but they sure could run, and they displayed character and heart in winning some very important races. He also had spirit, as witnessed by visitors to the Oshawa farm the morning after Victoria Park won the Queen's Plate. E.P. Taylor hosted a garden party that day, and one element of the festivities was to parade some of the stallions out in a walking ring for Taylor's guests to view. Chop Chop, then twenty years of age, came out and spotted a couple of attractive mares in a paddock. He whinnied and hollered at them, reared up to get their attention and proceeded to drag his groom around the walking ring.

By the end of his stud career, Chop Chop had sired twenty-nine stakes winners, which was 14 percent of his total foal population. Eighteen of the stakes winners were bred by E.P. Taylor. Chop Chop was leading sire in Canada seven times. He is a member of the Canadian Racing Hall of Fame due to his influential stud career.

Windfields

Chop Chop blood mixed very well with that of the Taylors' beloved horse Windfields. Everybody in racing and breeding, no matter who they are, has a first love in this wonderful world. For the Taylors, it was Windfields. He was not only named after their estate, but also shared the name of their racing and breeding empire. He was a kind and engaging horse to be around, and he made a substantial contribution to the success of the farm.

Although he was unable to compete in the Queen's Plate, Windfields had a notable affiliation with the classic race. His sire had won in 1938, while his son Canadian Champ won in 1956. Canadian Champ sired two winners of the race, Canebora (1963) and Titled Hero (1966). Canebora also went on to win the Canadian Triple Crown. One of Windfields' daughters produced a Queen's Plate winner, Victoria Park, who in turn sired three winners of the classic race. Windfields' name appears up close in the pedigree of five Canadian Horse of the Year champions bred by E.P. Taylor, and he continues to appear in the ancestry of many more down the line to further generations.

Retired from breeding in 1964, Windfields lived another five carefree years on the Oshawa farm before dying of old age on September 23, 1969. His life and contributions were thoroughly appreciated. He is buried in the main cemetery at the Oshawa farm, in a place of significance and honour. Windfields is a member of the Canadian Racing Hall of Fame.

The aforementioned Ciboulette, by Chop Chop, was out of Windfields' daughter Windy Answer. Ciboulette was purchased at the 1962 Windfields yearling sale by Canadian businessman and keen horseman Jean-Louis Lévesque. Lévesque would tap into Windfields breeding very successfully, with Ciboulette being a cornerstone of his racing and breeding achievements.

Windy Answer was a genuine "blue hen" mare in Windfields Farm breeding history (a blue hen is a mare who continually produces high-quality foals, no matter what stallion she is bred to). Her dam was Reply, a seminal foundation mare in the farm's success. Windy Answer won four stakes races, including the important Selene Stakes. She produced not only Ciboulette but also champion Cool Reception and Princess Elizabeth Stakes winner Breezy Answer.

Cool Reception was a classic tragedy of racing. This stunning horse, with a cinnamon-coloured coat, wide blaze on his face, white sock on his left rear leg, and flaxen mane and tail, was fast, social and radiated class. Canada's reigning champion two-year-old of 1966, he was well in the lead of the 1967 Belmont Stakes when he broke his right front leg during the stretch run. He still managed to finish second to Damascus (who went on to become a Racing Hall of Fame legend). Cool Reception was operated on successfully, but when he came out of anaesthesia, he stood and broke his leg again, right above the cast. This damaged his leg beyond repair, and he was humanely euthanized. Dr. William Reed, the lead vet during the operation, was shocked at the tragic turn of events. He had performed the same procedure many times and had never lost a horse to the circumstances that took Cool Reception.

Larkin Maloney had purchased the colt at the 1965 Windfields yearling sales for $40,000, giving Cool Reception to his daughters to race. E.P. Taylor followed the colt's career and was in attendance on that fateful afternoon at Belmont. Had Cool Reception survived, he would have retired to Windfields for stud duty. Given that his sire was Nearctic and his dam line became known as a sire-producing line, Cool Reception's death was a blow to the breed.

Windy Answer did go on to produce a very good sire in Northern Answer (by Northern Dancer).

Some of the other daughters of Windfields who became essential contributors to the quality of the farm's breeding program were Flaming Wind (out of Taylor's foundation mare Flaring Top), unraced Victoriana (out of the great broodmare Iribelle) and Willow Lake (out of the foundation mare Compensate). Flaming Wind's progeny are covered in Chapter Four. Victoriana produced stakes winners Bull Vic, Victoria Regina, champion Northern Queen and Hall of Fame champion

Victoria Park. Willow Lake produced champion Victorian Prince and major producing daughters Northern Lake, Northern Willow and Willowfield. Many more stakes winners have descended through generations from each of these daughters of Windfields.

Menetrier

Many of the descendants of Windfields' daughters were bred to Menetrier. Taylor purchased this stallion from his friend François Dupré, who bred and raced the horse, and stood him in France for his first few years at stud. Menetrier was a well-bred multi-stakes winner, who won such significant European races as the Prix d'Ispahan, Prix Edmond Blanc, Prix de la Forêt and Prix de la Jonchère (twice). Carrying as much as 143 pounds, he made twenty-nine starts over three racing seasons, won thirteen times and was unplaced only three times.

Menetrier was sired by the outstanding Fair Copy, a son of the legendary Fairway. Bred by Lord Derby in 1934 from the same family that gave the breeding world Hyperion, Fair Copy led the French sire list in 1952 and also sired Sayani, the leading French sire of 1953, who was eventually exported to Brazil and became a leading sire there. Menetrier's dam was La Melodie, a stakes-winning daughter of sprint champion Gold Bridge. La Melodie came from a fine family of French stakes winners.

The dark bay or brown Menetrier had already sired Virgule, winner of the Poule d'Essai des Pouliches, as well as United Nations Handicap winner Blue Choir, when Taylor acquired him for his Oshawa farm. Menetrier was not an easy horse to be around. Actually, he was downright savage. As a precaution, a loaded shotgun was kept close at hand when bringing the stallion into the breeding shed to perform his duties. A specially designed stall was constructed to house Menetrier. It had a low wire ceiling, several feet under the actual roof, that prevented him from jumping or rearing in the stall, thus making it difficult for the crusty stallion to batter the walls or handlers. Even so, there were many hoofprints embedded in the ceiling.

Menetrier's idiosyncrasies and volatile nature were tolerated because of his consistent ability to pass on his speed and class to great effect, thus improving the offspring bred at Windfields.

Victoria Regina was undoubtedly his masterpiece and solidified the name of Menetrier in pedigrees around the world. She produced only three foals, all colts. Two of the colts were sired by Northern Dancer—Canada's 1968 Horse of the Year Viceregal, and thirteen-time leading Canadian sire Vice Regent.

Sadly, Victoria Regina was one of twelve mares to perish in a massive barn fire in Maryland in 1968.

Menetrier also sired Menebora, the dam of Canadian Triple Crown winner Canebora. Canebora was a chip off the old block, not only looking like his maternal grandfather, but also having a big dose of his personality. The champion Windfields runner was in a constant snit around the barn, straining relationships with his human handlers. Even at feeding time, Canebora was a tricky horse to attend to.

Canebora despised music, bugle music in particular, which is unavoidable for a racehorse. He would react violently when he heard the track buglers play the call to the post as the field made its way to the post parade before a race. The tune, sweet to most ears, must have sounded like fingernails on a chalkboard to Canebora. However, there was no denying his speed and racing ability, as his Triple Crown achievement attests.

Menetrier sired Canadian Oaks winner Menedict, who was out of yet another foundation mare, Queen's Statute. Menedict won stakes races in each of her three seasons on the track.

Orchestra was a multi-stakes winner sired by Menetrier for Windfields Farm, who would become a foundation mare in her own right, producing Allegro, Victory Chant and Orchestrina, stakes producers all.

Menetrier sired only nineteen stakes winners, but this was actually 12 percent of all his foals. Today, stallions of noteworthy achievements in the breeding shed can service large books of mares, sometimes more than two hundred per breeding season. In part, this is because breeders now have the advantage of modern medical equipment that lets them determine the optimum time to cover a mare, thus requiring only one cover to complete the task. When Menetrier was plying his trade, old-fashioned husbandry was the prevailing method, and a stallion often had to cover mares two or three times before conception was achieved.

Menetrier led all Canadian sires in earnings in 1955. Many of his get were important in the development of the Windfields breeding program, making valuable contributions to the improving status of Canadian breeding in general.

Bull Page

The fourth pillar stallion was one of E.P. Taylor's early high-priced yearling purchases. Bull Page was acquired at the 1948 Keeneland yearling sales for what was then a princely sum of $38,000. This was actually considered a low price, given his pedigree. His sire was five-time leading US stallion Bull Lea, the foundation patriarch of the great Calumet Farm dynasty. Bull Lea's son Citation won the US Triple Crown the year E.P. Taylor obtained the yearling colt, who was out of Our Page, the excellent producing daughter of Blue Larkspur. Our Page, who won the 1942 Spinaway Stakes, later became a broodmare of the year.

Although the colt was the third-highest-priced yearling in the sale, the perceived low price led Bert Alexandra to ask Taylor, "Why did you get the colt so cheap? Is he lame on all four legs?" Alexandra's suspicions were confirmed when he saw the colt for the first time. Bull Page had very suspect legs, straight in front and short in the pasterns. Such conformational liabilities threatened a short racing career, as they severely reduced the possibility a horse would withstand the rigours of racing.

Bull Page demonstrated his speed early in his training, but those legs became sore after his speed-trial workouts. The colt did not start a race until he was three. Bull Page was fast, winning three of five races, and Alexandra was impressed with him. At the same time, it was a challenge to keep the colt sound enough to compete. Bull Page ended his three-year-old season with a broken bone in his left front foot.

After a successful operation to repair the damage, Bull Page came back in 1951 as a four-year-old and had a terrific record. Starting in sixteen races, the son of Bull Lea won six times, with five seconds and three third-place finishes thrown in. He won the Canadian Championship Stakes, the forerunner of the prestigious Canadian International, as well as the Autumn Handicap. His consistent high placing in top Canadian stakes races was enough to earn him the first Canadian Horse of the Year honours.

Retired to the National Stud in Oshawa, Bull Page lived up to his impressive pedigree and became a solid sire, contributing some very important offspring. He sired four winners of the Canadian Oaks: Air Page, Yummy Mummy, Maid O' North and Flaming Page. The latter also won the Queen's Plate in 1962, becoming the first filly to win both important Canadian classics. Flaming Page went on to become one of the wonderful broodmares in racing, as she is the dam of the great English Triple Crown winner Nijinsky, as well as his champion full brother Minsky. Flaming Page's daughter Fleur also produced an Epsom Derby winner, The Minstrel. Windfields Farm's breeding program reached a pinnacle with the outstanding contributions of Bull Page's daughter Flaming Page.

Bull Page sired 1959 Canadian Triple Crown winner New Providence, who captured three other stakes races, including the important Cup and Saucer Stakes as a two-year-old. This handsome 16.2-hand bay was another unsold yearling who raced for Windfields Farm and later became a key contributor to future E.P. Taylor–bred champions.

Among Bull Page's many other noteworthy offspring are Windfields-bred multiple stakes winners Censor and Bull Vic; his daughter Countess Angela, dam of Queen's Plate winner Titled Hero; and Princess Elizabeth Stakes winner Breezy Answer, who produced top two-year-old Arctic Blizzard.

The contributions of Bull Page and the other three "pillar" stallions to Windfields Farm's breeding program ushered in a new level of excellence. E.P. Taylor was beginning to see the fruits of his investments, and the farm was poised to attain new levels of racing success.

Sons of the Pillars: New Providence and Victoria Park

Although the Four Pillars begot several worthwhile racing sons, only two were similarly successful when they entered stud. These two, New Providence and Victoria Park, continued the tradition of siring daughters who became important broodmares. Unfortunately, the tail male line has not progressed much beyond the Four Pillars' sons. The strength of their contributions lies in the females of the line.

When Bull Page's son New Providence was retired from racing to the National Stud, he replaced his sire, who was sold to a Western Canadian breeding farm. The tall bay New Providence most famously made his mark on worldwide breeding through his daughter South Ocean, who defeated the great Fanfreluche in the Canadian Oaks. When Windfields bred her to Northern Dancer in 1977, South Ocean produced Storm Bird, one of the best two-year-olds ever seen in England. He was purchased as a yearling for $1 million by Robert Sangster. Put into the exceptional hands of trainer Vincent O'Brien, at Ballydoyle Racing

Stable, Storm Bird was unchallenged as a two-year-old in 1980. As a three-year-old, he had to endure a savage attack by a former Ballydoyle employee with a vendetta, who hacked off the colt's mane and tail in a late-night raid. This and a series of nagging injuries restricted his 1981 season to one unplaced appearance on the track. However, at stud he became a great stallion and is most prominently known as the sire of Storm Cat. This is one of the more important male sire lines in the world today.

New Providence got many winners from his limited foal crops. Nineteen of his first twenty foals not only made it to the track but also became winners—an extraordinary feat. He sired another Canadian Oaks winner, Happy Victory, who was the champion three-year-old filly in 1972. New Providence was retired from breeding following the 1975 season and lived on the farm as a cherished pensioner until his death in 1981. He is buried in the cemetery in front of the stallion barn on the Oshawa grounds and is enshrined in the Canadian Racing Hall of Fame.

Another descendant of one of the Four Pillars to continue the legacy is Chop Chop's son Victoria Park. Victoria Park actually represents two pillar stallions, as his dam is Victoriana by Windfields. Offered as a yearling at the annual farm sale in 1958 for $12,500, Victoria Park was not sold and remained with Windfields Farm, to be raced under the famous colours.

Victoria Park was on the small side—15.3 hands at full growth—and had a distinctly toed-in front left foot, with suspect knees. These conformation defects were undoubtedly a concern for prospective buyers and could explain why he was not sold. Victoria Park was also somewhat hard to deal with. He was a determined fellow, which proved to be his greatest asset when he raced. Racing manager Joe Thomas once remarked, "Victoria Park always showed up. He gave his all in training and in his races."

Despite his conformation faults, Victoria Park was a very fast colt. Nicknamed "Ol Pigeon Toes" by the racing press of the day, and "Parkie" by Windfields Farm staff, Victoria Park became the champion two-year-old in Canada in 1959. He won the Clarendon Stakes and the two most important races for Canadian two-year-olds, the Coronation Futurity and the Cup and Saucer Stakes. Trainer Pete McCann then sent him to Aqueduct to win the Remsen Stakes and set in motion the possibility of campaigning toward the US Triple Crown.

E.P Taylor had envisioned that one day he would have a horse capable of competing for the Kentucky Derby. In Victoria Park, he had a genuine prospect for the first time. Taylor was excited at the possibilities. Parkie was put into the training barn of Horatio Luro to take advantage of his experience on the American circuit.

In his first race as a three-year-old, Victoria Park defeated Bally Ache in an allowance race at Hialeah. He set a new track record for the 8.5-furlong test. A runner-up finish in the important Flamingo Stakes and a third in the Florida Derby confirmed his credentials to run on the first Saturday in May at Churchill Downs. In the 1960 Kentucky Derby, Victoria Park became the first Canadian-bred to finish on the board when he came third to Venetian Way and Bally Ache.

Sent to Pimlico two weeks later for the Preakness Stakes, Parkie improved his final position to finish second to Bally Ache, ahead of Venetian Way. Many in the racing world were impressed by the Canadian colt's determined efforts in the first two American Triple Crown races and pegged him as the likely winner of the upcoming Belmont Stakes. There was, however, a problem.

The 1960 Belmont Stakes was scheduled for June 11, which just happened to be the same day as the Queen's Plate at Woodbine. E.P. Taylor had a dilemma. He could keep Victoria Park in the United States and take a legitimate shot at winning the third leg of the American Triple Crown, becoming the first Canadian to win such a race. Or he could return home and try for another Queen's Plate triumph. Taylor was always a proud Canadian and chose the latter. Victoria Park proceeded to win the Plate in a record time that would stand for thirty years. Meanwhile, the Belmont Stakes was won by Celtic Ash, whom Parkie had never finished behind in their previous encounters. To his credit, E.P. Taylor never lamented the decision to skip the Belmont Stakes. He did not view it as a missed opportunity, but as confirmation that his breeding program was on the right path to achieve international competitiveness.

Parkie made one more start before his racing career was cut short by a bowed tendon. He dominated the 9-furlong Leonard Richards Stakes at Delaware Park in track record time. Luro was preparing him for a campaign on the tough California circuit when Parkie sustained his career-ending injury.

Victoria Park was a harbinger of racing success to come. And he played a significant role in that success.

Sent to the National Stud in Oshawa to begin the 1961 breeding season, Victoria Park became an important and successful stallion, siring twenty-five stakes winners, including three consecutive Queen's Plate winners in Almoner, Kennedy Road and Victoria Song. Parkie also sired the very consistent and durable Victorian Era, who later stood at Windfields Oshawa beside his father. In a curious twist that would interest people who follow genetics, Victoria Park was a dominant bay and thus did not sire any chestnut offspring.

His Victorian Era, born in 1962, was the epitome of a fast and durable racehorse. Although he was purchased by Allan Case from the Windfields yearling sale for $25,000, Taylor reacquired the horse in September 1966 for an undisclosed price. Victorian Era, out of the Nasrullah mare Ivy, went on to become Canada's Horse of the Year in 1966. He made forty-eight starts in a four-year career, winning twenty-three races, eighteen of which were stakes races. He added twelve second-place finishes and placed third six times. Victorian Era won with as much as

136 pounds on his back and is a member of the Canadian Racing Hall of Fame.

Many daughters of Victoria Park became outstanding brood-mares, carrying on his line. Victory Chant, Chou Fleur, Arctic Vixen, Flaming Victress, Greek Victress, Solometeor, Song Of Victory, Victorian Queen and Floral Victory all produced champions or daughters that produced champions.

Among the fifty stakes winners from Victoria Park mares are Northern Taste and the great Epsom Derby winner The Minstrel. Northern Taste was out of Lady Victoria, a daughter of foundation mare Lady Angela. The uniquely coloured colt—a bright orange-red chestnut with a white blaze that almost covered his face, two white stockings on his right front and left hind legs, and white socks around the pasterns on the other two legs—was purchased as a yearling by Zenya Yoshida and won the Group One Prix de la Forêt for him. Yoshida retired Northern Taste to his Shadai Stallion Station in Hokkaido, Japan. Here, the flashy stallion became a revelation in Japanese breeding. He led the sire list an unprecedented ten consecutive years and established himself as the most successful sire in Japanese breeding up to that time.

The dam of The Minstrel was Fleur, a daughter of two Queen's Plate winners, Victoria Park and Flaming Page. Three of the pillar stallions appear in the pedigree of this undisputed champion—Chop Chop, Windfields and Bull Page. His sire was Northern Dancer, and he was trained in Ireland by Vincent O'Brien for the syndicate headed by Robert Sangster. The Minstrel won seven of nine races, finishing second once and third once. He was undefeated as a two-year-old, then went on to win the Epsom Derby and Irish Derby, a rare Derby double. In his last race, he bravely won the prestigious King George VI and Queen Elizabeth Stakes as a three-year-old against the top older horses in training.

The Minstrel later stood at Windfields Farm in Maryland and became a great success as a stallion. He encapsulated all the advances Windfields Farm was achieving in Thoroughbred breeding, the genesis of which was the success of the Four Pillars that stood at Windfields in Oshawa.

Although, as mentioned, there is no continuation of the Four Pillars' tail male lines in today's breeding circles, two very prominent horses bred by E.P. Taylor have solidified the names of these stallions. Storm Bird and Vice Regent are sons of Northern Dancer, and each one represents two separate pillar sires close up in his pedigree.

Menetrier's daughter Victoria Regina, out of the mare Victoriana, by Windfields, gave us the previously mentioned Vice Regent, who carved out a wonderful stud career at the Oshawa Farm. Vice Regent is the sire of two-time leading North American sire Deputy Minister, who in turn is the sire of Breeders' Cup Classic and Queen's Plate champion Awesome Again. The latter horse sired Hall of Fame inductee Ghostzapper, who is one of the leading sires at time of writing.

Bull Page's granddaughter South Ocean and her famous son Storm Bird bring in not only her sire, New Providence, a son of Bull Page, but also pillar sire Chop Chop, who is the sire of South Ocean's dam, Shining Sun. Storm Bird's son Storm Cat was also a two-time leading sire in North America and successfully carried the line to worldwide prominence through his son Giant's Causeway and many others.

Both Deputy Minister and Storm Cat have been leading broodmare sires, in keeping with their lustrous heritage, and both have been game changers in the breeding industry. In retrospect, it is amazing that E.P. Taylor collected the Four Pillars and stood them together at the dawn of his breeding empire. The odds against such an occurrence—to stand four stallions during the early stages of a breeding program who end up having such a profound influence on future breeding around the world—are overwhelming, and yet it happened.

Another key ingredient for the success of Taylor and his Windfields Farm was having the foundation of mares from the Four Pillars to be bred to Nearctic and his son Northern Dancer. We'll turn to those mares, both purchased and homebred, next.

E.P. Taylor, the founder of Windfields Farm. PHOTO CREDIT: KEENELAND ASSOCIATION LIBRARY/THOROUGHBRED TIMES COLLECTION

Windfields Willowdale Farm scene. Note the emerging skyline in the background. PHOTO CREDIT: WINANTS BROS./DRUMMER BOY PUBLICATIONS

Top Parkwood Gates circa 1940's. PHOTO CREDIT: PARKWOOD NATIONAL HISTORICAL SITE

Bottom Chop Chop, with Johnny Longden up, in the winner's circle after defeating Princequillo in the Empire City Handicap. PHOTO CREDIT: KEENELAND ASSOCIATION LIBRARY/SIRICO COLLECTION

Above Colonel R.S. "Sam" McLaughlin on his mount Brilliant Moon. PHOTO CREDIT: PARK-WOOD NATIONAL HISTORICAL SITE

Facing Top Lady Angela with foal on the Oshawa Farm. PHOTO CREDIT: CANADIAN FILM CENTRE/JEFFERSON MAPPIN

Facing Bottom E.P and Winnie Taylor attending the races. PHOTO CREDIT: KEENELAND ASSOCIATION LIBRARY/THOROUGHBRED TIMES COLLECTION

George Blackwell of the British Bloodstock Agency, circa 1954. PHOTO CREDIT: KEENE-LAND ASSOCIATION LIBRARY/THOROUGHBRED TIMES COLLECTION

{ 4 }

FOUNDATION MARES I: PLANTING THE SEEDS

AS IMPORTANT AS the pillar sires are, no breeding operation can survive without high-quality broodmares. Many experts in breeding claim that, more times than not, the dam is far more influential to the resulting foal than the sire. E.P. Taylor and his team of horsepeople knew this. Right from the start, gathering fine producers for the broodmare colony at Windfields paid dividends, establishing the foundation to further the farm's success in the breeding world. As the old saying goes, "Breed the best to the best and hope for the best."

Buying and breeding quality broodmares takes time, expertise and a great deal of good luck. This is where the study of pedigrees and conformation becomes the key to a successful breeding enterprise. Taylor had the resources to finance the collection of an extensive array of bloodlines in order to discover the most useful lines, which could take Canadian horses to the top of the breeding pyramid.

As we trace the descendants of foundation mares, we will, of course, skip back and forth in time. In these foundation mare chapters, we are highlighting mainly Grade/Group One stakes winners and champions. Chronological charts of all stakes winners and producers are displayed at the back of the book.

Nandi

Nandi was one of the first draft of horses Bert Alexandra acquired from the claiming ranks in his Pimlico raid of 1936. Although claimers (horses who run in races where they are offered for sale) are often viewed as the lower ranks of the Thoroughbred world in terms of class, on occasion fillies or mares who run for a claiming tag go on to become successful stakes producers as broodmares. Very few of them have had the incredible impact on breeding that Nandi did.

Nandi was sired by Stimulus, a son of the very good and successful sire Ultimus. Ultimus was a closely inbred grandson of American foundation sire Domino. How close was the inbreeding, you may ask? Well, Ultimus's sire and dam, Commando and Running Stream, were both offspring of Domino. Nandi's dam was Golden Feast, sired by Golden Sun. Looking further along the dam side of her pedigree, we see the names St. Simon and Bend Or in the fourth generation. These two important sires of the nineteenth century were considered essential in pedigrees around the time Nandi was racing. So Nandi had a potent mix of acclaimed American and English bloodlines working for her. In all likelihood, this escaped Bert Alexandra's attention when he claimed her at Pimlico. He was just on the lookout for useful racehorses his new boss could campaign.

But the value of her pedigree kicked in when Nandi retired. We have already seen that her son Windfields, sired by Bunty Lawless, became a major stakes winner and important sire. Nandi's stakes-placed daughter Nandina, sired by pillar stallion Bull Page, also continued the family's influence.

Nandina produced a filly named Cut Flower, by pillar sire Chop Chop, in 1960. Cut Flower was a modest racehorse, winning only two races, though she did start in a number of stakes races under Windfields colours. At retirement, she was sent to the Windfields Farm broodmare band. Her second foal, in 1966, was a filly named Chilly. Sired by Nearctic, Chilly did not set the world on fire at the track either, winning only once in nine tries. As a broodmare she produced ten winners, of which three won stakes races. We'll examine her contribution in depth in Chapter Eight.

Nandi's influence was a catalyst for the future domination of Windfields breeding. As the dam of Windfields, she cemented her own value as a key contributor, while her daughter Nandina took the family to wonderful heights in the years to come.

Iribelle

Iribelle has been previously mentioned as a full sister to E.P. Taylor's first major stakes winner, Mona Bell. The sisters were sired by the imported English stallion Osiris II. Colonel Sam McLaughlin had bought this multiple-stakes-winning son of the great stayer Papyrus to stand at his Parkwood Stud in Oshawa. Osiris II became a four-time leading sire in Canada, earning his final sire title in 1947, the year he died. His pedigree shows he was inbred 4x4 to the great breed-shaping sire St. Simon. (This means St. Simon shows up twice in his pedigree, in the fourth generation.)

Belmona, Iribelle's dam, was a daughter of King James. King James was an extensively campaigned son of Plaudit, who in turn was by Himyar. This sire line had deep influence in

American breeding in the latter part of the nineteenth century and on into the early twentieth century. King James won some prestigious races, including the Metropolitan Handicap, the Brooklyn Handicap and the Toronto Cup twice. He was named the champion handicap horse of 1909.

Iribelle made thirteen starts, winning only two races, so she was not as accomplished a racer as her sister (though she did place third in the Plate Trial Stakes). However, when she became a broodmare, Iribelle set down a remarkable legacy of stakes winners that has carried on for generation after generation. This legacy is particularly remarkable given that Iribelle produced only four foals. The first three were stakes winners Bennington (by Boswell), Britannia (by Bunty Lawless) and the great Canadiana (by Chop Chop).

The gelding Bennington made sixty-eight starts in his racing career, winning fourteen. The highlights were victories in the King Edward Gold Cup and the Durham Cup Handicap.

Britannia came a year later, in 1948. As a two-year-old, she won the two most prestigious races for both genders when she captured the Princess Elizabeth Stakes and the Coronation Futurity. Britannia joined the broodmare ranks, producing two stakes-winning daughters by Chop Chop. Myanna won the Vandal Stakes as a juvenile over colts, while Rule Britannia captured the Prix Rabelais in France.

Canadiana was the first international stakes winner bred by E.P. Taylor. The mating that produced her, however, was a dose of the Taylor luck at full strength. Iribelle was to be bred to Boswell, but the stallion dropped dead right before the tryst was to take place. Windfields Farm hastily sent Iribelle to Chop Chop, who was standing at Trafalgar Farm. The result was Canadiana, whose racing career is described in Chapter Three.

The fourth foal from Iribelle's brief life was an unraced daughter by Windfields named Victoriana, whom we touched on in Chapter Three. This bay filly was destined to be a grand producer as she had both Nandi, the dam of Windfields, and Iribelle in her blood. It is through the example of Victoriana's offspring that we see the generational improvement in class for Windfields Farm horses.

Victoriana was bred to Chop Chop in 1956, and a year later produced Victoria Park, E.P. Taylor's first US-classic-placed stakes winner (discussed at length in Chapter Three). Victoria Park consistently lowered track records around North America and gave the Taylors and the racing world a glimpse of the future as he demonstrated his speed and class on the racetrack. E.P. Taylor knew from this colt that he was on the right path to achieving success at the highest levels in racing.

The success of the Iribelle clan did not stop with Victoria Park. His dam, Victoriana, was bred to Menetrier in 1957 and produced a daughter, Victoria Regina. This lovely chestnut filly won eight races in total, four of them stakes, including the prestigious Princess Elizabeth Stakes and the Nettie Handicap. Victoria Regina was always compared to her half-brother Victoria Park by the local press. Her head was exquisite, with a near Arabian look, and she had a delicately feminine air about her. If she were human, she would have been a pin-up girl.

Victoria Regina formed a very successful partnership with Northern Dancer when she retired from racing to the breeding arena. Her first foal from the alliance was the stunningly handsome champion Viceregal. The colt injured an ankle in a paddock accident as a youngster, and the joint never fully healed. The injury probably put off many prospective buyers when Taylor offered the chestnut son of Victoria Regina, from the first crop of Northern Dancer foals, for a $50,000 price tag. His looks made everyone take double and triple views. He was a stunning individual, but, oh, that ankle! Viceregal battled this chronic injury throughout his brief racing career.

Sent to Pete McCann for training, Viceregal had a juvenile campaign that is the stuff of legend. McCann was constantly challenged to keep Viceregal sound, but he did a masterful job, guiding the colt to champion two-year-old honours and a Canadian Horse of the Year title. The campaign began with a resounding win in a maiden race. Viceregal demonstrated what would become his signature racing style—a come-from-behind dash that was thrilling to behold.

The next race was the Victoria Stakes at Woodbine. Again, Viceregal came from behind to win, and he equalled the track record for the 5.5-furlong distance. Viceregal then continued his winning ways, taking the Colin, Vandal, Summer and Clarendon Stakes in succession. Next up was the prestigious Cup and Saucer Stakes, an 8.5-furlong test on the grass. He had already run on the surface in his Summer Stakes victory, and he put in one of his most exhilarating performances, coming from far back to win going away from his archrival, Grey Whiz. The public was in love with Viceregal, as was the Windfields staff. His start in the top two-year-old race, the Coronation Futurity, brought a capacity crowd to Woodbine. Viceregal did not disappoint the masses, winning the race in superb fashion.

At this point, E.P. Taylor believed that Viceregal might be the best horse he had ever bred. The decision was made to train the colt toward the Kentucky Derby the following May.

Unfortunately, at this point the racing gods decided to abandon E.P. Taylor. The colt broke his coffin bone in his first race as a three-year-old and was retired from racing. Viceregal took up stud duty at the Oshawa farm and actually led the Canadian sire list before he was sold to a French stud farm because his brother Vice Regent was outperforming him as a stallion. (We will highlight Vice Regent's career as a stallion in Chapter Thirteen.) Viceregal eventually ended up in Japan and died there in 1984 at the age of eighteen. He was a generally quiet, good-natured stallion but had two phobias of note. One was claustrophobia. He despised tight quarters, such as shipping crates, and destroyed the crate he was in during his trip to France. The other was that Viceregal was not happy when dental cleaning was performed. Windfields had a policy that all horses on the farm had their teeth "floated" twice a year—that is, a vet or dental technician would file any sharp points off their teeth to make the chewing surface smooth. Viceregal hated this process, and we're sure many readers can relate to him on this point.

Three more links from Victoriana in the chain of Iribelle's line were Victoriana's daughters Northern Queen, sired by Nearctic; Victorian Dancer, sired by Northern Dancer; and Victorian Heiress, also by Northern Dancer. Northern Queen was named Canadian champion three-year-old filly in 1965 when she won the Canadian Oaks and the Wonder Where Stakes, which is two-thirds of the Canadian Triple Tiara for three-year-old fillies. Later in the year, she captured the Nettie Handicap, and as a two-year-old, she had won the Shady Well Stakes. Northern Queen produced six winners, including stakes winners Buckstopper and Against All Flags. Victorian Dancer was a modest racehorse but later produced Imperial March by Forli. Imperial March won the Queen Anne Stakes at Royal Ascot. Victorian Heiress was bred to Windfields' Maryland farm sire Snow Knight and produced Northern Blossom in 1980. Northern Blossom went on to become the champion three-year-old filly in Canada, winning the Nassau, Wonder Where, Bison City and Ontario Colleen Stakes during the year. She produced Italian St Leger winner Jape and the dam of High Accolade, who finished second in the English St Leger.

Compensate

During his renewed involvement in acquiring racing stock following his war commitments, E.P. Taylor purchased a yearling filly by Reaping Reward, out of Niblick by Fairway, for $8,000.

The Taylors named the filly Compensate. She came from a storied family, as she was a direct female descendant of the legendary mare Chelandry, and was also inbred to Phalaris 3x3: her sire was a grandson and her dam was a granddaughter.

Compensate had two important offspring. The first was Censor, a 1953 colt sired by Bull Page. Censor ran under Mrs. Taylor's name and was a solid stakes winner, taking the Toronto Cup, Connaught Cup, Canadian Maturity and Jacques Cartier Stakes. He later stood at stud at the Oshawa farm but was not successful in the role.

Two years after producing Censor, Compensate gave birth to a brown filly by Windfields. The filly was named Willow Lake, and she would become the main link to the success of future generations in the family. Willow Lake won four of eleven races and earned minor black type when she finished second in the Fury Stakes (when horses win or place in major races, these results appear in bold type, or black type, in sales catalogues, pedigree charts, etc.).

Willow Lake produced two stakes winners and three daughters who moved the family on to greater success. The stakes winners were Miss Snow Goose, by Nearctic, and Victorian Prince, by Victorian Era. The latter was the champion older horse and turf horse in 1976. Victorian Prince won the Arlington Handicap, Lakeside Handicap, Bunty Lawless Stakes and Ultimus Stakes during his championship season.

The three daughters of Willow Lake who became fine broodmares were Willowfield, by Stratus, and the full sisters Northern Willow and Northern Lake, by Northern Dancer. Willowfield was unsold as a yearling and never raced. She became a broodmare at the Oshawa farm and, in 1971, produced a daughter by Victoria Park named Victorian Queen. Victorian Queen was an honest racehorse, winning the Canadian Stakes and the Ontario Sire Stakes. She also placed second nine times in graded stakes around the North American continent.

Victorian Queen became a very good broodmare. She produced three Grade One winners from three different sires. The first was Judge Angelucci, by Honest Pleasure. Judge Angelucci was bred by Tom Gentry and won the Californian Stakes and the San Antonio and Mervyn Leroy Handicaps. He kept good company, as his second place to Ferdinand in the Hollywood Gold Cup and third place to Ferdinand and Alysheba in the Breeders' Cup Classic will attest. In different races, Judge Angelucci defeated Ferdinand, Alysheba, Simply Majestic, Tasso and Snow Chief.

The next Grade One winner produced by Victorian Queen was a bay son of Majestic Light named War. He was one of the highly touted entrants in the 1987 Kentucky Derby after winning the Blue Grass Stakes and the Lexington Stakes leading up to the first Saturday in May. In the Derby, however, he was mugged going around the clubhouse turn and stumbled badly, causing him to lose his momentum and the race. War was never the same after that unfortunate incident.

The third Grade One winner from Victorian Queen was Peace. Sired by Naskra, Peace was better on grass than on dirt and won the John Henry Handicap, earning his place as a Grade One winner.

Another descendant of Victorian Queen who has brought the family to the forefront of the breeding world came from her daughter Saviour, a full sister to War. Saviour was bred to Danehill in 1997, and the following spring, she produced a bay filly, Speirbhean. This filly became a stakes winner in Ireland and then was bred to the incredible sire Galileo, producing Teofilo, the European champion two-year-old of 2006. Teofilo was undefeated as a juvenile, the only season he raced. He began his stud career at Kildangan Stud, Ireland, in 2008 and is already the sire of eighty-three stakes winners, of which fifteen are Group One winners. This is only from his first seven crops of racing-age foals. Among his best foals are 2013 Irish Derby winner Trading Leather and 2018 Melbourne Cup winner Cross Counter.

An examination of the pedigree of Victorian Queen shows that she was inbred to Windfields 3x3. Such a breeding pattern, highlighting the first stakes winner bred by E.P. Taylor, is unusual but may have contributed to the success of this mare.

Returning to Willow Lake, we now look at her daughter Northern Willow. This filly presented a shockingly bold white face to the world, but she did not cover herself in glory on the track. She made four starts and could only muster a fourth-place finish in one race, to earn a paltry $140. However, as a broodmare she produced two stakes winners: May Combination, by Right Combination, and a beautiful chestnut filly with flaxen mane and tail by champion racehorse Dr. Fager. The latter filly was sent to the Saratoga yearling sales in 1976 and was bought by leading Canadian owner/breeder Jean-Louis Lévesque for $102,000. Lévesque named the filly L'Alezane, which is French for "the chestnut."

L'Alezane became the darling of Canadian racegoers the following year. She won her first five races in impressive fashion. This included three stakes races: the Shady Well and the Grade Two Schuylerville and Adirondack Stakes. L'Alezane suffered her first loss in the Grade One Spinaway Stakes, then went to Manitoba to take the Winnipeg Futurity over the boys. She cemented her position as the top filly in Canada with her seven-length victory in the Princess Elizabeth Stakes. Following a second place in the Natalma Stakes, which was run on a very heavy turf course, with L'Alezane carrying eleven pounds more than her conqueror, the filly returned to the United States to win the Grade Two Alcibiades Stakes at Keeneland. She was named the top two-year-old in Canada and also took home the Canadian Horse of the Year title, wrapping up a very memorable season.

The following season was good but not as dominating as her juvenile campaign. L'Alezane won the important Selene Stakes, then placed second to La Voyageuse in the Canadian Oaks and third to Regal Embrace and Overskate in the Queen's Plate. She battled various nagging injuries throughout the year. Lévesque decided to bring her back for a four-year-old campaign, and she seemed to be over her ailments when she made her seasonal debut in an allowance race at Hialeah Park on March 7, 1979. Unfortunately, L'Alezane broke the sesamoid bones in her left front ankle. The injury was too severe to be corrected through surgery, so the stunningly beautiful L'Alezane was humanely euthanized to end her suffering.

Another daughter of Northern Willow to make a name for herself and her family was Bay Willow, by Fappiano. Bay Willow was a foal of 1985 and was not a winner on the track, placing only once in four races. As a broodmare, she became a winner when she moved to Australia and produced a bay filly by Rory's Jester named Aragen. Aragen won the Group One QTC Sires' Produce Stakes and the Group Two AJC Silver Shadow Stakes.

Willow Lake's daughter Northern Lake was bred to Maryland farm sire Smarten and, in 1981, produced a dark bay colt who would go by the name of Southern Arrow. Southern Arrow won a pair of stakes races in Italy as a juvenile, then captured the Group One Premio Parioli (Italian 2000 Guineas) the following season.

Northern Lake's daughter Tintaburra, by Oshawa farm sire Bold Agent, produced a filly by Queen's Plate winner Regal Intention in 1992. Given the mouthful name Woolloomooloo, the filly improved with age to become the Sovereign Award champion older mare and turf mare in Canada in 1997.

Flaring Top

Purchased from the Claiborne Farms consignment of horses to the 1948 Keeneland Summer Yearling Sale, Flaring Top cost E.P. Taylor $8,500. She was a daughter of Menow, out of Flaming

Top by Omaha. Menow was the champion two-year-old of 1937 due to his important victories in the Champagne and Futurity Stakes. Omaha was an American Triple Crown winner. Flaring Top won three of fourteen races in her career before becoming an important broodmare. Her first two foals were Gleam, by Oshawa sire Tournoi, who became the second dam of Grade One winner Royal Ski by Raja Baba; and Top Tourn, a durable multiple-stakes winner, who made 108 starts in his seven-year racing career.

Her first foal to further the line to high-level excellence was Flaming Wind, by Windfields. Flaming Wind won three of twelve races. Her first foal was a daughter by Ace Marine, born in 1960, named Flaming Issue. Unraced, she produced a New Providence filly named Dobbinton, who won stakes races in Western Canada before producing a pair of daughters to further the family fortunes. Ferdeleh, by Viceregal, was sent to Venezuela for broodmare duty. After a meeting with Heron Bay, a son of Alleged, she produced a bay daughter named Ferd d'Ferh. This filly won the Group One Caracas City Classic at two, and at three the Clàsico Internacional Propietarios La Rinconada and the Clàsico Prensa Nacional, both Group One races, to become the champion three-year-old of Venezuela in 1989.

The other daughter of Dobbinton to mention is Dobbinee, by Oshawa sire Ruritania. Stakes-placed in the Mademoiselle Handicap, Dobbinee produced a daughter by Vice Regent named Rosedon. This one became the dam of Benburb, Canadian Horse of the Year in 1992. The grey gelding sired by Dr. Carter defeated a pair of stellar horses during his championship season. In the Prince of Wales Stakes, Benburb beat Queen's Plate winner Alydeed, who had romped in the first Canadian classic and finished second in the Preakness. Later, Benburb proved that his Prince of Wales victory was not a one-off when he won the Molson Export Million, defeating none other than

Belmont winner A.P. Indy. The latter was named Eclipse Award Horse of the Year at the end of the season.

Rosedon also produced stakes winner Lady Aloma, by Cozzene, who in turn is the dam of Canadian champion grass filly Chopinina, by Lear Fan.

Returning to Flaring Top, we follow the path of her descendants to an interesting horse bred in 1975. Cool Victor was from the Flaming Victress branch of Flaring Top's family. Flaming Victress was by Victoria Park, and when she was bred to Nearctic, she had a daughter named Polar Victress. This one was bred to Tentam, and the result was Cool Victor. Cool Victor won four of fifteen races for his owner, Steve Stavro, who had purchased the colt as a yearling from Windfields in 1976.

Cool Victor had exceptional breeding, but he was an ordinary runner, winning only allowance races. He was used as a teaser on the Oshawa farm—a stallion who will interact with the mares so they will show the handlers they are ready to be bred—and he also test-bred a few of Stavro's mares who were boarded at Windfields in Oshawa. Once the foals from those matings began to race, however, people noticed that the offspring of the farm teaser were winning some class races. Cool Victor sired only seventy horses, but fourteen of them won stakes races. Victor Cooley won the Queen's Plate and was named the Sovereign Award champion three-year-old in 1996. Apelia won the Grade Two Genuine Risk Stakes twice, as well as seven more stakes, and was named the champion sprinter in Canada. Sometimes you just never know when a stallion of quality will come along.

The Flaring Top family made a significant contribution to Windfields' international popularity. Flaming Page contributed mightily, but Friendly Relations put forth a branch that has contributed to Australian Group One success. Friendly Relations, by Nearctic, had a daughter by Elocutionist named Elzevir. This descendant of Flaring Top relocated to Australia, where she produced a brown colt by the stallion Bellotto named Bellzevir, the winner of the 1997 Group One Goodwood Handicap.

Flaming Page was the best direct offspring of Flaring Top to race. She also became one of the greatest broodmares of the twentieth century. By Bull Page, she was a big, masculine-looking filly, strong of bone, and fast. After she went unsold for $20,000 at the yearling sale, Flaming Page was retained by Windfields for racing. She won the Shady Well Stakes as a two-year-old and showed exceptional promise, placing second in the Princess Elizabeth and third to stablemate Choperion in the Coronation Futurity.

Horatio Luro thought she would be a good prospect for the Kentucky Oaks, run the day before the Derby at Churchill Downs. Flaming Page made it to the Oaks and finished second to champion Cicada. She returned to Canada to win the Canadian Oaks over Caledon Belle, thus fulfilling her potential. She one-upped herself in the following race, when she beat the boys in the Queen's Plate. In doing so, she became the first filly to win the Oaks/Plate double.

Luro noted that Flaming Page preferred to run from behind and did not like to be too close to the pace during the early stages of a race. Her Queen's Plate jockey, Jim Fitzsimmons, stated after the race, "From the break, I took her right back to last. We passed one horse early, then with maybe five-eighths of a mile to go, I let her start picking up horses on the outside, which is important with a filly, to keep her clear of trouble. I never set her down, let her head loose, even once. Go over to the barn and you won't find a mark on her. She won as easy as a horse can win." Rival jockey Hugo Dittfach on King Gorm said, "Get this, Fitzy had her under a pull when they flew by me." Fitzsimmons concluded, "Actually, she could have won by more." And Bill Hartack, on second-placed Choperion, said, "When

Flaming Page went by me, I thought she would win by five." The actual margin of victory was two lengths.

Flaming Page made one more start when she ran a week later in the Coaching Club American Oaks at Belmont Park. The field for the 10-furlong race was stellar, with Cicada as the favourite. Bramalea and Flaming Page set the pace, battling for the lead, which was not the way Flaming Page liked to conduct her racing. These two kept at it for the first mile, until the top of the home-stretch, when Cicada made her move and challenged the leaders. Flaming Page fell back, and Bramalea edged out Cicada to win in the fast time of 2:02 ⅗, one-fifth of a second off the track record. Flaming Page was fourth, two-and-a-half lengths behind Brama-lea, with Cicada and Firm Policy second and third. The race was significant in retrospect for the fact that both Flaming Page and Bramalea later produced Epsom Derby winners (Nijinsky and Roberto, respectively). The Coaching Club American Oaks was also the final race of Flaming Page's career. She went on from there to the pinnacle of Windfields' breeding program.

Her first foal was Fleur, a filly of 1964 by Victoria Park. Fleur won only three races from twenty-one starts, and though the bay filly ran in many stakes races, she did not win a single one. Her best stakes result was a third-place finish in the Summer Stakes as a juvenile. Fleur made amends in a huge way by producing four stakes winners, including a daughter who produced a stakes winner of her own. Fleur visited Northern Dancer on five occasions, with three of those trysts producing stakes winners.

The most famous was her son The Minstrel, who was champion three-year-old in Europe following his victories in the Derby Stakes at Epsom, the Irish "Sweeps" Derby and the King George VI and Queen Elizabeth Stakes. Full siblings to The Minstrel were stakes winners Far North and Pilgrim, while Flower Princess, by Majestic Prince, produced stakes winner Dance Flower, by Northern Dancer.

Flaming Page met Northern Dancer before her daughter did, and the result was legendary. In 1967, she produced a bay son whom many people consider one of the greatest Thoroughbreds in the long history of the sport. His name was Nijinsky. Chapter Nine is devoted predominantly to Nijinsky and The Minstrel, detailing their substantial accomplishments.

Minsky, a full brother to Nijinsky, was born in 1968. While not quite as talented as his brother, he was no slouch, but Minsky's timing was unfortunate. He was part of a deeply talented crop that included legends Mill Reef and Brigadier Gerard. Minsky won two stakes in Ireland as a two-year-old, took the Gladness and Tetrarch Stakes at three, and then transferred to his homeland to win the Durham Cup in Canada. He added a second Durham Cup victory later in his career. Minsky was just slightly below the best of his generation, as his fourth-place finishes in both the 2000 Guineas and the Washington D.C. International indicate.

Flaming Page had only the aforementioned offspring. She twice gave birth to stillborn foals: twins in 1966 and another colt in 1969. The last troubled birth caused severe damage to her. Windfields decided to retire her from further breeding so as to not risk her life. Flaming Page was only ten when the decision was made. She went on to a career as a mentor for newly retired younger mares embarking on a broodmare career, and she spent paddock time with her daughter Fleur for many years. Flaming Page lived until she was twenty-five, enjoying her status as one of the great females in Windfields history, if not Thoroughbred history in general.

Stalina

In 1955, George Blackwell purchased a bay stakes-winning mare by Stalino named Stalina. Stalina won the Epsom Produce and Minting Produce Stakes in England, and she had produced a colt by Sayajirao before she entered the sales arena in foal to Lord Derby's champion sire Alycidon. Blackwell was looking for top-quality bloodlines that E.P. Taylor could use in his quest to improve Canadian racing quality, and Stalina seemed to fit the bill.

Stalina had the Alycidon foal in Canada. Given the name Sunday Sail, the bay colt won the Horometer Stakes at three and placed in several other Canadian stakes races, including the Prince of Wales and Cup and Saucer Stakes (the latter as a two-year-old). Stalina's next foal was a daughter of Windfields named Missy R, who was stakes-placed. Cut Steel by Chop Chop came next. The extensively raced son won the Carleton Stakes to become a black-type winner.

Stalina was bred to Censor and produced a massive colt named Grand Garcon in 1961. This big boy came from the same Windfields yearling crop as Northern Dancer. He was sold, while Northern Dancer was not. The two met in the Cup and Saucer Stakes in 1963. Grand Garcon towered over Northern Dancer by one and a half hands. He also received a break in the weights, since Northern Dancer had already won the Summer Stakes. Grand Garcon became the only Canadian-bred horse to beat Northern Dancer when he took the Cup and Saucer by a half length. He added the Canadian Maturity Stakes two years later to his stakes-winning total.

In 1963, Stalina had a chestnut filly by Nearctic who was named Speediness. This filly won a few races and was stakes-placed in the Natalma Stakes at two. Her son Speedy Zephyr, by Restless Wind, was a distinctively bright red chestnut colt. He set new track records in the Manitoba Derby on dirt and the Heresy Stakes on grass, and he equalled the track record in the Toronto Cup, also on grass. Speedy Zephyr was a versatile, fast horse who campaigned in the United States with some success in graded stakes races.

The most pervasive branch of the Stalina family has come from her daughter Drama School, born in 1966, a chestnut filly from the first crop of Northern Dancer foals. Drama School was on the trail to the Canadian Oaks after winning the Star Shoot and Selene Stakes, but she went unplaced in the big event. Her first foal was a stakes-placed daughter by Victorian Era named Stagetime. Her second was a champion.

Norcliffe was sired by the great racehorse and sire Buckpasser. He sold for $80,000 at the Saratoga yearling sales to Bud Baker, who named the exceptionally well-conformed horse after his stable. Norcliffe broke his maiden with a sixteen-length victory. He later won the rich Coronation Futurity, ran second in the Cup and Saucer and third in the Summer Stakes during his juvenile campaign.

Coming out like a tiger at three, Norcliffe became the Sovereign Award Horse of the Year after he won the Queen's Plate, Prince of Wales Stakes, Carling O'Keefe Handicap and four other stakes races. At four, he repeated his Carling O'Keefe victory, finished one length behind Forego in the Nassau County Handicap and added the Canadian Maturity to his resumé, as well as another Sovereign Award as the top older horse in Canada.

At stud, Norcliffe sired Eclipse Award champion sprinter Groovy. The dam of Groovy, Tinnitus, was a daughter of Restless Wind; recall how well the blood of Restless Wind worked with the Stalina family in the case of Speedy Zephyr. Groovy twice broke the 130 Beyer speed barrier with back-to-back 133 and 132 races in 1977.

Another son of note sired by Norcliffe was At The Threshold. Winner of the Grade One Arlington Classic and American Derby, At The Threshold also took the Ohio Derby and Jim Beam Stakes, and finished third in the 1984 Kentucky Derby. His son Lil E Tee won the 1992 Kentucky Derby to avenge his father's defeat eight years earlier.

Returning to Stalina's daughter Drama School, we find the latter's daughter L'Insatiable, by Maryland farm sire Caveat.

L'Insatiable's son Lodge Hill, by Breeders' Cup Mile winner Cozzene, won the Canadian classic Breeders' Stakes. Drama School's daughter Vaguely Dramatic had a daughter by champion Damascus called Dam Dramatic. That one was sent to Argentina, where she produced El Sultan. This colt was sired by Morning Bob and won the Group One Gran Premio Montevideo and the Gran Premio Santiago Luro on his way to being named the champion two-year-old in Argentina.

Fair Colleen

The infusion of British bloodstock into E.P. Taylor's breeding program continued throughout the 1950s. Fair Colleen was a stakes-winning daughter of Preciptic, a winner of fifteen races in England and Ireland. Preciptic was a son of Ascot Gold Cup winner Precipitation, who in turn was a son of the great stayer Hurry On. This line was noted for its ability to win top-level races at longer distances than the average. The Gainsborough blood Preciptic received from his dam, Artistic, also strengthened the staying ability.

The bottom half of Fair Colleen's pedigree reveals that her dam, Fairvale, was a daughter of Fairford, who in turn was a son of the great Fairway. By breeding Preciptic to Fairvale, a 4x4 inbreed to the great Thoroughbred speed source The Tetrarch was created. This well-crafted pedigree was just what E.P. Taylor was in search of as he tried to improve the quality of Canadian horses.

The first foal from Fair Colleen was Canadian Triple Crown winner New Providence (his racing and stallion career is described in Chapter Three). Not only did New Providence win the Plate, the Prince of Wales and the Breeders' Stakes, but he also captured the Cup and Saucer at two, and the Inferno, Ultimus and Seagram Cup Handicaps. His place in worldwide pedigrees is cemented as the sire of South Ocean, the dam of the great sire Storm Bird.

New Providence had a full sister in 1958, Maid O'North. This filly was sold at the Windfields yearling sale, likely due to the success of her older brother. Maid O'North did the family proud when she won the Canadian Oaks for Shermanor Farm. However, the dark side of the racing game came to the fore when Maid O'North was fatally hurt in a race not long after her Oaks triumph.

The year after Fair Colleen produced Maid O'North, she gave birth to another filly, this time by Oshawa farm sire Queen's Own. The filly was a chestnut and went unsold at the annual yearling sale. Racing under the colours of Windfields with the name Own Colleen, the filly won four of twenty-eight starts, with no black type to report. She was the pacemaker for stablemate Flaming Page in the Canadian Oaks, and she took the same role in other stakes races.

Once retired from competition, Own Colleen became an important contributor to the family's future. Her son Winlord, by Oshawa farm sire Canebora, won the Summer Stakes in 1970. Three years later, Own Colleen produced a chestnut filly by champion Viceregal. Royal Colleen was a real trooper on the track, winning seven races, placing second four times and third fifteen times. She earned black type with a third-place finish in the Nassau Stakes. When she went on to her breeding career, she made a name for herself. Royal Colleen was bred to Ontario-based stallion Bold Ruckus, standing at Park Stud, and produced Grade One winner Beau Genius. Beau Genius was an honest top-flight horse, who made forty-two starts over a four-year racing career. He won nineteen races, thirteen of them stakes. The most prestigious win came in the Grade One Philip H. Iselin Handicap at Monmouth Park. He also took the Michigan Mile and One-Eighth, Autumn Handicap, Display Stakes,

Arlington Challenge Cup and Churchill Downs Handicap. Beau Genius was then retired to stud in California, where he became a very busy and successful sire. He is currently best known as the damsire of Grade One stakes winner Cupid.

Kathie's Colleen, by Woodman out of Royal Colleen, won the Grade Two Monmouth Oaks and was second in the Canadian Oaks for her breeder, Gus Schickedanz. Kathie's Colleen was then bred to Schickedanz's champion sprinter Langfuhr. The result was a big beautiful chestnut colt whom Gus named Wando. Wando took the Canadian racing public by storm when he captured the Canadian Triple Crown, generating publicity similar to that for past champions such as Dance Smartly, With Approval and even the great Northern Dancer. Wando was named the Sovereign Award Horse of the Year in 2003.

Evensong

George Blackwell was a busy man for E.P. Taylor. In 1957, he purchased, on Taylor's behalf, an unraced mare, Evensong, by The Phoenix, out of Angelus by Blandford. Evensong was in foal to King George VI and Queen Elizabeth Stakes winner Vimy at the time of the sale. She had the Vimy foal in Canada, a dark bay filly who would go by the name Song Of Even.

Song Of Even became another no-sale at the Windfields annual yearling sale, so she raced under the turquoise and gold colours. She had an affinity for racing on the grass, and her come-from-behind style endeared her to many race fans. Song Of Even raced against male competition consistently and beat them in the Prince of Wales and Breeders' Stakes, setting a new course record in the latter. She also won the Achievement Handicap, was second in the Niagara Handicap and was third in both the Cup and Saucer and Heresy Stakes. All of these races were against the boys.

Evensong was bred to Victoria Park and gave the world a bay filly in 1962, from the first crop of foals by the Canadian champion. This filly, Song Of Victory, went unsold at the following year's sale and remained in the Windfields domain. She won three of eighteen races and then joined the Windfields broodmare colony. Here, she produced only one foal, a filly by New Providence named New Tune. New Tune won the Yearling Sales Stakes before producing Sound Reason.

Sound Reason, sired by the Hail To Reason stallion Bold Reason, was bought by leading Canadian owner/breeder Jack Stafford from the Windfields consignment to the CTHS sale of 1975. Sound Reason became Stafford's third Queen's Plate winner. He won an additional nine stakes races, was named the champion two-year-old of 1976 and later became a successful stallion in New Zealand.

New Tune also produced an unraced filly by Damascus named Breezy Stories. This Taylor-bred became a Grade One producer when her daughter Desert Stormer, by Storm Cat, defeated a stellar field in the 1995 Breeders' Cup Sprint. Desert Stormer carried on the family line with her first foal, Sahara Gold, by Seeking The Gold. Sahara Gold won the Grade Two Beaumont Stakes before becoming the dam of Better Lucky, by Ghostzapper. Better Lucky won the Grade One First Lady and Matriarch Stakes.

Breezy Stories produced a full sister to Desert Stormer named Desert Stormette. This sister was also bred to Seeking The Gold, and the resulting filly was stakes winner Desert Gold. Desert Gold kept up the family tradition when her Dynaformer filly, named White Moonstone, won the Group One Fillies Mile at Newmarket. This was her fourth win in four races. It was also her final career race as she hurt herself in training for the 1000 Guineas the following year and never recovered well enough to resume racing.

One more descendant of Evensong to mention here is her grandson Victoria Song. Sired by Victoria Park and out of Arctic Song, by Nearctic, Victoria Song became the third of three consecutive Queen's Plate winners sired by Victoria Park.

Lady Angela

Since we are studying mares acquired from Europe by George Blackwell on behalf of E.P. Taylor, let us look at the most famous now. We have already touched on Lady Angela and will again when we discuss her famous son Nearctic in depth. However, Lady Angela had other important offspring who have added to Windfields Farm's laurels.

Lady Angela was bred twice to Bull Page and produced a pair of sisters. The second sister was Countess Angela, winner of three races and stakes-placed in the Princess Elizabeth Stakes. Countess Angela's first three foals were sired by Canadian Champ. The second was a black—and we do mean black, not dark brown—colt who became a champion. He was sold for $15,000 at the Windfields annual sale to Peter Marshall, who named him Titled Hero.

Titled Hero was trained by veteran Pat MacMurchy. One morning he sent out the colt, then an unraced two-year-old, for some training in the starting gate on the main Woodbine track. Jimmy Lynn was on the colt as he approached Windfields trainer Pete McCann, also working in the starting gate, and asked if he could tag along. McCann, aboard the very fast Muskeg, and his assistant Bill Reeves, on Daring Bull, asked Lynn whom he was riding.

"Oh, just some green two-year-old of MacMurchy's," said Lynn.

"Come along," said McCann, thinking it would be fun to kick some dirt in the face of the two-year-old.

While in the gate, McCann pretended to need a whip to straighten his mount. He borrowed Jimmy Lynn's and made sure the doors flew open before he offered the piece of equipment back. The two Windfields horses were off in a flash, leaving the black two-year-old flat-footed. However, Lynn and his mount were soon gliding up to the Windfields pair, and even though Lynn did not have his whip, he had no trouble keeping up to the older horses.

McCann gasped, "I thought you said this was a green two-year-old!"

"It is," said Lynn.

"What's his name?" asked Pete.

"Titled Hero" was the response.

Titled Hero made believers out of more than Pete McCann and Bill Reeves. He won the Coronation Futurity, Summer Stakes, Grey Stakes and Colin Stakes, four of his eight wins as a juvenile from twelve starts, and was named the Canadian champion two-year-old. He followed that up with a brave campaign in which he battled foot trouble throughout the year. He won the Queen's Plate after being given a masterful ride by Avelino Gomez. Gomez also expertly guided Titled Hero to win the 12-furlong Breeders' Stakes. With additional wins in the Plate Trial Stakes and the Friar Rock Stakes, Titled Hero earned his second consecutive divisional championship.

E.P. Taylor and Peter Marshall struck a deal to stand Titled Hero at Windfields following his four-year-old campaign. Unfortunately, the black colt sustained an irreparable injury and was humanely euthanized. It was a tragic blow to Canadian racing.

Countess Angela's next foal was a full sister to Titled Hero named Titled Heroine. Unlike her brother, Titled Heroine was a bright chestnut. She certainly did not emulate her brother's racing accomplishments either, winning only one race from twelve starts. She did have a breeding career, and this is where she established a solid position within the family accomplishments. Having been sold a couple of times as a broodmare,

Titled Heroine produced a daughter by Impressive in 1976 who was named Titled. She produced multiple-graded-stakes winner Fit For A Queen, by the Bold Ruler–line stallion Fit To Fight. Fit For A Queen's daughter Gold Rush Queen, by Seeking The Gold, produced multiple stakes winner Ender's Sister, by A.P. Indy. And Ender's Sister is the dam of Grade One stakes winner A.P. Indian, by Indian Charlie. A.P. Indian won six stakes races in 2016, including the Grade One Forego Stakes and Alfred G. Vanderbilt Handicap.

Titled Heroine is also the dam of champion three-year-old filly Hungria. The chestnut daughter of Nodouble was imported to Mexico and earned her championship in her adopted country with a resounding win in the Clàsico Dalia.

Returning to the great Lady Angela, we see her dark bay son by Chop Chop, named Choperion. Winner of the Coronation Futurity at two, Choperion was highly regarded for a three-year-old campaign but had the unfortunate luck of being born the same year as Flaming Page. He ran second to his stablemate in the Queen's Plate, but did take the Durham Cup later in his career to add another stakes win to his total.

Sent to the National Stud in Oshawa, Choperion proved to be a shy breeder and only got a handful of foals. He certainly was not like his half-brother Nearctic, who was as eager as any stallion who ever lived when it came to meeting the ladies. Choperion does have one long-ranging influence in breeding through his daughter Prize Answer, the fourth dam of recent Australian champion sprinter Brazen Beau.

One more daughter of Lady Angela worth mention is her Victoria Park–sired filly Lady Victoria. Lady Victoria won the Princess Elizabeth Stakes at two and the Tattling Handicap and Maple Leaf Stakes at three. She was an honest racer, placing in the money for fourteen of her twenty races. We have already introduced her son Northern Taste but did not describe in detail how influential Northern Taste has become in his adopted homeland of Japan. No other stallion had dominated the Japanese sire ranks as Northern Taste did during the late 1970s and through the '80s. When Sunday Silence came along to eclipse Northern Taste's records, he did so using many Northern Taste mares as the springboard to success.

In other words, Northern Taste broodmares helped Sunday Silence rewrite the Japanese sire records that Northern Taste had set.

The influence of Lady Angela is deeply felt throughout the world.

{ 5 }

FOUNDATION MARES II: SO MANY SEEDS

T HE EIGHT MARES introduced in the previous chapter exerted considerable influence on the success of both Windfields Farm and the breeders who bought descendants of these mares for their own programs. Several more mares from the same era have been just as important, and in this chapter, we'll look at seven more foundation mares who shaped Windfields fortunes and became revered names in the stud book.

Reply

E.P. Taylor searched the globe for top-quality mares he could bring to his farm. But searching the globe also means looking through one's own neighbourhood. In Ontario, he found a daughter of his stallion Teddy Wrack, out of the Alsab mare Alaris, bred by local breeder Charles Robson. Taylor purchased the filly as a yearling, and she was given the name Reply. She never raced, but Reply did become a valued mare in Windfields Farm history.

Reply was bred to Windfields (the stallion), and, in 1955, she produced a bay filly, Windy Answer, who we met in Chapter Three when we talked about her sire. Windy Answer won ten of twenty-one races in a successful track career. Her biggest moments came in the Star Shoot, Selene, Nassau and Maple Leaf Stakes. She was also second in the Canadian Oaks. Pete McCann considered her to be the best filly he trained since Canadiana.

As a broodmare, though, Windy Answer became a legend. She had six foals, four daughters and two sons. Five of her six foals have outstanding records in either racing or breeding. Her first foal was a daughter by Bull Page named Breezy Answer. This filly won the Princess Elizabeth Stakes at two and finished second in the Canadian Oaks. Breezy Answer's son by Nearctic, Arctic Blizzard, was the champion two-year-old colt in Canada in 1967, after winning the Cup and Saucer and the Coronation Futurity.

Windy Answer's second foal was a filly by Chop Chop who was sold to Jean-Louis Lévesque in the 1962 Windfields annual yearling sale. Lévesque named her Ciboulette, which means *"chive"* in French. This filly also won the Princess Elizabeth Stakes as a two-year-old and added the Duchess, Maple Leaf and Shady Well Stakes to her resumé. Ciboulette later became the cornerstone mare for Lévesque's breeding operation.

Ciboulette's first foal was a memorable one on many levels. Born April 9, 1967, on the Windfields Oshawa farm, Fanfreluche was a beautiful bay daughter of Northern Dancer from his second crop. Fanfreluche raced two years, winning the Princess Elizabeth, Natalma and Fleur de Lys Stakes in her juvenile season. The following year "Fanny" became Canada's Horse of the Year after capturing the Selene Stakes, Bison City Stakes, Quebec Derby, Manitoba Derby and prestigious Alabama Stakes at Saratoga. She finished second to Almoner in the Queen's Plate and to South Ocean in the Canadian Oaks. Fanfreluche added US champion three-year-old filly honours to her resumé also.

Lévesque then retired her for broodmare duty, and here she exceeded her track accomplishments. Her first foal was two-time Sovereign Award Canadian Horse of the Year L'Enjoleur. A son of champion Buckpasser, L'Enjoleur won such important races as the Queen's Plate, Coronation Futurity, Laurel Futurity, Summer Stakes, Cup and Saucer Stakes, Prince of Wales Stakes and R.S. McLaughlin Handicap. He later sired thirty-two stakes winners.

The second foal from Fanfreleuche was L'Extravagante, a stakes-placed bay filly sired by Le Fabuleux. L'Extravagante's name appears as the second dam of Group One Sun Chariot Stakes winner Majestic Roi, and as the third dam of sprint star Russian Revolution, winner of multiple Group One Australian stakes.

Fanny was bred to Epsom Derby winner Sir Ivor and produced a chestnut filly, Grand Luxe, who would win the Fury Stakes and set a track record at Calder racetrack before becoming the pipeline to future important Thoroughbreds in the family. Grand Luxe's 1984 daughter by Mr. Prospector, named Rolls, produced a filly by Star Way named Shoal Creek. This one is the dam of Group One winning Encosta De Lago, a champion Australian sire. Encosta De Lago was sired by Fairy King, a full brother to Sadler's Wells, the great son of Northern Dancer.

Rolls was not done there. Her own son by Danehill, named Flying Spur, was a three-time Group One winner in Australia, which included victories in the prestigious Golden Slipper

Stakes and Australian 2000 Guineas. Flying Spur also became a champion sire in the land down under.

Another daughter of Grand Luxe to make an impression in future breeding was Islands, by Forli. Forli was an Argentinean legend before he took up stud duty at famed Claiborne Farm. Islands' granddaughter Historia, by French Deputy, a son of Deputy Minister, was bred in Argentina and produced three Group One winners—Hinz, Hispanidad and Hi Happy—all sired by Storm Bird's grandson Pure Prize. Hi Happy was Argentina's Horse of the Year as a three-year-old in 2015. He captured four Group One races in his homeland before he came to the United States to win the Grade One Man O' War Stakes and prove his mettle against top-calibre competition in the northern hemisphere.

Fanfreluche was just getting warmed up in her broodmare career. The next foal after Grand Luxe was a dark brown, almost black, filly who Lévesque named La Voyageuse. Sired by Windfields' Maryland farm stallion Tentam, La Voyageuse became the second champion produced by Fanfreluche. Fanny's daughter was an honest and durable racehorse, making fifty-six starts over a five-year career. La Voyageuse won twenty-six of these races and placed in a further seventeen. Her biggest triumphs were the Canadian Oaks, thus avenging her mother's upset loss, and the Nearctic Handicap against males.

The next foal from Fanny, and her third champion, was her doppelgänger son of Secretariat named Medaille d'Or. He was the Sovereign Award champion two-year-old of 1978 and had his biggest moment on the track when he won the Coronation Futurity. Medaille d'Or later stood at Windfields Maryland and was beginning a promising career when he died at the age of ten from injuries in a paddock accident that were too severe for surgery.

Fanfreluche had five foals sired by Secretariat. Her fifth, and her only daughter by the great champion, was L'On Vite, who was unraced. L'On Vite had fifteen foals, six by the outstanding sire Danehill. Her sixth foal by Danehill, and only son, was multiple Group One winner Holy Roman Emperor. L'On Vite produced four stakes winners in total. Holy Roman Emperor entered stud at Coolmore in Ireland in 2007, and the early returns show him to be a promising stallion.

Before Fanfreluche produced L'On Vite, she was bred back to Secretariat not long after producing Medaille d'Or, and came in foal at Claiborne Farm in Kentucky. While there, she was horsenapped (abducted). The news made headlines all around the continent. An exhaustive search led by the FBI turned up nothing. Finally, after five months, she was discovered at a small farm in Tompkinsville near the Tennessee border. She had been found wandering the road by the McPherson family, who owned the farm. Not knowing who she was, they adopted the mare as a family pet and named her Brandy. Larry McPherson willingly gave the FBI the mare once her true identity was revealed. The FBI charged a man with the kidnapping and obtained a conviction.

In total, Fanfreluche had eighteen foals. Five were major stakes winners, and three became champions. Her son L'Enjoleur and daughter La Voyageuse have joined her in the Canadian Racing Hall of Fame. Fanny tended to produce her foals in their sire's image. L'Enjoleur looked very much like Buckpasser. Grand Luxe was so named because of her close resemblance to the impeccable Sir Ivor. Medaille d'Or was a carbon copy of Secretariat, and La Voyageuse was very much in the image of Tentam. Fanfreluche lived to the ripe old age of thirty-two, after leading an unusually colourful and eventful life. She certainly is one of the most memorable Canadian horses.

Returning to Ciboulette, we find her son Coco La Terreur, by Nearctic, who won the Queenston and Woodstock Stakes, as well as a full brother to Fanfreluche called Barachois. Barachois was a flashy red chestnut with plenty of white markings. He won the Plate Trail and finished second in the Plate itself.

Two more Ciboulette offspring are Somfas, her 1978 filly by What A Pleasure, and Night Shift, a bay full brother to Fanfreluche. The latter was not a stakes winner, but he is one of the few stallions to become a very important sire despite a lack of stakes wins. Night Shift sired eighty-nine stakes winners, including multiple Group One winners In The Groove, Daryaba and Azamour. Somfas produced four Group winners and is the grandmother of two more recent such winners. A recent descendant of note is Charm Spirit, who captured three Group One races—the Queen Elizabeth 11 Stakes, the Prix Jean Prat and the Prix du Moulin de Longchamp—during a scintillating three-year-old campaign.

This is the legacy of the Ciboulette branch in the Reply story, and a very successful branch it has become. Now we return to Windy Answer, Ciboulette's dam, and the rest of her enormous contributions to the family fortunes.

Cool Reception, Windy Answer's foal by Nearctic, was covered in Chapter Three, so all we will say here is that Cool Reception's tragic early death was arguably the most devastating loss to Canadian racing. He was a brilliant colt and would have made a fine addition to the stallion ranks.

Prize Answer, by Choperion, was unraced due to injury and remained as a Windfields broodmare. She produced stakes winner Noble Answer, by Viceregal, and unraced Nearctic Answer, by Nearctic. The latter was sent to Australia and is the third dam of the brilliant champion Brazen Beau.

Finally, with regard to Windy Answer, we find her son Northern Answer, by Northern Dancer. Due to his family tree, Northern Answer was pre-priced at $175,000 in the 1967 Windfields yearling sale. There were no takers so he remained with Windfields. He made only one start, in which he fractured a sesamoid. He was successfully operated on and was retired to stud. Northern Answer stood initially at Nashville Stud in Ontario, but he was always owned by Windfields, and after three years, he moved to the Oshawa farm until the 1978 breeding season. Then he was sold to Japanese interests and transferred to the land of the rising sun.

The most important progeny of Northern Answer sired in Canada are Greek Answer, Eternal Search, Victorious Answer and Ocean's Answer. Greek Answer won the Grade One Arlington-Washington Futurity and eight additional graded stakes races. He was a very fast colt and was the champion sprinter in Canada in 1975.

Eternal Search was also a Canadian champion: champion sprinter in 1981 and twice champion older mare, in 1982 and 1983. She won fifteen stakes races in four seasons of competition, never failing to win at least one stakes race each year. She became a very good broodmare and will be highlighted in the section on her ancestor Orchestra later in this chapter. Victorious Answer also came from the family of Orchestra and will be reviewed there too.

Ocean's Answer won the Natalma Stakes and is a female-line descendant of Solar Display. Her stellar broodmare record will be highlighted under her ancestor, in the next section of this chapter.

We have mentioned the best get of Northern Answer here to highlight the successful blending of the families developed by Windfields through several generations. There are many more examples to come.

Another key contributor to the family of Reply is her daughter Respond, by Canadian Champ. Respond produced a filly by Secretariat in 1980 named Devinette. That one produced a daughter, Hey Hazel, by Oshawa farm sire Ascot Knight. Hey Hazel won at least two stakes races in each of her four racing seasons and was a popular fixture at Woodbine during her career.

For fans of breeding nicks, the Nearctic over Reply pattern (seen in Cool Reception) had another success when Northern

Dancer was bred to Respond to get the filly Cold Reply. Among her many stakes winners and her stakes-producing daughters, Cold Reply gave the world three standouts: Question d'Argent, by Tentam; and full sisters Halo Reply and Halory, by Halo.

Question d'Argent was remarkable in that she never placed or won in her eight races on the track but became the grandmother of multimillionaires. Her stakes-winning daughter Croupier Lady, by What Luck, is the dam of the Sunday Silence colt Genuine, winner of Satsuki Sho (Japanese 2000 Guineas), the Mile Championship and more than $5 million in purse earnings. Genuine's full sister Croupier Star earned over $1 million and is the dam of Asakusa Kings, the 2007 champion three-year-old in Japan. He won more than $4 million in his racing career.

Halo Reply won the Yearling Sales Stakes at two and the Ontario Colleen at three. She later became the dam of stakes-placed Prayer Wheel, by Conquistador Cielo, who in turn is the dam of Grade One winner Strategic Maneuver, by Cryptoclearance. Strategic Maneuver won the Matron and Spinaway stakes to earn her Grade One–winning status.

Though Halory started fourteen races, she never won one. However, she made amends in a big way by producing ten winners, five of whom won stakes races. Each stakes winner was sired by a different stallion from different breeding backgrounds. This is remarkable considering multiple-stakes-winning offspring from the same mare generally come from sires with similar breeding patterns. The five Halory produced were Van Nistelrooy by Storm Cat, Brushed Halory by Broad Brush, Halory Hunter by Jade Hunter, Key Lory by Key To The Mint, and Prory by Procida.

One more horse to mention in the Halory branch of the family is stakes-winning millionaire International Star. This son of Fusaichi Pegasus is a great-grandson of Halory and won the

Louisiana Derby, Grey Stakes and Risen Star Stakes on the Kentucky Derby trail in 2015.

Solar Display

In 1952, E.P. Taylor attended the yearling sales in Lexington, looking for good fillies to race and eventually become farm broodmares. He decided to go all in on a half-sister to champion two-year-old Battlefield, consigned by top breeder John Bell. The chestnut filly was by Sun Again, out of Dark Display by Display. However, the filly, named Solar Display, did not make it to the races. If she was to pay for herself, she would have to be a good producing mare.

Solar Display produced four stakes winners, including her first two foals, Dr. Em Jay (by Chop Chop) and Men At Play (by Menetrier). Her two stakes-winning fillies came later and were sisters sired by Victoria Park. Solar Park won the Mazarine Stakes and placed in the Princess Elizabeth Stakes, Coronation Futurity and Wonder Where Stakes. Full-sister Solometeor, on the other hand, won the Princess Elizabeth Stakes and followed up the next year by winning the Canadian Oaks.

Solometeor has been a source of stakes horses through her daughters Solartic, by Oshawa stallion Briartic, and Victoria Star, by Northern Dancer. Solartic was a hard-knocking filly who won seven races from fifteen starts, five of which were stakes wins. She was second to the good filly Par Excellance in the Canadian Oaks and was unplaced only once in her career. Solartic did produce two stakes winners in her breeding career, but no Grade One stakes winners.

Victoria Star entered the yearling sales with a reserve of $50,000, but due to her good looks and fine pedigree, she sold for three times as much, at $160,000. At stud, Victoria Star produced three stakes-placed sons in Bucksplasher, Cogency and

Potentiate. The latter two were Grade One placed, while Bucksplasher was Grade Two placed. Bucksplasher found fame as the sire of multiple Grade One winner Buck's Boy (Breeders' Cup Turf, Turf Classic Stakes).

Victoria Star also produced Stellaria, by Roberto. Stellaria was purchased by Prince Khalid bin Abdullah for his Juddmonte Farms operation, for which she won the Group Two Rose Bowl Stakes. Stellaria later became the dam of the exceptional Observatory, by the Mr. Prospector stallion Distant View. Observatory won the Group One Queen Elizabeth II Stakes, defeating Giant's Causeway and Best Of The Bests, and the Prix d'Ispahan. Observatory won six of ten races in top-level company. He stood at Banstead Manor, Juddmonte's stud farm, where he sired, among others, Twice Over, the European champion older horse of 2010 who won the Champion, International and Eclipse Stakes.

Returning to Solar Display, we find her unraced daughter by Menetrier, named Solarism. This full sister to Men At Play produced Champ de Soleil, by Champlain, who in turn produced Every Effort. This one is the dam of multiple stakes winner Valiant Jewel, who is the dam of Friendly Michelle, by Artax. Friendly Michelle won the Grade One Prioress Stakes and the Grade Three La Troienne Stakes and placed third in the Grade One Acorn and Las Virgenes Stakes. Her sire, Artax, was an Eclipse Award champion sprinter in his day and is a son of multiple Grade One winner Marquetry, himself a grandson of Vice Regent and Lover's Walk.

The daughter of Solar Display who would move the family to worldwide acclaim was Shining Sun, by Chop Chop. Shining Sun was born blind in her right eye, a disability that compromised her racing career. Joe Thomas recalled a race in which she finished second to stablemate Canada Princess. At the start of the race, Shining Sun was cut off by other rivals when the gates opened. Thomas said, "She showed me something. Because she has only one eye, she is usually cautious in behind horses. This time she had to come through the pack, and she did. She's a game little thing."

Perhaps because of his memory of Shining Sun's display of heart, Thomas advised Charles Taylor to purchase a yearling filly out of Shining Sun (by New Providence) at the 1968 CTHS Yearling Sales four years later. The bidding had stalled and Thomas wanted Charles to keep her in the family at the low price. Charles was successful in buying back the filly and named her South Ocean.

South Ocean produced twelve foals. Nine of them became starters, eight became winners, four won stakes races and two were champions. She was enshrined in the Canadian Racing Hall of Fame due to her outstanding broodmare production. Every one of her foals was sired along the Northern Dancer sire line: seven by the patriarch himself, four by his sons and one by a grandson.

The most famous of all South Ocean's offspring was the very memorable Storm Bird. We mentioned his racing achievements in Chapter Three, as well as the frightening attack he endured in Ireland, which caused him to mistrust humans. Storm Bird was a kind soul before the trauma. His record as a stallion at Ashford Stud in Kentucky, following his syndication for a then record $28 million, has stamped Storm Bird as one of the best sons of Northern Dancer as a sire.

Storm Bird will live on due to his incredible son Storm Cat. This exceptional stallion has carried the line to great heights throughout the world with the likes of Giant's Causeway, Harlan, Tale Of The Cat, Bernstein, Forestry, Bluegrass Cat, Hennessy and Stormy Atlantic as sires. Among the prominent names from Storm Cat daughters are Shared Belief, Speightstown and Dialed In. However, Storm Bird's claim to fame hangs on more than just Storm Cat.

Preakness Stakes winner Summer Squall, a half-brother to A.P. Indy, has been a very desirable and successful stallion, despite fertility issues. Champion sprinter Bluebird proved to be a sire of quality at Coolmore in Ireland. Mukaddamah was a champion three-year-old in France. Prince Of Birds was the champion miler in Ireland in 1988. The wonderful filly Balanchine won the Epsom Oaks and the Irish Derby, and Indian Skimmer captured the Prix Saint-Alary, Prix de Diane and both the English and Irish Champion Stakes against the boys during her championship racing career. Clearly, Storm Bird was a world-class sire.

South Ocean's other champion offspring was Storm Bird's older full sister Northernette. Sold as a yearling to Syl Asadoorian and Sam Cosentino for $50,000 in 1975, the Windfields-bred became the champion filly the next year as a juvenile, then followed that with another championship as a three-year-old. Northernette won the Canadian Oaks, the Selene Stakes and the Fury Stakes at her home track, Woodbine. She was sold to Peter Brant, who put her into the barn of Hall of Fame trainer Frank Whiteley. He sent her out to win the Chrysanthemum Stakes on the Laurel Race Course turf course.

Returning for another racing season, Northernette won the Grade One Top Flight Handicap and the Grade Two Apple Blossom Handicap, and finished second to Tempest Queen while giving that one three pounds in the Spinster Stakes. Retired to the breeding arena, Northernette produced Grade One winner Scoot (Flower Bowl Handicap), by Mr. Prospector; Grade Two winner Gold Crest, Scoot's full brother; and stakes producers Fextal, Midnight Oasis, Wyndalia and Limbo.

South Ocean's daughter Ocean's Answer, by Northern Answer, represents two exceptional female families. This descendant of Solar Display won the Natalma Stakes, for her only black-type victory. As a broodmare, Ocean's Answer played a big part in furthering the family fortunes, although she did not produce a stakes winner. Her daughters did, however, and there are many.

Soundings, by Mr. Prospector, produced four stakes winners, including the classic Poule d'Essai des Poulins and the Prix d'Ispahan winner Green Tune. Green Tune claims 2012 Eclipse champion turf female Zagora (Breeders' Cup Filly and Mare Turf, Diana Stakes) as his best offspring as a stallion. Pas de Reponse, by Danzig, the European champion two-year-old filly of 1996 (winner of the Cheveley Park Stakes), is another important foal out of Soundings. A daughter of Pas de Reponse, Saying, by Giant's Causeway, produced Dicton, who defeated Almanzor in the 2016 Prix de Fountainbleau, then finished third to Almanzor in the Prix du Jockey Club and third to The Gurkha in the Poule d'Essai des Poulins.

Another daughter of Ocean's Answer is Devil's Oceanette, by E.P. Taylor–bred champion Devil's Bag. This chestnut mare is the third dam of Grade One winner Dr. Zic, by Milwaukee Brew.

The final daughter of South Ocean who we will feature, Stormette, by Assert, is the dam of Hollywood Turf Handicap winner Storm Trooper, by Diesis. There is a wealth of Grade Two and Grade Three stakes winners descending from Solar Display, and we refer you to the family tree chart at the back of the book for more details.

Orchestra

When tracing a successful family back to the key, or foundation, mare, we generally arrive at a purchase from outside the Windfields Farm breeding program. These mares were usually from families that had some success, but this success was elevated to new heights through the individuals introduced to the stallions available through Windfields.

Orchestra came to Windfields via a slightly different route. She was in utero when E.P. Taylor purchased her dam, Abondance. Her sire, Menetrier, stood in France. When Orchestra was born, Taylor and Gil Darlington were very impressed with the dark brown daughter of the stallion, leading them to ask François Dupré if Menetrier could be purchased and relocated to the National Stud in Oshawa (see more about Menetrier in Chapter Three). Orchestra proved her good looks were more than skin deep, going on to a successful racing and breeding career.

Unsold as a yearling, Orchestra raced under the turquoise and gold of Windfields, capturing three stakes victories. She took the Star Shoot Stakes and beat the boys twice, in the Woodstock and Friar Rock stakes races. One of the colts she defeated was multiple stakes winner Bunty's Flight, who would later become known as the damsire of Deputy Minister. However, it was as a broodmare that Orchestra made her biggest contribution to the success of Windfields.

Orchestra's second foal was a daughter of Chop Chop named Allegro. This stakes-placed filly formed a productive alliance with Northern Dancer. The first foal from the combination was Swinging Apache, one of the second crop of Northern Dancer foals. Sold to Frank McMahon as a yearling, Swinging Apache made six starts in his career and was never beaten. His most important victories came in the Canadian Derby, the Ascot Sophomore Stakes and the Harbour Handicap. Unfortunately, Swinging Apache was gelded so did not breed on.

Seven years after Swinging Apache, Allegro produced another son of Northern Dancer. Going by the name Dance In Time, the colt placed in the important Cup and Saucer Stakes at two, then won the classic Prince of Wales and Breeders' Stakes the following season. He added the Friar Rock Stakes and was named the Sovereign Award champion three-year-old colt of 1977.

The year after Allegro was born, Orchestra produced Orchestrina by Nearctic. E.P. Taylor had a small stable of runners with trainer Ron Smythe, who was based at Epsom Downs in Surrey, England. Orchestrina carried the Windfields colours in England

and won one race from ten starts. She came back to Canada for broodmare duties. Her first foal, and her only stakes winner, was New Pro Escar, sired by New Providence. He won the classic Prince of Wales Stakes.

Orchestrina's next foal was a filly by Victoria Park. Sold to Jean-Louis Lévesque at the 1970 CTHS yearling sales, the filly acquired the name Chou Fleur, which translates to the endearing nickname "Cabbage." Chou Fleur won three allowance races but did not earn any black type. She had only two foals, neither of whom won stakes races. You may ask why she is mentioned here. Well, her daughter Bon Debarras is a very good reason.

Sired by Oshawa farm stallion Ruritania, Bon Debarras was given a not very endearing name, which translates to "Good Riddance." She was never considered for racing and was actually bred to Northern Answer when she was only two years old. By this time, Bon Debarras was under the banner of the North American Bloodstock Agency. Essentially shunned from birth, Bon Debarras turned things around with her first foal, Eternal Search, a dark bay filly by Northern Answer, who became a multiple champion on the track, a producer of stakes winners and a member of the Canadian Racing Hall of Fame. Eternal Search was fast, durable and very game. She made forty-four starts, winning eighteen, fifteen of which were stakes races. She had a further eleven second-place finishes. Eternal Search won three Sovereign Awards, once as champion sprinter and twice as the top older mare.

With the success of Eternal Search, Bon Debarras became a frequent acquaintance of sons of Northern Dancer. In 1984, she produced a bay daughter by The Minstrel, later named Vevila. This one produced a daughter by Bold Ruckus named Embur Sunshine, who is the dam of champion older mare Embur's Song. Embur Sunshine also foaled a filly named Dawn Raid. Dawn Raid was bred to two-time Eclipse Award Horse of the

Year Curlin, and the result was 2016 Preakness Stakes winner Exaggerator. Exaggerator also added the Grade One Santa Anita Derby and the Haskell Stakes to his impressive racing resumé.

Savethelastdance is another daughter of Bon Debarras who has taken the family fortunes to latter-day success. She was a four-time allowance winner and placed seven times in stakes competition but did not win a stakes race. Her first foal was an unraced daughter of Forty Niner named Sue's Last Dance. This one produced Island Sand, a Grade One winner (Acorn Stakes) sired by Tabasco Cat. Savethelastdance also gave us Queen's Plate winner Niigon, by Unbridled.

Returning to Orchestra, we find her bay filly Victory Chant, from the first crop sired by Victoria Park. Victory Chant produced three stakes winners, including one champion, and three stakes-producing daughters. This branch of the Orchestra family has prospered around the world. Victory Chant's son Malvado, by Nearctic, became a five-time leading sire and three-time leading broodmare sire in his adopted home of India.

Giboulee is the champion son of Victory Chant. Sired by Northern Dancer, Giboulee became the only offspring of the Kentucky Derby winner to run in the famous race (he finished seventh). His credentials include wins in the Coronation Futurity and a second to Seattle Slew in the Flamingo Stakes prior to his Derby participation. Giboulee went on to win the Manitoba Derby and Calumet Purse as a three-year-old, then won his Sovereign Award the following year as the top handicap horse in the country.

Victory Chant's daughter Victory Songster is the link to some fine recent Grade One winners. Sired by Oshawa stallion Stratus, Victory Songster appears in the bloodlines of 2012 Sovereign Award Horse of the Year Uncaptured, Italian Derby winner Bahamian Knight and three-time Grade One stakes winner Curalina. The latter's pedigree is full of Canadian-influenced breeding, and she was sold as a broodmare prospect in 2016 for $3 million.

Another generational Grade One winner from the Victory Chant branch is Camp Victory, winner of the 2012 Triple Bend Handicap. The gelded son of the mare Victory Trick was sired by Deputy Minister's son Forest Camp. Victory Trick is out of Victorious Answer, a daughter of Victory Chant.

Queen's Statute

George Blackwell purchased Queen's Statute on E.P. Taylor's behalf at the 1955 Newmarket yearling sales. The daughter of Le Lavandou, out of the Son-In-Law mare Statute, set Taylor back £5,000, but it turned out to be a fortuitous acquisition that has paid dividends for many generations around the world.

Queen's Statute did not start in a race due to injuries. However, she covered herself in glory many times over with her incredible broodmare production. She gave the world six stakes winners and a pair of daughters who have brought the family to the forefront of world breeding acclaim. Her first three foals, all fillies, won stakes races. Epic Queen, by E.P. Taylor's first Queen's Plate winner Epic, was the first. Menedict, by Menetrier, won the Canadian Oaks, and Court Royal, by Chop Chop, won several high-class stakes at Woodbine.

Menedict produced a daughter by Roman Line, a grandson of the great stallion Sir Gallahad III, named Bye Bye Mercedes. Bye Bye Mercedes was unraced but became the dam of Grade One stakes winner Mercedes Won, by Air Forbes Won, who was a Grade One–winning great-grandson of Bold Ruler. Mercedes Won captured the Grey Stakes at Woodbine and the Hopeful Stakes at Saratoga during his juvenile season. He followed those successes with a win in the Florida Derby at three. He was named champion two-year-old colt in Canada.

The most successful stakes winner produced by Queen's Statute was Dance Act in 1966. From the first crop of Northern

Dancer foals, Dance Act was not a big horse, took his time to mature and was gelded—putting up with cranky Northern Dancer sons and saving their breeding ability had not yet become standard practice. Dance Act made up for lost time when he won back-to-back handicap championships in Canada at age four and five.

Dance Act's full sisters, Royal Statute and Falafel, are the avenues to modern stakes winners along the Queen's Statute line. Royal Statute's first foal, by Damascus, was a filly named Konafa. A winner of one race, Konafa placed second in the 1000 Guineas but did not win a stakes race. Her Group Two–winning daughter Proskona, by Mr. Prospector, is the third dam of Act One, who won five of his six lifetime races (including Criterium International, Prix Lupin). The only loss of this son of In The Wings was a close second to Sulamani in the French Derby. Proskona is also the second dam of the Manduro colt Ultra (winner of the Prix Jean-Luc Lagardère).

Konafa gave the world stakes-winning German champion Keos and full sister stakes-winner Korveya by Riverman, a stallion Windfields held syndicate shares in.

Korveya produced three Group One stakes winners and two daughters who produced winners at the highest levels. Shanghai, by Procida (a son of Mr. Prospector), won the classic Poule d'Essai des Poulins. Korveya had a brother and sister duo sired by Woodman, another son of Mr. Prospector, who each won Group One events. Hector Protector won the Prix Morny, Prix de la Salamandre and the Grand Critérium at two, to be named champion in France in his age group. He came back at three to win the Poule d'Essai des Poulins and the Prix Jacques Le Marois. His sister Bosra Sham won divisional championships in each of her three racing seasons. Among her major wins are the 1000 Guineas, the Champion Stakes and the Fillies Mile Stakes.

For fans of breeding nicks, Korveya seemed to have a good relationship with sons of Mr. Prospector. Her daughter Tapatina, by Mr. Prospector son Seeking The Gold, did not win a race from three starts. However, she did produce Del Mar Oaks winner Internallyflawless, by Giant's Causeway. Another Korveya daughter, Gioconda, by Nijinsky II, met up with Woodman to produce Grade/Group One winner Ciro. Ciro won the Grand Critérium at two and the Prix Lupin and Secretariat Stakes at three. He also finished third in the Irish Derby.

Konafa had a full sister to Proskona named Kamaina. This chestnut daughter of Mr. Prospector won only one race from eight starts but later produced Kalpita, a daughter of the cantankerous stallion Spinning World. Also a one-time winner, Kalpita was bred to the grey stallion Highest Honor, a three-time champion sire in France. The name of the grey colt who came from the match was Portus Blendium, and he won two races in France and placed third in a pair of minor stakes races. He was purchased by Hong Kong Thoroughbred owner Howard Liang Yum Shing. As is the practice with many horses imported to Hong Kong, his name was changed in his new home. Now racing as California Memory, the grey gelding won important races for his new connections: the Group One Hong Kong Cup, Champions & Chater Cup and the Hong Kong Gold Cup. California Memory became a popular fixture at Sha Tin and Happy Valley Racecourses and was named Hong Kong champion stayer three times.

Konafa had a liaison with British-bred stallion Sharpen Up, which produced stakes winner Carnet Solaire. When retired to broodmare duty, Carnet Solaire produced stakes-placed winner Beyond The Sun, by Kingmambo, another son of Mr. Prospector. Beyond The Sun is the dam of Red Giant, by Giant's Causeway. Red Giant became the world record holder for 10 furlongs when he sped around the Santa Anita grass track in 1:57.16 to win the Grade One Clement L. Hirsch Turf Championship.

One more descendant of Konafa to mention is Grade One San Juan Capistrano Handicap winner Passinetti. He is a son of Slew O' Gold, out of Cloelia by Lyphard. Cloelia is a daughter of Konafa.

Returning to Royal Statute, we find her son Akureyri, sired by the legendary Buckpasser. Akureyri was a graded stakes winner of the Fountain of Youth Stakes. He also crossed the wire first in the Grade Two Remsen Stakes but was disqualified and placed third due to interference. Akureyri was fast and athletic but also volatile, and his temperament was his undoing in many races. He was firmly on the Triple Crown trail, beating eventual Kentucky Derby winner Pleasant Colony three times in four meetings, and losing only in the Grade One Florida Derby, when he was second. However, he was retired following this race when it was discovered that he had chipped a knee.

Akureyri inherited his temper from his mother. Royal Statute was a very territorial mare and had to be kept in her own paddock. She would attack other mares and foals if they came too close to her or her foal. In 1978, she was bred to another known cranky horse, Snow Knight. The result was the wonderful Awaasif, England's champion three-year-old filly of 1982. Awaasif, a bay with a white star on her forehead and three white socks, was purchased by Sheikh Mohammed bin Rashid Al Maktoum for $325,000 at the Fasig-Tipton Kentucky yearling sales in 1980. Racing in Europe, she won the Yorkshire Oaks against fillies and the Gran Premio del Jockey Club against mixed company, and finished third to Akiyda and Ardross in the Prix de l'Arc de Triomphe. Sent to the Sheikh's broodmare colony, Awaasif became a foundation mare for his emerging breeding empire.

Snow Bride was undoubtedly Awaasif's most important offspring. Sired by the impeccable Blushing Groom, Snow Bride won the 1989 Epsom Oaks as well as four listed, or Grade Three, races. In the breeding shed, Snow Bride produced a horse of amazing accomplishments in Lammtarra.

Lammtarra started in only four races but won them all. After his only race as a two-year-old, Lammtarra was put away in preparation for his three-year-old campaign. His connections picked his spots perfectly. The Epsom Derby, the King George VI and Queen Elizabeth Stakes, and the Prix de l'Arc de Triomphe all fell to this big beautiful chestnut son of Nijinsky II, and he was named European champion three-year-old. His campaign was not only unique but also remarkable in that he trained to each big event and did not race in preliminary races for fitness. Saeed bin Suroor was the training mastermind behind Lammtarra's path to greatness.

Sheikh Mohammed bred Snow Bride to Sadler's Wells and got a filly, Abhisheka, in 2003. She made ten starts, winning three times, and later produced for the sheikh a Distorted Humor colt named Aesop's Fables. Aesop's Fables won the Group One Prix Jean Prat to add another high-level winner to the family accomplishments.

Going back again to Royal Statute, we find her daughter Victoress, by Conquistador Cielo. A winner of one race from four attempts, Victoress produced an unraced daughter of Darshaan named Gwynn. Gwynn produced Pour Moi, by Montjeu, who won the Epsom Derby, adding another winner of the world's most famous race to the Queen's Statute family.

As mentioned earlier, Royal Statute's full sister Falafel produced another branch of the Queen's Statute line to examine. Falafel was sold as a yearling and won once in five starts in France. She came back to North America for broodmare duties. Bred to Honest Pleasure, Falafel produced a 1982 colt, Again Tomorrow. This bay son attained Group One–winning status when he captured the Premio Parioli, otherwise known as the Italian 2000 Guineas.

Falafel later foaled a son by Irish River named Brief Truce. Here, we have a very honest, hard-knocking horse who was never off the board in his ten career starts, always at the top level of competition. Brief Truce won the Group One St. James's Palace Stakes, placed second in both the Prix du Moulin and the Queen Elizabeth II Stakes, and was third in the Irish 2000 Guineas and Breeders' Cup Mile.

The latest member of this high-level family to achieve Grade One–winning status is Condo Commando, winner of the 2014 Spinaway Stakes. Condo Commando is a five-time winner from eight starts and is a fifth-generation descendant of Falafel.

A little-known branch of the Queen's Statute family springs from Queen's Law, sired by Oshawa stallion Queen's Own. Queen's Law is the dam of Principle, by Viceregal, who is the granddam of the prolific Group One producer Miss Bio, by Principle's son River Mist. Miss Bio has produced two outstanding sons in Silverwave (Grand Prix de Saint-Cloud) and champion miler Stormy River (Prix Jean Prat).

Clearly the family of Queen's Statute has been front and centre in world breeding. She is the matriarch of some of the top stakes winners and is considered one of the premier broodmares of the twentieth century.

Heliostrings

E.P. Taylor cast his eyes to Kentucky for the 1956 yearling sales and found a well-bred daughter of leading sire Heliopolis that both he and Joe Thomas, a new employee at the time, liked. The dam was No Strings, by Occupation, a Belmont Futurity winner sired by Bull Dog. No Strings was popular that year due to her very fast two-year-old son Nail, who had won the Futurity Stakes at the time of the sale.

There was one catch to the filly, however, which was that she was a twin. Thoroughbred twins are not desirable because both offspring tend to have weaknesses. As with everything pertaining to equine genetics, though, exceptions aren't unheard of. Taylor liked the filly very much, as did other buyers, and he had to go to $20,000 in order to buy her. He was buoyed soon after when Nail was crowned champion juvenile of that year.

The filly was named Heliostrings, and she won three races from thirteen starts, finishing in the money another five times. Not bad considering her twin status. The daughter who brought this family to Grade/Group One level is Heliostrings' 1965 foal by Victoria Park named Greek Victress. This one produced two stakes winners, including Canadian champion sprinter Greek Answer.

Greek Answer won the Grade One Arlington-Washington Futurity and eight additional graded stakes races, including the Swynford Stakes, Fountain of Youth Stakes and Plate Trial. He was a very fast colt and was named the champion sprinter in Canada in 1975. He appears as the damsire in the pedigree of Grade One winner Captain Bodgit.

Grecian Victory, by Dr. Fager, won two stakes races and produced two stakes winners. Her stakes-winning daughter Valid Victress continued the stakes-winning line when she gave birth to Perfect Sting, a daughter of Red Ransom. Perfect Sting became the Eclipse Award champion turf female in 2000 when she won the Breeders' Cup Filly and Mare Turf, the Diana Handicap and three more graded stakes races on the grass. A year earlier, she had announced her presence with wins in the Grade One Garden City Handicap and the Queen Elizabeth II Challenge Cup.

Another daughter of Greek Victress to lead to a major winner is Midi Skirt, sired by Canebora. Midi Skirt is the third dam of Sovereign Award champion sprinter Field Commission, through her daughter Water Spider (by Briartic) and granddaughter Tearfull Moment (by Oshawa stallion Schossberg). Field Commission, a Minshall Farms–bred son of Service Stripe, himself a son of Deputy Minister, won the Nearctic Handicap during his championship season.

Midinette II

From Italy came a stakes-winning mare who E.P. Taylor purchased for his Oshawa farm. Midinette II was a daughter of Prix de l'Arc de Triomphe winner Tantieme, a stallion with a very impressive racing resumé, as he was also victorious in the Poule d'Essai des Poulins, the Grand Critérium, Coronation Cup and Prix Lupin. Midinette II was out of the stakes-winning Italian mare Milonga, who represents a strong line of Italian stakes-winning producers.

The second dam of Midinette II, Michela, won the Italian Oaks and was the Italian champion three-year-old in her year. The fourth dam of Midinette II was Fausta, one of the great female Thoroughbreds in Italian racing and breeding history. Bred and raced by the incomparable Federico Tesio, Fausta not only won the Italian Oaks, but also beat the boys in the Italian Derby. As a broodmare, she produced three Italian Derby winners in Meissonier, Michelangelo and Melozzo Da Forli. Midinette II came from a powerful family.

The first foal Midinette produced was a bay daughter of Victoria Park named Buena Notte. Unsold at the 1965 Windfields yearling sale, Buena Notte raced under the turquoise and gold Windfields colours twelve times, bringing those colours to the winner's circle only once. She was retired for broodmare duty, and among her eight foals was Puerto Rico's 1978 champion three-year-old colt Shake Shake Shake.

Buena Notte had a daughter by Maryland sire Search For Gold. This one did sell as a yearling to Pennyacres Farm at Timonium, Maryland, was named Pot Of Gold and won a single race. However, when bred to Maryland sire Tentam, Pot Of Gold produced a dark bay, almost black, colt who was purchased by the BKY Stable in Ontario. Given the name Ten Gold Pots, the great-grandson of Midinette won twelve stakes races and earned a Sovereign Award as Canada's champion older horse in 1985.

Buena Notte was bred back to Maryland sire Dancing Count and produced a full sister to Shake Shake Shake named Count On Bonnie. Bred to the Mr. Prospector stallion Woodman, Count On Bonnie produced a colt of exceptional class, a lovely bay named Hansel. At two, Hansel won the Grade One Arlington-Washington Futurity and Grade Three Tremont Stakes. The next year, he was the favourite in the Kentucky Derby but faded badly to finish tenth. He bounced back to win the Preakness Stakes by seven lengths, then won the Belmont Stakes by a head over the Derby winner Strike The Gold.

Dancing Count, Count On Bonnie's sire, and her dam, Buena Notte, had scarcely any form of note as runners. However, the best of their genes would manifest in Hansel. Accomplishments from the breeding shed are as unpredictable as prowess on the track.

Lachine

Just as he did with Lady Angela (see Chapter Four), E.P. Taylor purchased Lachine in England in foal to a highly regarded sire. She had the foal in England and was bred back to the same stallion. Once she was certified in foal, she and her suckling daughter were brought to Canada. The sire in question here is Match II, winner of the Washington International, the King George VI and Queen Elizabeth Stakes, and the Grand Prix de Saint-Cloud. Match II was a Horse of the Year in England and was also a son of Tantieme, a sire line that Taylor had a keen interest in.

The daughter Lachine bore in England was named Lachute. The daughter she carried in utero and delivered in Canada was Matcher. Shawnee Farm purchased Matcher at the last Windfields private yearling sale and took her to England, where she made two unplaced starts. Matcher eventually resided in Ireland and produced a stakes-winning daughter by Pampapaul named Myra's Best.

The second foal from Myra's Best was a chestnut filly by Ahonoora named Waky Na. Waky Na won a pair of stakes races in Germany and later produced a Grade One stakes-winning son by Alzao who went by the name of Waky Nao. This one captured the Premio Vittorio di Capua and several German group stakes during a very successful racing career.

Matcher herself was also bred to Ahonoora and produced the very fast and game filly Park Express. Park Express won the Group One Irish Champion Stakes against the boys as well as the Lancashire Oaks and the Nassau Stakes. After her stellar racing career, Park Express became a decorated broodmare, being named as an Irish broodmare of the year.

Park Express's first stakes winner was the Green Desert colt Shinko Forest, winner of the Japanese Group One Takamatsu-nomiya Kinen. Her next stakes winner was European champion two-year-old filly Dazzling Park, by Warning, who won the Irish Matron Stakes and was second in the Irish Champion Stakes and third in the Irish 1000 Guineas. Dazzling Park is the second dam of Group One stakes winner Alfred Nobel (Phoenix Stakes), by Danehill Dancer.

The third stakes winner from Park Express was also her last foal: Cartier European champion two-year-old of 2007, New Approach. Sired by Galileo, New Approach won the Group One Dewhurst Stakes and Irish National Stakes, and went a perfect five for five as a juvenile. In his first two starts as a three-year-old, he finished second in the English and Irish 2000 Guineas to Henrythenavigator. He redeemed himself with a stirring victory in the Derby Stakes at Epsom, finished third to Duke Of Marmalade in the International Stakes, and then captured both the Irish Champion Stakes and the Champion Stakes at Newmarket to complete his very impressive racing career.

Retired to stand at Dalham Hall Stud in Newmarket, New Approach got off to an impressive start with his first crop of foals. In this crop was European champion two-year-old Dawn Approach, winner of the Vincent O'Brien Stakes, Dewhurst Stakes and Coventry Stakes during his juvenile season. Dawn Approach followed up the next year with wins in the 2000 Guineas and the St. James's Palace Stakes. Also in the first crop by New Approach were the Group One winners Talent (Epsom Oaks), Sultanina (Nassau Stakes) and May's Dream (Australasian Oaks, VATC 1000 Guineas).

Park Express produced a full sister to Shinko Forest named Alluring Park. This stakes-placed winner would produce 2012 Epsom Oaks winner Was, from a cover by Galileo. Park Express has been a prominent mare in recent breeding circles.

Returning to Lachine, we find two sons by Northern Dancer. The first was Grand Chaudiere, a stakes-placed winner who faced the likes of Mill Reef, among others. His claim to fame is as an ancestor, fifth generation, of the great undefeated sprinting mare Black Caviar. The second son, Grand Lachine, was a stakes winner in National Hunt races—that is, in steeplechases. This success was originally overlooked while compiling Northern Dancer's sire records. It was later recognized, making Grand Lachine the 147th recorded stakes winner for his sire.

One more notable descendant of Lachine comes through Quick Selection, her stakes-winning daughter by Viceregal. This one's grandson Bandari, by Alhaarth (himself a grandson of Northern Dancer through Unfuwain), was a sound and consistent racehorse. Bandari won the Princess of Wales's Stakes, Great Voltigeur Stakes and six additional graded or listed stakes. He placed third in the St Leger Stakes.

Lachine was a daughter of the very important sire Grey Sovereign, a son of Nasrullah. Her outstanding pedigree has been a key to her founding a successful family that has crossed back to Europe, from whence she came.

$\{\,6\,\}$

ENTER NEARCTIC AND NATALMA

IF ONE COULD pinpoint a specific time in Windfields history that definitively shaped the future, it would have to be the arrival of Nearctic. Even with so many well-bred and highly regarded bloodstock entering the Windfields domain, the purchase of Lady Angela and Nearctic (in utero) from a repeat cover by Nearco is a key moment. As mentioned in Chapter Two, E.P. Taylor spent countless hours in negotiations, and dug deep into his pockets, to secure a second foal from a Nearco–Lady Angela union. And this was only for the speculative chance that one of the two foals might amount to much. Two previous foals from the same match had not been successful.

More drama would unfold in this story, and more of the Taylor good fortune was in play, when Lady Angela and her son arrived in Montreal. The crew of the ship she travelled on had little experience handling horses, especially a mare with a suckling at her side. The crate that carried equines to the dock was only large enough for one horse at a time, so the crew tried to unload the mare first. She became frantic when they tried to separate her from her son.

Luckily, Windfields management had sent experienced horseman Harry Green to collect Lady Angela, and when he saw the chaos developing, he quickly took charge. Harry had the colt led to the crate to be taken down to the dock first. He then went back and loaded the mare. Lady Angela quietly went on her ride to the dock and rejoined her son.

Lady Angela's panic attack could have induced a miscarriage, but, fortunately for the future of Thoroughbred breeding, the foal was safe, for it was none other than Nearctic. He was born February 11, 1954, at Windfields. The colt was black, like his sire, and had a similar temperament. (Note that Nearctic was officially registered as dark bay due to the prevailing laws of colour identification set by the Jockey Club, which is hesitant to proclaim a foal is pure black. That colour is very rare in the Thoroughbred breed. Many horses who look black under certain lighting conditions are actually dark bay or dark brown. But Nearctic was so close to black, we refer to him as such.)

As seems to happen in many stories of Thoroughbred lore, the fourth breeding of Lady Angela to Nearco proved to be fortuitous. The older foal, who came to Canada at Lady Angela's side, was a chestnut colt who was somewhat weak and light boned. Given the name Empire Day, this older brother of Nearctic won a few races and was quickly forgotten. Nearctic, on the other hand, was a strong, spirited colt, powerful and very fast.

A Real Handful

Growing up on the Willowdale farm after he was weaned, the robust black colt became an object of constant attention. He was obviously well made and possessed a lively character, seldom standing still when he was out in the paddocks. Farm staff would spend their off-duty hours watching this son of a legend out of the daughter of another legend. He could be hard to handle, unless you were a seasoned and talented horseman, and he could fray the nerves of anyone. In short, he was charismatic.

Nearctic was offered at Windfields' private yearling sale in 1955. A buyer could have snapped him up for $35,000, a hefty sum in those days. This high price tag for a Canadian-bred scared off all who attended the sale.

Consequently, as was E.P. Taylor's policy for unsold yearlings, the well-bred colt joined the Windfields racing stable to compete under the famous turquoise and gold colours. A foal of 1954, Nearctic was one of many exceptional colts to race from a remarkable generation that included such memorable racehorses as Bold Ruler, Round Table, Gallant Man, Iron Liege, Clem, King Hairan, Gen. Duke and Barbizon.

Four years before Nearctic's racing debut, Bert Alexandra had retired from training, fourteen years after he made his first attempt to do so. The parting with the Taylors' stable was bittersweet on both sides. Alexandra was a master of the claiming game and had done an impressive job for the Taylors, which they appreciated very much. But Bert was a meat-and-potatoes type of man, who relished the challenge of haltering another trainer's up-and-coming horse from a claiming race, or dropping a horse into a lower-class race in order to have someone else claim the horse away.

The ambitious E.P. Taylor was in search of bigger prizes. He wanted to develop top-calibre stakes winners. Bert did train

Taylor's first King's Plate winner, Epic, but the pomp and pageantry in the winner's circle was not to his taste. During the post-race interviews, when the public address announcer proclaimed that this was the first Plate win for the owner, the jockey and the trainer, Bert grabbed the microphone and famously said, "This was also the first for the horse."

When Bert retired, E.P. hired Gordon "Pete" McCann as his new stable trainer. McCann was an ex-jockey, like Alexandra, and was as dedicated to his horses as any man has ever been. Pete was a soft-spoken, unassuming man with two passions in his life, his family and his horses. Taylor could not have found a better or more caring person for his racing stable.

McCann had already trained two Plate winners for his new boss—Major Factor and Canadiana—by the time the blue-blooded Nearctic entered his barn. Part of Pete's training regimen was to exercise his horses himself, thus giving him first-hand knowledge of the horse's action, speed and running style. He was a brilliant horseman and had an uncanny ability to get into the psyche of his charges, which allowed him to devise specific training programs for each horse in his care, preparing them for racing and bringing them to their peak fitness.

Within the first couple of workouts aboard Nearctic, Pete knew that he had a fast but headstrong colt on his hands. There was plenty of speed and ability to tap into. But Nearctic had his own idea of how he wanted to race, which was to blast out of the gate as soon as it opened and go as fast as he could as long as he could. Nearctic had no interest in being rated (obeying his jockey's commands) to conserve energy for a longer distance. McCann knew he faced a challenge to get Nearctic to compete successfully at classic distances—a mile and a quarter to a mile and a half—and not just sprints.

Racing Career

Nearctic made his racing debut on May 10, 1956, at Old Woodbine in a 4.5-furlong maiden two-year-old event. The son of Nearco burst from the starting gate as if he had been shot out of a cannon and gradually increased his lead throughout the race to win. He won his next four races in similar fashion, with the last three wins coming in the Swansea Plate, Clarendon Stakes and Victoria Stakes. In these races, he was piloted by Avelino Gomez. The combination of McCann and Gomez would be the right mix for Nearctic to perform at his best, but the two men were not always available for the colt.

With a perfect five-for-five record, the decision was made to take Nearctic to the United States to test him against the top American two-year-old colts at Saratoga Race Course in New York State. McCann did not like to travel and was reluctant to go to Saratoga, since he had many other Thoroughbreds in his Toronto barn who needed his attention. So Nearctic went to the famous spa with his groom, while Pete stayed back in Toronto.

Complicating matters for Nearctic was the fact that the Cuban-born Gomez was not licensed to ride in the United States. He refused to go into the American military and was considered a draft dodger. Gomez began his riding career in Chicago, moving back to Cuba in 1951 and then on to Toronto two years later to resume riding. He was drafted by the United States when he was back in his native land, did not report and was handed the banishment. It would take until 1961 for Gomez to actually enter the United States without threat of imprisonment.

With Charlie Shaw as trainer in place of Pete McCann, Nearctic made three starts at Saratoga. He won the second race, which was the Saratoga Special, but ran unplaced in the other two. He also suffered bucked shins (an inflammation of the forelegs) while at Saratoga.

Nearctic was sent back to Windfields Farm for treatment, then returned to the barn of Pete McCann.

Pete got him ready for the 7-furlong Carleton Stakes at Woodbine, and Nearctic duly won with Gomez aboard. However, another injury surfaced in the form of a developing quarter crack on his left front hoof. Pete wanted time for the crack to grow out and heal, but it was now September and the prestigious two-year-old races were just around the corner. Nearctic stayed in training.

Charlie Shaw was again the trainer of record when Nearctic raced in New York, at Belmont Park, during his second cross-border foray. Nearctic faced the top two-year-old in Bold Ruler, and he ran dismally. He could no longer endure the pain in his left front hoof and stopped cold in the Belmont Futurity.

That was the end of Nearctic's two-year-old season, and the quarter crack, an equine version of split toenails, kept resurfacing during his three-year-old campaign. He did, however, win the International Handicap on the Fort Erie grass course to salvage an otherwise disappointing season.

Nearctic came back the following year and reasserted himself as one of the best in his remarkable generation. He won seven stakes races, including a win over future Hall of Fame inductee Swoon's Son in the Michigan Mile Handicap. He also took the Canadian Maturity, Bold Venture Handicap, Jacques Cartier Stakes and Vigil Handicap. He won on dirt and grass courses and was named Canadian Horse of the Year for 1958. He set track records in four of his victories.

Back for another campaign, the five-year-old Nearctic still presented Pete McCann with difficulties as his trainer tried to harness his headstrong desire to go all out from the starting gate. Nearctic was becoming increasingly obstinate, which compromised his chances. He won his second Vigil Handicap for his only stakes victory in an abbreviated season. The wear and tear was beginning to show, so Taylor and his advisors decided to retire the powerful black horse to stand at the Oshawa farm.

Stud Influence

When Nearctic began his stud career, he instantly became the most regally bred stallion in the Dominion. Still, even though Gil Darlington set a modest $2,500 stud fee, Canadian breeders were hesitant to send mares to him, likely due to his being an unproven stallion. American breeders did not send mares either, as they continued to believe that Canadian horses were inferior. However, the actor Don Ameche, who was a Thoroughbred breeder/owner, saw Nearctic while visiting E.P. Taylor at the farm and said, "Now there is a sire for my money. He has to be great. No matter what Taylor has accomplished so far in this field, it has to be overwhelmed by what is yet to come."

The stallion manager at the farm was Harry Green, the man who helped Nearctic's mother, Lady Angela, calmly disembark from the ship after her long voyage. Harry called the stallion "Nicky," and the two became the best of friends, with a bond of trust between them. Nearctic could be a handful, but with Harry he was calm and polite, responding to his friend's voice at all times.

Nearctic's first crop of foals were born in 1961 and came of racing age in 1963. From only seventeen named foals, sixteen of his first crop started in races, and all sixteen were winners, five of them stakes winners. Nearctic became the leading first-crop sire in Canada and the overall leading sire of two-year-olds. The quality of Nearctic-sired colts and fillies ushered in a new level of class in Canadian racing, for in that first crop was a small bay colt who was passed up at the Windfields yearling sale in 1962. The colt was retained by Windfields, and Winnie Taylor named him Northern Dancer. We tell the story of his mother later in this chapter, and Northern Dancer himself is featured in Chapter Seven.

Northern Dancer was not the only top-class colt or filly from neophyte sire Nearctic. Pierlou was the son of a mare named Windka. Jean-Louis Lévesque purchased the colt as a yearling from Windfields and won four stakes races with him, including the Colin Stakes and the Quebec Derby.

Langcrest was bred and raced by Sydney Langill and captured seven stakes races, including the Kingarvie Stakes twice, the Durham Cup Handicap and Canadian Maturity. Langcrest later sired Coronation Futurity winner Great Gabe.

Ontario breeder W.A. Graul bred and sold Arctic Hills as a yearling to Mrs. V.G. Cardy. Arctic Hills won the Breeders' Stakes, Toronto Cup, Heresy Stakes and King Edward Gold Cup in her colours.

Belarctic was the fifth stakes winner in the first Nearctic crop. Owned by Viscount Harding, the filly won the Fury Stakes.

Another noteworthy daughter of Nearctic from his first crop was Orchestrina (covered in the "Orchestra" section of Chapter Five). Although she won only one race from ten starts, this brown mare later produced Prince of Wales Stakes winner New Pro Escar, as well as the dam of major broodmare influence Bon Debarras.

Breeders who had not patronized Nearctic earlier were now clamouring for his services. Following Northern Dancer's victory in the Kentucky Derby in 1964, Gil Darlington was besieged by breeders nominating their mares for a visit with the emerging hot Canadian sire. By 1965, Nearctic's stud fee had risen to $7,500, and he was receiving a full book of mares. American breeders took note and began sending high-quality broodmares across the border to Oshawa. It was the beginning of the worldwide recognition that Windfields Farm would earn over the next four decades.

Nearctic continued his impressive output as a sire. We have already touched on his champion daughter Northern Queen and his terrific though tragic son Cool Reception in Chapters Four and Three, respectively. Cool Reception's brave second-place finish to Damascus in the Belmont Stakes on a broken leg is a testament to the quality and courage passed down by his sire.

From Nearctic's 1963 crop came a chestnut colt, bred by hockey legend Conn Smythe, named Bye And Near. Out of the Bunty Lawless mare Bye Bye Bunty, Bye And Near would become a stakes winner for Smythe taking the Dominion Day Handicap twice as well as the Plate Trial and Seagram Cup. He was placed in twelve additional stakes races and then retired to stud at Smythe's farm in Ontario, siring five stakes winners from only thirty foals.

Jean-Louis Lévesque purchased a full sister of Northern Dancer from the Windfields Farm 1964 yearling sales for the then-astronomical price of $100,000. Given the name Arctic Dancer, the promising filly finished second in the My Dear Stakes, her first race, and ran unplaced in her next start, sustaining a career-ending injury. Arctic Dancer was later bred to Buckpasser and produced the wonderful Hall of Fame filly La Prevoyante for Lévesque. La Prevoyante had a perfect twelve-for-twelve season as a two-year-old and earned not only champion two-year-old honours in the United States but also Horse of the Year honours in her native Canada. La Prevoyante (whose career is covered in more depth later in this chapter) was a harbinger of things to come for the daughters of Nearctic when they became broodmares.

The ratio of winners sired by Nearctic, whether male or female, was astounding. Three other horses from the 1964 crop that included Cool Reception were James Bay, who won eight stakes races, including two wins in the Connaught Cup; Battling, who won the Canadian classic Prince of Wales's Stakes; and Northern Blonde, who won the Star Shoot Stakes.

The 1965 crop contained twenty-two winners from twenty-eight named foals. In this crop was the bay filly Nangela, bred by E.P. Taylor. Nangela did not attain her reserve price at the Windfields yearling sales. She went on to win the Carleton Stakes under Windfields colours and later became an important broodmare for the farm. Also in this crop was the Gardiner Farms–bred Lady Known As Lou, who later produced Loudrangle, a foundation mare to the then new Sam-Son Farm breeding and racing outfit in Ontario.

The 1966 crop had thirty-six representatives. Thirty-three became starters, with twenty-seven winners, five of whom won stakes races. In this crop was the wonderful three-time divisional champion daughter of Nearctic named Not Too Shy, bred by Conn Smythe. Another full sibling to Northern Dancer, a brother this time, named Northern Native came from the crop of 1966. Northern Native did not meet his reserve price at the Windfields yearling sale and raced for the farm stable. Pete McCann considered him "potentially one of the best horses I ever trained," but the colt could not stay sound throughout his racing career. Northern Native stood at Windfields in Oshawa for six years before being sold to an English stud farm. He later completed his stud career in Japan.

A Change to His Passport

By 1967, Nearctic had become a highly valued stallion. Four years earlier, E.P. Taylor had acquired a substantial tract of farmland near Chesapeake City, Maryland, which he was developing as a training centre. With the emergence of Nearctic and his son Northern Dancer, however, Taylor switched gears and decided to turn the property into a breeding centre. The Maryland branch of Windfields offered closer access to many of the top breeders in Kentucky and other nearby states, but it was not out of reach for Canadian breeders.

Nearctic was transferred to Allaire du Pont's Woodstock Farm, essentially across the street from the Windfields location in

Maryland. Northern Dancer went to the new Windfields Maryland Stallion Annex. In these locations, the two E.P. Taylor–bred stallions could be visited by some of the best mares. The sire line was not abandoned in Canada, however.

From the final crop sired by Nearctic in Canada came Briartic, who won some important races in Canada and the United States during his sixty-three race career, then was a successful stallion who stood at Windfields in Oshawa. He sired Queen's Plate winners Steady Growth and Son Of Briartic.

The 1969 crop was the first sired by Nearctic in Maryland. An outstanding member of this crop was Icecapade. The grey colt was bred along the same cross as Northern Dancer, as he was out of the Native Dancer–sired broodmare Shenanigans. (Icecapade's future half-sister Ruffian became one of the most loved, but tragic, fillies in racing history.) Icecapade was a multi-graded stakes winner himself and captured some fine races, such as the William du Pont, Jr. Handicap and the Nassau County Handicap.

Later standing at Gainesway Farm in Kentucky, Icecapade became an important and successful stallion, siring seventy-three stakes winners, which equates to 12 percent of his foals. Among his top-rated runners are Canadian champions Izvestia and Kingsbridge, as well as Clever Trick and Wild Again. The latter won the inaugural Breeders' Cup Classic in a memorable race and has been an outstanding sire of eighty-eight stakes winners, including Wilderness Song, Milwaukee Brew and Sarava. Clever Trick sired seventy stakes winners, including Phone Trick, the sire of Eclipse Award Horse of the Year Favorite Trick. Icecapade has been instrumental in furthering the tail male line from Nearctic.

Another important son of Nearctic is Nonoalco. A winner of four Group One races in an abbreviated career, Nonoalco won three of those races as a two-year-old and then captured the classic English 2000 Guineas, defeating the great miler Apalachee in the process. One of the jockeys to ride Nonoalco in his races was the legendry Lester Piggott, who proclaimed the colt to be the fastest two-year-old he had ever ridden.

Many of Nearctic's offspring inherited his feisty manners. Windfields' chief veterinarian, Dr. Rolph de Gannes, noted that Nearctic's daughters were uncooperative with the palpation methods he pioneered for determining the optimum time to breed. His sons, including blue-chip boy Northern Dancer, generally had classic dominant stallion tendencies. Nearctic's legacy as a stallion is equally important on both sides of a pedigree chart. He parleyed his royal bloodlines into a highly influential career, proving E.P Taylor to be correct in his request to breed Lady Angela to Nearco once more when he acquired her.

Nearctic's stud career came to an early end in 1973 when he succumbed to chronic lymphangitis at the age of nineteen. After learning of Nearctic's failing health, the horse's groom, Harry Green, came to Maryland for a touching and heartwarming reunion. Nearctic nuzzled his old friend after hobbling over to greet him, looking for a treat, and of course Harry had come prepared, with a pocket full of Nicky's favourite snacks. Of all the people the headstrong stallion met, Harry Green was by far his most trusted friend. Nearctic died on July 26, 1973.

Nearctic sired forty-nine stakes winners, which may sound a rather small amount today. His time as a stallion came before the advent of large per-season books. In Nearctic's day, stallions averaged thirty-five to forty foals a year. Today's successful stallions average close to one hundred a year. Nearctic's stud career also preceded the modern technology that helps breeders determine the optimum time to breed. Old-fashioned husbandry was the prevailing method in the 1960s and 1970s. Nearctic still sired 14-percent stakes winners from his entire foal output, a number not attained by today's top sires.

The great stallion had a regal air. He carried his head high, like his maternal grandsire, Hyperion, and also had a similar prancing swagger when he walked. Nearctic also had plenty of his sire Nearco in him. His coat colour, his temperament and his speed all came from the great Italian stallion. Many of the older employees in the Windfields family regarded Nearctic as their own personal favourite.

Descending from world-class breeding, Nearctic's sire was bred by the incomparable Italian breeder Federico Tesio, while his damsire was bred by another turf legend, the 17th Lord Derby. Both of these turf luminaries are regarded as among the greatest breeders in the history of Thoroughbred horse racing. Nearctic went a long way to adding E.P. Taylor to this list. He was the first of an extensive and prestigious line of world-class stallions bred by Windfields Farm. The predominant branch of his tail male descendants has come from his brilliant son Northern Dancer, but there are many other important lines and broodmare families that trace back to Nearctic. Many were bred by E.P. Taylor, while other top breeders who wisely acquired Nearctic's blood for their own breeding programs prospered. Nearctic was the pivotal stallion in Windfields Farm history. He was the catalyst that took the operation from a dominant Canadian-only breeding farm to one of the dominant breeding operations in the world.

Let's Buy a Nice Filly

If the arrival of Nearctic is seen as the definitive point at which Windfields Farm became a major global breeding enterprise, then the purchase of Natalma can be seen as Exhibit 2. In the summer of 1958, right after Nearctic won the Michigan Mile, E.P. Taylor was at Saratoga for the annual yearling sales. Joe Thomas said to his boss, "Why don't we use that money Nearctic won in Detroit and find ourselves a nice filly to race and breed." Taylor thought it a good idea, and the two set about looking through the catalogue and barns for a nice filly.

They came across a lovely bay filly who was bred in Virginia by Daniel G. Van Clief and his aunt, Mrs. E.H. Augustus. The yearling was a daughter of the great grey champion Native Dancer, out of Almahmoud, the daughter of another notable grey, Mahmoud. Almahmoud was known then as the dam of the good stakes winner Cosmah. Mahmoud was entering legendary status as a sire of fantastic broodmares, while Native Dancer was beginning to fulfil his promise as a sire of note after his Hall of Fame racing career. The stars were lining up for E.P. Taylor.

The bidding was brisk for this bay offspring of Thoroughbred royalty, but E.P. held sway and got her for $35,000. Taking the first three letters of her sire's name and the first four letters of her dam's name, the filly became Natalma. She was smoothly made, refined but a little back at the knee, and she was sent to Horatio Luro to be broken to saddle and trained to become a racer.

Natalma showed some spirit and speed early in her career. After breaking her maiden and winning an allowance race, Natalma was entered in the Grade One Spinaway Stakes. She crossed the finish line first, but because she had ducked in to avoid the sting of jockey Bobby Ussery's whip, she was disqualified and placed third behind Irish Jay and Warlike. After that race, Natalma refused to go on the track, fearing she would be the recipient of pain from her rider with that whip. She would go as far as the track entrance and then just stand there. Luro was a good horseman and understood the problem. He knew it might take time before Natalma would acquiesce to go on the track and stop associating the oval with pain.

By the time Natalma started coming around, most of the quality three-year-old races leading up to the Kentucky Oaks had passed by. Her first start as a three-year-old came on April 9, 1960, at Keeneland. Natalma set the pace and carried the lead before she backed up suddenly to finish out of the money. It appeared that she had needed the race, as she again showed speed in her next event two weeks later. This time she kept going, under jockey Bill Hartack, to win by a length. However, she came out of the race with a chipped knee.

Taylor, Thomas and the rest of the Windfields brain trust debated whether to keep her as a racehorse or send her to the breeding shed. Natalma had missed her chance at the Kentucky Oaks because of her whip phobia, was not eligible for the Canadian classics for fillies and now had an injury that would require surgery before any attempt could be made to race her again.

E.P. Taylor had bought the filly with the intention of breeding her but had also wanted to see if she could win stakes races. Natalma had shown she was talented enough to be a stakes winner, but her opportunity to prove it would now have to wait until the next year. As a result, Taylor decided to breed Natalma to Nearctic, even though it was late June—which is late for Thoroughbred breeding. This was Nearctic's first year at stud, and though it was going well, with the stallion covering mares and getting most of them in foal from first covers, Gil Darlington was disappointed there was not a bigger book for him. Natalma would be one more good mare for him. And if she did not catch at first mating, she would be left barren for the year.

On June 30, Natalma and Nearctic met in the breeding arena at Windfields Farm in Oshawa. The rest, as they say, is history.

A colt was born at 12:15 a.m. on May 27, 1961, in Barn Six on the Oshawa farm. Natalma had walked and sweated for an hour and a half before she came into labour, with her actual labour lasting twenty minutes. The birth was described as "a tight but normal foaling." The foal was a bay, with an angled white blaze down his face (described as a star stripe and snip) and three white feet. He was also quite small. Natalma had carried her little boy for 331 days; now she would nurse and protect him as he grew. He was a sturdy colt and quickly stood to find his mother.

Of course we are now talking about Northern Dancer.

Natalma got off to an incredible start to her broodmare career. Northern Dancer went on to become the most heralded

Thoroughbred ever born in Canada. His popularity stems from his racing achievements and his worldwide domination as a sire. However, as legendary as her son became, Natalma was no one-trick pony as a broodmare. She is the head of an illustrious family that stretches beyond Northern Dancer's realm, and she has become a legend herself.

Matriarch to a Legacy

The next foal produced by Natalma was her son Native Victor, sired by Victoria Park. Native Victor had an attitude similar to his famous half-brother, but he did not escape the vet's knife and was gelded. Unsold as a yearling, Native Victor took a little time to find his form. He won the Fairbanks Handicap as a three-year-old, the Canadian Handicap at four and the King-arvie Stakes at five, and he placed in many high-class stakes throughout his career. Native Victor was a durable sort, making 105 starts, winning eighteen races, placing second fifteen times and third six times, and racing until he was nine years old.

Nearctic and Natalma met again, and the resulting foal, a full sister to Northern Dancer, was sold for the then record price of $100,000 as a yearling to Jean-Louis Lévesque. Lévesque named the filly Arctic Dancer. Her colour and markings were not as distinctive as her brother's, as she had only a small star on her forehead. Placed in the barn of trainer Duke Campbell, Arctic Dancer displayed exceptional talent and speed. Campbell was in awe of her since she was not only expensive but also the sister of a champion. He was asked at the time if she was as good as Northern Dancer, to which he replied, "Yes, in the filly class."

Arctic Dancer was somewhat mean around other colts but was generally a perfect pet and easy to handle. She needed extra schooling in the gate, as she became agitated in the close confines, but once she learned her lessons, she showed her ability.

Campbell reported early training times of 34 ⅗ seconds for 3 furlongs, 48 flat for 4 furlongs and 59 ⅖ for 5 furlongs. Speed was no problem for this young filly. She made her race debut in the My Dear Stakes at Woodbine. Prize Jive was a little more seasoned and defeated Arctic Dancer by two lengths, but this was a solid first outing for the daughter of Natalma. Two weeks later, Arctic Dancer started in the Clarendon Stakes. She was somewhat rank when she entered the gate but was eventually coaxed in. Unfortunately, she had a habit of squatting on the back of the gate, which she now did. Jockey Benny Sorenson alerted the starter to his predicament with the filly, but to no avail. The starter pressed the button to open the door. Arctic Dancer injured herself and finished last. The injury was serious enough to retire her from racing. Sorenson was later fined $200 by the stewards for complaining about the start.

With a pedigree as glittering as hers, Arctic Dancer was retired for breeding. Lévesque bred her to the best stallions available to him. The third foal produced by Arctic Dancer, a lovely bay daughter by champion Buckpasser, would demonstrate the high class of Thoroughbreds now being bred in Canada. Her name was La Prevoyante.

La Prevoyante

La Prevoyante was the author of one of the most remarkable juvenile campaigns in racing history, if not *the* most remarkable. She made twelve starts and won them all. Not only did La Prevoyante win these races—she was never headed. She beat the best from her native land, and also the best on the entire continent.

La Prevoyante burst onto the scene on May 31, 1972, at Woodbine, where she pulverized a field of two-year-old filly maidens by eight-and-a-half lengths. The performance was a sign of things to come. After winning her next race, a 5-furlong allowance on grass, La Prevoyante won her first stakes race, capturing the My Dear Stakes at Woodbine, the race in which her mother had finished second.

Her next start came at Blue Bonnets racetrack in Montreal, where she beat a solitary colt in the Fleur de Lys Stakes. She beat the boys again in the Colin Stakes at Fort Erie. La Prevoyante was just warming up, so it was on to the famous spa at Saratoga and a crack at some of the best of her age in the United States. La Prevoyante became the talk of the Saratoga backstretch after dominating the Schuylerville and Spinaway stakes races. Her combined margin of victory for the two events was nine lengths.

Returning to Woodbine, the emerging star took on the best of the Canadian juvenile fillies in the Princess Elizabeth Stakes. La Prevoyante simply toyed with the field, winning by seven-and-a-half lengths. She was ten lengths in front at the top of the homestretch and cruised home unchallenged.

With nothing left to prove in her home country, La Prevoyante went back to the United States. The four most important us races for two-year-old fillies are the Matron, Frizette, Selima and Gardenia Stakes. La Prevoyante swept them all. It wasn't just that she won, but the manner in which she won that caused the racing fraternity to stand up and take notice.

In the Matron, La Prevoyante zipped around the Belmont track in 1:23 ⅗ and won by seven-and-a-half lengths. In the one-mile Frizette, also at Belmont, she won by two lengths on a sloppy track. At Laurel, she sped around in 1:46 ⅖ on a sloppy track to win the Selima by fourteen lengths. Finally, at Garden State Park in New Jersey, La Prevoyante took the Gardenia by two lengths after being in front by as much as eight. She coasted to the line with plenty of energy to spare. The most remarkable aspect of these wins was that she was never in danger of losing any of the races.

That La Prevoyante won the Sovereign Award as Horse of the Year in Canada was a foregone conclusion. She was not only the unanimous winner of the US Eclipse Award in her division, but she also finished second on the Horse of the Year ballot. Who beat her? A juvenile chestnut colt named Secretariat. Only an immortal legend could have prevented the Canadian filly from becoming US Horse of the Year. Unfortunate timing on her part. And the first time a two-year-old won the Eclipse Horse of the Year Award.

The public took to La Prevoyante as if she were a movie star. It was revealed that she had a sweet tooth and her favourite treat was Tootsie Roll candy. She was called "Tootsie" by her stable helpers, a nickname taken up by the press and public alike.

Unfortunately for her connections and fans, La Prevoyante never duplicated her sensational juvenile form. She won the Quebec Derby and La Troienne Stakes as a three-year-old, showing some of her scintillating speed, but could not keep up in some other big events, such as the Canadian Oaks, where she was third. She ran unplaced in the Queen's Plate.

Coming back for a campaign as a four-year-old, La Prevoyante slipped further down the ladder. She did win quite a few allowance races but was ineffective in stakes competition. On December 28, 1974, La Prevoyante made her last start at Calder Race Track in the Miss Florida Handicap. That day is still painful to remember. Tootsie assumed command from the start and drew off to a seven-length lead after 5 furlongs. But the race was a mile and a sixteenth on the grass, and the field began to close on her near the far turn. By the top of the stretch, it had caught up.

Jockey Chris Rogers stated after the race, "Coming to the eighth pole, I could feel her body tighten under me. I didn't know what was wrong, but I knew she was in trouble. She finished under her own courage." La Prevoyante collapsed just beyond the finish line. She was revived using cold water spray and walked to the receiving barn under her own power. It was initially thought that she was suffering from heat exhaustion.

Back in her barn later that day, the great La Prevoyante collapsed again and died. The cause was a ruptured lung. Shaken and devastated, her trainer John Starr said he simply did not see this coming. "She trained so good for the race," he said when interviewed, adding, "If I knew there was the slightest thing wrong with her, I would not have run her. I imagine the rupture represented a weakness in her lung which was undetected. She looked great before the race."

The loss of La Prevoyante was not only a devastating blow to her connections and fans, but also to Thoroughbred breeding. Given her pedigree, she would likely have been an outstanding broodmare. Lévesque had stated that she was to be bred to Secretariat the following spring. Only our imagination can dream of the quality foals she might have produced.

Lévesque bred a full sister to La Prevoyante named Danseuse Etoile. This daughter of Arctic Dancer became the dam of Drums Of Freedom, by Green Forest. Bred to Gone West, Drums Of Freedom is the dam of Lexington Stakes winner Proud Citizen. Proud Citizen finished second to War Emblem in the Kentucky Derby and was third in the Preakness to the same competitor. Retired to stand at Airdrie Stud in Kentucky, Proud Citizen sired Kentucky Oaks winners Proud Spell and Believe You Can.

Spring Adieu

Due to the success of La Prevoyante, E.P. Taylor used one of his breeding rights to Buckpasser and sent Natalma to meet him. In 1974, she produced a bay filly who was entered in the Saratoga yearling sales, the same sale in which Natalma was found and purchased. In a what-goes-around-comes-around scenario, the filly was purchased for $260,000 by Daniel Van Clief, the man who had consigned Natalma to the sale seventeen years earlier. Van Clief named Natalma's filly Spring Adieu.

Spring Adieu won three races from seven starts before entering her owner's Nydrie Stud. Her first foal was a filly by Roberto named You're My Lady. A two-time winner from six races, with no black type, she went to South Africa and produced four stakes winners. Before her export to South Africa, You're My Lady produced a winning daughter named Gabbing Gloria. This one went to Australia, where she was bred to Brief Truce, the result being Diatribe, winner of the Rosehill Guineas and Caulfield Cup. Diatribe also finished second in the W.S. Cox Plate to the legendary Sunline. Ace High, son of Epsom Derby winner High Chaparral and winner of the 2017 VRC Victoria Derby and the ATC Spring Champion Stakes, is also a member of this branch of the family.

The second foal from Spring Adieu carried her name to the elite level in Thoroughbred breeding. She was bred to the Ribot stallion His Majesty, a brother to Graustark, and the resulting filly, born in 1981, was named Razyana by her new owner Prince Khalid bin Abdullah, the master of Juddmonte Farms. Razyana would not cover herself in glory on the track, placing second twice from three attempts. However, she made up for her lack of racing success when she produced a colt by Northern Dancer's son Danzig in 1986. Prince Khalid named the colt Danehill and watched him win the Group One Sprint Cup in England three years later. Danehill also won the Cork and Orrery Stakes and European Free Handicap. He finished third to Nashwan in the 2000 Guineas and to Cadeaux Genereux in the July Cup. Juddmonte syndicated Danehill to stand at Coolmore Stud in Ireland, and a new level of stallion excellence was soon achieved.

Danehill was one of the first successful "shuttle stallions," standing on either side of the equator in the same calendar year. Such stallions stand in the northern hemisphere from February 15 to mid-July, then travel to the southern hemisphere for the rest of the year (from September 15 to January). Danehill set the bar for shuttle sires so high that no other stallion has even approached his success. He was the champion sire seventeen times in various jurisdictions, nine times in Australia alone, and he sired 355 stakes winners from 2,409 foals. This equates to well over 14 percent of his foal output becoming stakes winners. Given the fact that he plied his trade year-round, Danehill had remarkable virility and was as prepotent as any stallion who ever lived.

Eighty-four of Danehill's stakes winners were successful at the Grade/Group One level, including such notables as Dylan Thomas, Duke Of Marmalade, Desert King, Danehill Dancer, Redoute's Choice, Exceed And Excel, Fastnet Rock, Flying Spur and Banks Hill. While this is only a partial list, you can see the extent of Danehill's influence. His sons are becoming leading sires around the world, taking the mantle and carrying on the line.

To add further to his sire credentials, Danehill has become an important broodmare sire. The likes of Frankel, Danedream, Teofilo, Siyouni and Intense Focus are all out of Danehill daughters.

Danehill is a son of Natalma's grandson Danzig, out of her granddaughter Razyana. His 3x3 inbreed to Natalma is the significant aspect of his pedigree. While there are many breeders and Thoroughbred experts who are strictly against close inbreeding, there are also those who swear by it. In the case of Danehill, such a breeding pattern has been a grand success. To further complicate matters, Danehill has worked very well with broodmares on the Northern Dancer sire line, adding another cross of Natalma to the resulting foal's pedigree. His daughters have mixed well with similar lines, with the incomparable Frankel leading the way. Danehill must be considered one of the most remarkable stallions in turf history.

Raise The Standard

Another daughter of Natalma who has exerted influence and kept the tail female line in the breeding news is the cleverly named Raise The Standard. Her sire is Hoist The Flag, hence the apropos name. When she was unsold as a yearling, Windfields retained her for breeding. Trainer Mac Benson remembers Raise The Standard as having good size and bone, but her ankles were an issue, so she never raced.

When Raise The Standard was bred to Halo in 1981, she produced a filly who was purchased by Stavros Niarchos at the Keeneland July yearling sale in 1983. Niarchos named her Coup De Folie. She raced in France, displaying her class by winning the Group Three Prix d'Aumale and finishing third in the Group One Prix Marcel Boussac. Niarchos retired her to his outstanding broodmare band, where she made her mark emphatically with her first foal, a son of Mr. Prospector who would go by the name Machiavellian.

Machiavellian was the 1989 champion two-year-old in France, where he won the Group One Prix Morny and the Prix de la Salamandre. He took the Prix Djebel in his first start as a three-year-old but went down to his first defeat in the classic 2000 Guineas at Newmarket. Machiavellian finished unplaced in his next two starts, both Group One events, indicating a lack of interest to compete. He was retired to stud at Dalham Hall in Newmarket.

In the role of stallion, Machiavellian prospered. He has established one of the major branches of the Mr. Prospector sire line in the world today, and he has sired seventy-eight stakes winners, which is 10.3 percent of his entire foal count. Among the best of his get is a pair of Dubai World Cup winners, Street Cry and Almutawakel, as well as Grade/Group One winners Best Of The Bests, Medicean, Invermark, Vettori and Rebecca Sharp. Street Cry and Medicean have continued the line with distinction.

Street Cry is the sire of Kentucky Derby winner Street Sense and two sensational racing mares. As this book was being written, Winx was wowing the world, especially fans in her native Australia, with a dominating thirty-two-race winning streak against top competition. Winx has won twenty-four Group One races. She took her time to reach her potential but has now become the darling of the racing world.

The other world-famous racing daughter of Street Cry is the legendary Zenyatta. A huge horse at seventeen hands two inches, Zenyatta made an equally huge mark on the racing world when she won her first nineteen races. She did so in the same manner every time. She danced to the gate with jockey Mike Smith on board, left the gate slowly and trailed the field, got her long legs going down the backstretch, gathering speed as she did so, and zoomed past the leaders in the homestretch to take victory.

Zenyatta lost her last race, the 2010 Breeders' Cup Classic, by a diminishing head to the very good horse Blame. She had previously won two Breeders' Cup races and twelve other Grade One events. She earned three Eclipse Awards as champion older mare, as well as the 2010 Eclipse Horse of the Year award. The popularity of Zenyatta and Winx has vaulted both to a status normally reserved for movie stars.

We should also mention Machiavellian's son Medicean, out of the Storm Bird mare Mystic Goddess. Medicean has been a very good sire, with ten Grade/Group One stakes winners to his credit so far. Among his top get are Middle Park Stakes winner Dutch Art, E.P. Taylor Stakes winner Siyouma, and Coronation Stakes winner Nannina. Medicean stands at Cheveley Park Stud, where his son Dutch Art has joined him.

Returning to Coup De Folie, we find her Group One Prix Jacques Le Marois–winning son Exit To Nowhere, by Irish River, and her Group Two Prix d'Astarté–winning daughter Hydro Calido, by Nureyev. Hydro Calido also finished second in the classic Poule d'Essai des Pouliches. Coup De Folie's next foal, Salchow, was an unraced daughter by Nijinsky II who would produce a Group One winner. Salchow was bred to Woodman and gave the Niarchos family Grand Critérium winner Way Of Light, who would also be named the 1998 champion two-year-old in France. Salchow is also the third dam of Canadian champion sprinter Calgary Cat.

The fifth foal from Coup De Folie became her second champion. Sent to Mr. Prospector in 1990, Coup De Folie produced a daughter, Coup De Genie, who emulated her full brother Machiavellian by winning the Prix Morny and Prix de la Salamandre, capturing divisional championship honours in France. Coup De Genie also won the Group Three Prix de Cabourg and Prix Imprudence. As a broodmare, she has done the family proud.

The first foal from Coup De Genie was a daughter of Nureyev named Moonlight's Box. Unraced due to a pelvis injury, Moonlight's Box made up for this by producing Prix de l'Arc de Triomphe winner Bago. Sired by Nashwan, Bago also won the Group One Grand Prix de Paris, Prix Jean Prat, Critérium International and Prix Ganay among his eight wins. Bago was named champion two-year-old in Europe and followed up with a championship year as a three-year-old.

Moonlight's Box also produced a son by the outstanding German stallion Monsun in 2008. The dark bay colt, named Maxios, took his time to find himself as a racehorse, but when he did, he was sensational. Maxios won stakes races at two and four, but as a five-year-old he won the Group One Prix d'Ispahan and Prix du Moulin de Longchamp. Maxios was bred by the Niarchos family and now stands stud at Gestüt Fährhof in Germany.

Coup De Genie's second and third foals were both by A.P. Indy. The first, a colt named Snake Mountain, won four stakes races. The second was a daughter named Glia, who won two stakes races. Glia produced a daughter by Touch Gold whom the Niarchos family sold to Juddmonte Farms. Juddmonte named the filly Soothing Touch, and she, in turn, is the dam of Emollient, by Empire Maker. Emollient won the Grade One Ashland Stakes, Spinster Stakes, Rodeo Drive Stakes and American Oaks.

As impressive as these representatives of the Coup De Genie branch of the family are, perhaps the most successful on the track was Denebola. Sired by the prolific Storm Cat, Denebola became another family champion two-year-old in France. Her title year was 2003, when she won the Prix Marcel Boussac and Prix de Cabourg. She ran third in the Prix Morny against the boys. Denebola's daughter Beta Leo, by A.P. Indy, has brought the family back to the top with her 2017 Prix de Diane winner Senga.

Raise The Standard's son El Moxie, sired by Conquistador Cielo, was no great concern on the racetrack. However, El Moxie was quite successful at stud when sold to Emirates Park Stud in Australia. His major claim to fame as a sire comes in his gelded son Silent Witness. A two-time Horse of the Year in Hong Kong, Silent Witness won seventeen consecutive stakes races, which included nine Group One races, and he was considered the best sprinter in the world in 2003–2005. He retired to much fanfare at Living Legends, located at Woodlands Historic Park in Greenvale, Victoria, Australia.

Bonita Francita, a daughter of Windfields-bred champion Devil's Bag, was the sixth foal from Raise The Standard. She has added to the family's success with her son Orpen, by Lure. Orpen became the champion two-year-old in Ireland and claimed the Group One Prix Morny during his juvenile season.

Bonita Francita is also the second dam of Bluemamba, who won the Poule d'Essai des Pouliches, adding yet another classic winner to the Natalma family.

We would be remiss if we did not mention the last foal Natalma produced. Born A Lady was a June 1, 1981 foal sired by Tentam. She won the Pearl Necklace Stakes for owners Brushwood Farm, who bought the filly from Windfields. Born A Lady traces in tail female to Australian Group One stakes winner Amanpour, a daughter of the Northern Dancer line stallion Northern Meteor. Another recent major stakes winner along the Born A Lady branch is Rapper Dragon, who swept the 2017 Hong Kong Classic Mile, Classic Cup and Derby. These races are called the four-year-old series and hold considerable prestige.

Rapper Dragon's sire is Street Boss, which means he is inbred to Natalma 6x6.

Natalma was bred to Nearctic for eight breeding seasons. On May 16, 1965, she foaled a brown filly by Nearctic who would unfortunately die as a yearling. Two years later, the full brother to Northern Dancer and Arctic Dancer was unsold at the yearling sale. Perhaps the $200,000 price tag was a bit much for prospective owners at the 1967 sale. The colt, who looked very much like Nearctic but with four white feet, was retained by Windfields and named Northern Native. He was stakes-placed from thirteen starts, won four allowance races and then took up stud duties at Windfields in Oshawa. He was later sold to a Japanese stud farm where he lived the rest of his life.

Two years later, another full brother was born. This one sold as a yearling for $100,000. Given the name Northern Ace, the colt failed to win as a two-year-old, which is strange considering the family heritage. He did win races as a three-year-old and four-year-old, though none were black-type events, and was then sold to stand in Denmark. He became a leading sire in his adopted homeland.

When Nearctic and Natalma got together in 1970, the result was a barren year. They had another son two years later, Transalantic—and that is not a spelling mistake. Another unique aspect to this colt is that he was the only chestnut from their liaisons. Transalantic raced three times in France, winning once and placing second once. As an eight-year-old, he went to Japan for stud duty after he had begun his career in France.

The final mating of Nearctic and Natalma resulted in twins, a colt and a filly, in 1973. Unfortunately, both foals died. The colt was dead at birth, while the filly died a week later despite the valiant effort by Windfields' veterinary staff to save her.

Natalma passed away in 1985, thirteen years after Nearctic. She is buried at the Northview Stallion Station in Chesapeake City, the former site of the Windfields Maryland farm, where she had relocated. Her productive broodmare career and fruitful partnership with Nearctic gave the Thoroughbred world one of the greatest legacies in the history of the sport, an everlasting bequest.

Both Nearctic and Natalma are enshrined in the Canadian Racing Hall of Fame, largely due to their breeding accomplishments.

From here, Windfields would scale the heights of breeding greatness.

Top Scene from the Oshawa Farm circa 1960's. PHOTO CREDIT: WINANTS BROS./DRUMMER BOY PUBLICATIONS

Bottom Nearctic conformation photo. PHOTO CREDIT: PETER WINANTS/DRUMMER BOY PUBLICATIONS

Top Attending the Keeneland Yearling sales. In the forefront of the picture is E.P. Taylor with Joe Thomas. Sitting behind are Paul Mellon and Jock Whitney. PHOTO CREDIT: KEENELAND ASSOCIATION LIBRARY/THOROUGHBRED TIMES COLLECTION

Bottom Oshawa Farm core view from the Stallion barn of Barn six, the foaling barn. PHOTO CREDIT: WINANTS BROS./DRUMMER BOY PUBLICATIONS

Facing Top Natalma, with Bobby Ussery up, and groom Bill Brevard in 1959. PHOTO CREDIT: KEENELAND ASSOCIATION LIBRARY/MORGAN COLLECTION

Facing Bottom Victoria Park at Keeneland Race Course, 1960. PHOTO CREDIT: KEENELAND ASSOCIATION LIBRARY/FEATHERSTON COLLECTION

Top Windfields Farm manager Peter Poole, circa 1970. PHOTO CREDIT: WINANTS BROS./ DRUMMER BOY PUBLICATIONS

Bottom Nearctic portrait photo. PHOTO CREDIT: WINANTS BROS./DRUMMER BOY PUBLICATIONS

{ 7 }

THE LITTLE ROCKET
TO THE STARS

AS IMPORTANT AS Nearctic's success as a sire and Natalma's legacy as the head of a powerful family were, they were overshadowed by their brilliant son Northern Dancer. His accomplishments propelled him to such astronomical levels that he became, quite simply, the most important Thoroughbred of the twentieth century. And his influence has not yet subsided. He may be even more revered today than he was during his lifetime.

The gods of Thoroughbred racing smiled on E.P. Taylor and his Windfields Farm when it came to Northern Dancer, though there were minor flaws as well. He was small but muscular and powerful. He was headstrong and determined, but not vicious. He was fast, but not completely sound. He was prepotent as a sire, but had fertility issues. Northern Dancer was a dynamo, like an equine rocket. He took Windfields Farm to the stratosphere of success and became the brightest star of the Thoroughbred universe. Simply put, Northern Dancer was more than any breeder could hope for, no matter how fertile an imagination that breeder had.

Throughout his development on the farm, the little colt attracted a lot of attention from farm employees. His domination of the herd as a weanling, his feisty character and constant movement are remembered by Windfields staffers of the day. He had a way about him, and that certain look in the eye that comes along very rarely, proclaiming him as something special. The little Nearctic–Natalma colt just drew your attention to him. He obviously had an abundance of charisma, but, man, was he small.

The success of Northern Dancer hung in the balance on multiple occasions.

First off, his mother was acquired with the funds his father earned from a big stakes victory. Northern Dancer was the result of a late-in-the-season breeding that came about due to his mother's racing injury. He was conceived the day before Canada's ninety-third birthday and was due on June 5, 1961, but entered the world nine days early.

The little Nearctic–Natalma colt was offered at the Windfields yearling sales in 1962. E.P. Taylor and his manager, Joe Thomas, put a $25,000 price tag on him. There was some interest due to his pedigree, but prospective buyers could not get over his diminutive size and passed on the colt. His size would come into question throughout his racing life and in the early days of his breeding career, until he established himself as the pre-eminent sire in the world.

Windfields retained him for its own racing stable, to compete under the turquoise and gold colours, and Winnie Taylor named him Northern Dancer.

The colt was strong and wilful and constantly displayed his impatience throughout his remarkable life. During his early lessons to become a racehorse, Northern Dancer refused to be broken to saddle and was known to dump his riders. Other than a few bumps and bruises, no one was seriously hurt. However, many became leery of climbing on his back. Horatio Luro and his team were entrusted with training Northern Dancer. Luro found the colt difficult and suggested to E.P. Taylor and Joe Thomas that he should be gelded to make him more manageable.

"No" was the immediate response to the trainer's request.

A Legend Begins His Journey

Luro had horses under his watch at numerous racetracks throughout the continent, so Northern Dancer was entrusted to Luro's able assistant Tom "Peaches" Fleming and top stable groom Bill Brevard at Woodbine. Natalma's colt made his first race appearance in a maiden special weight event on August 2, 1963, at Fort Erie Race Track. Ridden by future Hall of Fame jockey Ron Turcotte, who was an apprentice at the time, Northern Dancer won the race by six-and-three-quarter lengths. He was two-tenths of a second off the track record.

Turcotte was impressed with the colt, as he would later recall: "We were just lazing along with the other horses and he did go to the leader when I asked him, but he was not giving much of himself. I was told to not touch him with the whip so I switched over to my left hand, so as to not be seen from the stands, and just gave him one little tap on the shoulder at the sixteenth pole. He just exploded from there and I feel we could have won by twenty lengths if I had done this at the quarter pole!"

The press in the next day's newspapers had much to say about the debut race of Northern Dancer. "We may have seen an outstanding two-year-old colt in Windfields' Northern Dancer, easy winner of the third race yesterday. This one is by Nearctic out of Natalma by Native Dancer." (Coincidentally, on August 3, a three-year-old filly named Goofed started in the Heresy Stakes on the Fort Erie lawn. Six years later, Northern Dancer and Goofed got together to create the outstanding runner and sire Lyphard.)

Northern Dancer graduated to a stakes race for his next start, thanks to his impressive first outing. He faced the then dominant and more seasoned Ramblin Road, an American-bred who had won the Victoria Stakes earlier in the year, equalling the track record. Although the Dancer had a two-and-a-half length lead at the half mile, he eventually finished second to Ramblin Road by four lengths in the 6.5-furlong race.

The Summer Stakes at Fort Erie was the next outing on his dance card. The course came up very soft for the one-mile race, the longest two-year-old race so far in the season. Northern Dancer won the event by one-and-a-quarter lengths over Slithering Sam, with stablemate Windlesham third. The race favourite had been another son of Nearctic, Pierlou, until then undefeated. Jockey Paul Bohenko said after the race that Northern Dancer, who had led the entire race around the two-turn grass oval, was a "game little guy."

Going to Woodbine for the prestigious Cup and Saucer Stakes, also on the grass but a half furlong longer, Northern Dancer entered the starting gate as the favourite at 8/5 and carried 124 pounds as the high weight. Bohenko was again the jockey. This time, Northern Dancer was worn down in the stretch by Grand Garcon, a huge colt who towered over the diminutive Dancer by almost two hands and was beaten by three-quarters of a length. Grand Garcon, a 45/1 long shot, had been purchased the year before at the Windfields yearling sale for $10,000 and carried only 113 pounds in the race. The Cup and Saucer was the last race Northern Dancer did not win in his juvenile campaign.

The Coronation Futurity was the next big outing on the agenda, but Luro decided to give him a prep race in the interim. Northern Dancer won the Bloordale Purse, at a mile and seventy yards, handily as the race high weight over Northern Flight, a Nearctic-sired colt bred by Conn Smythe. These two were twenty-five lengths ahead of the rest of the field at the wire. The race did more than add to the Dancer's bank account. It also showed he could come from behind to win his races. He overcame an eight-length disadvantage to Northern Flight to capture victory.

Ron Turcotte was back on Northern Dancer for the Coronation Futurity. Grand Garcon was also back, and the two combatants generated a lot of pre-race press. The press consensus was that Northern Dancer was an exceptional youngster along the lines of Victoria Park. Horatio Luro, who had taken over the day-to-day training, stated, "This time, they are at even weight, so we will know which one is the better colt." He added that the Dancer had been exhibiting consistent daily improvement.

In a field of fifteen, Northern Dancer won by six-and-a-quarter lengths over Smythe's colt Jammed Lively. Third was Pierlou. Turcotte's post-race comment was "I had trouble holding him back in the early stages. He is a little guy, but he is strong, and he pulled the saddle forward. He won going away." Legendary jockey Sir Gordon Richards was in attendance on the day and observed, "He is a grand little model. Except for the colour, he is a replica of Larkspur, last year's Epsom Derby winner." (Larkspur was trained by one Vincent O'Brien—remember that name.)

At this point, it seemed the juvenile career of Northern Dancer was running on a track parallel to that of Victoria Park four years earlier. Not only were they both tended to by a wonderful groom, Bill Brevard, but they both followed similar paths to championship glory as two-year-olds. As they had with Victoria Park, the Windfields team aimed for the Remsen Stakes at

Aqueduct in November as a target to challenge Northern Dancer's class and speed. They decided to use the Carleton Stakes, at Greenwood Raceway, as a prep for the New York event.

The track on the day of the Carleton was a sea of slop. Again carrying at least five pounds more than any other horse in the race, the Dancer won by two-and-a-half lengths, though he came out of the race with a tender left front hoof.

Jim Fitzsimmons was in the saddle for this race and said, "He slipped a number of times, but slipping does not stop him trying. He does his best to do just what you ask him." Joe Thomas added, "Northern Dancer is a little tiger who digs in and tries. He wants to run."

Northern Dancer was shipped to New York and settled into Luro's barn at Aqueduct. Luro wanted to give the Dancer another tune-up race before the Remsen, so he entered the Windfields colt in the one-mile Sir Gaylord Purse. Northern Dancer was the third choice in the betting as the local punters were not convinced of his ability, but he won the race by a smashing eight lengths over the accomplished New York stakes winner Bupers. Luro's confidence soared.

In the Remsen a week later, Northern Dancer went off as the favourite—the locals now convinced—and was also the high-weighted entrant. He won by two lengths over Lord Date, in stakes record time. Manuel Ycaza had the mount and said in his post-race comments, "I never cocked my whip, but just tapped him on the shoulder a couple of times at about the three-sixteenths pole and the furlong pole. He ran easy."

Although the win was a significant achievement, there was not much in the way of celebration in the press due to the pall of gloom from the shocking events of five days earlier. The entire world was reeling from the assassination of President John F. Kennedy in Dallas.

So ended Northern Dancer's juvenile campaign. He was named champion two-year-old colt in Canada and was firmly on the radar for the upcoming Kentucky Derby. In the meantime, Northern Dancer went for a rest at Luro's farm in Georgia.

E.P. Taylor was full of confidence in this little stick of dynamite. He anticipated the upcoming racing year with excitement and hope. Victoria Park had showed that Taylor was capable of breeding a Kentucky Derby contender in Canada. Northern Dancer was to prove Taylor could breed a winner of the fabled race.

The Road to the Derby

Following the Carleton Stakes, a situation with Northern Dancer's left front hoof escalated into a full-blown concern. Brevard discovered a quarter crack, the equine equivalent of a split toenail, had developed, which worsened over time and two more races. The usual method to heal such an injury was to let the hoof grow out and then trim it off beyond the crack. This obviously takes time, which is not ideal if you are trying to get a horse ready for a race. Valuable training is missed while the hoof heals.

Horatio Luro had learned of a new treatment designed by blacksmith Bill Bane in California. Luro contacted Bane, and the blacksmith flew across the continent to apply a vulcanized rubber patch to the cracked hoof. This material would allow the hoof to grow but would also keep the crack from becoming worse by letting the hoof flex normally during activity. The new treatment helped immensely in accelerating the healing process.

Even though Northern Dancer could be a handful at times, he was never foolish. He exhibited his considerable intelligence by allowing the treatment to be administered and then adapting to the odd feeling in his left foreleg with minimal fuss.

With Northern Dancer's foot healing better than expected, E.P. Taylor began to get excited about the Kentucky Derby again. Luro put Northern Dancer back into training, at Hialeah Park, two weeks after Bane had treated him and planned his program to get the Dancer to the Derby on the first Saturday in May. Ironically, the early favourite for the Kentucky Derby, a colt named Hurry To Market, had a quarter crack similar to Northern Dancer's. He didn't make it to the big race because his connections decided to use the old method of time and growth to heal the problem.

Another issue with Northern Dancer was his penchant for food. Luro stated, "He would keep eating as long as there was anything in sight that he could eat. We have to cut down on his eating a week before a race. When we cut down on his hay, he goes for the straw bedding in his stall. So we then replace the straw with peat moss, which he won't eat. It is the only way we can keep him from eating his way out of shape." Bill Brevard kept a very close eye on the Dancer's food intake, making sure the colt had enough nourishment for an active athlete, but no more than would be required.

In January, early contenders on the Derby trail were already winning important races. Bupers won the Hibiscus Stakes and Roman Brother won the Bahamas Stakes, both at Hialeah. Luro needed to get the Dancer into a race, so he entered the colt in a 6-furlong allowance race called the Buccaneer Purse, at Hialeah Park on February 10. Also in the race was highly regarded Chieftain, ridden by Bill Hartack. Bobby Ussery was given the mount on Dancer.

When the gates opened to start the race, Bazaar slammed into Northern Dancer, causing a loss of many lengths. Then, at the sixteenth pole, he was blocked off, so Ussery began to beat on Dancer with his whip. Chieftain was long gone and won the race, with Mom's Request second and Dancer third after his troubled trip. Luro was livid, his Latin blood coming to a boil when he met with Ussery after the race. He fired the jockey on the spot for using the whip.

Northern Dancer was also upset. He paced and stomped in his stall for hours after the race. Luro had, as one of his hobbies, a talent for playing the violin. Now he played the instrument outside Dancer's stall, which seemed to soothe the headstrong colt.

Bill Shoemaker came in to take the reins on Northern Dancer. Two weeks after the rough season opener, the Canadian colt went to the Hialeah starting gate for a non-wagering three-horse race of 7 furlongs that carried no purse. Chieftain was back, along with Trader, to round out the small field. This time, Northern Dancer got a clean break but was behind the others, as per Luro's orders. Shoemaker then brought Dancer up to take command after 2 furlongs and was never headed, winning by seven lengths. The time for the race was 1:23 ⅖, but Shoemaker kept Dancer going to do the mile in 1:36 ⅖ and the 9 furlongs in 1:50 ⅘. Luro was very happy with the times, and Shoemaker was impressed by the Dancer's speed, stating, "I would be out of my mind if I did not ride this colt in the Flamingo."

The Flamingo Stakes came a week after Northern Dancer's win/workout. He had a morning workout during the week, but Dancer was not a morning horse. He did not impress anyone in his workouts, according to Luro. The Flamingo attracted a deep field that included Roman Brother, Quadrangle and Mr. Brick. (Earlier, Roman Brother had won the Everglades Stakes by a nose over Mr. Brick.)

From the off, Mr. Brick assumed the pace and set a scorching first half mile in 45 ⅗, with Northern Dancer a half length back in second. At the 6-furlong mark, the time was 1:09 ⅖. This was when Shoemaker let Dancer loose. The little colt gained the lead and went to the mile mark in a sizzling 1:34 ⅗, carrying on to win the Flamingo Stakes by two lengths over Mr. Brick in 1:47 ⅘. Quadrangle was ten lengths back in third place. The fourth-place finisher, Journalist, was another six lengths in arrears, while Roman Brother dead-heated for fifth with Dandy K.

Northern Dancer displayed his class on the day. Hall of Fame trainer Jimmy Jones had kept his Derby hopeful Kentucky Pioneer, a Calumet Farm colt, in the barn. Jones said of Northern

Dancer, "This is one runnin' son of a gun. He is a dangerous horse at three-eighths or a mile and a half. It doesn't seem to make any difference. Well, he proved that I was well off keeping my horse in the barn, because I wouldn't have been gettin' nothin'."

Meanwhile, in California, a big impressive colt was winning the Santa Anita Derby. Hill Rise won that important race with a display of class and speed, setting a new track record. Racing journalists were pegging Hill Rise as the probable winner of the upcoming "Run for the Roses," though other horses were still in the hunt. Jones sent Kentucky Pioneer out to win the Hutcheson Stakes at Gulfstream Park, while Chieftain won the Governor's Gold Cup at Bowie. Roman Brother and Dandy K came back to face each other in the Fountain of Youth Stakes at Gulfstream, with the latter winning while getting a twelve-pound weight advantage.

Dancer's next race was the Mrs. Florida Purse, an allowance event at Gulfstream Park that cut back in distance to 7 furlongs. Here, Northern Dancer would meet another well-regarded colt aimed at the Derby, The Scoundrel. Manuel Ycaza was back on board, substituting for Shoemaker. Dancer broke cleanly and settled in fifth while a hot first quarter in twenty-two seconds flat ensued ahead of him. After a 44 ⅗ half mile, Ycaza asked Northern Dancer for his run. The colt "ran right from under me," according to the jockey. Dancer crossed the line four lengths ahead of The Scoundrel in 1:22 ⅖, equalling the track record. He galloped out the mile in 1:36 ⅖. Luro was none too pleased with the race, saying, "I did not want him chasing those speed horses so soon."

Luro was training Dancer to not burn off his speed too early. "My horse always has had a world of speed, but I have tried to not use it too much. I've tried to teach the horse to rate himself." The day before the Florida Derby, Luro sent Dancer out for a short workout of five-sixteenths of a mile, but the exercise rider misinterpreted the instructions and worked the colt five-eighths instead. This error in judgment created a chain of events that changed Northern Dancer's inner circle just weeks before the Kentucky Derby.

The eleven-horse field for the Florida Derby included Roman Brother, Dandy K and The Scoundrel as well as Northern Dancer. The race was not a fast one, and the Dancer won by one length, ridden out, over The Scoundrel. The form chart commented that the second-place horse was not good enough in an all-out effort. Dandy K was five lengths back, with Roman Brother fourth.

Shoemaker, who was back aboard Dancer for the Florida Derby, noted that his mount tired in the stretch and lugged in near the finish line. At the time, "The Shoe" was debating which horse to choose as his Derby mount, with one option being the consensus Kentucky Derby favourite Hill Rise. After the Florida Derby, the jockey announced that he would pilot Hill Rise in the Derby. Bill Shoemaker was unaware of the taxing workout Dancer had put in the day before the Florida Derby, and he made his decision thinking that Northern Dancer did not have the stamina needed to win at 10 furlongs. One wonders if he would have made the same decision had he known about the workout.

Another major prep race for the Derby was the Wood Memorial, run at the same 9-furlong distance as the Florida Derby, but taking place at Aqueduct. Quadrangle won the event under the guidance of Bill Hartack. Finishing behind Quadrangle was second-placed Mr. Brick. The race favourite, Roman Brother, was third. Chieftain also ran in the race but was unplaced.

With Shoemaker's departure, Windfields needed to find a new jockey. Northern Dancer had had six different riders up to this point in his career. Luro knew Bill Hartack well, as they had won the 1962 Derby together with Decidedly, and he put a call out to him. Hartack said he wanted to ride the horse first before he made any commitment, since he was also the regular rider of Quadrangle, who was headed for Churchill Downs as well.

The Blue Grass Stakes, run nine days before the Derby at Keeneland, was the final prep race for Northern Dancer and a chance for Hartack to assess the horse. This was also the fourth time Dancer was required to run 9 furlongs, and he was to carry 126 pounds in this race. Bet down to ⅖, Northern Dancer won, as described in the chart, "cleverly without benefit of pressure and with complete authority," thoroughly impressing his new jockey. Bill Hartack declared Northern Dancer as his Derby mount.

Hero to a Nation

The lead-up to the Kentucky Derby is full of obstacles not associated with the average major horse race. The press coverage is intense. The parties and galas of Derby Week are strenuous for the connections who have a horse in the field. Trainers are challenged to keep their prized steeds calm and relaxed during this increased focus, relying heavily on their staff. Luckily for Luro, he had long-time Windfields groom Bill Brevard watching over Northern Dancer 24/7. This is not an easy task when you have a high-strung three-year-old colt. But Horatio Luro had been through this process many times before. He understood the pressure that comes with having a Kentucky Derby contender— he had won the race two years earlier. He knew what to expect and how to keep Northern Dancer fit and content as they prepared for the race.

The Dancer's daily routine consisted of some sort of work every day. On a warm morning, he would go for an exercise gallop at 6:45 a.m. On cooler days, this would start at 8:30. "I am training him conservatively since he is a late foal," Luro stated. "This horse is holding his flesh and doing very well, better than all winter.

"Northern Dancer is a tough little horse, with a remarkable constitution. A race takes nothing out of him. I have him galloped two miles almost every day. I will breeze him every fifth or sixth day. I am trying to build up his capacity, lung power and energy. I believe in everyday exercise and not too much breezing. His disposition is improving every day. Last year, he was very playful, bucking and squealing all the time and trying to run off. His attitude is much kinder this year. You have to be very careful. I trained both his mother and father and neither liked the whip. They gave you everything they had on their own."

Luro went on to say, "Northern Dancer is small but solid. He is fed at 10:30 a.m. after his workout. After the feeding, he usually lies down and takes a two-hour nap. He is fed again at 5:00 p.m. and he retires at night at 11:00 and gets to his feet around 2:00 a.m. when he hears the night watchmen come into the barn. The men have to feed Dancer first, or he will tear the barn down in protest."

During Derby Week, Luro said, "[He] slept like a baby, because that is precisely what he is at this stage. He is an intelligent horse who knows which days are for work and which days are for rest. On the rest days, he relaxes. I believe much of his smallness can be attributed to his youth. He is always a good doer [eater], which I attribute to his relaxed attitude." Luro predicted that if the track came up fast on Saturday, the race could be run close to two minutes flat.

Northern Dancer was very calm following his final pre-Derby work on the Thursday. Luro had him out grazing and noted, "He doesn't resent people. He is looking for sugar most of the time, but this grass is great. It is just like a salad to him and this grazing is very soothing for him. It is more relaxing than nourishment."

Northern Dancer was in the best shape of his life. His racing form had never been better. He was ready for the big stage.

Hill Rise came to Churchill Downs on the wave of a winning streak. He continued his fine form when he won the 7-furlong Forerunner Purse at Keeneland and the one-mile Derby Trial Stakes at Churchill Downs on the Monday before the first

Saturday in May. Roman Brother finished second in the Trial. Bill Shoemaker rode Hill Rise in both races and said after the Forerunner, "I like this horse. He does want to play around a bit, and I had to whack a couple. I can see this one is a little lazier than Northern Dancer. You have to keep his mind on his business."

Bill Finnegan, the trainer of Hill Rise, said, "Hill Rise has gained weight and keeps developing all the time. He is in wonderful condition, everything about him pleases me." Hill Rise stood 16.2 hands and weighed between 1,050 and 1,100 pounds during his racing career. He had a seventy-two-and-a-half-inch girth. Don Pierce, who had ridden Hill Rise in the Santa Anita Derby, said, "I have never ridden a better horse in my life." This, coming from a jockey who had ridden the likes of Tomy Lee, Decidedly and Kelso, was high praise.

Hill Rise seemed a little more agitated in Kentucky than he was back in California. Finnegan had to line the horse's stall with foam rubber because "the colt tried to kick his stall to pieces. He had never done nothing like this in California." Shoemaker noted that Hill Rise seemed nervous in the gate for the Derby Trial, so Finnegan ordered gate schooling for the colt. Despite this, Shoemaker still believed he had made the right choice for his Derby mount.

Saturday, May 2, 1964, broke with warm sunshine, which lasted the entire day. The weather was perfect for the grand stage that was the Kentucky Derby. The track was rated fast, the crowd overflowed and the anticipation built to a crescendo as the twelve horses for the Derby came on the track to the glorious tradition of the tune "My Old Kentucky Home." Canadian history was about to be made.

Northern Dancer broke from the number seven stall alertly and in good order. Hill Rise was unhurried from stall eleven and was bumped twice along the front straight past the twin spires into the first turn. Mr. Brick, after brushing Quadrangle out of the gate, set the early fractions of 22 ⅖ for the first quarter and 46 flat for the half mile. Fast times, indeed. Hartack took Northern Dancer to the rail to save ground around the first turn in sixth place, four-and-a-quarter lengths behind the leaders.

Along the backstretch, Northern Dancer continued to let the leaders set the pace, but he began to move up midway down the lane. He left Hill Rise behind by a couple of lengths, and Hartack asked him for more as they entered the far turn. The Scoundrel had come to the head of Mr. Brick and took the lead entering the turn, with Northern Dancer bearing down on the outside. Dancer took the lead near the end of the turn and gained control as the field entered the homestretch. He was four lanes wide of the inside rail.

Through the stretch drive, Northern Dancer maintained his relentless speed and pulled away from The Scoundrel, but Hill Rise loomed on his outside. The big horse began to cut into Dancer's advantage. You could literally see the will and determination of Northern Dancer as he held off his larger foe and crossed the Churchill Downs finish line a neck ahead of Hill Rise. Northern Dancer had won the Kentucky Derby in style, setting a new track record of two minutes flat for the 10-furlong distance. An entire country began to celebrate.

Finishing third, some three-and-a-half lengths back, was The Scoundrel, with Roman Brother another nose back of him. Quadrangle finished fifth, a neck behind Roman Brother, with Mr. Brick three lengths farther back in sixth.

Northern Dancer pranced to the winner's enclosure as E.P. Taylor led the full-of-himself colt in. Horatio Luro and the entire Windfields team joined in the celebrations at Churchill Downs, while, back in Canada, people were out in the streets, proclaiming "Our Horse" was the greatest of them all. Northern Dancer posed with his garland of roses, proud as a peacock.

Post-race comments and tributes came pouring in. Bill Hartack said, "I knew I had a horse with speed. I didn't want to press him early. When the gates opened, I took him in hand immediately. When The Scoundrel made his move around the last turn, I let him pace me and we left Hill Rise. With a quarter mile to go, I felt I had to make my move. Luro told me if I hit the horse to hit him only on the shoulder, and not hard. I did and he reacted to it. From the quarter pole in, I hit him hard on the rear, and he responded to that too. So I put him to a hard drive, hitting hard all the way. In the Blue Grass, I rode him to see what he was made off. I learned he is agile. I knew he would be well trained. This horse is all blood and guts." Hartack added, "After the Blue Grass, I was never more confident in a Derby ride than I was with Northern Dancer."

E.P. Taylor commented, "It is a great day for Canada. Northern Dancer has given me my greatest thrill in racing." Horatio Luro said, "Northern Dancer is consistent, honest and has a big heart."

When interviewed, Shoemaker said, "I am not sorry I chose Hill Rise over Northern Dancer. If I had to do it over, I would do the same thing. The race was very close. My horse ran as good as expected. I was gaining at the wire, but Northern Dancer was a lot of horse. The ground ran out on us before we could catch him. Hartack had a ton of horse under him, while in contrast I was punching at my horse to get him going."

Bill Finnegan felt that both horses ran their best race in the Derby, but said that he needed to train more speed into Hill Rise in order to combat the speed and agility of Northern Dancer. He eagerly awaited a rematch.

Sports fans in Canada, especially in Toronto, were celebrating not only Dancer's historic victory, but also the third consecutive Stanley Cup triumph of their beloved Toronto Maple Leafs the week prior. Heady days, indeed. While Canada celebrated, Northern Dancer went back to the barn, ate his post-race meal and had a sound, deserved nap. He had achieved all of this more than three weeks before his actual third birthday.

Proving His Point

Northern Dancer came out of the Kentucky Derby in perfect health, so it was on to Pimlico Race Course, just outside Baltimore, for a start in the second jewel of the Triple Crown, the Preakness Stakes. Dancer arrived at Pimlico two days after his win in Kentucky, following a sixteen-hour van ride. Hill Rise was flown in. Dancer settled in the stall reserved for Derby winners entering the Preakness, as the vultures in the press began circling, stating that the Derby had taken too much out of the little Canadian and that the next race would have a different result. Again, Northern Dancer's resolve and determination were underestimated.

The focus intensified at Pimlico after the record-setting Derby victory, and the Windfields contingent fielded all sorts of questions from the press. A turf writer from Chicago saw Northern Dancer in the flesh for the first time. His printed comment was comical: "This has got to be an imposter. A colt that size couldn't do what he has done." The latest Kentucky Derby winner's appearance played against the notion that a champion racehorse had to be big and imposing.

Horatio Luro was asked by a columnist about Dancer's personality. "He just likes to have fun. He has taken my shirt off and my pants, but what's the difference as long as he is paying for them, eh! He could be any kind of horse. He has beautiful muscles and a beautiful face."

Preparing Northern Dancer and dealing with the press took all Luro's time, and he gave Pimlico officials several anxious minutes as they waited for him in the racing secretary's office moments before nominations closed for the Preakness. Luro arrived with his nomination form for Northern Dancer with three minutes to spare.

From a field of twelve in the Derby, only six started in the Preakness. One was a new contestant, Big Pete, while the top five finishers from two weeks before came for a shot at winning the Woodlawn Vase. Hill Rise went into the gate as the favourite again at ⅕, while the Derby winner was second choice at 2/1. Quadrangle, The Scoundrel and Roman Brother made up the rest of the field.

The newcomer, Big Pete, assumed the lead from the off, while Northern Dancer was between Quadrangle and Hill Rise and being squeezed ever so slightly. Big Pete carried the lead through the first turn, with Quadrangle on his hip. Hartack had Dancer in third, with Shoemaker in close proximity on Hill Rise. Quadrangle relieved Big Pete of the lead as they approached the far turn, while Shoemaker asked Hill Rise for more and came to Northern Dancer. Hartack saw this move and let out some rein, and the Derby winner responded immediately.

Northern Dancer took the lead from Quadrangle midway through the far turn and put some distance between himself and Hill Rise as well. Down the stretch they came as Northern Dancer increased his lead and powered through off a hand ride to win by a commanding two-and-a-quarter lengths over The Scoundrel, who made a late charge to get second place. Hill Rise finished a head back of The Scoundrel in third, and Quadrangle was another head back in fourth.

Many people consider Northern Dancer's Preakness his finest racing performance.

Bill Shoemaker commented after the race, "This time I got beat legit. I have no excuse whatsoever. We had a good position on the backstretch and couldn't keep up with Northern Dancer then. Hill Rise moved when I asked him, and we had another shot at him, but we couldn't stay with the top horse. He's just the best, that's all."

Braulio Baeza was asked if his horse, Quadrangle, had any trouble. "We all have one big trouble. The big trouble is we could not keep up with that Canadian. We could not handle him. Other than that, my horse had no trouble."

Bill Hartack by now was in complete awe of his mount. "I had a labouring horse under me at the end, but the others were also tiring on the deep track. Dancer gives a rider great confidence. He runs kindly and responds when you want him to. Some horses, when you push the Go button, they just don't go. Dancer goes. This horse is an agile and free-running short strider. He gives you his run when you ask for it. He is willing and game, and I don't think he will come up empty in the Belmont."

The Belmont Stakes, the final leg of the Triple Crown, is the most gruelling race of the series. At a distance of one and a half miles, or 12 furlongs in turf parlance, the three-year-olds are asked to run farther than they have ever raced before. That it comes so soon after they have run two demanding and fiercely contested races (the Belmont is just three weeks after the Preakness) imposes another physical demand that at times goes unnoticed by the average racing fan. The Belmont Stakes has earned its nickname, "the Test of Champions."

Luro had made a headline-grabbing statement at the gala celebrations following Northern Dancer's victory in the Preakness. He stated that he felt the Belmont was beyond the horse's limits, and he did not want to enter him in the race. E.P. Taylor countered this a few days later when he told the press, "We have come too far not to try for the triple."

The last Triple Crown winner prior to 1964 was Citation in 1948. Tim Tam in 1958 and Carry Back in 1961 were the only horses to have won the first two legs of the triple and tried for the sweep since Citation. Now, here was another challenger in the diminutive powerhouse Canadian colt.

We know that Northern Dancer failed in his bid to capture the Triple Crown. It would be another nine years before the drought of Triple Crown winners was ended when the great Secretariat ran to immortality. Quadrangle, who had finished second to the six-year-old Olden Times in the Metropolitan Mile between his Preakness and Belmont appearances, won the classic race (which was held at Aqueduct Racetrack, as the Belmont Park grandstand was undergoing renovations). Roman Brother, who seemed to race every week and had won the Jersey Derby between his Preakness and Belmont appearances, finished second. Hill Rise was fourth in the Belmont, again behind Northern Dancer.

Fans were disappointed, but the sheen of the Churchill and Pimlico wins did not lose its lustre. E.P. Taylor said, "Quadrangle won a fine race today. We have no excuses." Hartack stated, "My horse ran his heart out for me. I'm sorry he didn't win, but he just wasn't good enough." And Luro said, "We didn't lose the war, just one of the battles."

Quadrangle was coming into his own and ran the final quarter in 24 ⅖. He proved himself genuine when he won the Travers Stakes later in the year at Saratoga. Roman Brother would become the Horse of the Year the following season.

Northern Dancer came home to Canada to a hero's welcome. E.P. Taylor had bred a Kentucky Derby winner right in the heart of the nation, defying the naysayers who said that such a horse could not be raised in Canada. The racing fans at Woodbine and around the country praised Taylor for his accomplishment. The Queen's Plate was the next race on the Dancer's card and would give his countrymen a chance to see him on their own soil. However, an old problem was beginning to resurface.

The quarter crack that had caused so much concern at the end of the previous year was showing signs of returning. Luro contacted local blacksmith Carl Grguric, who had established himself at Woodbine as a master farrier. Grguric was an intuitive blacksmith and knew his craft well. He cut the quarter crack out right up to the coronet band to relieve the pressure. Northern Dancer's team had caught the emerging problem early enough to avoid the loss of substantial training time. Luro was thrilled with Grguric's work and had Dancer back on the track four days after the treatment. Here was another moment that could have altered the legend of Northern Dancer, as it would have been a massive disappointment if the Canadian star could not start in his home country's biggest race.

The Dancer's rivals in the Queen's Plate consisted of a fine group of three-year-olds. Pierlou came into the race unde-feated on the season and had won a division of the Plate Trail by twelve-and-a-half lengths, while Grand Garcon won the other division by two-and-a-half lengths over Brockton Boy. All three of these would-be challengers to the Windfields flag-bearer had been sold by Windfields as yearlings two year prior. Brockton Boy was sold for $25,000, the same price Northern Dancer was offered for, and passed over at.

On a beautiful spring afternoon at Woodbine, spectators lined up twenty to thirty people deep around the oval walking ring. Everyone strained to watch Northern Dancer as Bill Bre-vard led the new national hero around. A record crowd filled the grandstand to overflowing and cheered their equine hero as he made his appearance on the track with Hartack in the saddle. Never before had a Canadian horse inspired so many people to attend the races in such large numbers.

Luro was a bit disappointed with post position one, which Northern Dancer had drawn. And Dancer gave his adoring public quite the scare as he entered the first turn past the big grandstand in last place. E.P. Taylor later said, "I was uneasy during the early running. I would have hated to see him beaten. I felt much better after I saw Hartack make his move."

Hartack did make his move along the back straight, and they began to pick off horse after horse as the field entered the far turn. Dancer had the lead midway through the turn, and under a hand ride, with one little shoulder tap from Hartack, Northern Dancer won the Queen's Plate by seven-and-a-half lengths over fellow Nearctic son Langcrest, with Grand Garcon third.

As E.P. Taylor led Northern Dancer to the winner's circle, the cheering and celebrations from the packed grandstand became louder. This was a 180-degree turnaround from the previous year, when Canebora was led in for his Queen's Plate trophy and the fans booed Taylor unmercifully. The press had fuelled the antipathy toward Taylor due to the perception that he was dominating the Canadian classic. He also offered every horse he bred for sale, so he was winning the race with horses who had been rejected by buyers. All that was now in the past. Taylor was adored by his fellow Canadians for his accomplishments with Northern Dancer.

Post-race comments were predictable. Hartack said it was just too easy. "I did not ride him out because I did not have to. He was never boxed in. I chose my position, but found my horse going at his slowest and still overtaking the others. Luro wanted me to win with the least necessary effort."

Luro added, "The horse came out fast so we had to back off the pace because he was full of run and we wanted someone else to make the pace. Don't forget Dancer passed six horses in an eighth of a mile when he moved."

Rival jockey Jim Fitzsimmons, who had ridden Northern Dancer as a two-year-old, was on third-placed Grand Garcon. "My horse travelled as fast as he could, but when Hartack passed us, he still had Northern Dancer's head bowed."

A rest was in order for Northern Dancer, so Luro shipped him back to his main string at Belmont. The horse had won all his big races save one. He was the darling of an entire country, praised as the greatest Canadian horse ever bred. Now he would be aiming for the American Derby in two months at Arlington Park.

However, fate stepped in and prevented Northern Dancer from ever racing again.

In August, Northern Dancer had an easy, controlled 7-furlong breeze to keep his fitness level up. The track was a bit deep due to morning rain. Luro was reluctant to carry out the work, but if Dancer was to make the American Derby, the colt needed it. As

Dancer came off the track from his breeze, Luro noticed a slight bump on the left foreleg. Heat was also present, and treatment was immediately administered. There was definitely something amiss with Dancer's left front tendon. It did not seem bowed but did appear to be strained. Northern Dancer missed the American Derby and was shipped back to Woodbine. He was not in dire pain, but the tendon was not in racing condition.

On October 24, Northern Dancer was on the Woodbine main track. He was not in a race but was paraded in front of his adoring public on Canadian International day. Ron Turcotte was given the chance to ride the champion. "It was an honour Mr. and Mrs. Taylor gave me to ride Northern Dancer that day," he said many years later. "We just lightly jogged, but that little competitor wanted to run. He was more mature than when I rode him the year before. He was all heart."

The racing career of Northern Dancer had come to an end. The awards came pouring in. Horse of the Year in Canada. Champion three-year-old colt in Canada and the United States. These honours were expected. The big surprise came when Northern Dancer was awarded the Lou Marsh Trophy as Canadian Male Athlete of 1964, beating out hockey legend Gordie Howe. To this day, Northern Dancer is the only non-human to win a Lou Marsh Award. He was also the first horse to be inducted into the Canadian Sports Hall of Fame.

Northern Dancer was retired to stand at stud at Windfields Farm in Oshawa. A national hero would soon become a worldwide phenomenon, to be treasured by more than just his compatriots.

{ 8 }

FOUNDATION MARES III: DEVELOPING NEW FOUNDATIONS

ITH THE WORLDWIDE acclaim given to the stallions and great runners coming from Windfields, many people tend to forget where all these runners came from, and who bore the stallions' great offspring. Following a female family is one of the keys to a successful breeding enterprise, and numerous valuable foundation mares sent Windfields breeding to exalted heights. It is no coincidence that outstanding matriarchs produce outstanding matriarchs. In some cases, greatness skips a generation or two, but it eventually reappears with foals from a descendant of some famous broodmare.

Offering every yearling for sale sometimes took a toll on the continuation of excellent female families developed by

Windfields, though there were always a few descendants ignored by prospective buyers and retained by the farm, while others were reacquired once they were finished racing.

E.P. Taylor knew that in order to stay on top, he had to bring in new blood. He reinvested much of the earnings from yearling sales in fillies who would be retained for breeding, and a transition of sorts took place in the Windfields realm.

Chilly

Chilly, a bay daughter of Nearctic born in 1966, was a great-granddaughter of foundation mare Nandi. Both Chilly and her dam, Cut Flower, were unsold at Windfields yearling sales and thus stayed with the farm as broodmares once they finished racing. Chilly would become a new-generation foundation mare.

The first stakes winner from Chilly was a dark bay daughter by Impressive, named Impressive Lady. Impressive Lady won eight of sixteen races, with her victories in the Mazarine, Star Shoot, Selene and Yearling Sales Stakes her biggest triumphs. She was also second in the Fury Stakes and Canadian Oaks to Square Angel, finishing ahead of La Prevoyante in the latter. A third-place finish to males in the Manitoba Derby was another notable performance.

Impressive Lady had three stakes winners from eleven foals as a Windfields broodmare: the colts Impressive Prince, by Kamaraan II, and Imperial Colony, by Pleasant Colony, and a filly named Supertam, by Tentam. While these three brought immediate laurels to the family, two other daughters, both winners, took the family fortunes to further heights. The first of the two was Caucasienne, by Maryland farm sire Caucasus. The second was Chilly Hostess, by Oshawa farm sire Vice Regent.

Caucasienne won three of her five races, none of which were stakes events, and was retired due to an injury. She produced only two foals before dying at the age of eight. The two foals were both fillies. The first, a bay named Adorned, remained with Windfields after she was removed from the yearling sales due to an injury. She eventually became the dam of three stakes winners, including Queen's Plate winner and champion three-year-old Archer's Bay. That one became a stallion at the Oshawa farm when his racing career ended.

Chilly Hostess contributed to South African breeding in a big way. Her stakes-winning son Western Winter, by the excellent sire Gone West, was the leading sire in South Africa several times. At the time of his passing in 2013 due to complications from colic surgery, Western Winter was the all-time leading sire by prize money and Group One winners in South African history. He sired seventy-six stakes winners, including two South African Horse of the Year winners in Yard-Arm and Winter Solstice, and many sons that are continuing the line. His daughters have become sought-after broodmares.

The success of Western Winter is an example of the pervasive influence Windfields breeding has had globally. Previously, the dominant sire in South Africa was Northern Guest, a Windfields-bred son of Northern Dancer, out of Sex Appeal (we will look at Sex Appeal's influence later in this chapter).

Returning to Chilly, we find another daughter who has been important to Windfields' breeding success. Stage Queen, by Oshawa farm stallion Ruritania, was a foal of 1976 and sold the following year at the CTHS yearling sales to leading Canadian owner Jack Stafford for $102,000, the second-highest price of the sale. The grey filly won three races from seventeen starts and was stakes-placed. Assimilated into the Stafford Farms broodmare band, Stage Queen produced a chestnut filly by Oshawa sire Lord Durham, later to be named Stage Flite. Stage Flite, one of the last Thoroughbreds to run under the red-and-white colours of Stafford Farm, became the Sovereign Award champion two-year-old filly in 1985 after winning the Nandi, Mazarine and Princess Elizabeth Stakes.

Stage Queen was sold to Minshall Farms and for them produced in 1990 a bay filly by Bold Ruckus. Given the name Bold Ruritana, the Minshall Farms runner became a champion and earned over $1 million during her notable racing career. Her best performance was a track-record outing on the Woodbine grass in the King Edward Gold Cup. She ran the 9 furlongs in a scorching 1:45 ⅕ over a stellar field of male competition. She kept company with top-level horses, as evidenced by her win in the Dance Smartly Stakes. She also had two wins in both the Nassau Stakes and Victoriana Stakes, and placed twice in the E.P. Taylor Stakes and once in the Grade One Yellow Ribbon Stakes. Bold Ruritana also won the Canadian Handicap, Ontario Damsel Stakes and Providian Mile during her career.

Bold Ruritana has kept the line going through her unraced daughter Preemptive Attack. Sired by Canadian-bred champion Smart Strike, Preemptive Attack produced Sky Treasure from a cover by Sky Mesa. This chestnut filly went on to win the Grade Two Nassau Stakes and almost half a million dollars. Surgical Strike, a son of Preemptive Attack, by world-record-holder Red Giant, won the 2016 Arlington Classic.

One more offspring of note from Chilly is her 1975 filly by Oshawa sire Right Combination. This dark bay was named Right Chilly and found a home in Western Canada, winning ten stakes races including the British Columbia Oaks. Her daughter Darcia, by 1983 Canadian Horse of the Year Travelling Victor, won four western stakes races. In a unique tie to Darcia's Windfields heritage, Travelling Victor was sired by former Oshawa sire Hail To Victory; thus, Darcia had Windfields-influenced breeding on both sides of her pedigree.

Impetuous Lady

A daughter of Hasty Road, out of an Argentine mare named Escocesa, by Nigromante, Impetuous Lady carried a very different pedigree than one would normally see in Windfields breeding. E.P. Taylor was never afraid to mix different bloodlines with his existing stock to find the next champion. However, Impetuous Lady was not a champion, nor a race winner. She did, however, become the matriarch to a very fine family of stakes winners and producers. She herself is the dam of four individual stakes winners.

The first stakes winner from Impetuous Lady was her son by Northern Dancer named Northern Fling, who won three graded stakes races. Her second was a daughter named Regal Gal, sired by the Dancer's son Viceregal, who won seven stakes races and produced graded stakes winners herself. The third Impetuous Lady stakes winner became the line to some very good Grade One stakes winners.

Impetuous Gal, by Briartic, won four stakes races. When she was introduced to Nijinsky II, she produced Banker's Lady. A top New York–based handicap mare, Banker's Lady won eight of ten races, including the Ladies, Top Flight and Shuvee Handicaps. Banker's Lady is the third dam of Grade One winner Personal Diary, by City Zip, and has several other graded stakes winners among her tail female descendants.

Impetuous Gal is the second dam of two additional Grade One winners. Her daughter Devil's Dispute is the dam of Daisy Devine (Jenny Wiley Stakes), by Kafwain; while another daughter, Daring Danzig, is the dam of Ecton Park (Super Derby), by Forty Niner.

The fourth stakes winner from Impetuous Lady was Countess North, a full sister to Northern Fling. Countess North produced Palangana, by His Majesty, who in turn is the dam of 2009 Eclipse Award champion female sprinter Informed Decision.

This fleet filly, sired by Kentucky Derby winner Monarchos, won the Breeders' Cup Filly and Mare Sprint, the Madison Stakes and the Humana Distaff Stakes as a four-year-old. She won an additional eight graded stakes races.

Nangela

One of the emerging families in breeding during the 1950s and '60s was that of Sister Sarah. Sister Sarah was a great-granddaughter of the immortal Pretty Polly. E.P. Taylor had already bought into the family when he acquired Lady Angela, dam of Nearctic, and we have seen how that mare has influenced the breed. Other well-bred descendants from Sister Sarah include Great Nephew, sire of Epsom Derby winners Grundy and Shergar.

Taylor had a chance to get another filly in the family and did so in 1961 by purchasing a bay daughter of Tim Tam, out of Great Niece, a full sister to Great Nephew, as a yearling. The filly was aptly named Angela's Niece, as she was a niece of Lady Angela, and became an allowance-level winner on the track. Angela's Niece was introduced to Nearctic after her racing days ended, and on April 19, 1965, she produced a bay daughter who would go by the name Nangela.

Offered at the Windfields annual yearling sale in 1966, Nangela was yet another unsold youngster who went on to further the fortunes of the farm. During her juvenile season at the track, Nangela won the Carleton Stakes against the boys and another three races. She inexplicably went off form as a three-year-old and didn't place in eight races, winning only $210 from one fourth-place finish after her promising juvenile year. This prompted her retirement from the track to the Windfields broodmare colony.

As a broodmare, Nangela founded a family rich in stakes winners and success at the highest levels in racing worldwide. Her first foal launched Nangela's broodmare career with a resounding triumph. In an interesting twist of irony, Nangela was bred to Belmont Stakes winner Quadrangle, the horse who had stopped Northern Dancer's Triple Crown bid in 1964. E.P. Taylor had bought shares in Quadrangle for breeding, bearing no grudge when it came to the stallion's promising breeding career.

The resulting foal, a bay filly, was sold as a yearling for $20,000 at the 1971 CTHS sales to General W. Preston Gilbride. Given the name Square Angel, the Windfields-bred became a major force on the track and in breeding. She won the Shady Well Stakes as a two-year-old and placed second in two other stakes races. She came into her own at three, winning the Canadian Oaks over Impressive Lady and reigning two-year-old champion La Prevoyante. Square Angel also won the Fury Stakes and the Nettie Handicap. (The latter race underwent a name change a decade later and is now known as the E.P. Taylor Stakes, a prestigious Grade One race on the world racing calendar.) Square Angel was named the Sovereign Award champion three-year-old filly.

E.P. Taylor bought her back from General Gilbride after her racing career and added her to the Windfields broodmare population. Here, Square Angel became one of the most accomplished broodmares of the latter part of the twentieth century. Her second foal, Kamar, was sired by Key To The Mint and became a chip off the old Square Angel block, not only looking like her but also having a similar racing and breeding career. Kamar emulated her dam by winning the Canadian Oaks and being named the Sovereign Award three-year-old filly in 1979. Kamar's first foal was a son by Wajima named Key To The Moon. This colt won the Queen's Plate and was the champion three-year-old colt in Canada. He was the first of many high-class stakes winners to come.

Kamar's most successful foal as a racehorse was Gorgeous, a daughter by Eclipse Award champion Slew O' Gold. Gorgeous had a consistent record of 8-4-1 from fourteen starts. She ran in elite company, winning the Grade One Hollywood Oaks, Ashland Stakes and Vanity Handicap. Gorgeous was second three times to champion Bayakoa in the Breeders' Cup Distaff, Spinster Stakes and Santa Margarita Invitational, and she also finished just behind another champion, Open Mind, in the Mother Goose Stakes.

As a broodmare, Gorgeous and her daughters continued the family line. Her first foal was a daughter by Mr. Prospector named Dreamboat. A winner of one race, Dreamboat produced Group One winner Music Show (Falmouth Stakes), by Noverre. Music Show raced against top company: her second-place finish to three-time Breeders' Cup winner Goldikova in the Prix Rothschild, and a third in the classic Irish 1000 Guineas give a great indication of her class.

Gorgeous had a pair of fillies sired by Seeking The Gold, a son of Mr. Prospector, named Fabulous and Glasgow's Gold. Fabulous did not enhance the family on the track, being unplaced in one start, but her granddaughter Turbulent Descent has done the family proud. This bay daughter of the A.P. Indy sire Congrats won four Grade One races, the Hollywood Starlet Stakes at two, the Santa Anita Oaks and Test Stakes at three, and the Ballerina Stakes at four. Turbulent Descent acquired her name when she survived a near-fatal plane trip on her way from the yearling sales to her new home.

Gorgeous's other Seeking The Gold filly, Glasgow's Gold, did win one race, but later contributed to the family fortunes by producing Swift Temper (by Giant's Causeway), winner of the Grade One Ruffian Handicap. Swift Temper added three more stakes wins to her resumé, including the Delaware Handicap.

Kamar was bred to Alydar and produced a chestnut filly, Hiaam, who won the Princess Margaret Stakes to earn more black-type honours for this regal family. Hiaam produced Oaks

Trial Stakes winner Munnaya, by Nijinsky II. This one, in turn, is the dam of multiple-graded-stakes-winning Alpha, by Eclipse Award champion Bernardini. Alpha emulated his sire by winning the Grade One Travers Stakes, albeit in a dead heat with Golden Ticket, as well as the Grade One Woodward Stakes for Godolphin Racing. Alpha showed his class as a two-year-old when he finished second to future Belmont Stakes winner Union Rags in the Champagne Stakes.

Kamar produced a three-quarter sister to Gorgeous in 1987. Seaside Attraction was by Triple Crown winner Seattle Slew, the sire of Slew O' Gold. Though the filly was not quite as successful as her sister, she did win the Grade One Kentucky Oaks, beating Go For Wand. In the role of broodmare, Seaside Attraction has excelled. As with other members of this family, Mr. Prospector and his son Seeking The Gold have had a huge influence.

The first foal from Seaside Attraction was Cherry Hinton Stakes winner Red Carnival, by Mr. Prospector. This one's son Desert Lord, sired by Green Desert, was a top-class sprinter and took the Group One Prix de l'Abbaye de Longchamp as his biggest prize.

Golden Attraction, a full sister to Red Carnival, became the Eclipse Award champion two-year-old filly of 1995. Her season was outstanding as she was the winner of the Grade One Spinaway, Matron and Frizette. In the Breeders' Cup Juvenile Fillies, she ran a close third to My Flag and Cara Rafaela. Golden Attraction won eight of eleven lifetime starts, placing second and third once each. In her only non-placing race, Golden Attraction was injured, and she did not race again.

Seaside Attraction was bred to Seeking The Gold and produced Florida Derby winner Cape Town. Cape Town later sired Kentucky Oaks winner Bird Town, out of a Storm Bird mare.

Staying with the Kamar branch, or should we say tree, we now come to her daughter Wilayif, sired by Danzig. This one was a modest winner of one race and later produced Morning Pride, by Machiavellian. This daughter won the Prix du Bois and then became the dam of Grade One winner Flashing. Sired by A.P. Indy, Flashing won the Test Stakes and the Gazelle Stakes as a three-year-old. She won six of ten races and also finished third to Rachel Alexandra in the Mother Goose Stakes.

A pair of recent Grade One stakes winners from the Kamar family descended from her first daughter, Forli's Key. Sharp Azteca won the 2017 Cigar Mile, and Bowie's Hero took the 2018 Frank E. Kilroe Mile. Both colts are out of granddaughters of Forli's Key.

One more daughter of Kamar deserves mention. Jood was sired by Nijinsky II and was only placed on the track. In the breeding shed, however, she produced 2001 Horse of the World Fantastic Light. This son took his time to learn the racing craft, but once he got the hang of it, he was something to behold. Sired by Rahy, a son of Blushing Groom and Windfields-bred champion Glorious Song, Fantastic Light raced in top events around the world, facing most of the elite runners of his generation. He won six Grade/Group One races, finished second in six more such events and earned in excess of $8 million. In America, his Grade One wins came in the Breeders' Cup Turf, setting a new course record, and the Man O' War Stakes. In England, he captured the Tattersalls Gold Cup and Prince of Wales Stakes. In Ireland, he won the Irish Champion Stakes, defeating Galileo, and at Sha Tin, he won the Hong Kong Cup. Fantastic Light finished second twice in the King George VI and Queen Elizabeth Stakes, once to Montjeu and once to Galileo. Other second-place finishes were behind such top performers as T.M. Opera O, Stay Gold and Daliapour. Clearly, Fantastic Light lived up to his name.

Jood had a liaison with Mr. Prospector, like many others in the family, and produced a daughter named Wanice. Wanice won her only race, in France, and later went to Australia for broodmare duty. There, she produced a daughter, Zembu, by the Sunday Silence sire Fuji Kiseki. Zembu is the dam of Group One BTC Cup winner Your Song, a son of Fastnet Rock.

That is the extensive list of Grade/Group One–winning descendants from the Kamar branch. It is not hard to believe that Kamar is a former Kentucky broodmare of the year, in keeping with the remarkable achievements attained by this branch of the family. Now we return to Square Angel to continue tracing the family of Nangela.

Stellarette, sired by Maryland farm sire Tentam, would add further plaudits for this regal family. Sold to Frank Stronach at the 1979 CTHS yearling sales, the Taylor-bred Stellarette captured a pair of graded stakes races and then became an excellent producer, in keeping with family tradition. Her first foal, a daughter of Mr. Prospector—there's that name again!—was given the name Graphite. Graphite won one race, was bred to Lammtarra and produced a filly named Rose Quartz. This filly also won only one race, but upon her tryst with Linamix, she produced Rosawa, who in turn is the dam of Prix Marcel Boussac winner Rosanara. This grey filly also finished second in the classic Prix de Diane to Sarafina.

Graphite also had a daughter by English champion miler Kris named Clovis Point. Another winner of only one race, Clovis Point produced a stakes-winning daughter in Japan, sired by Arc winner Carnegie. This horse, Temple Of Peace, is in turn the dam of Whobegotyou, winner of the Group One Caulfield Guineas and Yalumba Stakes. The well-raced son of Street Cry won an additional seven graded stakes races and placed in seven further Group One stakes, all in Australia. He was named the champion three-year-old colt/gelding for the 2008–2009 season.

Back to Stellarette, we find her daughter Nuryette, by Nureyev, himself a leading-sire son of Northern Dancer. Nuryette was bred to Canadian Horse of the Year Afleet, a son of Mr.

Prospector, and produced multiple-graded-stakes-winning Northern Afleet, one of the most popular and successful sires currently breeding at time of writing. Northern Afleet has sired eleven Grade/Group One stakes winners, including Preakness and Belmont stakes winner Afleet Alex, and Breeders' Cup Sprint winner Amazombie. Both are Eclipse Award recipients. Nuryette is also the dam of Grade One Gazelle Handicap winner Tap To Music, by Pleasant Tap.

Stellarette had a full sister to Graphite named Cuddles, who won the Hollywood Starlet Stakes at two and several graded stakes races at four.

Speaking of full sisters, Square Angel produced a full sister to Kamar who was sold to Del and Gail Chase at the Keeneland yearling sales in 1982. The Chases named their new filly Love Smitten. Love Smitten took her time to reach the top of her game but did so with authority when she won the Grade One Apple Blossom Handicap as a five-year-old. She went on to great things in the breeding shed as well.

Love Smitten is the dam of two-time English champion older horse Swain. Sired by the remarkable double classic winner Nashwan, Swain also took his time to reach the pinnacle of racing success. When he did, he was as genuine as his cousin Fantastic Light. Swain won the prestigious King George VI and Queen Elizabeth Stakes (twice), Coronation Cup, Irish Champion Stakes and several Group Two and Three races. He ran second to Helissio in the Grand Prix de Saint-Cloud, second to Silver Charm in the Dubai World Cup, and third to Lammtarra in the Arc and to Awesome Again in the Breeders' Cup Classic. Swain was strong, consistent and successful on all sorts of surfaces in all sorts of conditions.

Another son of Love Smitten who has had an impact is Water Poet, by Sadler's Wells. While not a world beater on the track—he won a listed stakes in France—Water Poet became a revelation in his adopted country, Venezuela, as a sire. Water

Poet led that country's sire list nine times, eight times consecutively. He sired two Venezuelan Triple Crown winners and is credited with fifty-six stakes winners from 301 foals (18.6 percent). While Venezuela is not considered a top-flight racing jurisdiction, Water Poet's achievements are noteworthy.

This concludes the extensive Grade/Group One list of Square Angel's branch of the Nangela family.

Returning to Nangela herself, we find her daughter Miss Nanith, by Victoria Park. Unplaced as a racer, Miss Nanith had a pair of daughters who have brought the family additional Grade One stakes winners. Loose Wire, sired by Oshawa farm sire Ruritania, is the dam of Tastetheteardrops. This one produced a dark bay colt who would be named Taste Of Paradise, by Conquistador Cielo. Taste Of Paradise won the Vosburgh Handicap and finished second in the Breeders' Cup Sprint. He won three additional graded stakes and was placed in several more.

Miss Nanith had a daughter sired by Dance Spell, a son of Northern Dancer out of champion broodmare Obeah. Given the name Spell Victory, the filly won once in twenty-one attempts. Bred to Native Prospector, another son of Mr. Prospector, Spell Victory produced Susan Powter. This one is the dam of Triple Bend Handicap winner Joey Franco. A full sister to Susan Powter named Molly's Prospector is the dam of Malibu Stakes winner Bob Black Jack. Bob Black Jack set a world record of 1:06.53 for 6 furlongs when he won the Sunshine Millions Dash at Santa Anita in 2008.

The family of Nangela has exerted considerable influence on the breed.

Gay Meeting

In 1968, E.P. Taylor and Joe Thomas were at the Keeneland July yearling sales and found a bay daughter of Sir Gaylord, out of Secret Meeting by Alibhai, who was to their liking. They purchased her for $26,000. Named Gay Meeting, the filly made only two starts the next year, winning once and placing second in her other start. Her only win was a stakes race, the Blue Hen Stakes, so she added black type to her pedigree. She suffered an injury and was retired from racing.

Bred the next year to Buckpasser, Gay Meeting produced a bay filly at the Maryland farm. Unsold as a yearling, the filly acquired the name Passing Look and raced for Windfields, winning four races and placing in a pair of stakes. She became another quality broodmare at Windfields, relocating to the Oshawa farm. Passing Look formed a strong alliance with farm stallion Vice Regent. The two had four daughters together, three of whom became stakes winners.

The first daughter from this partnership came on May 22, 1982, and was a chestnut filly. Ernie Samuel's Sam-Son Farm purchased her at the CTHS yearling sale the following year and named her In My Cap. The filly became a solid high-class competitor on the Woodbine circuit, winning the Princess Elizabeth Stakes and Ontario Lassie Stakes as a juvenile, and following up the next year by winning the classic Bison City Stakes and Wonder Where Stakes. She added the La Prevoyante and Maple Leaf Stakes to her resumé, as well as a second place to La Lorgnette in the Canadian Oaks.

In My Cap's contribution as a broodmare to the Gay Meeting family lies with her daughters, one of whom was Bright Feather by Fappiano. This stakes-placed filly was bred to Kentucky Derby winner Go For Gin, and the resulting foal was a colt named Albert The Great. Here, we have a hard-knocking runner who kept up with top-level company in his career.

Albert The Great won the Jockey Club Gold Cup as a three-year-old and defeated More Than Ready and Red Bullet in the Dwyer Stakes. His four-year-old campaign was solid, if somewhat frustrating. He won both the Brooklyn and Suburban Handicaps, but those two historic races had by then been downgraded to Grade Two status. In his five Grade One races that year, Albert The Great was second four times and third in the Breeders' Cup Classic to Tiznow and Sakhee.

A granddaughter of In My Cap named Autumnal produced a bay filly by More Than Ready in 2015. Given the name Rushing Fall, this descendant won the prestigious Breeders' Cup Juvenile Fillies Turf in 2017. She followed up with a win a year later in the Grade One Queen Elizabeth II Challenge Cup. Rushing Fall won six of her seven starts, placing second in her only non-winning appearance.

Passing Look's second daughter by Vice Regent, named Trumpets Blare, captured the 1989 Arlington-Washington Futurity to earn Grade One–winning status. She added four more stakes victories before her retirement to Bluewater Farm in Lexington. Her full sister Passing Vice was a graded stakes winner who finished second in the Grade One Hollywood Starlet Stakes.

In keeping with the family's penchant for hard-knocking types, Gay Meeting's second foal was a gelded son of Northern Dancer named Gay Jitterbug. He won eighteen of his forty races and captured three stakes, placing in several more.

Deceit

The year after purchasing Gay Meeting, Taylor and Thomas were back at Keeneland and bought a dark bay daughter of highly regarded sire Prince John, himself a son of three-time leading sire Princequillo. The dam of the filly was Double Agent, a Double Jay–sired daughter of multiple stakes winner Conniver. Conniver was bred by Alfred Vanderbilt and was a daughter of his great weight-carrying champion Discovery. The filly Taylor purchased came with excellent genes.

Given the name Deceit, the filly was put into the barn of Del Carroll, who trained her to win many important races for female Thoroughbreds. Deceit was one of the best of her generation and won the Astarita, Fashion, Colleen and Polly Drummond Stakes in her juvenile year. At three, she took the Acorn, Matchmaker and Mother Goose Stakes. Deceit regularly faced her main foe, Forward Gal, with each one winning her share. During her racing career, the system of grading races based on their importance was not yet in place, but many of Deceit's wins came in races that have since been established as Grade One.

Having a stellar race record was a huge bonus to Windfields when Deceit was retired to begin her broodmare duties. The farm had by this point shifted its focus to selling yearlings without setting pre-sale prices or reserves, save for a select few. The offspring of a new broodmare with the pedigree and race record of Deceit would attract buyers with the deepest pockets, especially when you consider the stallions Windfields had access to.

Deceit's first suitor was Northern Dancer, and the result was a filly, Slight Deception, who did not attain her reserve price at the yearling sale and so went unsold. She was also unraced. She joined the Windfields broodmare colony, and in 1978, she had a daughter by Halo. Halo Dancer won four races and was stakes-placed in four additional races from fourteen starts. Halo Dancer's first two foals were both stakes winners, but her final foal, Classiest Carat, by Pleasant Colony, became the dam of Sovereign Award–winning champion older mare Impossible Time. Bred and raced by Charles Fipke, Impossible Time was sired by his own stallion Not Impossible, a son of Sadler's Wells.

Deceit produced four stakes winners. Her most accomplished was her daughter Deceit Dancer, by Vice Regent. Deceit Dancer won three stakes races as a two-year-old to earn the Sovereign Award as the champion in her division. Deceit's daughter Diana Dance, a full sister to Slight Deception, went to Germany and won three stakes races there. Her granddaughter Deva became Germany's high-weighted older mare in 2003, winning multiple group stakes races. Deva's full sister Divya became the dam of 2017 Grosser Preis von Berlin winner Dschingis Secret.

Lover's Walk

Another yearling filly purchase for eventual replenishment of the broodmare band was Lover's Walk. She was sired by Never Bend, the 1962 champion two-year-old from Nasrullah's final crop. Never Bend was having a solid career as a sire, with his emerging best son, Mill Reef, starting to display his potential in 1970, the year Taylor bought Lover's Walk. Her dam, Honey Lake, was a stakes-placed daughter of Argentinean-bred Miss Grillo, a very accomplished race mare who won important races in her native land and then races such as the Diana Handicap, San Juan Capistrano Handicap and Pimlico Cup Handicap (twice) when she relocated to Horatio Luro's barn in North America.

Lover's Walk won only two races, but in the breeding shed, she produced two stakes winners and three daughters who moved the family to high level. Her stakes winners were the colts Lover's Answer, by Northern Answer, and Le Promeneur, by Tentam.

Her daughter Lovely Briar was born in the year between the two colts and was sired by Briartic. Lovely Briar won three races and was stakes-placed. Her daughter Our Dani is the dam of five-time Grade One winner You. Sired by a son of Kris S named You And I, the daughter You won the Frizette Stakes at two and the Santa Anita Oaks, Test Stakes, Acorn Stakes and Las Virgenes Stakes the following year. You was also second in six Grade One stakes races. She won nine races and came in second eight times from twenty-three starts.

Lover's Walk produced two fillies by Vice Regent. The first was stakes-placed Regent's Walk in 1981. This one's first foal was a chestnut son of Conquistador Cielo who had a wide white blaze down his face, three white socks and a unique white patch just below his knee on his left foreleg. He was named Marquetry. A three-time Grade One winner, Marquetry won the Hollywood Gold Cup, Eddie Read Handicap and the Meadowlands Cup Handicap among his ten wins from thirty-six races. At stud, Marquetry sired a pair of Eclipse Award sprint champions in

Artax and Squirtle Squirt. A half-sister to Marquetry by Seeking The Gold named Spain Lane won a pair of graded stakes in France and was third to Coup De Genie in the Prix Morny.

The other Lover's Walk daughter by Vice Regent to make a splash in breeding is Lover's Talk. Following a brief racing career in which she won once from three starts, Lover's Talk became a Canadian Broodmare of the Year, with four stakes winners by four different sires.

Shake A Leg

E.P. Taylor came up with another yearling sales gem in 1971 when he bought a bay filly by Raise A Native, out of the Fleet Nasrullah mare Fleeting Doll, bred by Verne Winchell in Kentucky. Given the name Shake A Leg (a name co-author Michael Armstrong had suggested to Windfields the year before pertaining to a Tambourine–Allegro filly), she would become a stakes winner and stakes producer.

Shake A Leg raced in Ireland with success, capturing the Waterford Testimonial Stakes and finishing second in both the Railway and Anglesey group stakes races. She was returned to the United States and won the Grade Three Miss Woodford Stakes and the listed First Lady Handicap. Shake A Leg won nine of twenty-one starts and finished second five times, including the Friar Rock Stakes in Canada. Then she entered the Windfields broodmare colony, her destiny from the time she was purchased.

Her second foal was a daughter by Vaguely Noble, purchased at the 1977 CTHS sales by Stafford Farm for $132,000. The filly was named Vaguely Modest and became a stakes winner when she finished ahead of the pack in the Selene Stakes at Woodbine. Vaguely Modest would exceed her name and produced a more-than-modest stakes winner in Australian-bred Danarani, by Danehill. Danarani won the Group One Flight Stakes and the

Group Two Tea Rose Stakes. The filly also placed in the Australasian Oaks and MRC One Thousand Guineas.

Shake A Leg produced a bay colt by Northern Dancer in 1980, thus creating a 3x3 inbreed to Native Dancer. The colt was purchased by Danny Schwartz for $1 million and named Danzatore, which means "dancer" in Italian. Schwartz shipped Danzatore to Ireland, where the colt entered the barn of Vincent O'Brien. Danzatore went undefeated in his juvenile campaign and was named the champion of his age in Ireland. On retirement, he stood at Sir Patrick Hogan's Cambridge Stud in Waikato, New Zealand. His success there was nominal, but he did sire Australian Derby winner Wonder Dancer. Danzatore was sent to Spendthrift Farm in Kentucky, where he stood for a few years before moving to nearby Prestonwood Farm, now known as WinStar. While there, he sired Breeders' Cup Sprint winner Reraise. Danzatore sired twenty-five stakes winners before his passing in Roswell, New Mexico, following his move to that state.

The year after Shake A Leg gave the world Danzatore, she produced a full sister named Nadia Nerina. A winner on the track, Nadia Nerina produced six foals for Sheikh Mohammed Al Maktoum. Her daughter Zorina, by Shirley Heights, raced in Ireland for Gestüt Riepegrund. Moving to Germany for broodmare duty, Zorina was bred to that country's favourite son, Lomitas. The resulting filly was named Zaza Top, a stakes winner of four races. Zaza Top was bred to French Derby winner Shamardal to produce Group One stakes winner Zazou. Zazou was the highweight three-year-old of 2010 and held the same distinction as a four-year-old and five-year-old in his native Germany.

Sex Appeal

E.P. Taylor and his team of bloodstock experts went shopping at the Keeneland Summer Yearling Sale in 1971. They purchased five fillies at the sale for racing and restocking the breeding colony. The second most expensive of the fillies was a chestnut daughter of champion Buckpasser, the first foal from stakes-winning broodmare Best In Show. She was named Sex Appeal.

The purchase of Sex Appeal gave Windfields an entree to one of the emerging strong families that, in a short time, would become a force on the world racing scene. Although she was unraced, Sex Appeal became one of the notable contributors to the success of the family, if not the most important. Her strong pedigree and correct conformation gave her the ticket to be bred to the top stallions in the Windfields domain.

Sex Appeal's second foal was a colt by Northern Dancer, born in 1975 and sold to Robert Sangster the following year at the Keeneland Summer Sales for $185,000. Given the name Try My Best, the bay colt won the Larkspur Stakes in Ireland and then went to England to capture the important Dewhurst Stakes, going on to become the champion two-year-old in England and Ireland following an undefeated campaign. At three, he came out to win the Vauxhall Trial Stakes, but stunningly ran unplaced as the heavy favourite in the 2000 Guineas. It was discovered that Try My Best had contracted a virus, which compromised his performance in the classic event.

Try My Best never raced again. He was retired to stand at Coolmore in Ireland. Here, he sired Last Tycoon, a sprint demon on the top courses in Europe. Last Tycoon won the King's Stand Stakes and the Sprint Championship Stakes, both 5-furlong races, before he came to the United States to stretch out and win the 1986 Breeders' Cup Mile over a strong field at 3⅘ odds. At stud, Last Tycoon had success on both sides of the equator, getting the likes of Eclipse and International Stakes winner Ezzoud, Marju (St. James's Palace Stakes, Craven Stakes), Bigstone (Queen Elizabeth II Stakes, Prix d'Ispahan), and Taipan, a two-time champion in Italy and Germany. In Australia, Last Tycoon sired Australian Horse of the Year Mahogany, Blue

Diamond Stakes winners Knowledge and Lady Jakeo, and AJC Galaxy winner Magic Of Money.

Another son of Try My Best to mention here is Waajib. Waajib won at the Group Three level on the track, but at stud he sired Royal Applause. Winner of the Middle Park and Gimcrack Stakes during his juvenile year, Royal Applause missed most of his three-year-old season. At four, he made amends by capturing the Group One Haydock Sprint Cup and three additional Group Three races, and finished second and third, respectively, in the top Group One sprints July Cup and Prix de l'Abbaye.

Royal Applause in turn sired Acclamation. This one was a Group Two winner but has been a steady sire of stakes winners at stud. Acclamation sired the exciting 2018 Breeder's Cup Mile winner Expert Eye, as well as Dark Angel, a winner of the Middle Park Stakes as a two-year-old, like his grandsire Royal Applause. Dark Angel is currently in fashion as a stud at Yeomanstown Stud in Ireland and has sired the likes of Mecca's Angel (Nunthorpe Stakes twice) and two-time Group One winner Lethal Force.

Returning to Sex Appeal, we find her third foal, and first filly, Solar, by Halo. Solar became the first stakes winner sired by Halo when she won a pair of Group Three races in Ireland as a two-year-old. She was named the high-weighted filly of her year. The first foal produced by Solar was a daughter named Solariat, sired by Secretariat. Unraced, Solariat had a daughter by Nijinsky II in 1991 who went unraced as well. Her name was Margot. Margot had a daughter by Kingmambo named Queen Mambo who also was unraced. This one had a daughter by Lode, in Argentina, named Queen Tango, who was the fourth consecutive unraced daughter in the family tree. We are mentioning this because Queen Tango had a son by Bernstein named Que Vida Buena who won the Group One Gran Premio Ciudad de Buenos Aires and is a full brother to two other group stakes-winning fillies. This branch of the family has made a resurgence in Argentina.

Solar had another unraced daughter, this one by Deputy Minister, who has carried the family fortunes to high acclaim. Shining Through was a 1989 foal, who in 1995 gave the world her son Bahamian Pirate, by Housebuster. This gelded son won the Nunthorpe Stakes, a race that seems to be dear to the family, and two other group stakes, and placed second in the July Cup and Prix de l'Abbaye.

The next foal of note from Sex Appeal is Northern Guest, a full brother to Try My Best. Coolmore agents saw the little fellow on the Windfields Maryland farm when he was five weeks old and were smitten. Having seen their current two-year-old Try My Best dominate his age group, Coolmore made an offer Windfields could not refuse. Coolmore bought the colt for $1 million and had him shipped to Ireland after he was weaned from his mother.

For those who are believers in breeding nicks—the idea that breeding mares sired by a particular stallion to a stallion with success covering mares from that stallion line will produce more successful foals—the Northern Dancer/Buckpasser nick ranks very high indeed. In another of what seems an endless procession of unraced foals who bred to success in the family, Northern Guest went to stud without competing on the track. When the colt crashed into a fence on the Ballydoyle gallops, a wood splinter skewered his foot and the wound never healed properly. Northern Guest walked with a limp for the rest of his life.

He was sold to a then new South African stud farm named Summerhill and proceeded to take the country by storm in the breeding shed. In his adopted land, Northern Guest was the country's leading sire three times and won two juvenile sire championships and ten broodmare sire championships. While his brothers had fertility issues, Northern Guest displayed none of those traits. He was known to have a wonderful temperament and passed this attitude on to his get.

Among the top runners Northern Guest sired was five-time Group One winner Senor Santa; November Handicap winner Northern Princess, who also defeated Senor Santa in a widely watched match race at South Africa's Germiston racetrack; Gentleman Jones (Administrator's Handicap); Travel North (South African Derby); as well as J&B Met winners Imperious Sue and Angus. As a damsire, Northern Guest counts Durban July winner Pomodoro, international sprint star JJ The Jet Plane, and Emerald Cup winner The Mouseketeer among the stakes winners produced by his daughters. Northern Guest is a legend in South African breeding.

Sex Appeal visited Northern Dancer frequently. Her next foal was a son named Compliance. While this one did get to the races, he never won in three starts, although he did finish second twice. His claim to fame is as the sire of full brothers Fourstars Allstar and Fourstardave. The first brother is the only American-based horse to win an Irish classic race, the Irish 2000 Guineas, while the latter became a popular grass runner at Saratoga, with multiple graded-stakes victories. The fan favourite won a race at Saratoga for eight straight years and has a Saratoga stakes race named in his honour.

The most successful foal from Sex Appeal was her son El Gran Senor. Sired by Northern Dancer, El Gran Senor was bred in partnership by Windfields and Coolmore after Coolmore bought a half interest in the mare. Named in honour of Horatio Luro, the trainer of Northern Dancer, El Gran Senor was a nose short of winning all eight races he competed in. The only loss came in the Derby Stakes at Epsom Downs, when Secreto, another Windfields-bred Northern Dancer colt, bested him in the great race. El Gran Senor was the highest-rated horse in the world at three, was the champion two-year-old the season before and went to stud at Windfields Maryland with high expectations.

Unfortunately, fate stepped in. El Gran Senor had trouble getting his mares pregnant due to his low fertility. When word of his troubles spread around the breeding world, many breeders sent their top mares elsewhere. Windfields agreed to move El Gran Senor to Coolmore's Ashford Stud in Kentucky. Coolmore owned a large share in the stallion, and the feeling was that breeders might be less inclined to worry about fertility issues if they didn't have the extra expense of shipping their mares to Maryland. The loss of the great champion was a blow to the farm's annual income.

However, El Gran Senor was not a failure as a stallion. While he continued to struggle to get his mares in foal, he did end up having a remarkably successful stud career. Of the 397 foals he sired, fifty-five won stakes races, or 13.8 percent of all foals. Lit De Justice, Belmez, Corrazona, Helmsman, Rodrigo De Triano, Saratoga Springs, Senor Tomas, Spanish Fern and Toussaud were all Grade/Group One stakes winners, and the latter has become one of the key broodmares in recent breeding history.

Toussaud is the dam of Arlington Million winner Chester House, who died at a young age after a successful beginning at stud; Honest Lady, who won the Santa Monica Handicap and later produced Forego Stakes winner First Defence; and Chiselling, who captured the Secretariat Stakes. Another of Toussaud's offspring, Empire Maker, became her fourth Grade One stakes winner. Empire Maker won the Belmont Stakes, Florida Derby and Wood Memorial. He was second in the Kentucky Derby as the race favourite. At stud, he is flourishing, responsible for Santa Anita Derby winner Pioneerof The Nile (sire of Triple Crown winner American Pharoah), as well as Royal Delta, Emollient, Bodemeister and ten more top-level stakes winners.

The daughters of Sex Appeal are not to be ignored. Three of them—Golden Oriole and Bella Senora, both by Northern Dancer, and Lotta Lace by Nureyev—have carried the family to future generational Grade/Group One success. Golden Oriole is the second dam of Brazilian Group One stakes winner Estrela Monarchos. Bella Senora is the second dam of Breeders' Cup Mile winner Domedriver, while Lotta Lace is the dam of Queen Elizabeth 11 Commemorative Cup winner Fusaichi Pandora in Japan. Fusaichi Pandora, in turn, is the dam of 2018 Japanese Filly Triple Crown winner Almond Eye.

Sex Appeal is one of the key names in many outstanding pedigrees in fashion today.

Noble Fancy

An interesting mare on a number of fronts is Noble Fancy. Her sire was Prix de l'Arc de Triomphe winner Vaguely Noble, a stallion of importance on the Hyperion sire line. Noble Fancy's dam was the well-raced stakes winner Amerigo's Fancy, by the Nearco sire Amerigo. Amerigo was also an interesting horse in that he was one of his sire's cranky sons and did not display his true talent until he was a four-year-old. He had shown flashes of brilliance before, but his temperament became his undoing in many races. Amerigo won some big races, such as the San Juan Capistrano and Hialeah Turf Cup handicaps. He was versatile as well, winning from 6 furlongs to 14 furlongs and all points in between.

Another interesting note to Noble Fancy was that she was bred by movie and television star Desi Arnaz at his ranch in California. Arnaz, known around the world as the husband of Lucille Ball and as Ricky Ricardo from the famous *I Love Lucy* television show, was a keen patron of the turf and had bred and raced many winners. Noble Fancy had a pedigree that would intrigue a horse breeder of E.P. Taylor's stature.

Noble Fancy was bred to Northern Dancer often, producing three foals by the world's top sire. Her second foal, a daughter named Katsura, was stakes-placed but set in motion a series of producers that led to one of the best racehorses in recent memory. Kastura is the dam of Rambushka, by Roberto. Rambushka, in turn, is the dam of Tugela by Riverman. Tugela is the dam of the great three-time winner of the Melbourne Cup, Makybe Diva. Makybe Diva shows three crosses in her fourth generation of Northern Dancer, as her sire, Desert King, is by Danehill, out of a mare by Nureyev.

Makybe Diva not only won three Melbourne Cups, a feat of extraordinary merit; she also won four other Group One races: the Cox Plate, Sydney Cup, Australian Cup and the BMW Stakes. She was twice the Australian Horse of the Year and won seven additional divisional awards. Makybe Diva is, deservedly, in the Australian Racing Hall of Fame. She was a remarkable racer.

Another descendant of Noble Fancy to mention came through Katsura's daughter Ranales, by Majestic Light. Ranales had only two foals, both daughters, but in 2005 her Fame At Last, by Quest For Fame, produced a colt by Dansili for Juddmonte Farms who went by the name Famous Name. Here, we have a throwback of sorts to a time when horses raced more often and for longer careers. Famous Name won stakes races from age three to seven, five consecutive years. He made thirty-eight starts, winning twenty-one and placing second an additional eight times and third five times. Famous Name was consistent and never quit in any race. However, he could not quite win a Group One race. He finished second in the French Derby (the Prix du Jockey Club) and in the money three times in the Tattersalls Gold Cup, and he came up short against the likes of So You Think, Aqlaam, Durban Thunder and Campanologist. Twenty of Famous Name's twenty-one wins came in Group Two or Three races, and he did defeat Group One winners in many of those starts.

Noble Fancy's daughter Regent's Fancy, by Vice Regent, became another link in the chain to a recent Group One winner. Regent's Fancy is the dam of stakes winner Roses 'N' Wine, by

Broken Vow. After her racing career, Roses 'N' Wine was bred in Australia to Redoute's Choice and produced a bay colt named Hampton Court. Hampton Court won the 2014 ATC Spring Champion Stakes, setting a new course record. He is currently a shuttle sire between Kentucky and Australia for Spendthrift Farms.

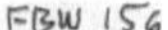

Above 1964 Horse of the Year "PEB" cartoon of Northern Dancer. PHOTO CREDIT: KEENELAND ASSOCIATION LIBRARY/PEB COLLECTION

Facing Top E.P. Taylor, Northern Dancer, and Horatio Luro. PHOTO CREDIT: PETER WINANTS

Facing Bottom Weanlings in west border paddock of the Oshawa farm. "Do they expect us to go that fast?" PHOTO CREDIT: COLIN NOLTE

MAXIMUM
70
km/h

Top The Kentucky Derby trophy, won by Northern Dancer in 1964. PHOTO CREDIT: CANADIAN FILM CENTRE/JEFFERSON MAPPIN

Bottom Vice Regent with his best friend Al Kerr, 1983. PHOTO CREDIT: COLIN NOLTE

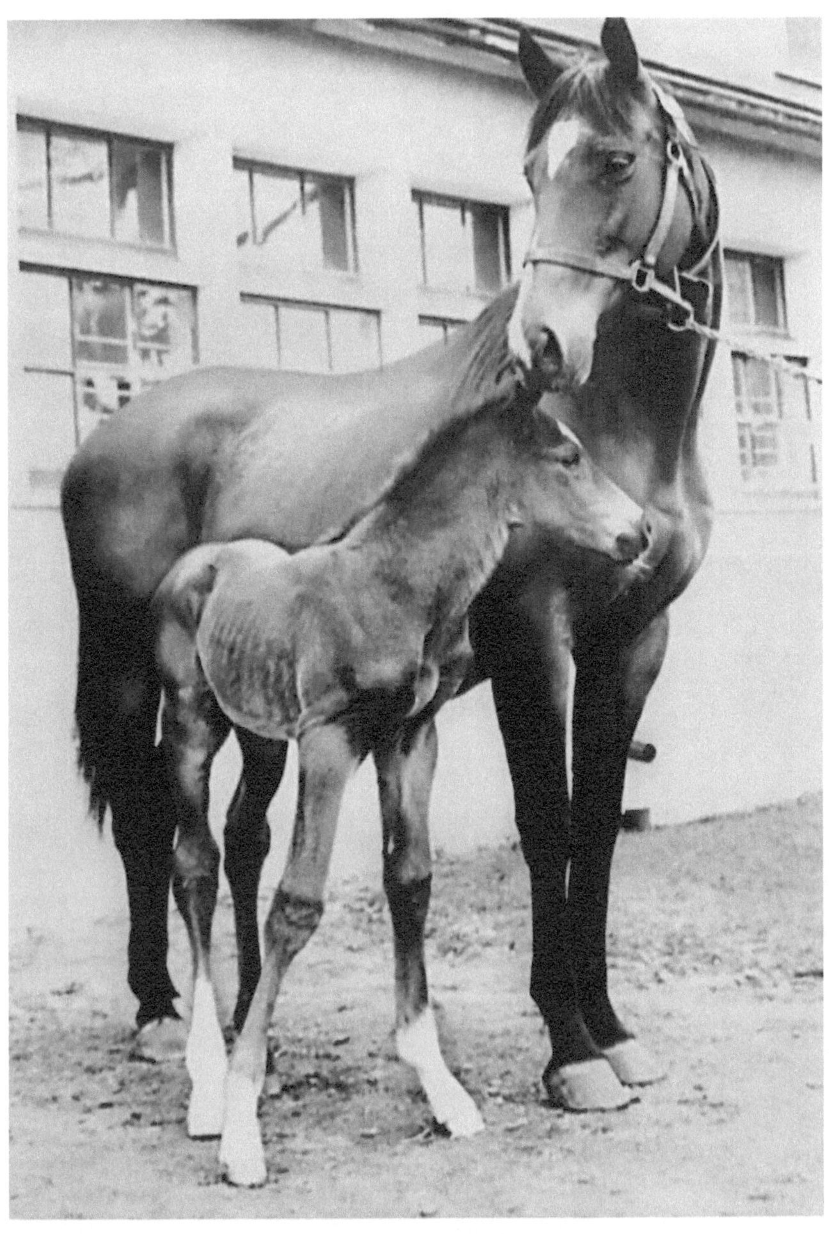

Natalma and her son Northern Native, a full brother to Northern Dancer. PHOTO CREDIT: PETER WINANTS

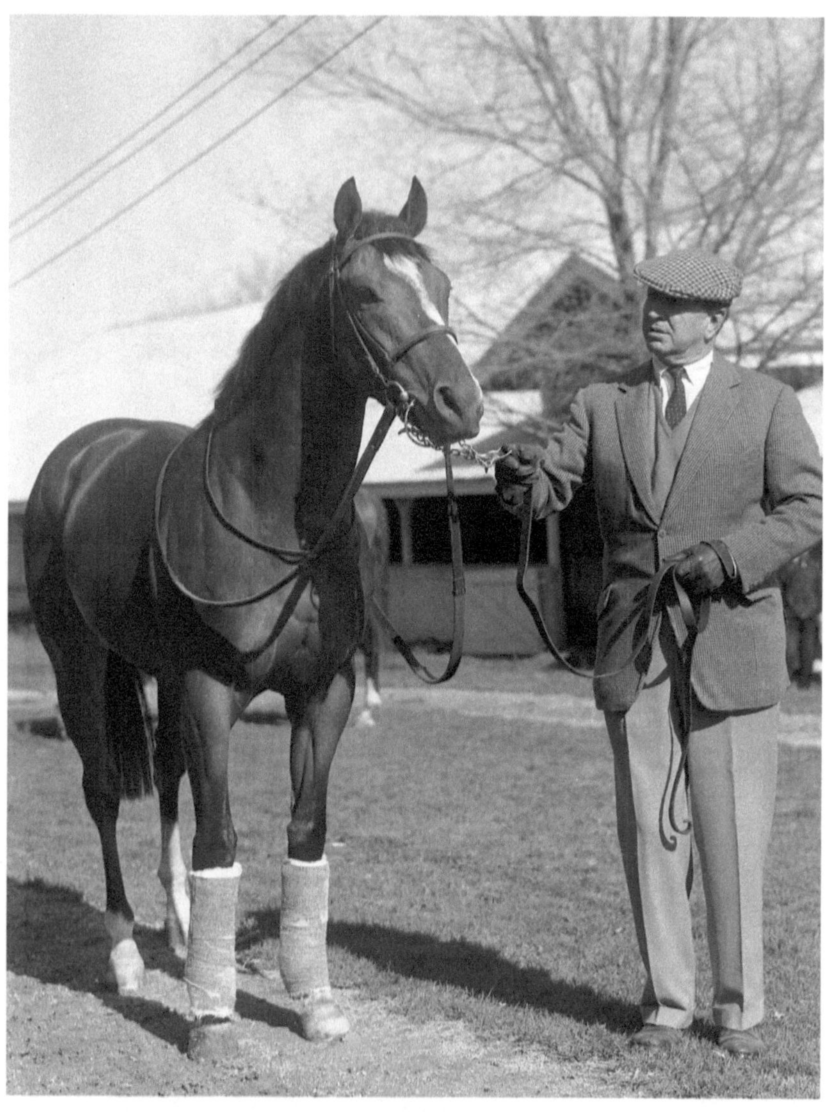

Above Northern Dancer with trainer Horatio Luro. PHOTO CREDIT: KEENELAND ASSOCIATION LIBRARY/MEADORS COLLECTION

Facing Top Northern Dancer in training. PHOTO CREDIT: KEENELAND ASSOCIATION LIBRARY/MEADORS COLLECTION

Facing Bottom Northern Dancer with stud manager/groom Harry Green. PHOTO CREDIT: PETER WINANTS

Victoria Park. PHOTO CREDIT: PETER WINANTS/DRUMMER BOY PUBLICATIONS

{ 9 }

TRIPLE CROWN AND GLOBAL SUCCESS

VINCENT O'BRIEN IS in the record books as one of the elite trainers in racing history. The Irishman began his training career in National Hunt racing and became one of the greatest at his craft in that discipline. He gradually switched over to flat racing during the 1950s and then proceeded to have success after success on the world stage. O'Brien was a remarkably gifted horseman, with an astute eye and the innate ability to get the best out of his charges. He was known to all who worked at Ballydoyle, his training centre in County Tipperary, Ireland, as "The Boss."

In 1968, one of O'Brien's major clients was platinum magnate Charles Engelhard. Engelhard was a keen racing patron and had a love of the great racehorse Ribot. He was on a quest to acquire the best of Ribot's get on offer in yearling sales around the world. Engelhard was also a good friend of E.P. Taylor. When he learned that Taylor had bred a colt by Ribot out of the good mare Northern Queen, a daughter of Victoriana, he asked O'Brien to fly to Toronto and look over the colt to assess whether he would be a good addition to the racing stable.

O'Brien arrived at the Windfields Willowdale farm where the yearlings were housed and saw the Ribot colt. He did not like him. However, he could not take his eyes off a big, robust bay colt in another paddock. O'Brien asked the farm staff about this colt and learned that he was from the second crop by Northern Dancer, out of champion Flaming Page. He didn't know much about either parent, but he could not get past his gut feeling that this yearling might be something special. He advised Engelhard to buy the Northern Dancer–Flaming Page colt and pass on the Ribot–Northern Queen colt.

The Flaming Page colt entered the CTHS Woodbine yearling sale with a $60,000 reserve price. The bidding quickly rose to a final bid of $84,000, with Charles Engelhard the winning bidder. The colt was sent to Ballydoyle and given the name Nijinsky, in honour of the famous Russian ballet dancer who once said he would be reincarnated as a horse.

A Chip Off the Old Block

Upon arrival at Ballydoyle, Nijinsky proved to be just as wilful and headstrong as his sire-line ancestors. He refused to eat the oats fed to him by O'Brien's staff, as he had never eaten such meals before. Exasperated, O'Brien called Windfields management and asked for a shipment of the feed the colt was used to eating. On the day the feed arrived, Nijinsky decided that oats were okay and tucked into his Irish cuisine.

Nijinsky was not an easy horse to manage. "He had to be specifically trained with good handling and patience," O'Brien said of him when recalling his champion years later. "He needed to be worked alone before the other horses. Nijinsky got impatient if he was kept waiting, so I think if he had been trained at a public training ground like Newmarket or the Curragh, he could have easily gone the wrong way." Nijinsky eventually trained with another Engelhard colt, Riboprince, as his companion.

Vincent O'Brien and his top-notch staff worked with the promising colt and reaped the rewards of their patience and good horsemanship. Nijinsky reeled off four consecutive victories at the Curragh, a racecourse in County Kildare, Ireland, between July 12 and September 27 during his juvenile campaign in 1969. All four races were stakes—the Erne, the Railway, the Anglesey and the Beresford Stakes—and he was never seriously challenged in any of them. O'Brien decided to take Nijinsky to Newmarket and test his young star in the Dewhurst Stakes, against the best of the two-year-old crop in training.

Nijinsky dominated the Dewhurst with style and class. The English turf hierarchy was stunned by the performance and voted him champion in the division. He also won the Irish juvenile championship. Nijinsky was the top-rated colt on the year-end Free Handicap and was installed as the early favourite for the upcoming classic races.

The Gladness Stakes at the Curragh was the scene for Nijinsky's return to racing at the start of his three-year-old campaign. Barely breaking a sweat, the big bay colt cruised to an easy win. All was set for the 2000 Guineas at Newmarket and a chance to become the first Canadian-bred to win an established English classic race.

Nijinsky swept to victory as he had done in all his prior races, taking the fabled race on the Rowley Mile course with a performance that appeared to be no more than a training session to him. Lester Piggott partnered Nijinsky and said after the race, "He won the Guineas comfortably enough. He could have beaten any of them at any distance." Following the Guineas victory, Nijinsky's odds for the upcoming Derby Stakes were lowered from 4/1 to 5/2. The bookmakers in England had not been convinced that the Canadian colt could handle the 12-furlong distance until after his domination on the Rowley Mile.

As impressive as his Guineas performance was, Nijinsky still had his detractors. William Hill, the most widely known of the English bookmakers, needed more convincing. His agency determined that Nijinsky did not have the pedigree to stay a mile and a half on the fabled Epsom Downs Racecourse, citing his sire's failure in the Belmont Stakes at the same distance. O'Brien and Piggott had no such qualms about Nijinsky's ability. The main challengers to the unbeaten Canadian included Gyr, a huge and talented colt sired by the great racehorse Sea-Bird, who was garnering plenty of support. Approval, Stintino and Meadowville were also earning pre-Derby respect from the oddsmakers.

The 1970 Derby Stakes at Epsom

O'Brien did not make his final preparations for Nijinsky's Derby at Ballydoyle. There was an outbreak of coughing at the home training centre, and the master was taking no chances with his star before the biggest race in the world. Nijinsky trained at Sandown Park, arriving five days before the big event. All was going well as Nijinsky trained with his buddy Riboprince over the Surrey course.

Nijinsky travelled to Epsom Downs the day before the Derby and had a leisurely gallop over the course. He returned to his assigned stable, and while he was being rubbed down, the powerful Canadian colt started pawing at the floor. Nijinsky continued to paw, then lay down in his stall and began to sweat. He was showing the signs of a colic attack. O'Brien had been watching these developments. Even though it was a hot day, the sweating increased abnormally. It was definite. Nijinsky, on the day before the Derby Stakes, had been struck with colic.

The Boss told his travelling head lad to contact a local vet but to keep it quiet so as not to alert anyone to the colt's discomfort. O'Brien then phoned veterinarian Bob Griffin back at Ballydoyle to come ASAP. He described to Griffin exactly how Nijinsky was behaving.

"It sounds as if he has at least a slight twinge of colic," Griffin told The Boss. "Even if I came over, I can't treat him because we can't give him medication the day before the race."

When the local vet arrived, he confirmed the diagnosis. It seemed at this point that all they could do was hope the symptoms might pass.

O'Brien sent some of his stable lads to fetch fresh grass from the other side of the racecourse. This was mixed with carbonated soda and bran, then offered to Nijinsky in the hope that he was not too distressed and would eat it. The colt tucked into the snack and soon appeared a bit more relaxed. O'Brien, who hadn't left Nijinsky's side during the crisis, and his staff let out a giant sigh of relief when they saw their star Thoroughbred return to normal. The entire ordeal lasted ninety minutes, but to the trainer and his staff, it must have felt like ninety hours.

Few people knew of the colic attack Nijinsky suffered the day before the Derby, surprising as this may seem. Bookmakers always have spies around to report anything that might affect the preparations of Derby horses, and they will adjust the odds accordingly. But somehow they missed the emergency at O'Brien's barn.

Derby day brought glorious English sunshine and the usual throng of over a quarter of a million people to the downs at Epsom. Nijinsky, feeling like himself again, went through his pre-race routine and appeared in the paddock in top condition. Lester Piggott was given a leg up by O'Brien and cantered the colt in company with other entrants toward the starting gate at the far end of the course. The anticipation reached a crescendo as the horses loaded, one by one, into the starting stalls. Nijinsky was slotted into stall nine.

From the off, Piggott settled Nijinsky in sixth position as the field moved up the hill to the crest at the top of the course. Cry Baby led the race along the decline to Tattenham Corner, followed by Great Wall and Meadowville, who assumed command as they went around the famous left-hand corner leading onto the 4-furlong uphill straight to the finish post. Gyr had made a move to relieve Meadowville of the lead after they straightened for home, with Stintino in hot pursuit. Nijinsky was improving his position in the middle of the pack, and Piggott had him poised for his bid.

Two furlongs from home, Lester Piggott gave Nijinsky the signal to go, and go he did. Nijinsky switched to another gear and zoomed past the top three in a flash. The race was over. There was no drama, nor was there any doubt as to which horse was the best on the day. Nijinsky cruised to the finish post at Epsom two-and-a-half lengths in front of Gyr, with Stintino another length back in third. Nijinsky covered the distance in 2 minutes, 34.6 seconds, which was only ⅘ths of a second off the record set by Mahmoud thirty-four years earlier (though handheld timers were used for Mahmoud's race, as opposed to the advanced timer recording gear used in 1970). And Nijinsky still had plenty left in the tank if needed.

The win was a sweet reward for Charles Engelhard, who had finish second in the classic race three times in previous years. Engelhard was a great patron of the turf, and the victory by his outstanding colt was well received. As is the custom for Derby-winning connections, Engelhard, O'Brien and their families in attendance were invited to the Royal Box after the race. The excited team was on its way to meet the Queen when Charles Engelhard had what might be called a wardrobe malfunction. In his hour of glory, the winning owner's suspender broke. He had to greet Queen Elizabeth II, the Queen Mother and the rest of the royals holding his top hat in one hand and his pants up with the other. The Queen Mother, noticing his difficulty, offered to hold his hat while he shook hands with all the dignitaries, and thus Engelhard avoided any more embarrassment.

E.P. and Winifred Taylor were also in attendance at Epsom to watch the horse they bred win the biggest race in the world. The Taylors kept a house near Epsom—they had horses in training there—and must have felt as proud as anyone that day. The great Italian Thoroughbred breeder Federico Tesio once stated, "When you breed a horse, you have one thing in mind, and that is a piece of wood. The piece of wood is the finish post at Epsom. You want your horse to run past that piece of wood before any other on Derby day. Then you know you have succeeded." E.P. Taylor had just accomplished what many breeders who have spent a lifetime in the game have never achieved.

One of the Greatest of All Time

Nijinsky came out of his Derby victory in wonderful condition. O'Brien would now point his star toward his home country's Irish Derby, to be run at the Curragh in front of adoring fans. On a rain-soaked course, Nijinsky again dominated the proceedings and won by three lengths over Meadowville. Liam Ward was in the irons on the day, as O'Brien customarily had Ward ride his horses in Ireland. There was an omen of things to come, however, as Nijinsky seemed agitated in the paddock before the race. The increased attention unsettled him, and he sweated quite badly.

Then it was back to England and a start in the prestigious King George VI and Queen Elizabeth Stakes at Ascot. This would be Nijinsky's first race against older horses. He was the only three-year-old to make the start and would be facing his toughest challenge to date. Included in the field was Blakeney, the previous year's Derby winner; Crepellana, who had won the French Oaks; the highly regarded Washington D.C. International winner Karabas; as well as Coronation Cup winner Caliban and

Italian Derby winner Hogarth. Nijinsky again sweated and seemed tense in the paddock. But with a performance described by Lester Piggott as the best he ever had, Nijinsky won the great Ascot race by two easy lengths ahead of Blakeney. Piggott had actually eased his mount before the finish since he had such a commanding lead at that point. This was Nijinsky's tenth consecutive victory, and he seemed unstoppable.

The Prix de l'Arc de Triomphe is the big prize for the top horses in European racing. Run traditionally on the first Saturday in October at Longchamp in France, the "Arc" is unofficially the champion-defining race on the European calendar. Nijinsky won the King George on July 25, so it would be ten weeks between the events. However, everyone connected to Nijinsky would be challenged to get him to the Arc after what happened the week after the win at Ascot.

Nijinsky contracted a condition known as ringworm, a skin disease that is generally brought on by horses sweating freely, making them prone to the fungus. The bout Nijinsky came down with was very severe. He lost a lot of hair around the saddle and girth area. It was impossible to put a saddle on him because of pain where the rash was located, so regular training was curtailed. O'Brien could only lunge Nijinsky in the yard, running him in a circle at the end of a line, to try to keep his fitness level up.

Treatment for Nijinsky's ringworm was working well enough, but the loss of serious training time was a concern for O'Brien. Then Englehard contacted the trainer and asked, since Nijinsky had won the first two legs of the Triple Crown, could the colt be ready in time for the St Leger Stakes, the third leg? No horse had won the Triple Crown since Bahram, thirty-five years earlier.

O'Brien had hoped to have Nijinsky run in a race before the Arc, but the St Leger? At one mile, 6 furlongs, 170 yards, this was the longest race for three-year-olds on the calendar. It required a very fit horse, especially if there were serious challenges at the finish. Vincent O'Brien would have to use all of his knowledge and training expertise to get Nijinsky ready for the St Leger and then have him at his peak for the Arc three weeks later. It was a tough ask.

Nijinsky did make it to Doncaster for the St Leger, winning the race, and thus the Triple Crown, when he finished a length in front of Meadowville. In the forty-nine years since Nijinsky's Triple Crown achievement, no horse has been able to duplicate the feat. Taking into account the thirty-five-year drought before he captured the Crown, Nijinsky is the only English Triple Crown winner in the past eighty-four years.

But the St Leger took its toll on Nijinsky. Piggott reckoned that the race was a bit beyond his best distance. Nijinsky lost thirty pounds in the race, so even though he was not severely tested by the other horses, the race itself was a challenge to him. He was also still recovering from his ringworm bout, so Nijinsky was not coming to the Arc in the best condition.

The eleven-race winning streak would be put on the line at Longchamp. A powerful field had been assembled for the Arc. In the paddock before the race, the crush of press and fans taking pictures and popping flashbulbs around Nijinsky unnerved the Triple Crown winner. He was clearly agitated by the chaotic masses swirling around him, and he became a washy mess. Not a good sign.

In the race, French Derby winner Sassafras, guided by the redoubtable Yves Saint-Martin, was placed in a perfect stalking position and asked for his run at the right time. Piggott on Nijinsky came down the homestretch with a furious run, but Nijinsky just was not himself on the day. Sassafras won by a diminishing head lead at the finish line.

Immediately, the press started asking what had happened to the horse everyone considered unbeatable. They threw blame around indiscriminately, and rather than praising Sassafras for his exceptional run, they seemed to focus on Nijinsky's failure to win the Arc.

The fact is, Sassafras was a very good horse who beat an exceptional horse when the latter was not at 100-percent fitness. He took advantage of Nijinsky's weakness and won with his own courage and talent. What Nijinsky lacked in the race was his higher-than-average cruising speed, so when it was time for him to make his bid to win, he had much more to do than usual. Coupled with his loss of fitness and his nervousness before the race, it all caught up to him. Nijinsky was mortal after all.

Charles Engelhard said it best in the post-mortems that abounded after the Arc. "Nijinsky did not fail us, we failed him."

Nijinsky had already been syndicated for stud duty and was scheduled to join the outstanding stallion barn at Claiborne Farm in Paris, Kentucky, the following year. However, his connections wanted him to retire with a victory, so Nijinsky was entered in the 10-furlong Champion Stakes at Newmarket. In an echo of what had happened to his famous ancestor Hyperion, a well-intended idea backfired when Nijinsky ran perhaps the worst race of his career. He finished second to Lorenzaccio when he could not find his late speed to overtake the winner in the stretch.

Nonetheless, Nijinsky was voted European Horse of the Year in all the polls and now embarked on his new career as a stallion. He excelled in this new role and perhaps gained even more admiration from the Thoroughbred world as a sire than he had done in his racing career.

To Paris for Ooh La La

Not only had Nijinsky changed his home address from Ballydoyle in Cashel, County Tipperary, to Claiborne Farm in Paris, Kentucky; he also had to change his name ever so slightly. There was another horse in America called Nijinsky, and he had first dibs on the name. So during his stud career, the Windfields-bred son of Northern Dancer and Flaming Page was known as Nijinsky II.

The stallion roster at Claiborne when he arrived represented many of the great living racehorses and stallions of the day. Buckpasser, Bold Ruler, Forli, Damascus, Sir Ivor, Round Table and Herbager were all standing at the great farm. Soon to join Nijinsky II would be Ack Ack, Secretariat, Hoist The Flag, Danzig, Spectacular Bid and Mr. Prospector. Claiborne has been one of the most successful stud farms for over a century. Nijinsky II became one of the elite of the elite stallions, and his great stud career added to the historic reputation of Claiborne Farm.

When his career totals are added up, he sired 851 foals in a twenty-two-year career. Of those, 155 became stakes winners, for a strike rate of 18.2 percent. And it was not just the number of stakes winners Nijinsky II sired that is to be lauded, but also the quality and class of many of the individuals. The list is impressive.

Three of his offspring won the Derby Stakes at Epsom: Golden Fleece in 1982, Shahrastani in 1986 and undefeated Lammtarra in 1995. The year Shahrastani won, Nijinsky II also sired the winner of the Kentucky Derby, Ferdinand, becoming the first stallion in history to sire the winners of both major world classic races in the same year. This is another of Nijinsky II's accomplishments that has not been duplicated since.

One more record that Nijinsky II still holds is the price for the most expensive yearling ever sold at auction anywhere in the world. Born in 1984, Seattle Dancer was sold a year later at the Keeneland yearling sales for a record $13.1 million.

Nijinsky II's outstanding offspring include the very fast Royal Academy, winner of the 1990 Breeders' Cup Mile. This was a significant win also because it marked the final time Lester Piggott rode a major stakes winner to victory for Vincent O'Brien. Royal

Academy also became the son of Nijinsky II who sired the most stakes winners in his stud career, totalling 167 such runners.

In no particular order, Caerleon, Green Dancer, Sky Classic, King's Lake, Ile de Bourbon, Baldski, Dancing Spree, Niniski and many more sons of Nijinsky II became champions in racing or breeding or both. They won major stakes races around the world and spread the Windfields Farm excellence to all ports of call in Thoroughbred breeding when they entered stud, also around the world.

Windfields stood a pair of Nijinsky II sons, Caucasus and Dancing Champ, for many years. Canadian Thoroughbred breeder/owner Ernie Samuel, through his powerful Sam-Son Farm, bred and raced Sky Classic to championship awards in both Canada and the United States. Lammtarra won not only the Derby Stakes but also the King George VI and Queen Elizabeth Stakes, as well as avenging his sire's defeat in the Prix de l'Arc de Triomphe. Vincent O'Brien also had major success with the offspring of his great champion, training Golden Fleece, Royal Academy, King's Lake, Solford and Caerleon.

Nijinsky brought Windfields Farm to the pinnacle of the Thoroughbred breeding world. That the farm retained this lofty position for the next two decades confirmed that his success was no fluke. Windfields had been steadily building to breed a horse like Nijinsky for more than three decades. E.P. Taylor had created a powerhouse Thoroughbred breeding establishment, which has given the world many of the finest animals to ever grace the turf.

Singing The Minstrel's Praises

We have touched on the second Epsom Derby winner bred by Windfields in Chapters Three and Four. The Minstrel was a flashy chestnut with four white socks and a wide blaze down his face.

His markings caused concern for many prospective buyers at the Keeneland yearling sales in 1975 due to an old saying: "One white foot, buy a horse; two white feet, try a horse; three white feet, look well about him; four white feet, do well without him."

Vincent O'Brien was smitten with the animal, however, and looked past his socks. He could see the quality and desire in the eyes of the chestnut son of Northern Dancer. O'Brien also knew that the colt's dam, Fleur, by Victoria Park, was a half-sister to his great Triple Crown winner Nijinsky, so he was well aware of the class of this colt's family. Fleur's son was on the small side, quite different from Nijinsky in conformation. He had more of his sire's build. O'Brien had trained and won his first Derby with Larkspur, a colt of similar stature. He knew that quality came in all sizes.

When Fleur was carrying The Minstrel, she suffered what appeared to be a significant injury to her shoulder. It was not clear how she was injured. When her handlers came to collect her one morning after she had been in her paddock for the night, she was lame. Dr. Rolph de Gannes administered bute (an anti-inflammatory) to keep her comfortable and avoid the possibility of an aborted pregnancy. The treatment worked, and on March 11, 1974, she produced her chestnut son.

Dr. de Gannes noted that he had to use scissors to cut open the birth sack to help the foal emerge, and he said the afterbirth from which The Minstrel emerged was somewhat thicker and heavier than usual. Normal equine afterbirth for a foal carried to full term generally weighs eight to ten pounds. Fleur had produced her son carrying a thirty-two-pound birth sack.

During The Minstrel's formative time on the Oshawa farm, he displayed a social and inquisitive nature. After Fleur's little son passed his first birthday, a number of yearlings in his paddock escaped their confines and went on an adventure. The Minstrel discovered a freshly dug grave that was ready for a horse due to be euthanized because of a severe and untreatable disease. The Minstrel was found perched precariously at the edge of this big hole in the ground, looking as if he was about to fall in. His curiosity almost became his downfall.

E.P. Taylor closely followed the colt's progress after his sale to Robert Sangster and his transfer to Vincent O'Brien's training stables. The Minstrel displayed his competitive spirit during his early training sessions on the Ballydoyle gallops. He would get keyed up and want to run as soon as possible—shades of his grandfather Nearctic and his hell-bent-for-leather running style.

The Minstrel made his race debut on September 8, 1976, in the Moy Stakes at the Curragh. He won by five lengths in track record time. Three weeks later, The Minstrel took the Larkspur Stakes at Leopardstown Racecourse near Dublin. After another three-week interval, the O'Brien-trained colt went to Newmarket and captured the Dewhurst Stakes. Such an outstanding year would normally see a colt as fast and successful as The Minstrel named champion two-year-old, but in 1976 another very fast and accomplished two-year-old usurped the title. J.O. Tobin was named the top juvenile for the year. Ironically, J.O. Tobin was bred at Windfields Maryland by George Pope, the same man who bred and raced Northern Dancer's archrival Hill Rise.

The Minstrel flourished through the winter, getting stronger and displaying his iron constitution and physique. He reappeared at the races for the 2,000 Guineas Trial Stakes at Ascot. The ground was a deep quagmire—"barely raceable," said O'Brien—but The Minstrel slogged through to win. The race took a lot out of every horse in the race: none of the other competitors would ever win another race, and two never raced again, but The Minstrel went on to new heights.

Four weeks later, in the 2000 Guineas at Newmarket, The Minstrel suffered his first defeat, finishing third, two lengths behind the winner, Nebbiolo, with Tachypous in second place.

Two weeks later, he seemed to be recovering from his arduous Ascot race when he was beaten by a short and diminishing head by Pampapaul in the Irish 2000 Guineas, with Nebbiolo two lengths behind in third.

Although he had now lost two classics, the ones it seemed he would have been best suited for, Lester Piggott told O'Brien that if he was taking The Minstrel to Epsom for the Derby Stakes, he, Piggott, wanted the mount. The great jockey had faith in The Minstrel's courage and ability.

The Minstrel did enter the 198th Derby Stakes, and Lester Piggott was his jockey. Vincent O'Brien, remembering how Nijinsky had become anxious around large crowds, like the ones that traditionally flock to the Downs for the big race, decided to take precautionary measures. He instructed his head assistant, John Gosden, to stuff the colt's ears with cotton wool to drown out the noise that came with the boisterous throng of humanity. Once The Minstrel was beyond the crush of people and noise, Gosden would remove the earplugs, and Piggott could get him settled for the start.

Twenty-two hopeful combatants entered the starting stalls for this Derby. The favourite was Blushing Groom, a colt from France belonging to the Aga Khan IV. Piggott had The Minstrel well placed and cruising effortlessly as they went up to the top of the hill and then down the steep decline into Tattenham Corner. At the famous left-hand corner, Milliondollarman held a slight lead from Hot Grove, while Piggott waited on the outside of second choice Caporello, with Blushing Groom three lengths behind these two. With 2 furlongs left to go, The Minstrel came to the flank of Hot Grove, who had assumed the lead. The Minstrel on the outside and Hot Grove on the inside waged a furious prolonged battle to get to the winning post first. Lester Piggott used every bit of his considerable experience and ability as a rider to get every ounce of courage and speed from The Minstrel, who had his ears pinned and his neck fully extended. Both colts ran as one for the final 2 furlongs, neither giving nor expecting an inch from the other. With twenty yards to go before they crossed the winning post, The Minstrel got his head in front, winning the Derby Stakes by a close neck over the game Hot Grove. Blushing Groom could only watch from third place. The spectacle is fixed in the memory of all those who saw the race and is considered one of the greatest Derbies of the twentieth century.

Although both Lester Piggott and Vincent O'Brien had each won the Derby multiple times before, and twice together, this was the first win for turf patron Robert Sangster, whose blue and green colours The Minstrel carried. An exhausted but obviously happy horse and rider came back to the winner's enclosure to receive their hard-earned reward. The Minstrel, although completely spent, came back bouncing on his toes and relished the adulation. Piggott, a man not noted for a broad smile, was beaming with pride.

The Irish "Sweeps" Derby, three weeks later, was the next big race. The Minstrel had had four demanding races in less than two months, and the press was convinced that the little colt would have nothing left for the Irish Derby. However, The Minstrel had remarkable recuperative powers and came to the Curragh as fresh as ever for his adopted home country's big classic. He won what was perhaps his easiest race by one-and-a-half lengths from Lucky Sovereign and Classic Example.

O'Brien pointed his star colt to the King George VI and Queen Elizabeth Stakes, to be run four weeks after the Irish Derby. Before the latter race, O'Brien had thought this would be too gruelling a task for the colt, but since the Curragh race had taken very little out of him, he felt The Minstrel would come to Ascot in fine fettle. As it turned out, the Windfields-bred chestnut son of Northern Dancer needed all of his resolve and talent to win, just as he had at Epsom.

The Minstrel was taking on older horses for the first time in the King George, and the field was stellar, including five other winners of classic races. Fellow three-year-old Crystal Palace, four-year-olds Exceller and Crow, and five-year-olds Orange Bay and Bruni entered the starting stalls at Ascot on July 23, 1977, for the 12-furlong race.

The Minstrel took the lead with 2 furlongs to go and then came under relentless pressure from an on-form Orange Bay, piloted by Pat Eddery, who got to The Minstrel's neck. As his sire did in the Kentucky Derby, The Minstrel drew on his courage and will and refused to let his challenger overtake him. Both horses were all out all the way to the finish post, with The Minstrel ahead by the slimmest of margins. Exceller made a furious rush to be third but could not catch the two in front. Determination and a willingness to leave everything he had on the track were the hallmarks of The Minstrel, and he showed them again on this day.

E.P. Taylor, who had followed The Minstrel's career, offered to syndicate the colt he had bred and bring him to stand at Windfields Farm in Maryland. The final price was $9 million, with Windfields buying half of the thirty-two shares. The son of Northern Dancer would stand beside his illustrious father in Maryland when he retired from racing.

The retirement came much sooner than expected. An outbreak of equine metritis had developed in England, and there were rumours that import and export of horses might be banned until the outbreak could be dealt with. This particular disease is more severe in stallions, so The Minstrel was retired and hastily sent to Chesapeake City to begin his new career. Fellow three-year-old Blushing Groom was also brought to the United States for the same reason. He stood at Gainesway Farm in Kentucky.

The Minstrel was named European Horse of the Year for 1977. He was an immediate hit with breeders and began to sire stakes winners and champions from his first crop. Among the many important winners are L'Emigrant (Poule d'Essai des Poulins), three-time Group One winner Minstrella, Melodist (Irish Oaks, Italian Oaks), Musical Bliss (1000 Guineas), Opening Verse (Breeders' Cup Mile), Treizieme (Grand Critérium), Bakharoff (William Hill Futurity) and Palace Music (Champion Stakes, John Henry Handicap). The latter became an excellent sire and claims as his most important offspring two-time Eclipse Award Horse of the Year Cigar.

When Windfields closed down the Maryland farm, it retained shares in The Minstrel and moved him to Overbrook Farm in Kentucky. He had two years there before he died at the age of sixteen due to laminitis.

The Minstrel was an engaging and delightful horse, and he possessed an almost human sense of fun. His favourite routine was to wiggle out of his halter and then elude his handlers as they tried to reattach the headgear before he came in to the barn. This gave him an extra fifteen to twenty minutes of outside time, and he was always pleased with himself when his handlers had to corral him before they could lead him out of his paddock. The Minstrel could entertain his handlers and visitors daily.

Derby One-Two for Number Three

The Minstrel won his Derby seven years after Nijinsky had won the race. Seven years after The Minstrel, the next Windfields-bred winner of the great race appeared. The favourite in the race was El Gran Senor, a son of Northern Dancer bred on the Maryland farm in partnership with Robert Sangster and associates. (The dam of El Gran Senor, Sex Appeal, was a daughter of the great Buckpasser, and Windfields had sold a half interest in her to Sangster.) Like The Minstrel, Sex Appeal's son was trained by Vincent O'Brien for the Sangster syndicate, of which the trainer was a prominent shareholder.

El Gran Senor came into the Derby as the reigning champion juvenile and was still unbeaten when he went to the post for the race. The colt had won the first English classic of the year when he showed his authority to a classy field in the 2000 Guineas. All in attendance at Epsom Downs that day thought him to be unbeatable.

To add to the interest in the race, there was another Northern Dancer son in the Derby, trained by another O'Brien. In the early 1980s, David O'Brien, Vincent's son, had taken out his training licence. He now had a good three-year-old colt in his barn named Secreto, by Northern Dancer, who had been purchased by Luigi Miglietti at the 1982 Saratoga yearling sales. Secreto was also bred on the Maryland farm and was out of the Secretariat mare Betty's Secret. He was a bigger horse than El Gran Senor and had lost only once—the Irish 2000 Guineas to Sadler's Wells—before his entry at Epsom. The two sons of Northern Dancer were about to stage an epic and riveting battle that resonated on many levels.

A seventeen-horse field lined up in the starting stalls for the 1984 Derby Stakes. El Gran Senor was the overwhelming favourite at ⅘, with Alphabatim, piloted by Lester Piggott, second choice at ⁴⁄₁, and Secreto, Claude Monet, Ilium and Kaytu next on the totes at 14⁄₁. Future multiple Group One stakes winner At Talaq was also in the field as an outsider in the wagering, and this improving colt had a five-length advantage as he led the field into the famous Tattenham Corner, which leads to the 4-furlong home straight to the finish post.

El Gran Senor and Secreto began their bids for Derby glory as they started the ascent up the long straight. Pat Eddery on El Gran Senor and Christy Roche on Secreto asked their mounts for everything, and another classic duel to the finish was underway. The difference this time was that both colts were sired by Northern Dancer and bred by Windfields Farm, with one trained by a legend and the other by his son. Secreto on the outside, nearer to the stands, and El Gran Senor on the inside, nearer the rail, waged a furious battle. It appeared that the favourite would just hold off his half-brother and take the glory.

With about fifty yards to go, Secreto found a little bit more and passed El Gran Senor, winning the Derby Stakes in a close photo finish. The two were five lengths in front of third-placed Mighty Flutter. The son beat the father. The lesser-regarded Northern Dancer son beat the heavily favoured son.

Windfields Farm had now bred its third Epsom Derby winner. Only three times in the long history of this classic had sons of the same sire finished one-two. Never before had they been from the same breeder, and never so close at the finish line. Windfields had achieved one of the rarest accomplishments in Thoroughbred breeding.

Secreto never ran another race. He had been entered in the Irish Derby but was withdrawn and retired. He stood initially at Calumet Farm in Kentucky but did not get off to a good start as a stallion and was subsequently sold to Japan, where he died at the age of eighteen. He did get 2000 Guineas winner Mystiko and Italian 1000 Guineas winner Miss Secreto among his thirty stakes winners (4.6 percent of all foals) during his stud career.

As mentioned in the previous chapter, El Gran Senor also got off to a slow start at stud, beginning at Windfields in Maryland and then transferring to Coolmore's Ashford stud after one season at his birthplace. El Gran Senor suffered from low fertility. Unfortunately, modern ultrasound and other electronic medical devices that determine the optimum time for a mare to conceive were not in place when he began his stud career. Had the technology been more developed, things might have been different for El Gran Senor.

However, one Northern Dancer son from the same crop as El Gran Senor and Secreto has become one of the all-time great stallions in history. Sadler's Wells, who defeated Secreto but not El Gran Senor on the track, was named the top miler in 1984. He went on to become a fourteen-time leading sire in England/Ireland and once led the North American sire list, while standing at Coolmore in Ireland. Sadler's Wells broke records: he sired 294 stakes winners and established the most successful tail male line descending from Northern Dancer through his phenomenal son Galileo. At time of writing, Galileo is the leading sire in the world. He is currently on a seven-year streak as leading sire and looks to break his illustrious father's records.

The dream of every breeder is to win the Derby Stakes at Epsom or the Kentucky Derby at Churchill Downs. E.P. Taylor and his Windfields Farm achieved the latter with Northern Dancer, and the former three times with sons of Northern Dancer. No other breeder in the over three-hundred-year history of racing can claim this feat. That is as close to a dynasty as could be accomplished in Thoroughbred horse racing.

{ 10 }

MARYLAND, MY MARYLAND

E.P. TAYLOR WAS always looking to expand the horizons of his racing and breeding empire. In the late 1950s, he had leased a farm in Kentucky, looking for a site to establish a presence in the United States. Kentucky, the epicentre of Thoroughbred breeding, with the best farms in the business, seemed a natural location. However, Taylor noticed that the foals born on this farm were no more advanced than the foals born in Ontario, so the Kentucky plan was scrapped.

Taylor had also leased a farm in Georgia to use as a winter training centre. This lasted a few years before he hit on an idea that would change the direction of Windfields and boost the name into the company of the elite establishments of the turf world.

One of the Taylors' closest friends in racing was Marylander Allaire du Pont. Du Pont bred and campaigned one of the greatest horses in racing history during the first half of the 1960s, the mighty Kelso. She talked to the Taylors about the merits of land in the Chesapeake Bay area of Cecil County, Maryland, and its central location near many of the East Coast tracks. Du Pont had her own Woodstock Farm in Cecil County, and she mentioned to the Taylors that there was good land available near her establishment. Eddie heeded her words and, after doing his due diligence, assessed that the area was a good place to set up a training centre.

On April 18, 1963, Taylor bought 674 acres of a former dairy farm and built a training facility on the land. A 5-furlong dirt oval was complemented by a 7-furlong grass oval around it. Barns with enough stalls to house forty horses, homes for employees and European-style gallops for training were constructed. This turned the property into a hybrid American/English training facility. The operation was up and running by May 1964, when Northern Dancer was winning the Kentucky Derby, Preakness Stakes and Queen's Plate.

The costs to run a large racing stable are enormous. Even for a man as wealthy as E.P. Taylor, such ventures can strain the bank account. The purses won in racing seldom cover the expenses. Take into account the high cost of stabling at various tracks, and it's clear why a central training facility appealed to Taylor. The operation in Maryland did help cut expenses, but not by a significant margin. E.P. Taylor began looking for ways to make his investment reap more success.

Around this time, Nearctic's stud career was creating a buzz in the industry, and in 1967, he moved to Maryland to stand at Allaire du Pont's farm. In 1965, Northern Dancer embarked on his historic stud career at the Oshawa farm. E.P. Taylor decided to change Windfields' focus from breeding and racing a large stable to becoming primarily a breeding enterprise. The

Maryland property, while central to many tracks, was also within reach of the fine established farms in Kentucky. Taylor and his advisors reasoned that if both Northern Dancer and Nearctic were standing in Maryland, they would be more accessible to the best mares in America, thus giving the stallions a better opportunity to succeed.

A new era in Maryland's rich history of racing was about to begin, and the Canadian E.P. Taylor would be the architect.

Change in Direction

In 1968, the Maryland farm was converted into a breeding centre, with Taylor purchasing additional tracts of land surrounding the original farm. The entire complex would eventually grow to encompass 2,600 acres of prime land.

One 170-acre property Taylor bought was originally known as the Maryland Stallion Station. He enlarged the site with an additional four hundred acres and built two twenty-four-stall barns to house incoming mares who were to be bred to the farm stallions. These barns were in addition to the existing fifty-four stalls from the original Maryland Stallion Station capacity. Later, this "commercial" section of the Maryland farm was further enlarged with additional barns for customer mares and new stallion barns to house more world-class stallions. The entire complex was split into two separate divisions: the Stallion division, which would be the commercial portion; and the Windfields private division, which housed the home mares and their offspring. The training area remained under the private portion and was in operation until the end.

There were four stallions standing at the Stallion division when Taylor bought it: Impressive (a champion sprinter bred and raced by Ogden Phipps), Royal Orbit, Nail and Eurasian were all retained by Windfields. In late 1968, Northern Dancer joined them.

Not everything went smoothly, however. One of the new barns that housed the mares to be bred caught fire the night after the mares arrived. Faulty electrical wiring ignited the blaze. The barn was built of wood, and once the fire started, the structure lit up quickly. There was no chance for staff or the local volunteer fire department to save the horses caught in the inferno. Twelve mares died in the blaze.

Among the twelve was the beautiful Victoria Regina, the dam of Viceregal and Vice Regent. She was in foal to Northern Dancer and was to be bred to Nearctic. Also lost in the tragedy were stakes producer Bally Free and Bill Beasley's Canadian Oaks winner All We Have. Many of the mares were young new additions to the broodmare colony, and many were to have been bred to either Nearctic or Northern Dancer in the following breeding season.

The Taylors and the farm staff were devastated. Following the tragedy, E.P. Taylor vowed to never build another barn structure of wood. Cement block and steel would be the only materials used to construct further homes for the horses. Contrary to the usual way he approached building, he allowed the new barns to be built quickly in order to convert the Maryland complex into a breeding farm. E.P Taylor was never one to repeat a mistake.

Fans in Canada were concerned that Taylor was planning to gradually pull out of his home country. He had sold most of his Willowdale property, which included the breeding farm, to land developers. He used the capital from the Willowdale land sale to fund additional land purchases for the Cecil County farm. Taylor did retain forty-five acres, keeping twenty for his estate and donating the rest to the city for parkland. He assured his fellow patriots that he was not leaving Canada, but the sale of the Willowdale farm was inevitable. The city was growing up around the land, engulfing it. There is a charming, but telling, picture of Nijinsky running in the fields as a yearling in 1968 that says it all. One can clearly see the North York skyline and high-rise buildings in the background. Local children would stop frequently to pet the horses in the outlying fields. While this was not a problem, it was concerning, as the children could be hurt if one of the animals were to bite or kick.

Another sign that worried Canadians was the relocation of Nearctic and the beloved Northern Dancer to Maryland. Taylor's reason for these moves was to give both fashionable stallions access to better-bred mares to enhance their stud careers. "It is a difficult decision to bring Northern Dancer to Maryland," he said, adding, "He is a Canadian hero and has done well here at home. In justice to his promising future, I think we must make him more accessible to the finest mares possible."

With the new Maryland division of Windfields Farm, E.P. Taylor brought a world-class breeding centre to a state that has a wonderful history of racing. Marylanders are passionate about their horses, and some of the elite Thoroughbreds in American history have been bred and raced there. Pimlico Race Course in Baltimore has been the scene of many historical races and is the home of the Preakness Stakes, second jewel of the American Triple Crown. Laurel Race Course, located between Baltimore and Washington, has also staged many world-class race meets and was home to the Washington D.C. International until 1994.

The state was home to many of the turf elite. The aforementioned Kelso spent his distinguished retirement at nearby Woodstock Farm. Native Dancer, the sire of Natalma and many other notable Thoroughbreds, was born and raised at Alfred Vanderbilt's Sagamore Farm in Maryland. He spent his stud career at Sagamore and is buried there. Vanderbilt also had the great champion Discovery, whose influential breeding career took place in Maryland. Turf legend William Woodward operated his fabled Belair Stud in Prince George County, Maryland. Woodward's famous colours, white with cherry-red dots and cherry-red cap, were seen in the winner's circle of many famous racetracks, carried by the winners of such renowned races as the Kentucky Derby, Belmont Stakes and Ascot Gold Cup. Elite horses like Nashua, Flares, Boswell and Granville were bred in the state. Triple Crown winners Gallant Fox and his son Omaha, although bred by Woodward in Kentucky, called the state home.

William Woodward was one of the turf's great ambassadors and a true gentleman. He had success in America and in England, with horses in his British stable trained by Captain Cecil Boyd-Rochfort. His American stable was trained by another legend, James "Sunny Jim" Fitzsimmons. Woodward knew E.P. Taylor for years before his passing in 1952. Taylor bred two Queen's Plate winners from Belair-bred stallions and later stood Flares' son Chop Chop with great success.

The Maryland government provided tax relief to Thoroughbred breeders, which would further entice a businessman like E.P. Taylor to seriously consider building a breeding operation in the state. The land is limestone based, similar to the geography in Kentucky, which adds to its fertility, and has gentle rolling pastures filled with lush grass for grazing. The setting is serene and conducive for raising horses. The climate is moderate, without extreme hot or cold spells, and with an annual average rainfall of forty-one inches.

Cecil County contained a thriving horse business, centred in the St. Augustine area. The addition of Windfields Farm began an exciting new chapter and brought even more elite Thoroughbreds to Maryland.

World-Class Stallions

As Windfields Maryland grew in both size and stature, it became a go-to farm for many stallion prospects when they retired from the track. By the late 1970s, the farm was not only home to leading sires Northern Dancer, Halo and The Minstrel, but also to highly regarded stallions such as Val de l'Orne, Snow Knight, Tentam and King's Bishop. Breeders had a wide variety of choices with the stallions Windfields stood in Maryland. They could also be certain that the stallions on the farm were from elite families and represented the top sire lines in breeding.

Val de l'Orne was an intriguing addition to the stallion roster at the Maryland farm. The bay son of leading French sire Val de Loir had won the Prix du Jockey Club (the French Derby) and three other races in an abbreviated five-race career. He represented a total outcross to North American breeding and passed his class on to many noteworthy foals. Windfields chief veterinarian, Dr. Rolph de Gannes, was dispatched by Joe Thomas to assess the horse in France while negotiations took place to purchase him. Dr. de Gannes's report was favourable, and so the deal was made.

Val de l'Orne was a high-withered bay of considerable scope and stamped his foals with these attributes. Among his best runners were consecutive Queen's Plate winners La Lorgnette and Golden Choice, Japan Cup winner Pay The Butler and Hollywood Derby winner Victory Zone. His daughter Adorned became the dam of Queen's Plate winner and Canadian champion Archer's Bay.

Snow Knight, while containing a completely different pedigree background, was similar to Val de l'Orne in that he was a total outcross to American breeding. Snow Knight had won the Epsom Derby and attracted the attention of Windfields, which subsequently purchased the chestnut son of Firestreak, out of Snow Blossom by Flush Royal. He raced in Windfields colours and was trained by Mack Miller, who got the headstrong Snow Knight to an Eclipse Award championship as the top grass horse of 1975. Snow Knight won the prestigious Canadian International, Man O' War Stakes and Manhattan Handicap during his championship season.

At stud, Snow Knight sired many durable and fast runners including Awaasif. Purchased by Sheikh Mohammed from the Windfields Keeneland yearling consignment in 1980, Awaasif was out of the regal mare Royal Statute, by Northern Dancer, and became the champion three-year-old filly in England in 1981. She was the first of many champions campaigned by Sheikh Mohammed and was the catalyst for him to continue shopping for Windfields-bred yearlings.

Tentam was another stallion who Windfields purchased while he was still in training and continued to campaign. The dark brown, almost black horse was as American as apple pie. His sire was Intentionally, a great-grandson of the legendary Man O' War. Tentam came through the War Relic branch. (Taylor had sought a stallion prospect by War Relic when he was interested in purchasing that one's son Relic for Windfields in 1950.) Tentam came from a very remarkable family that stayed in the spotlight of breeding importance after his birth. His three-quarter brother Known Fact won the English 2000 Guineas and become a strong sire. His half-sister Secrettame was a stakes winner and later produced Grade One winner Gone West, who in turn became an important sire.

Unfortunately, the unpredictable nature of racehorse breeding struck when Tentam died suddenly in 1981 at the age of twelve, while still in the early stages of a very promising career as a sire. Canadian champions New Connection and Ten Gold Pots, as well as Grade One winners A Phenomenon and Great Neck were some of his top sons. Canadian champion and Hall of Fame member La Voyageuse and multiple stakes winner Stellarette proved that Tentam could sire first-class daughters as well. Queen's Plate winner and champion three-year-old Regal Intention was out of Tentam's stakes-winning daughter Tiffany Tam.

King's Bishop was born in the same year as Tentam and, coincidently, died in 1981 as well. Sired by the legendary Round Table, King's Bishop brought his steady race record—in which he won five stakes races, including the race named after his sire—and a classy pedigree to Windfields Maryland. King's Bishop was also on the path to a very successful breeding career when he died too soon from an injury he sustained when a mare kicked his leg. The leg became infected, and the syndicate that owned him discussed the possibility of amputating the leg and replacing it with a prosthesis in order to save him. The idea was deemed unviable, so King's Bishop was euthanized. There is a Grade One stakes race run at Saratoga in his name to honour him.

During his brief stud career, King's Bishop sired a steady stream of stakes winners. King's Swan, winner of the Vosburgh Handicap, was a beloved performer on the New York racing scene. Cabrini Green, ten-time stakes winner Castelets, Possible Mate, Lady Lonsdale and King's Fashion were additional stakes winners by King's Bishop. His get were much like him, steady and fast.

King's Bishop became a Windfields stallion in September 1976 when the farm purchased the Northview Stallion annex from Allaire du Pont. Mrs. du Pont wanted to devote her equine energies to her own stock, and so she decided to relinquish her stallion division to Windfields. There were three stallions on the property at the time: T.V. Commercial, King Emperor and King's Bishop, all syndicated stallions who Windfields had shares in. The transfer was seamless and the horses did not have to relocate.

T.V. Commercial was a well-raced and durable multiple stakes winner sired by champion T.V. Lark, who in turn was a grandson of the dynastic stallion Nasrullah. T.V. Commercial sired a steady stream of winners who competed over a variety of distances and surfaces, much as he had when he raced. He became a paddock neighbour to Northern Dancer and lived to the ripe old age of thirty-one.

The Maryland stallion roster also boasted the likes of Master Willie, a British-bred champion on the Hyperion tail male line. Master Willie was a big, bright red chestnut who won three Group One races, including the Benson and Hedges Gold Cup and the Eclipse Stakes. He was inbred to the great stallion Hyperion 3x4, and Windfields management was convinced he would make a suitable outcross to the predominantly Nearctic/Northern Dancer mares who populated the farm.

Assert was a champion grandson of Northern Dancer who stood at Windfields Maryland. Bred in Ireland by Robert Sangster, Assert captured two derbies, the French and the Irish, as well as winning the Benson and Hedges Gold Cup.

Gregorian was another highly regarded stallion prospect who had won at the top level of competition and came to stud with a very desirable pedigree. Gregorian was sired by the successful stallion Graustark, a son of the immortal Ribot, and his dam was Natashka, a granddaughter of Hall of Fame champion Vagrancy. Gregorian's best offspring was Queen's Plate winner Imperial Choice.

Smarten stood at Windfields Maryland beginning in the 1980 breeding season. The compact, dark bay son of Cyane, a sire by Turn-to, who in turn was a grandson of the great Nearco, got off to a quick start at stud when his first crop contained Classy 'n Smart, the 1984 champion three-year-old filly in Canada. Classy 'n Smart was bred by prominent Canadian owner/breeder Ernie Samuel and went on to be the dam of the great Dance Smartly, as well as two-time leading sire Smart Strike. Smarten remained a steady source of good honest racehorses throughout his sire career.

One of the early stallion prospects to stand at the Maryland farm was a horse bred in 1969 named Search For Gold. The bay son of Raise A Native, out of Gold Digger by Nashua, ran impressively as a two-year-old, competing in five races. He won once, by seven lengths, and finished second three times. Among the vanquished in his lone victory was future Kentucky Derby winner Riva Ridge. Search For Gold was injured in his fifth race, which necessitated his retirement from the track. He entered stud at Windfields when he was three years old.

The Windfields brass was very keen on the colt during his juvenile campaign, so they decided to try to buy his year-younger full brother at the 1971 Keeneland July yearling sales. The bay brother attracted much fanfare when he entered the sales ring. The bidding was brisk, and the colt set a new record for top price for a yearling. When the auctioneer's hammer came down to end the sale, Floridian Abraham Savin was the highest bidder at $220,000. The immediate underbidder was Windfields. This colt would later be named Mr. Prospector and went on to become the closest rival in stallion supremacy to Northern Dancer during his stud career. Windfields came close to owning and standing both stallions.

During the heyday of Windfields' Maryland occupation, the quality of its stallions rivalled those in Kentucky, where most of the top names in breeding resided. The farm provided desirable stallions throughout its existence. Impressive, Protanto, King Emperor, Rambunctious, Dancing Count, Caucasus, Medaille d'Or, Caveat, Oh Say, Robellino and Two Punch all came from top-class families and top-class sire lines. Caveat and Caucasus were classic winners. Impressive and Medaille d'Or were divisional champions. Every stallion who stood in St. Augustine had merit, and the variety offered breeders a diverse array of pedigree combinations and conformation traits. It was a golden age for Maryland breeding.

Launch Point to the World

A large number of the stallions who stood at the Maryland farm had been raced in Europe before coming to the United States, and their Canadian- or American-bred offspring had great success when they raced in Europe. The back and forth between the two continents solidified the transition to the global breeding business that had begun in the early sixties. Although it was not the originator of the practice, Windfields Maryland became one of the leaders, if not *the* leader, in providing horses for this trans-Atlantic express of Thoroughbred bloodstock.

Many of the proven Canadian broodmares, such as Natalma, Nangela, Sex Appeal, Royal Statute, Sweet Alliance, Northern Sea and Pacific Princess, were shipped to the Maryland facility and stayed there. The reputation and breeding records of these mares dictated the relocation. They no longer needed to return to Ontario so their foals would be born in Canada in order to accommodate the home market for Canadian-breds. The high-rolling, big-spending European racing outfits invariably swooped in to buy these youngsters and whisk them off to England, Ireland or France for racing. Influential horses who made their name in Europe, like Shareef Dancer, El Gran Senor, Be My Guest, Try My Best and Istabraq, were born on the Maryland farm, and the St. Augustine area of the Chesapeake Bay region became a gold mine for quality Thoroughbreds. The American market was not shut out however, as we see star performers Southern Halo and Devil's Bag were both born on the Maryland farm, and raced in the US.

Many of the yearlings who were born in Canada were destined for the big sales in Keeneland and Saratoga. These youngsters were brought down to graze on the lush grass of the Maryland farm and were prepared by Don Coulter and his son Tom for these prestigious sales. Don and Tom were elite horsemen who knew how to have a well-bred yearling ready to impress the buyers. They were key contributors to the record-breaking prices achieved by Windfields yearlings. The Minstrel, Awaasif, Storm Bird, L'Alezane, Norcliffe and more Canadian-bred champions were given the royal treatment by Coulter's staff in Maryland before their appearance in the sales ring.

As they had done on the Oshawa farm, the leading buyers flocked to St. Augustine to inspect the yearlings Windfields had on offer. Don or Tom would take the bloodstock agents around to see the yearlings in action in the paddocks. The agents had their Windfields brochure in hand and made notes of the colts or fillies they inspected. The system appeared to work to perfection, judging from Windfields' success at the most prestigious sales venues on the continent.

As mentioned earlier, Windfields was not the first breeder to produce horses in the United States who were purchased and sent across the Atlantic to run in the big European races. Such horses as Sir Ivor, Mill Reef, Youth and Exceller became champions in Europe before Windfields' reign as chief supplier of European champions. But they were exceptions. The top sales yearlings tended to stay in America to race. However, Windfields consistently offered bloodlines that intrigued European owners. It made the Keeneland and Fasig-Tipton venues in Kentucky and Saratoga the places to find world-class quality. Windfields yearlings drew in the crowds as well as the money. And when these yearlings became Derby winners, Guineas winners, divisional champions and Grade/Group One winners in both Europe and America, the Windfields Maryland yearling department earned an enviable place at the top of the industry. Global breeding took root in large part thanks to the bloodstock bred and/or developed at Windfields Maryland.

The World's No. 1 Source of Stakes Winners

A yearling sale in the Thoroughbred world is much like a draft in professional sports. In baseball or hockey drafts, teams select unproven but promising athletes to restock their rosters. The teams then develop the players. The most promising are selected early, but some of the prospects selected later in the process have been known to develop into the finest players. And not every prospect selected in the early rounds becomes a contributor to a team's success.

In Thoroughbred yearling sales, the most promising yearlings are also the most expensive. The big racing stables with deep pockets often go to what seem like extreme lengths to acquire these yearlings. In the event that a high-priced youngster does go on to become a stakes winner or champion, the value of that horse skyrockets. But many times the high-priced yearlings do not become winners, let alone champions, just as the most promising young athlete does not always lead a sports team to glory. Both horse auctions and sport drafts are speculative worlds.

A selection process for each yearling sale is conducted throughout the year. A team of well-informed, astute horsemen visit the top-ranked breeding farms to inspect the young colts and fillies who are nominated by consigning breeders. The elite prospects go into the summer sales in Kentucky. This method provides a central location for the high rollers in the sport to converge at one place, spend their money and restock their racing stables.

During the late 1970s and into the first half of the 1980s, prices for well-bred yearlings set new records year after year for ten straight years. Millions of dollars were spent on individual unproven horses. The gradual rise in yearling prices began in the early 1970s. Bold Ruler was the undisputed king of sires at the time, but not many of his offspring made it to the sales. Those lucky enough to obtain a breeding to the "Ruling Stallion" did so via a foal-sharing arrangement, so they were more inclined to keep the colt or filly than to sell it. Also, the predominant racing stables were still private affairs, relying mostly on their own breeding programs. They only went to the sales when they needed to enhance their own stock with fresh bloodlines.

There were still plenty of well-bred and beautifully conformed yearlings at the sales, from stallions such as Raise A Native, Round Table, Damascus, Ribot, Buckpasser and other top sires. Breeders like Claiborne Farm and Spendthrift Farm had long-established records of selling prime yearlings at the sales. World-class champions, including Sir Ivor, Majestic Prince and Windfields-bred Nijinsky, were sold as yearlings in the 1960s. This was rare, however, because of the dominance of private stables that bred and raced their own champions.

When E.P Taylor decided to offer every Windfields yearling for sale, and placed a well-publicized reserve on only a select few, he essentially created an open market for buyers to acquire some of the best horses anywhere. With the public sales of two Epsom Derby–winning sons of Northern Dancer (Nijinsky and The Minstrel), yearling buyers realized they had prime prospects to choose from. Taylor had essentially created a viable global market by expanding the availability of sons and daughters of the hottest sire in the world.

Englishman Robert Sangster and his associates, Vincent O'Brien and John Magnier, were often the buyers of these expensive yearlings. In 1975, the first year Windfields consigned to the Keeneland summer sales, the UK trio paid $200,000 for a chestnut colt by Northern Dancer who they named The Minstrel.

Sangster and Associates did not get all the horses they wanted, however, because of the appearance of an equally determined and deep-pocketed Arab contingent of turf enthusiasts led by Sheikh Mohammed bin Rashid Al Maktoum and his family. These heavily financed and very motivated people spent enormous amounts of money at unprecedented levels. They were all keen to become major players in a short time, and they did so spectacularly. Today, the legacy of the Sangster team is the world-renowned Coolmore breeding and racing empire, while Sheikh Mohammed is the leader of the giant Darley breeding operation and the Godolphin racing stable. Coolmore and Darley are the major players in the world today, with breeding centres in Europe, America, Australia and Japan. Many of the world's top stallions are located on these farms, as are many of the top broodmares. But the seeds of success were planted with purchases from Windfields Farm's yearling consignments at the top sales in Kentucky, Saratoga and Canada.

Windfields horses sold to other buyers as well, and the farm was at the forefront of the yearling sales boom. The combination of Northern Dancer or one of his sons as a sire, the families of Windfields broodmare colony and E.P. Taylor's record as breeder ticked every box to make potential buyers feel comfortable they were going to get their next champion.

Windfields published annual yearling catalogues with the slogan "World's No. 1 Source of Stakes Winners" emblazoned on the cover and listings of the blue-blooded youngsters available for sale inside. The elite owners in the racing world would receive a copy from Windfields management weeks before the sales via mail, and they would converge on the barns at the sales to view the yearlings first-hand so they could assess the conformation and general presence of the animals.

The slogan was a well-earned fact. In 1977, E.P. Taylor broke a long-standing record for the number of stakes winners bred by one breeder. The record had been held by Harry Payne Whitney, with 192 winners. On June 22, 1977, Right Chilly became the 193rd stakes winner bred by E.P. Taylor. The record-breaking daughter of Oshawa farm stallion Right Combination, out of Nearctic's daughter Chilly, had been sold as a yearling the year before to Herb Doman and was a fourth-generation descendant of foundation mare Nandi.

For years, Windfields consigned its yearlings to four or five different sales venues—the CTHS sale at Woodbine in Ontario; the Maryland Thoroughbred Breeders Association at Timonium, Maryland; Fasig-Tipton sales at Saratoga, New York, and Lexington, Kentucky; and the Keeneland yearling sales at the beautiful venue in Lexington. The sales at Woodbine and Timonium were generally for horses bred in Ontario and Maryland for those respective markets. The Keeneland and Fasig-Tipton sales sold the cream of each yearling crop. The Keeneland venue, in particular, was where the elite yearlings were sold and was the site of the spirited bidding wars that caused the market to explode. Windfields' participation at Keeneland was key to the venue becoming the prime destination where upper-echelon buyers sought their next champions. Keeneland owes a great debt to the Canadian E.P Taylor and his operation. A king's ransom was paid for many unproven commodities based on conformation, pedigree and a breeder's reputation.

The appearance of E.P. Taylor, Charles Taylor, Joe Thomas and George Blackwell, as well as the horsemen and horsewomen dressed in Windfields livery at the Keeneland sales, caused a reaction akin to that created by a top rock band on a continental tour. People would flock to them, discuss the latest in racing and breeding news, and ask to be photographed in their company. Similar scenes played out many times during the heyday of the Windfields consignments at the venue, as the biggest movers and shakers in the industry acknowledged the enormous contributions and successes of the Windfields team.

The successes were indeed impressive. International champions Storm Bird, Awaasif, Secreto, Danzatore, Shareef Dancer, Devil's Bag and Try My Best were bred and sold during the heady days of the elite sales bonanza. They were in addition to the champions Windfields had sold in prior decades. The breeding practices of E.P. Taylor's Windfields Farm were reaching new heights.

Reinvesting in the Market

With the sales of regally bred yearlings, Windfields Farm needed to restock its breeding colony. No longer could the farm rely on keeping unsold daughters from its own breeding families for future breeding. The word was out and buyers were snapping up descendants of Windfields-developed bloodlines.

E.P. Taylor, his son Charles and Joe Thomas took the money from Windfields' sales and reinvested it, acquiring top-class stock offered by other breeders to reinvigorate their breeding colony for the future. Many yearling fillies purchased by Windfields at the big sales venues became foundation mares after their racing careers ended (see the highlights of this generation in Chapter Eleven).

Windfields also continued to invest in stallion prospects and bought shares in many syndicates for stallions who stood at other breeding centres as well as their own. Being part of these syndicates allowed Windfields to draw on a diverse array of bloodlines to breed future yearlings who would attract buyers. They could match mares, by conformation and bloodlines, to the very best stallions available, thus offering their clients outstanding prospects for future success. As well, the broad scope of the bloodlines available to Windfields added to the spectrum for buyers looking for certain nicks or breeding patterns.

The stallions Windfields held shares in paid big dividends. Sir Ivor, Nijinsky II, Buckpasser, Damascus, Round Table, Mr. Prospector, Secretariat and Conquistador Cielo all stood at Claiborne Farm. Each one of these stallions sired Windfields-bred Thoroughbreds who achieved great success either on the track or in breeding careers. Dr. Fager, Ribot, Key To The Mint, Exclusive Native, Hoist The Flag, Majestic Prince, Hawaii, Le Fabuleux, Kennedy Road, Arts And Letters and Foolish Pleasure were some of the other off-farm syndicated sires bred to Windfields broodmares.

E.P. Taylor was very aware of the need for diversity in the breed. As a student of genetics, he actively sought compatible outcrosses for his breeding stock. He stood outcross stallions to complement his broodmare colony and made these stallions available to fellow breeders. Taylor was firm in his belief that outcrosses were vital to keep the breed vigorous and improving, and to prevent its becoming too narrowly focused on a select few bloodlines. Inbreeding can produce spectacular results, but eventually too much of such breeding will stagnate improvement. Keeping a broader base within a pedigree increases the potential combinations for success in future generations. This belief was a cornerstone to Taylor's enormous achievements in the sport, and no one can argue with the success he achieved.

One of the stallions Windfields bought a share in was the tragically fated Shergar. He was only able to stand one breeding season before he was abducted and never found. Shergar sired thirty-four foals, five of whom became stakes winners. One of those stakes winners, Tisn't, was bred by Windfields, while three were bred by the Aga Khan iv, who bred and raced Shergar and held the highest percentage of shares in the breeding syndicate. The fifth stakes winner was multiple Group One stakes winner Authaal, bred and raced by Sheikh Mohammed and foaled from a mare by Nijinsky ii.

Windfields' reinvestment in bloodstock not only aided the breeders of the horses who were purchased, but also the buyers of future Windfields-bred yearlings. Buyers could confidently purchase a well-conformed yearling from Windfields, knowing that they were tapping into quality stock with desirable pedigrees. Owning a Windfields-bred was seen as a status symbol of sorts by new owners and those looking to establish a racing and breeding operation of their own.

By putting capital back into the sport, Windfields was a key contributor to the economic stability and growth of Thoroughbred racing. If Windfields had a successful sale, then other breeders would have success as well, due to Windfields having more capital to spend and reinvest in yearlings bred by other breeders. It was an an example of free-trade capitalism at its best.

Grassroots Availability

Windfields did not breed Thoroughbreds just to cater to the elite. There were broad ranges of affordability for stallion services and farm-bred yearlings for sale. All levels of Thoroughbred breeders and potential owners with various budgets had an opportunity to breed or own a quality racehorse.

The Chesapeake farm stood several affordable stallions to enrich the surrounding area markets. Windfields always considered all breeders, no matter their financial wherewithal: the small operations were just as important as the big-money spenders.

The Ontario and Maryland farms produced yearlings bred for more modest racing budgets. Local provincial and state racing programs gave horse owners of lesser financial means a chance to get involved in racing and enjoy the fruits of owning a well-bred and well-raised filly or colt. Windfields-bred horses were able to compete in these programs, thus stocking these jurisdictions with exciting racing prospects.

A plethora of exalted names in today's pedigrees have come from the yearling consignments Windfields sold at Woodbine and Timonium. These yearlings were not necessarily inferior to the yearlings on offer at the bigger sales; they or their families were just not as highly regarded. Many of these young colts and fillies came from generations of stakes-producing families nurtured in the Windfields breeding program. And remember that horses such as Nijinsky, Northernette, Square Angel, South Ocean, Kamar, Glorious Song and many more were sold in the Woodbine sales pavilion when they were yearlings. Several bargains obtained from Windfields consignments at the lower-end sales turned out to be champion racehorses and/or influential broodmares.

All the comments in earlier sections of this chapter about the advantages of standing well-bred stallions and having breeding shares in sires who were not standing at Oshawa or Maryland apply in this case too. Windfields had an assortment of riches to tap, and the proven quality of the farms' mare populations gave further confidence to yearling buyers at the Ontario and Maryland sales. Joe Thomas knew the market well and kept Windfields at the forefront on all levels.

Many of today's successful breeders shopped at Windfields and based their own breeding programs on the Windfields pattern and bloodlines. The wealth of outstanding equine families spread around the globe.

Top Northern Dancer with broodmare manager Ben Miller. PHOTO CREDIT: PETER WINANTS/DRUMMER BOY PUBLICATIONS

Bottom Maryland Stud barn, where Northern Dancer spent most of his life in residence. PHOTO CREDIT: PETER WINANTS/DRUMMER BOY PUBLICATIONS

Maryland Farm entry gate to the commercial section of the farm. PHOTO CREDIT: PETER WINANTS/DRUMMER BOY PUBLICATIONS

Above Nijinsky II in his paddock at Claiborne Farm, Kentucky. PHOTO CREDIT: KEENE-LAND ASSOCIATION LIBRARY/THOROUGHBRED TIMES COLLECTION

Facing Top Father and son. E.P. Taylor and Charles Taylor at Keeneland. PHOTO CREDIT: KEENELAND ASSOCIATION LIBRARY/THOROUGHBRED TIMES COLLECTION

Facing Bottom Secreto. PHOTO CREDIT: KEENELAND ASSOCIATION LIBRARY/THOROUGH-BRED TIMES COLLECTION

Portrait of the greatest stallion of the twentieth century, Northern Dancer. PHOTO CREDIT: KEENELAND ASSOCIATION LIBRARY

{ 11 }

FOUNDATION MARES IV: CONTINUITY OF EXCELLENCE

THROUGH THE PURCHASE of mares that reinvigorated a depleted colony of broodmares, new foundations were established for the high-class racing families emerging from Windfields. Outcross blood, as well as lines from proven winning families, gave Windfields additional resources to breed to their Northern Dancer–line stallions, as well as to the other fine stallions they stood or had breeding rights to. Another litany of champions and Grade/Group One winners descended from these well-bred and influential mares.

As we have seen, Windfields buyers searched the globe to find mares they felt would be successful. Many of these mares were purchased as yearlings, raced under the turquoise and gold colours, and then retired to fulfill the main purpose of their acquisition. Windfields employed this tried-and-true method for success throughout the years of operation.

Ballade

Windfields purchased a yearling bay filly by the French stallion Herbager, out of Miss Swapsco by Cohoes, for $55,000 at the 1973 Keeneland sales. The consignor was Walmac-Warnerton Farm. The filly was given the name Ballade, and she made eight starts, winning twice and finishing second four times and third once. She ran in allowance races and was consistent but did not earn any black type. Ballade was retired due to injury, and her first breeding was to new Maryland farm sire Halo. She was three years old when she met the fiery stallion.

Ballade's first foal turned out to be a memorable one. Purchased by Frank Stronach at the Woodbine yearling sale in 1977, the bay filly was named Glorious Song and went on to be one of the great Canadian-bred fillies of all time.

Glorious Song had a four-year racing career. She took a little time to get the hang of racing and had to overcome some issues of temperament, no doubt inherited from her father. When she did find her form, Glorious Song showed her speed, class and iron will to the racing public and earned her place in the Canadian Racing Hall of Fame with distinction. Glorious Song went to the United States and won some important Grade One races, earning an Eclipse Award as the champion older mare as a four-year-old. In her native Canada, Glorious Song won three Sovereign Awards, including a Horse of the Year title in 1980.

Among her many memorable races, Glorious Song gained wins in the Santa Margarita Invitational, Top Flight Handicap, Spinster Stakes, Dominion Day Handicap (twice), La Canada Stakes, Wonder Where Stakes and Canadian Stakes. She won seventeen of her thirty-four starts, became the first

Canadian-bred to break the $1 million mark in earnings and raced against the best of her generation, both male and female.

Glorious Song possessed a steely resolve, proven time after time. She gave Spectacular Bid all he could handle with her second-place finish in the Amory L. Haskell Handicap during the Bid's all-conquering perfect season. She also ran a close second to Winter's Tale in the Marlboro Cup, proving her toughness again. Fellow Windfields-bred Grade One winner Kamar edged her out in the Duchess Stakes. However, Glorious Song defeated thirteen separate Grade One winners during her career, and then passed on her will to win and her class to future generations.

As with Kamar, Glorious Song became a highly regarded broodmare. Unlike her dam, Ballade, Glorious Song's first foal was only a minor winner. Rivotious, by Riverman, won five of eighteen races and placed in one stakes race. Glorious Song's third foal, however, was a great contributor to the breed. Rahy, by Blushing Groom, won three stakes races in England and the United States, including the Grade Two Bel Air Handicap. As a stallion standing at Three Chimneys Farm in Kentucky, Rahy sired thirteen Grade/Group One winners and is a broodmare sire of importance.

Rahy was a small, 15.1-hand chestnut but is a big influence, counting the likes of Fantastic Light, Serena's Song, Dreaming Of Anna, Noverre, Tranquility Lake and Tate's Creek among his offspring. Another notable is Mariah's Storm, the dam of Giant's Causeway, Freud and Pearling. The latter is the dam of Group One winner Decorated Knight. Mariah's Storm is also the grandmother of 2000 Guineas winner Gleneagles. The recently deceased Giant's Causeway is a three-time leading sire, while Serena's Song, a thirteen-time Grade One winner, is the dam of Sophisticat and Harlington, and third dam of Honor Code.

The fifth foal of Glorious Song, her fifth straight colt, was Rakeen, by Northern Dancer. From the last full crop of his sire,

Rakeen raced in England and South Africa, winning the Group Two Allen Snijman Stakes. Rakeen became a sire of note in South Africa, getting the likes of Jet Master, North By Northwest and Young Rake among his twenty-three stakes winners.

The first filly Glorious Song produced was a full sister to Rahy named Morn Of Song. A winner of three races from seven starts, Morn Of Song produced Prix Vermeille winner Mezzo Soprano by Darshaan. Another daughter from Morn Of Song, this one by Nureyev, was called Halwa Song. She, in turn, is the dam of Halwa Sweet, a mare who has made a significant contribution to Japanese racing in recent times.

Halwa Sweet is the dam of three major Group One winners. Verxina is the first of the three. Sired by the great Deep Impact, this fleet filly twice won the Victoria Mile but was unfortunate to be born the same year as the wonderful Gentildonna, finishing second to that one on four occasions in major classic races such as the Japanese Oaks and the Oka Sho and Shuka Sho. The second major foal from Halwa Sweet was her 2012 colt by Heart's Cry named Cheval Grand, winner of the 2017 Japan Cup. The third major foal from Glorious Song's direct descendant was a full sister to Verxina and was given the name Vivlos. Vivlos captured the Shuka Sho at three and then travelled to Dubai, where she captured the important Dubai Turf Cup in 2017.

Glorious Song went back to producing colts and came up with a great one when she foaled a son of In The Wings in 1992. Singspiel became a top-level stakes winner in four countries, and placed second in two more countries. This world traveller won the Japan Cup, Canadian International, Dubai World Cup, Coronation Cup and Juddmonte International. He placed second in the Breeders' Cup Turf, Grand Prix de Paris and Eclipse Stakes. He was named the Eclipse Award champion turf horse in North America, and his Canadian International victory was welcomed by Canadian fans, due to his being a son of their beloved

Glorious Song. While slow to establish himself on the world scene as a sire, Singspiel has made an impact. Solow has been sensational, with wins in the Dubai Turf, Prix d'Ispahan, Queen Anne Stakes, Sussex Stakes and Queen Elizabeth II Stakes, all Group One wins. Dar Re Mi, Folk Opera, Hibaayeb and Lahudood are some of the fourteen Grade/Group One stakes winners sired by Singspiel at time of writing.

One more of Glorious Song's offspring to mention is her unraced daughter Ring Of Music. Sired by Sadler's Wells, this bay filly made up for her lack of racing credentials by producing Campanologist, by Kingmambo. Campanologist won three Group One races in Germany and one more in Italy. In Germany, he won the Preis von Europa, Rheinland-Pokal and Deutschland Preis, while in Italy he took the Gran Premio del Jockey Club. Campanologist also finished second to the outstanding So You Think in the Tattersalls Gold Cup.

Returning to Ballade, we come to her next foal, a colt born five years after his full sister Glorious Song. He was sold at Keeneland by Windfields for $325,000 to Hickory Tree Stable. Woody Stephens was the trainer of the well-bred colt, who was named Devil's Bag. A saucy sort, in keeping with his sire line, Devil's Bag was overwhelming as a two-year-old and became the undefeated Eclipse Award champion juvenile in 1983. He was also made the early favourite for the 1984 Kentucky Derby, and most horseplayers were in agreement that the race was his to lose if he made it to Churchill Downs. Comparisons to Secretariat were freely bandied about, and Stephens, a seasoned and astute trainer, said, "He is the best I have ever trained." However, after making his three-year-old debut with a seven-length win, Devil's Bag stunningly backed up in the Flamingo Stakes after taking the lead at the top of the homestretch. His fourth-place finish was seen as the most baffling loss by any horse in many years. Six weeks later, he returned to win the Forerunner Purse at Keeneland by a smashing fifteen lengths. Nine days after that, he made it to Churchill Downs for the Derby Trial with another winning effort. Unfortunately, his entry for the Derby was abandoned after a small fracture was discovered in Devil's Bag's right front knee.

Retired for a reported syndication of $36 million, Devil's Bag took up residence at Claiborne Farm and lived there until his passing in 2005. Forty stakes winners were sired by this son of Ballade, with the most prominent being Twilight Agenda, Japanese champion Taiki Shuttle and the consistent Devil His Due. The latter won five Grade One races, placing second in a further ten such events. He went on to sire Dubai World Cup winner Roses In May.

Ballade then kept company with Northern Dancer and his sons for her next five foals. A stunning dark bay colt by the great stallion, born in 1983, commanded a then record $8.25 million at the 1984 Keeneland yearling sale. He was named Imperial Falcon by his new owners, the Coolmore syndicate. The following year Ballade produced another Northern Dancer colt, Manshood. Imperial Falcon made three starts and won twice, but earned no black type. Manshood went unraced. Both were given a chance at stud, with Imperial Falcon beginning his career at Windfields Maryland, but both made little impact on the breed.

Vice Regent courted Ballade, and the result was a charming bay filly, sold at the CTHS sale at Woodbine for $1 million to agent Mike Ryan, working for Sheikh Hamdan Al Maktoum. The filly was named Thaidah by her new owner. After winning three of eleven races, one of which was the City of York Stakes, Thaidah eventually became the grandmother of Shakis, a much-travelled graded-stakes winner.

A full brother to Thaidah came the year after her birth. A chestnut who sold for $400,000 to agent Fred Seitz at Woodbine, he was given the name Nosferatu by his new owner, Jean-Louis

Beuzelin. The colt won five of fourteen races in France and Barbados, where he stayed to become a sire of great importance. Incitatus, Federico, Owen Taylor, Nicodemus, Gone Platinum and Swade are some of the big Barbadian winners sired by Nosferatu.

Halo came back into Ballade's life, even though he had now been shipped off to Stone Farm in Kentucky. The two produced two more foals together, a filly and a colt. The first was Angelic Song, who never raced. She later went to Ireland and was bred to Sadler's Wells to produce Hollywood Turf Club Stakes winner Sligo Bay. This horse has come back to his Canadian roots and stands at Adena Springs in Aurora, Ontario. Sligo Bay has been a good sire early in his career, with Canadian Horse of the Year Lexie Lou as his flag-bearer so far.

The Ballade–Halo partnership created one more gem in 1989 with the birth of a dark bay, almost black, colt who was part of the Windfields consignment at the Keeneland September yearling sale the following year. Although he was a full brother to two undisputed champions, he did not gain entry into the prime July sale because his front legs were crooked. This conformation deficiency resulted in his being purchased for $90,000 by Tartan Farms at the sale, a very low price considering his pedigree.

Tartan named the colt Saint Ballado and found that he could propel his crooked legs quite admirably. Saint Ballado had powerful hindquarters, good length to his body, and stood 16.2 hands at full growth. He won the Grade Two Arlington Classic and Grade Three Sheridan Stakes, which pales in comparison to the achievements of his full siblings who raced, but is noteworthy nonetheless. Saint Ballado was retired to stand at Ocala Stud in Florida and began a career that would propel him beyond his siblings.

From his first crop came Florida Derby winner Captain Bodgit. Following his win in the Wood Memorial, Captain Bodgit was made the favourite for the Kentucky Derby but finished a close second to Silver Charm. Captain Bodgit came third in another close finish in the Preakness Stakes, which would be his last race. The hard-closing son of Saint Ballado strained a tendon in his left front leg and was retired to stand at Margaux Farm in Kentucky.

On the heels of Captain Bodgit's success, Saint Ballado became very popular with breeders. He was moved to Taylor Made Farm in Kentucky in time for the next breeding season, and his stud fee was raised. Further success would follow.

Ashado was a brilliant filly who became a champion at three and four years old. She made a big noise as a two-year-old winning the Spinaway Stakes and finishing second in the Breeders' Cup Juvenile Fillies. At three, she won three Grade One events: the Kentucky Oaks, Coaching Club of America Oaks and Breeders' Cup Distaff. The next year, Ashado continued her assault on Grade One races, taking the Beldame, Go For Wand and Ogden Phipps Handicap for another Eclipse Award as the champion of her division.

Another big-ticket winner sired by Saint Ballado was his brilliant son Saint Liam. This colt was another who took his time to understand the racing game, but when he did, he was, in a word, breathtaking. Saint Liam did not win his first stakes race until he was a four-year-old. He served notice that he was improving toward the end of the season, when he finished second to Horse of the Year Ghostzapper in the 2004 Woodward Stakes. The next year, he reigned as the Eclipse Horse of the Year, winning the Donn Handicap in track record time and the Stephen Foster Handicap, finishing second in the Whitney and ending the year by winning the Woodward Stakes and the Breeders' Cup Classic. Saint Liam was retired following his powerful display in the Classic to stand at Lane's End Farm in Kentucky. Unfortunately, he would stand for only one season. In August 2006, he suffered an untreatable leg fracture in a paddock accident and had to be humanely euthanized.

Saint Liam covered a full book of mares in his one season of work and got a foal crop of 115 foals, 96 of whom made it to the races. One, in particular, became another Eclipse Award Horse of the Year to add to the family laurels. Havre de Grace came to hand in a fashion similar to her sire. Winning only one stakes race prior to her four-year-old season, Havre de Grace then captured the Apple Blossom Handicap and the Beldame Stakes, and beat the boys in the Woodward Stakes in her championship year.

The daughters of Saint Ballado are beginning to assert themselves as stakes producers, which, given the pedigree of their sire, is no surprise. Much-beloved Lady Eli became a grass-running demon, capturing the Breeders' Cup Juvenile Fillies Turf, Appalachian Stakes, Belmont Oaks and Flower Bowl Stakes, all of which are Grade One events. Her well-documented recovery from laminitis has given her a special place in the hearts of racing fans, to go along with her never-say-die racing performances.

Clearly, the family of Ballade is at the forefront of racing excellence. Her association with Halo has obviously been her big contribution, but the Northern Dancer line made her family prosper as well. Dr. de Gannes said, "Ballade was a wonderful mare to work with," and her contribution to Windfields' legacy is honoured at the Oshawa farm cemetery, in company with other all-time-great contributors.

The Temptress

In 1974, the Windfields team purchased a bay filly by Nijinsky II, out of La Sevillana by Court Harwell, for $130,000. The filly came from a sturdy and successful family. La Sevillana was bred in Argentina in 1966 and won the Gran Premio Selección (Argentine Oaks) and the Polla de Potrancas (1000 Guineas), as well as four other major stakes races in her native land. Her sire, Court Harwell, was a champion sire in England and Argentina and is a grandson of Prince Rose. Also in La Sevillana's pedigree are Hyperion, Precipitation and Son-In-Law, all highly revered names in class pedigrees.

The new Windfields filly was named The Temptress, and she made nine starts for her connections, winning once. In 1982, The Temptress produced a tall, rangy filly by Val de l'Orne. The filly came down with a bout of colic the night before her scheduled appearance at the CTHS yearling sale in the Woodbine pavilion and was subsequently retained by Windfields. She did not attract much attention.

Charles Taylor was now firmly in charge of Windfields. Charles's wife, Noreen, named the big lass La Lorgnette. Although she was a long-legged filly, a type that traditionally needs time to coordinate her physical build, La Lorgnette raced well as a two-year-old. She won the Grade Three Natalma Stakes, placed second to In My Cap in the Princess Elizabeth Stakes and placed third to eventual juvenile champion Bessarabian in the Ontario Debutante.

As a three-year-old, the filly who was described as "unattractive" became a champion in Canada. La Lorgnette won the Canadian Oaks, defeating In My Cap, and the Queen's Plate, defeating Imperial Choice. According to her trainer, Mac Benson, and owner, Charles Taylor, the big filly became "very attractive" following her Plate/Oaks double. La Lorgnette gave Charles the thrill his parents had had many times in the past, leading the Queen's Plate victor to the winner's circle. La Lorgnette was named the Sovereign Award champion three-year-old filly. Following the filly's success, Charles gave his wife a pair of diamond earrings as a gift from La Lorgnette.

La Lorgnette's first foal was a filly by Conquistador Cielo. Steve Stavro purchased the filly at the 1988 CTHS yearling sale for his Knob Hill Stable and named her Alexandrina. Alexandrina won the Yearling Sales Stakes the following year. Stavro added her to his broodmare colony, which he kept at the Windfields Oshawa farm, and bred her to Sky Classic, a champion son of Nijinsky II. The resulting colt was named Thornfield. Thornfield emulated his sire by winning the Canadian International and becoming a Sovereign Award Canadian Horse of the Year. Thornfield was a gelding, so he did not breed on.

La Lorgnette was part of the dispersal sale that Windfields had to undergo in 1996. She was not in foal at the time of the sale. Bloodstock agent Michael Brown purchased her for $350,000 on behalf of Hill 'n' Dale Farm, owned by Canadian breeder John Sikura. Three years after her purchase, La Lorgnette produced a bay colt sired by Woodman who Sikura sold as a yearling to Sue Magnier, daughter of Vincent O'Brien, who named the colt Hawk Wing. He was a consistent Group One performer and won four high-weight championships in England and Ireland. From twelve races, Hawk Wing won five and finished second five times, seven of which were Group One races. He won the Group One National Stakes in Ireland at two, the Eclipse Stakes at three in England and the Lockinge Stakes at four. In the latter race, Hawk Wing pulverized a quality field by ten widening lengths. His close second-place finishes in the Epsom Derby to High Chaparral and the 2000 Guineas to Rock of Gibraltar were also outstanding efforts.

Although not great in numbers, The Temptress's offspring made a significant contribution to the Windfields legacy.

Pacific Princess

E.P. Taylor was always looking for solid outcross families when he went shopping for prospective broodmares at the yearling sales. He was fully aware that his major stallions were along the Nearco sire line, including, of course, Nearctic and Northern Dancer. Taylor tended to blend a diverse array of bloodlines, looking for correct conformation along these parameters.

At the Saratoga yearling sale in 1974, Taylor found a well-proportioned bay daughter of Damascus and a dam who carried a very interesting pedigree. The filly was out of the Acropolis mare Fiji, who had won the Coronation Stakes during a four-for-five racing career. Acropolis was by Donatello, another great racer/sire bred by the incomparable Federico Tesio in Italy. The filly's second dam was by Mossborough. Taylor was not the only bidder liking what he saw in the filly, and he had to go to $75,000 to acquire her. She was given the name Pacific Princess.

Pacific Princess paid dividends on the track when she won the Grade One Delaware Oaks and the Grade Two Hempstead Handicap. Retired to the Windfields broodmare colony, Pacific Princess was bred three consecutive years to Northern Dancer. The third foal, a bay filly born in 1981, was one of many from an outstanding crop of memorable Northern Dancer foals that included the likes of Sadler's Wells, El Gran Senor, Secreto, Wild Applause and Northern Trick. While not adding to the stakes winner total on the track, the daughter of Pacific Princess, now named Pacificus, contributed mightily with her progeny.

Pacificus went to Japan and founded a legacy of her own. Her son Biwa Hayahide, by the grey stallion Sharood, who is a son of Caro, became the Japanese Horse of the Year in 1993, when he won the Kikuka Sho (Japanese St Leger) and placed second in three other Group One events, including the other two Triple Crown races. Biwa Hayahide followed up with another divisional championship the following year when he won the Tenno Sho (Spring) and the Takarazuka Kinen.

The year after Pacificus foaled Biwa Hayahide, she gave birth to another son, this one by Brian's Time. The colt was named Narita Brian, and he became a member of the Japanese Racing

Hall of Fame. Narita Brian won the juvenile championship in his two-year-old season after capturing the Asahi Hai Sansai Stakes. He followed up the next year with a Japanese Triple Crown sweep. Whereas his half-brother had placed in two of the races and won the other, Narita Brian won the Tokyo Yushun (Japanese Derby), the Satsuki Sho (2000 Guineas) and the Kikuka Sho. He also won the Arima Kinen (Japanese Grand Prix) against older horses. This outstanding season garnered Narita Brian a JRA Horse of the Year Award. So in the 1994 racing season, Pacificus was the dam of two JRA Award–winning champions.

The legacy of Pacific Princess was not done with Pacificus. Her daughter Catequil, by Storm Cat, was bred in Oshawa by Windfields and sent forth another branch of the family with Group One success in Japan. Catequil had a liaison with Brian's Time and delivered a daughter, named Phalaenopsis, in 1995. This dark bay filly took the Oka Sho (Japanese 1000 Guineas) and the Shuka Sho as a three-year-old. She later won the Group One Queen Elizabeth II Commemorative Cup at five.

Fifteen years after foaling Phalaenopsis, Catequill produced a colt by Deep Impact who would become a JRA Award winner. Kizuna won the 2013 Tokyo Yushun and three other group stakes races. He travelled to France for the Prix Niel, capturing that important prep for the Prix de l'Arc de Triomphe. In the big race itself, Kizuna finished a close fourth behind the great Treve.

Northern Sea

The year after he acquired Pacific Princess, E.P. Taylor was at it again. The venue this time was the Keeneland yearling sales, where he went to $260,000 for a daughter of Northern Dancer, out of Sea Saga by Sea-Bird, who had been bred in Virginia by Tom Evans. Sea Saga won three stakes races in her racing career, while her sire, Sea-Bird, is still considered one of the greatest runners ever seen in Europe. Taylor was purchasing the first foal produced by Sea Saga.

The expensive filly was given the name Northern Sea. She came out running in her two-year-old campaign, winning two stakes races and placing second in a pair of Grade One stakes. The following year, Northern Sea defeated Northernette in the Test Stakes and placed second in six other graded stakes. She was retired from the track for breeding.

Now, one might wonder why Windfields would buy a daughter of their stallion Northern Dancer when they were breeding many quality fillies from him themselves. The sales policy E.P. Taylor adhered to meant that every foal born on the farm was designated for sale as a yearling. He and Joe Thomas were always looking for quality fillies from other breeders to supplement the Windfields stock. Northern Sea is a prime example of Windfields going to great expense to maintain the high level of quality in the broodmare band.

Northern Sea was bred to Halo and produced a bay colt at the Maryland farm in 1983. The following year, the colt entered the sales ring at Keeneland, where he sold for $600,000 to the Irish branch of the British Bloodstock Agency, which was acting on behalf of Stavro Niarchos. The new owner named the colt Southern Halo.

The racing career of Southern Halo is a prime candidate to be recognized as one of the hardest hard-luck stories of all time. The son of Northern Sea never won a stakes race, but he placed second in two Grade One stakes as well as two other stakes events. He won five races and was in the money ten more times. In spite of his non-stakes-winning record, with his stellar pedigree he was given a chance to be a sire. This part of the Southern Halo story is no hard-luck case, for he has been sensational as a stallion.

Retired to stand at Haras la Quebrada in Argentina, Southern Halo made an immediate impact. He went on to lead the Argentinean sire list seven times, siring 173 stakes winners, of whom 57 are Grade/Group One winners, with 19 champions from 21 foal crops. He was repatriated to stand as a shuttle sire at Ashford Stud in Kentucky and also did a tour of duty in Japan.

Perhaps his most memorable offspring was the fleet filly Wally. This sprint star could be considered the Argentine version of Black Caviar. Wally won nineteen races, seven of which were Group Ones, and owned the top sprint race in the country, the Carrera de las Estrellas, three consecutive years. Wally is also the dam of Group One stakes winner Watch Her, by Mutakddim.

Additional notables to include under the Southern Halo body of work are Queen's Plate winner Edenwold, Fairy Magic, Spinster Stakes winner Miss Linda, undefeated Petit Club, Pryka and King's Bishop Stakes winner More Than Ready, to name just a few. More Than Ready has carried on the sire line as a shuttle sire between Kentucky and Australia with great success. He became one of the youngest sires in history to achieve 150 stakes winners and 1,000 race winners. He has sired graded stakes winners in twelve countries, including seven Grade/Group One winners.

Another of the quality Windfields sires standing at the Maryland farm who paid a visit to Northern Sea was Smarten. Their mating resulted in a filly whom John Mabee purchased from Windfields at the 1987 Keeneland July yearling sales for $100,000. Mabee named her Excellent Lady, and she won four of her thirteen races. She proved her purchase was a wise one when she produced two Grade One stakes winners. One of her nine daughters was Oak Leaf Stakes winner Notable Career. However, prior to this one, Excellent Lady produced a colt of excellent racing class.

We are talking here of General Challenge. This son of the Seattle Slew stallion General Meeting was a West Coast phenom.

General Challenge won the Santa Anita Derby and the Pacific Classic as a three-year-old. He proved himself the next season with a solid win in the Santa Anita Handicap, also known as "The Big Cap." The gelding had a pair of seconds in Grade One races and banked almost $3 million for his owners, Golden Eagle Farm.

Excellent Lady's daughter Jeweled Lady went unraced. However, this full sister to General Challenge became the dam of Jewel Of The Night, by Giant's Causeway. This one is the dam of Evening Jewel, by Northern Afleet. Evening Jewel won both the Ashland Stakes and Del Mar Oaks to add Grade One wins to the family. Evening Jewel's half-sister Maggie McGowan also paid a visit to Northern Afleet and became the dam of Denman's Call, winner of the Grade One Triple Bend Handicap.

One more foal from Northern Sea to mention in the Windfields legacy is her unraced grey daughter by Spectacular Bid named Northern Pageant. She was unsold and remained with Windfields. When Northern Pageant was bred to Oshawa stallion Silver Deputy, she produced a filly named Pageant Princess. Following a winning, but not black-type, racing career, this one went to Argentina. Pageant Princess met up with the fiery Luhuk, a grandson of Royal Statute, and produced Panacea in 2001. Moving forward, Panacea is the dam of Gran Premio de las Americas winner Panegirico. This horse carries five crosses of Northern Dancer within the first six generations of his pedigree.

Sweet Alliance

The acquisition of female Thoroughbreds from established stakes-producing families garnered another gem of a racer/ broodmare when Windfields purchased Sweet Alliance in 1975. E.P. Taylor had already bought her half-brother Dancing Champ and campaigned him successfully to multiple stakes wins, and he would soon stand that one at stud. The price for Sweet Alliance, two years after buying Dancing Champ, was $65,000—$5,000 more than was paid for the half-brother.

Sweet Alliance came from the well-established family of Legendra, her second dam, and was out of the Tom Fool mare Mrs. Peterkin. Windfields acquired several Thoroughbreds from this family, including half-siblings to Sweet Alliance, such as the aforementioned Dancing Champ (by Nijinsky II), Banderole (by Hoist The Flag), and Minstrelsy (by The Minstrel). Windfields also purchased Lady Roberta from this family, who was out of Farouche, another half-sister of Sweet Alliance. Clearly Taylor, Thomas and the rest of the Windfields decision makers had extreme confidence in the offspring of this family.

As well, Sweet Alliance had as her sire Sir Ivor, the 1968 Epsom Derby winner, who was establishing himself as a top-level sire, particularly with his fillies. Sweet Alliance would become one of the more celebrated members of this elite family as both a racer and broodmare.

Sweet Alliance raced fifteen times and was in the money on thirteen occasions, winning six of her starts. Among her notable wins were the Kentucky Oaks, La Troienne Stakes and the Pocahontas Stakes. She retired to stud with almost three times her purchase price in her bank account. And she takes pride of place in breeding as the dam of Shareef Dancer, the 1983 Irish Derby winner.

Shareef Dancer was sired by Northern Dancer, and Windfields sold him at the Keeneland July yearling sale for $3.3 million to Sheikh Maktoum Al Maktoum. He was the second-highest-priced yearling in the sale, only $200,000 behind the then world record price paid for another Windfields-bred son of Northern Dancer, later named Ballydoyle.

Shareef Dancer lived up to his lofty price with his Irish Derby victory, as he defeated a stellar field that included Epsom Derby winner Teenoso, who went on to win the King George VI and Queen Elizabeth Stakes and the Grand Prix de Saint-Cloud. Also among the defeated in the Irish Derby was Caerleon, who had won the French Derby and later took the Benson and Hedges Gold Cup. The fact that Shareef Dancer won what was, in essence, a showdown of Derby winners speaks volumes about his talent.

Retired with a record of three wins from five races, Shareef Dancer did not become one of the elite sires in the Northern Dancer line, but he has made a significant contribution nonetheless. His daughter Colorado Dancer, winner of a pair of group stakes races, became the dam of Dubai Millennium, by Seeking The Gold, one of the best horses to grace the turf in the past half century. He won nine of ten races, including the Dubai World Cup and the Prince of Wales Stakes, the Prix Jacques Le Marois and the Queen Elizabeth II Stakes. Sheikh Mohammed's favourite horse suffered his only loss in a baffling unplaced performance in the Epsom Derby.

Dubai Millennium was forced to retire from racing following a slight fracture of his right rear leg while in training. Sheikh Mohammed retired his champion immediately, and following successful surgery to repair the fracture, sent him to stand at Dalham Hall, the Newmarket stud the Sheikh owned that was the legendary stud farm once owned by Lord Derby. Unfortunately for racing fans, and for Sheikh Mohammed in particular, Dubai Millennium died from grass fever during his first season at stud. He sired fifty-six foals from his one and only crop, and he did get a great son to carry his name to future generations.

Dubawi has become one of the most heralded sires in the world today. He is out of E.P. Taylor Stakes winner Zomaradah, and he went on to win the Group One Irish National Stakes as a juvenile, then took the classic Irish 2000 Guineas and the Prix Jacques Le Marois at three. Dubawi is currently standing at

Dalham Hall and is establishing himself as an elite sire of classic winners and world Grade/Group One winners.

Again we see the fruits of Windfields breeding being enjoyed by a world leader in racing and breeding. If it were not for Sweet Alliance and her son Shareef Dancer, there would be no Dubai Millennium or Dubawi.

Country Romance

From the first crop of foals sired by Windfields Maryland farm sire Halo, a crop that included Glorious Song and Misty Gallore, came another stakes winner named Country Romance. Windfields sold the filly at the 1977 CTHS Alberta Division yearling sale at Spruce Meadows in Calgary, a venue Windfields patronized during the boom years of yearling sales in Canada. Knocked down by the auctioneer's hammer for $4,500, the chestnut filly was purchased by CFCW Radio, a frequent yearling purchaser at this venue.

Country Romance raced in Western Canada with stakes success. At two, she won the Stampede Futurity and Birdcatcher Handicap, beating the boys in both, as well as the Kindergarten Stakes. At three, she travelled between her home base in Alberta and her birth province of Ontario for various stakes races. Country Romance placed in several top-quality stakes races, including a third-place finish to Kamar in the Canadian Oaks. This placing in the classic Canadian event for three-year-old fillies is significant, due to the long-lasting effect runners from this race have had on world breeding excellence. Country Romance would add to this legacy.

The daughter of Halo was sold for breeding to Arthur Hancock III, the master of Stone Farm (where Halo would eventually move in 1984), and was bred to the quality stallions Hancock had access to. The third foal produced by Country Romance was a daughter of Kentucky Derby winner Gato Del Sol. A grey like her sire, Romanticat became the dam of Things Change, by Stalwart, who won the Grade One Spinaway Stakes at two.

The next foal from Country Romance was a son by Storm Cat, bred in partnership with W.T. Young, the owner of Overbrook Farm, where Storm Cat resided. The colt raced under the partnership and was named Harlan, but he was not cut from the same cloth as most Storm Cat offspring. Harlan took his time to reach his potential, unlike the majority of Storm Cat's get, who were widely known for their precocious two-year-old achievements. Harlan did not add stakes black type to his pedigree until his four-year-old season, when he finished second in the Forego Handicap. He garnered his first stakes victory the following year, in the Grade One Vosburgh Handicap, beating Cherokee Run, among others.

Harlan retired to stud at Stone Farm for what was, unfortunately, a short tenure. He died at the age of ten. Despite this brief career, Harlan made a significant impact in breeding. His son Menifee won the Grade One Blue Grass Stakes and the Haskell Invitational, defeating Cat Thief in both, as well as Forestry in the latter—both sons of Storm Cat. Menifee finished second to Charismatic in the Kentucky Derby and Preakness Stakes, and third to Lemon Drop Kid in the Travers Stakes.

Another notable son of Harlan was Harlan's Holiday. Winner of the Grade Three Iroquois Stake at two, Harlan's Holiday improved the next year to win the Grade One Florida Derby and Blue Grass Stakes. At four, he continued his Grade One–winning ways, capturing the Donn Handicap, and placed second in the Hollywood Gold Cup and Dubai World Cup. Harlan's Holiday was retired to stand at Airdrie Stud in Kentucky, shuttling to Haras La Mission in Argentina.

Harlan's Holiday was extensively bred on both sides of the equator. His most notable offspring was undoubtedly Shanghai

Bobby, winner of the 2012 Breeders' Cup Juvenile, as well as the Champagne Stakes that same year. Shanghai Bobby retired with $1,857,000 in the bank to Ashford Stud. He has stood five breeding seasons in Kentucky, and his first two crops have reached racing age. At the time of writing, there are five stakes winners in these two early crops. Shanghai Bobby was sold in November 2018 to Arrow Stud in Hokkaido, Japan, and will begin his Japanese stud career in 2019.

Another memorable son of Harlan's Holiday is Into Mischief, winner of the Grade One CashCall Futurity at two. Into Mischief came out of the breeding gate flying with his son Goldencents, a two-time winner of the Breeders' Cup Dirt Mile, who also has the Santa Anita Derby on his impressive resumé. In 2018, Into Mischief is one of the top five stallions in North America and commands a $100,000 stud fee. He has sired forty-three stakes winners, including three champions, with only six crops of racing age so far in his stud career.

A third son of Harlan's Holiday to mention here is Alfred G. Vanderbilt Handicap winner Majesticperfection. This son has also begun his stallion career on a high note as the sire of Lovely Maria, winner of the Kentucky Oaks and Ashland Stakes in 2015. Majesticperfection stands at Airdrie Stud and has replaced his sire, who passed away on November 1, 2013.

Harlan's Holiday was a productive stallion of quality and often stamped his get with a prominent blaze on the faces of his foals.

Betty's Secret

Windfields spent $230,000 in 1978 at Saratoga for a yearling chestnut daughter of Secretariat, out of Betty Loraine by Prince John. The filly, who Windfields named Betty's Secret, was from the productive family of Gay Hostess, dam of Majestic Prince. Sent to England for training, Betty's Secret did not race. She came back to Windfields Maryland and was bred to Northern Dancer, a union that produced a bay colt. Sold to Luigi Miglietti for $340,000 at Keeneland, the colt, now named Secreto, went to Ireland to be trained by David O'Brien, son of Vincent O'Brien.

In a race that could have been scripted for a Hollywood movie, Secreto won the 1984 Epsom Derby in a heart-pounding finish over fellow Northern Dancer son, El Gran Senor. The latter was trained by Vincent O'Brien. The son, David, beat his legendary father in the grandest race on the globe, and both had horses bred by Windfields Farm. This marked the third son of Northern Dancer to win this great classic and also the third to be bred by E.P. Taylor's Windfields Farm. The one-two finish is recognized as perhaps the greatest single race achievement by a breeder in racing history.

The year after Secreto was foaled, Betty's Secret produced a full sister who would eventually be named Catopetl. Like her mother, Catopetl went to the British Isles for training but did not make it to the races. Also like her mother, Catopetl returned to America and produced a Group One stakes winner. Bred by Robert Sangster's Swettenham Stud in Kentucky, the bay colt, named Close Conflict, by High Estate, won the Group One Gran Premio d'Italia.

Betty's Secret went back to England after Windfields sold her in a broodmare reduction sale to Shadwell Estate Company, owned by Sheikh Hamdan. The last foal she produced was a son of Sadler's Wells named Istabraq. Not having much success on the flats, Istabraq was sold to trainer John Durkan and switched to National Hunt racing over hurdles. Durkan was diagnosed with leukemia and had to relinquish training duties, but not ownership. Istabraq soon became a star in the division. Unfortunately, John Durkan passed away before seeing his horse achieve his greatest success.

Trained by Aidan O'Brien (no relation to Vincent), the now gelded Istabraq won twenty-three of twenty-nine races over fences, including thirteen Group One events and four wins at the Group Two level. He holds the Cheltenham course record over two miles, was named Champion Irish Hurdler four times and Smurfit Hurdle Champion three times, and is considered one of the greatest of all time in the discipline. Istabraq is the pride of Ireland.

Street Ballet

Street Ballet was purchased by Windfields at the 1978 Keeneland yearling sales from Claiborne Farm, acting as agent for breeder William T. Brady. The price for the daughter of Nijinsky II was $200,000. She was out of the Native Dancer mare Street Dancer, a full sister to Kentucky Oaks winner Native Street. Street Ballet won the La Centinela Stakes, though she made a habit of finishing second or third in most of her stakes race appearances. She had eight such finishes during her racing career.

In 1985, Street Dancer produced a daughter by Conquistador Cielo who would be named Arbela. This one was bought by Steve Stavro's Knob Hill Stable and went unraced. Her first foal was a dark bay, almost black, filly by Cool Victor who raced for Stavro, who named her Apelia. She was a multiple stakes winner and the Sovereign Award–winning Canadian champion sprinter of 1993. Apelia won twelve of her lifetime twenty-four starts.

Emulating her dam, Apelia's first foal became a Sovereign Award winner. Bred to Cure The Blues, Apelia produced in 1996 a bay filly who would be named Saoirse and would be the Canadian champion older mare of 2000.

Ponche, a grey son of Maryland farm stallion Two Punch, is the next foal of Street Ballet to look at here. Ponche won a couple of listed stakes races and placed in graded stakes. His claim to fame is as the damsire of Mucho Macho Man, a very popular recent Grade One stakes winner in America. Mucho Macho Man won the Breeders' Cup Classic as a five-year-old, the year after he finished second in the previous running of the Classic. He had built up his resumé with improving years as he aged. The son of Macho Uno also won the Grade One Awesome Again, a race named after his sire's half-brother.

The most notable foal produced by Street Ballet was her son by Smart Strike named Fleetstreet Dancer. This hard-knocking horse was very unlucky to not win a stakes race in America. He placed in several Grade One and Two races and faced the likes of Candy Ride, Pleasantly Perfect and Medaglia d'Oro. Fleetstreet Dancer went to Japan, however, and captured the Japan Dirt Cup to finally add a Group One win to his racing credentials.

Truly Bound

Windfields paid $300,000 at the 1979 Keeneland yearling sales to acquire what turned out to be a very fast filly by In Reality. From the potent family of champion Vagrancy, the bay filly was out of a granddaughter of that famous mare named Natashka, who was sired by the Princequillo stallion Dedicate. Named Truly Bound, the filly was a half-sister to Group One winner Gregorian and to notable producers Arkadina and Ivory Wand.

Truly Bound went to the post twelve times and won on nine of those occasions. The filly came out flying in her race debut, winning a 5.5-furlong maiden race by nine-and-a-half lengths in 1:06 ⅗, a new track record at Delaware. During her juvenile year, she won the Arlington-Washington Lassie Stakes and the Mermaid Stakes. As a three-year-old, Truly Bound captured the Ashland, Cotillion and two more stakes races. She finished a game second to Glorious Song in the Spinster Stakes when that famous mare was a five-year-old. Windfields retired Truly Bound to the breeding barn at the end of her three-year-old season.

She produced three stakes winners, but none of them won at the Grade/Group One level. However, her daughter Bound To Dance, by Northern Dancer, produced a filly in Japan by Brian's Time who did win at the highest level. Silk Prima Donna captured the Yushun Himba (Japanese Oaks) in 2000 to become a classic winner, adding to the family laurels. She also finished third in the Oka Sho (Japanese 1000 Guineas).

Another daughter of Truly Bound to add Grade/Group One–winning status to the family was Secret Truth, by Secretariat. Although she was unraced, Secret Truth, who had been sent to Australia, was bred to Giant's Causeway and produced Secret Cause, a modest winner of two races from fifteen starts. Given her strong pedigree, Secret Cause was visited by Casino Prince, a son of champion Flying Spur. This mating gave us Escado, the winner of the 2013 South Australian Derby and two more group races in the land down under.

Vadsa

The diversity of pedigrees in the Windfields broodmare colony was broad and contained some interesting names. E.P. Taylor was never afraid to acquire a well-conformed yearling with an outcross pedigree. In fact, he welcomed the opportunity to bring new bloodlines to his breeding program. In 1975, Taylor bought a yearling filly by Crème DeLa Crème, a stallion who was foreign to Windfields breeding, out of an Argentine mare named Lost Horizon. The latter was sired by Court Harwell, a stallion whose blood was seen occasionally in the Windfields pantheon. The third dam of the filly Taylor purchased was by Sideral, a legend in Argentina but pretty much unknown north of the equator. The filly cost $25,000 and was named Rainbow's Edge.

Rainbow's Edge won only once from seven races, with no black type. Her second foal after she was retired from racing was a bay filly by Halo who came into the world in 1979. The following year, she was sold for $50,000 at the Fasig-Tipton yearling sales. The filly went to France to race under the colours of Lagardère Elevage and was given the name Vadsa. She did not cover herself in glory, winning only once from twelve races. She had a penchant for finishing fourth, doing so six times. However, Vadsa became a foundation mare for two very successful breeding operations once her racing days had finished.

The second foal Vadsa produced was a daughter of Prix du Jockey Club winner Bikala and went by the name of Vadlava. While not a stakes winner, Vadlava did produce foals who were victorious in stakes events, including Breeders' Cup Mile winner Val Royal by Royal Academy. Vadlava's stakes-winning daughter Vadlamixa, sired by Linamix, has taken the family line to great heights.

Please bear with us as we continue the narrative of the Vadsa family, because the names are all similar and could become confusing.

Vadlamixa won a pair of listed stakes races in France. Her first foal when she retired from the track was a filly by Zafonic who would be christened Vadaza. This filly was in the money five times from seven races, winning once. She produced two Group One stakes–winning daughters, who both, by coincidence, won the Prix Saint-Alary in their respective three-year-old seasons. The first was Vadawina, sired by the Northern Dancer stallion Unfuwain, while the other was Vazira, sired by Epsom Derby and Prix de l'Arc de Triomphe winner Sea The Stars.

Vadlamixa produced her own Group One winner in 2001 when she gave birth to a bay son by Arc winner Trempolino. Trempolino was out of a mare sired by Viceregal, so the colt had Windfields breeding on both sides of his pedigree. Vadlamixa's colt was named Valixir by his owners, Godolphin Racing, who had purchased him as a yearling from Lagardère Elevage. Valixir raced against the best of his generation at three and four, winning the Prix d'Ispahan and the Queen Anne Stakes. He had third-place finishes in the Prix du Jockey Club, Prix Lupin and Prix Jacques Le Marois.

Another stakes winner produced by Vadlamixa, but not in a Group One race, was Prix Melisande winner Celebre Vadala. Her sire was Arc winner Peintre Celebre, a son of Nureyev. Bred to the great German sire Monsun, Celebre Vadala gave the world her Group One winner in the form of her son Vadamos. In 2016, Vadamos won the Group One Prix du Moulin and finished second in the Prix Jacques Le Marois. He has entered stud at Tally-Ho Stud in Ireland and will shuttle to Rich Hill Stud in Australia.

Vadlava had another daughter who moved the family fortunes along. This one is Vadlawysa, by the Danzig stallion Always Fair. Vadlawysa is the dam of stakes winner Valima, by Linamix. Valima, in turn, is the dam of Prix de Diane (French Oaks) winner Valyra. This lovely daughter of Azamour unfortunately died in a freak accident while exercising on the beautiful Deauville beach. Her loss was a tragic blow to the Aga Khan's outstanding breeding empire.

Returning to Vadsa, we find her daughter by Highest Honor, named, appropriately, Vadsa Honor. The first foal she produced was a classic winner. Bred to Linamix, the grey great-grandson of Lyphard who has blended well with other members of this wonderful family, the result was a grey named Vahorimix, who won the 2001 Poule d'Essai des Poulins (French 2000 Guineas) and the Group One Prix Jacques Le Marois.

Vadsa Honor is also the dam of Vadorga, by multiple Group One winner Grand Lodge. The filly was born in 2002 and was part of the 2003 dispersal of the Lagardère racing and breeding stock, which was purchased by the Aga Khan IV. For her new owner, Vadorga produced a filly named Voleuse de Coeurs, winner of the Irish St Leger over the boys. Her sire was Teofilo, a stallion by Galileo who has a strong Windfields connection close up in his pedigree. Voleuse de Coeurs, therefore, is chock full of Windfields breeding on both sides of her pedigree.

Looking closely at the broodmares Windfields bred or purchased, the number of world-class contributors is staggering. For one breeding operation to have so much influence on future bloodlines, with the magnitude of importance of Windfields-bred horses, is indeed a fantastic achievement. E.P. Taylor and his team of bloodstock advisors and farm employees had a great breadth of experience to draw on when making decisions for stallion choices and yearling purchases, and they created a powerful nucleus of equine families that breeders around the world could tap into with confidence.

The racing world owes a great deal of gratitude to these people for their foresight and dedication to the Windfields program. The proof, as they say, is in the results, and the results in this case are spectacular.

{ 12 }

GOODBYE, MARYLAND, AND THANKS

ORTHERN DANCER'S RETIREMENT from breeding in 1987 left a large void in the Windfields stallion ranks. Farm management had been planning for this inevitable day, and it was still standing his sons, The Minstrel in Maryland and the ageing Vice Regent in Oshawa, as well as emerging top sire Deputy Minister and a handful of first-rate stallions. However, some of the other expensive stallions were not producing with the expected level of success. Not every stallion is able to succeed at stud—in fact, the number may be as low as one in ten. And now the day had arrived when the big-ticket sire was no longer in service.

At the same time, the yearling sales market was in a freefall from the heady days of the early 1980s. Breeding had become a bigger gamble for established farms like Windfields, and the enormous expense of operating two large breeding centres was beginning to take a toll on the entire operation. Although Windfields offered boarding and breaking services, these were a break-even proposition at best. The operation made its capital from stallion services and yearling sales, and with these two major revenue streams in decline while costs were rising, the future looked bleak.

To add further pressure to Charles Taylor, who took over management of Windfields in 1980 after his father suffered a major stroke, Joe Thomas's death in 1984 left him without the man who had overseen the operation since the 1950s. There were still plenty of top-class horsemen from whom he could draw advice, but Charles had also learned that his own health was not 100 percent, which forced him to re-evaluate the wisdom of running such a large family-owned business in an increasingly risky industry.

Leading sire Halo was sold in late 1984 to Stone Farm in Kentucky, though there were no tears shed at his departure by the staff who had to handle him. The stallion was legendary as one of the most volatile stallions in history, and the common descriptor used by those who knew him was "mean." However, even though many were happy to see the back of Halo, the sale of a top stallion indicated the need to bring in new revenue.

The year after Halo's departure, El Gran Senor entered stud. Windfields hoped the well-bred champion son of Northern Dancer would be the successor to his esteemed father. Unfortunately, El Gran Senor displayed fertility problems during his first season. Word spread through the industry, and Windfields had to let him go to Coolmore's Ashford Stud in Kentucky. Windfields had bred the horse in partnership with the Coolmore Group and retained a percentage in the horse for El Gran Senor's stud career. Although he continued to have fertility issues, with the help of modern medical technology, which determined when a mare was at her peak time to conceive, he did become a successful sire of 14-percent stakes winners from limited foal crops.

The loss of these two stallions and the retirement of Northern Dancer, in conjunction with reduced stud fees for stallions who were purchased when prices were high, severely affected revenue for the Maryland farm. The breeding industry was in chaos and Windfields was feeling the effects. Although Windfields management had planned for the major changes they could see coming, the sudden dramatic downward trajectory in the breeding market and the failure of some very expensive stallions were crippling.

Charles decided that the entire Windfields operation needed to scale down in order to remain self-sufficient. It had always been a Canadian operation first, so, in August 1988, Charles made the hard choice to shut down the Maryland operation and concentrate entirely on the Oshawa farm. The decision to close the Chesapeake City farm came as a complete surprise to the staff and the Maryland breeding industry.

Windfields sold its shares in stallions Val de l'Orne, Master Willie, Robellino, Assert and Gregorian. All five were relocated to continue stud careers at other farms. Windfields also sold its interests in Smarten, Caveat and Two Punch, but these three were kept to stock the new Northview Stallion Station. Headed by Richard Golden and Allaire du Pont, this enterprise took over a portion of the Windfields commercial stallion property. Northview is still a successful operation today and now encompasses most of the former Windfields Stallion land.

T.V. Commercial was retired and, as part of the sales terms, kept Northern Dancer company in an adjoining paddock. Windfields retained its shares in The Minstrel, Deputy Minister and Imperial Falcon. The latter two were relocated to Brookdale Farm in Kentucky, while The Minstrel continued his stud career at Overbrook Farm, also in Kentucky. Ric Waldman oversaw Windfields' interests in these three stallions' stud careers.

The entire 2,600 acres of the farm was sold to a consortium that included the aforementioned Richard Golden and Allaire du Pont, but was then parcelled off to separate entities. Another investor involved was Thomas Bolden. Today there are several farms occupying the land that once was Windfields.

During the Maryland years, E.P. Taylor was credited with breeding his 300th stakes winner when Quitman, a full sister to Queen's Plate winner Regal Embrace, won the Grade Three Whimsical Stakes on April 27, 1986, at Woodbine Racetrack. The win marked the first time in the three-hundred-year history of the sport that one breeder had bred that many stakes winners. At the time, no other breeder had even gone over the two-hundred-stakes-winners mark.

Record after record was established or broken by Windfields during the Maryland years. One of the records was the fee paid for a breeding service to Northern Dancer. Beginning with the 1975 edition of the "Windfields' Classic Sirelines" stallion brochures, the fee for the great sire was listed as "private"—a not uncommon practice in the industry, which indicated the fee was significant. By the time of the yearling sales boom during the 1980s, there were reports that single breeding services by Northern Dancer were being sold privately for $1 million, without the guarantee of a live foal. The unprecedented figure has not been achieved by any stallion before or since.

Another record of sorts pertaining to Northern Dancer came in the form of an offer Windfields received from the breeding syndicate Horse France in 1981. The syndicate wanted to purchase Northern Dancer outright for the astronomical price of $40 million. Up to this time, no horse had been sold or even offered for such a sum. A few horses since have been sold for stud at this price, but they were newly emerging stallions, not a twenty-year-old horse who had his most productive years behind him.

For two decades, the Maryland farm was the place many of the emerging racing outfits visited to scout for their next superstar racehorse. When the end came, it left a large void. As well, many people were left without work, but Windfields management took care of them as best it could with generous severance payments and help in finding the staff employment in the industry. Some were hired by the owners of the North-view Stallion Station that took over the commercial breeding area of the farm. Others went to established farms in Maryland, Pennsylvania and Kentucky. Some of the veterans retired with a pension from Windfields. A glorious period in Maryland's Thoroughbred involvement had come to a close.

The King Is Gone

When the Maryland farm was sold, one of the stipulations was that Northern Dancer would live out his life in his home until his passing. Two years after the farm sale, on November 16, 1990, at 6:15 a.m., the great Northern Dancer died.

The news communiqué was brief but succinct: "Northern Dancer, the first Canadian-bred horse to win the Kentucky Derby, died today in Maryland." The news reverberated throughout the Thoroughbred world. Every publication in every racing jurisdiction—not just racing journals, but also the general press of the major racing countries—dedicated mountains of paper and rivers of ink to record their admiration of the greatest stallion of the twentieth century. Condolences and reminiscences came from every corner of the racing world. Northern Dancer had touched the lives of millions of people in a positive way, whether or not they had ever encountered him in the flesh.

Obituaries made front-page headlines in every newspaper in Canada. Both print and television media extensively covered the death of a legend. The country was in mourning.

Northern Dancer was the fourth major Windfields Farm family member to pass away within the decade, after E.P. and Winifred Taylor, and Joe Thomas. His death emphatically drove home the point that an incredible era in Canadian history was becoming just that, history.

Northern Dancer's body was returned to his home country in a special casket that barely fit into the trailer, clearing the walls with inches to spare on either side. The van had a minor breakdown en route but arrived at the US/Canada border at ten o'clock on the evening of November 18, 1990.

Charles Taylor and Bernard McCormack, the farm manager, waited at the border crossing near Kingston for the van to arrive and clear customs. The Department of Agriculture had already given Taylor clearance to bring Northern Dancer's intact body across the border. Such border crossings are strictly vetoed in most circumstances, but because Northern Dancer was seen as a national treasure, special measures were allowed to bring the country's greatest Thoroughbred back to his home for a proper burial.

At 1 a.m., the body of Northern Dancer arrived at his birthplace in Oshawa, where his final resting space had been prepared. The entire farm staff had assembled to greet and pay their respects to the horse. The press was not alerted to the arrival. Charles insisted that the only audience for the funeral would be the employees, the Windfields family. On that snowy cold night, Northern Dancer was laid to rest only a hundred feet from where it all began. There were many tears shed as a remarkable era in Canadian history officially ended.

There was a glitch, however, when they had trouble removing the casket from the van. With only inches to spare on either side, removal of a heavy casket containing a thousand-pound horse could not be done manually. The Brooklyn Concrete Company came to the rescue and, with a sense of the importance of the proceedings, extricated Northern Dancer and his coffin, graciously doing the job free of charge. The stone marking Northern Dancer's grave was commissioned from Brooklyn Concrete and is still there today.

The next morning, the press converged on Windfields en masse, including five television networks. They were there to record the funeral and were aghast to find that it had already taken place. Bernard McCormack described the media reaction as "surreal." He said, "The media had a hard time understanding that we chose to have a private burial for Northern Dancer. We did not expect such a massive response from the press, and with all the TV cameras looking to record the event. To many of us there, that experience was on the same level as when Armstrong walked on the moon."

A few details of Northern Dancer's final years were not widely known. While it was common knowledge that he lived out his life on the land he knew as home, roaming his paddock and enjoying a carefree lifestyle, Northern Dancer experienced a heart condition that required constant monitoring. His prepotency declined sharply before he was taken out of the breeding arena, but according to Ben Miller, "his desire never left him." He had his chum T.V. Commercial in an adjoining paddock, and he continued to be the king of the farm right up until the end.

Perhaps more widely known is the story of how Northern Dancer's breeding career in Oshawa began with a minor crisis when he was introduced to Flaming Page, one of his earliest mares. Flaming Page was very tall, and Northern Dancer's short stature created a problem. Windfields workers dug a pit in the sand-based floor of the huge breeding arena, where Flaming Page and other tall mares would stand while the Dancer did his duty. The pit was referred to, with tongue in cheek, as "Northern Dancer's Passion Pit." When he went to Maryland, a ramp was built so he could reach the tall girls. It was named "The Pitching Mound."

Trying to summarize the contributions made by Northern Dancer during his incredibly influential life can be exhausting. He was quite simply the greatest stallion of the twentieth century. From a commercial standpoint, Northern Dancer is still the undisputed king of the yearling sales. He became the first stallion to sire more than 100 stakes winners, finishing with a total 147.

These numbers have been surpassed by many stallions since, most of whom are sons, grandsons and great-grandsons of the Dancer. It must be said, though, that, since Northern Dancer's reign, the top stallions are bred to far more mares per breeding season than he was—in most cases, as many as five or six times more. Dancer sired a total of 636 foals in 23 crops. Many stallions today reach this number after only five crops.

However, in terms of percentages and average earnings per foal, today's stallions do not come close to his numbers. Northern Dancer had an average earnings index (AEI) just a shade under 6.00, with 23 percent of his foals becoming stakes winners. These numbers were not records even then, but only a handful topped these numbers, and no stallion before Northern Dancer topped more than one of these statistics. Today, the best stallions worldwide have an AEI of around 3.00, with around 13 percent stakes winners from total foals on average. One hundred of Northern Dancer's foals became champions on the track or in the breeding shed, or, in some cases, both. Those numbers are yet to be surpassed.

The success of Northern Dancer's sons in the biggest race in the world, the Derby Stakes at Epsom, solidified the little Canadian's position as the pre-eminent stallion of his generation. His sons Nijinsky II, Vice Regent, Lyphard, Northern Taste, Be My Guest, The Minstrel, Northern Guest, Nureyev, Danzig, Storm Bird, Dixieland Band, Sadler's Wells, El Gran Senor, Fairy King and Night Shift have all sired branches of the male line that have incredible influence today. Grandsons such as Danehill, Royal Academy, Deputy Minister, Storm Cat, Galileo, Alzao, Caerleon, Green Desert, War Front, El Prado, Montjeu, Dixie Union and many more have extended the line to every corner of the globe.

It is not just the numbers that are impressive but also the quality he has passed on and the long-lasting influence Northern

Dancer has had on the breed. Historically, the greatest stallions are acclaimed when they sire sons who continue the line at the top level. Most of the all-time greats had two or three or four sons who carried the torch. In Northern Dancer's case, fourteen or more have continued the line at the elite level of breeding. Those sons are branching off further multiple sons as leading stallions. It is in this realm that Northern Dancer has become the greatest of all in history.

And the beat goes on with the daughters of Northern Dancer, and on down through the generations from the distaff side. He is the broodmare sire of two hundred stakes winners, many of whom became champions. These Thoroughbreds have continued to excel at breeding. It is not uncommon these days to find a top-class stakes winner with a pedigree containing multiple crosses of Northern Dancer. In some cases, the Dancer's name may appear as many as five or six times within the first six generations.

Breed-defining stallions appear throughout the history of the turf. Eclipse, Herod, Matchem and Highflyer were the early stallion superstars. Later came Stockwell, West Australian, Lexington, Bend Or, St. Simon and Domino. The early part of the twentieth century saw Phalaris, Teddy, Swynford, Hyperion and Nearco. Northern Dancer, the only Canadian on the list, is considered to be on the same level as these, and many people consider him superior to all these immortal stallions of the racing world.

It is safe to say that there will never be another like Northern Dancer.

Winifred Duguid Taylor

Winnie Taylor passed away in 1982, eight years before her beloved Northern Dancer. The affable and kind Mrs. Taylor truly loved being around the horses. She came up with the names of many of the greats who raced under Windfields colours. Winnie was a charming, intelligent and witty woman who could always be counted on to provide warmth to anyone in her company. Her generosity was limitless.

During Northern Dancer's racing career, a twelve-year-old fan named Greg Robson, a student at the Ontario School for the Blind, told his mother that he would like to meet and touch Northern Dancer. Winnie Taylor learned of this and agreed to introduce Northern Dancer to him. She set up a meeting for the boy at the Woodbine barn where Dancer was stabled. Horatio Luro was nervous when the time came for this meeting because he had just had a frightening experience with the champion. The colt seemed to be in a rather nasty mood, and Luro barely got out of the stall in one piece after Northern Dancer threw a temper tantrum.

With a concerned Luro watching, Mrs. Taylor brought Greg over to Northern Dancer and took hold of the boy's hand to guide him to touch Northern Dancer on the nose. The colt stood calmly and allowed this friend of Mrs. Taylor to pet him. Dancer received some mints from Greg, his favourite treat, and was the epitome of good manners. He displayed his intelligence and his understanding of the situation, and gave the youngster an unforgettable thrill. Northern Dancer was always on his best behaviour around Winnie Taylor.

Another example of her kindness comes from the Second World War, when Winnie would drive an old station wagon full of the local children to school each day, then wait in the city to bring them home. Winnie could have driven back to her estate to wait there, then made a return trip to get the children, but she abided by the gas-rationing laws of the day.

While she was never a part of the decision-making process for the operation, Winnie did spend as much time as possible with her husband on the farms and at the races. The farm employees loved to have her around, and she took great pleasure in watching the foals develop and become racehorses. She always had time for everyone on the farm and in the training stables, no matter their standing in the pecking order, and her approachability endeared her to all. She spoke to people at their level, so they never felt uncomfortable in her presence.

Mrs. Taylor was one of the first to fall in love with Northern Dancer. "I always adored Northern Dancer," she said. "He certainly had character. I loved him dearly, but nobody else seemed to love him like I did because he was so small."

Peter Poole commented, "I think Mrs. Taylor always spoiled him a little bit, always giving him treats and things like that. He treated her the same way. Dancer would get all soft when Winnie was around. He could be tough unless she was there. Then he became just a big pussycat."

Winnie's sense of family pervaded Windfields. This facet of her personality was passed on to her son, Charles, and daughters, Louise and Judy, and they were much like their mother when associating with Windfields employees.

Mrs. Taylor was beloved by all who had the pleasure to meet her.

Joe Thomas

Late in 1984, long-time Windfields vice-president and operations manager Joe Thomas passed away. Joe had served Windfields since 1955 and was front and centre in the major decisions that shaped the fortunes of the vast racing and breeding enterprise—he was always seen sitting with E.P. and Charles at the major sales during his tenure. Ben Miller said the death of Joe Thomas was the beginning of the end of Windfields' glorious run at the top.

Thomas came to Windfields from the ranks of racing journalists. He wrote many articles about the Thoroughbred world for the *Lexington Herald* and the *Daily Racing Form*. Many of the articles found in Windfields publications, such as the yearling catalogues and stallion brochures, were penned by Joe. "There is such a fascination with racing. You can virtually create something and, within a relatively short time, find out if you are right or wrong," Thomas once said. His love of the sport was limitless.

Joe Thomas was an astute horseman, and he had a gift for identifying promising young horses and breeding pairings for future stock. His unofficial title among the Windfields community was "Vice President of Racing and Romance." Joe always got a good chuckle from that description of his job. He could anticipate what the market would require and made sure Windfields was ready for any shift in trends. Thomas did all of this with an engaging, affable personality—and with a plethora of fashionable, and novelty, hats that he always wore around the farm. He was loyal to all Windfields personnel, and he could make anyone laugh.

John Neville, manager of the yearling division, told the authors of this book, "Joe could get us laughing in stitches many times. He had a wealth of good jokes, but was so quick that he could make us laugh with off-the-cuff remarks. He was a great boss and wonderful to work with. He once wore a hat with a battery-powered fan on it for air conditioning. He broke us up with that one."

Thomas was the boss and had earned respect and admiration from everyone. Ben Miller told the authors of a time when Joe spotted him climbing up a ladder at his residence on the Maryland farm to adjust his TV antenna. "Benny!" Joe called, "Get down from there! You are no good to me with a broken leg and too valuable to be taking time off! I will get someone to adjust that contraption for you." Joe was not angry but was genuinely concerned for Ben's safety.

Joe Thomas had faith in his own ability to assess pedigrees and conformation, and in the talent the Windfields staff had in raising foals to become athletes. A case in point was when the organization purchased Snow Knight for eventual stud duty. The horse had won the Epsom Derby, but his pedigree was completely unfamiliar to North American breeders at the time. Windfields campaigned Snow Knight in North America to demonstrate his class as a runner, and he won some important races, including the Canadian International, Man O' War Stakes and Manhattan Handicap. The chestnut was named the Eclipse Award champion grass horse of 1975.

Thomas bought some well-selected young broodmares to breed to Snow Knight for his first two breeding seasons. He then sold some mares in foal to Snow Knight after the second-year mating at the Keeneland October breeding stock sales. The foals from the mares who were retained sold very well when offered as yearlings. The entire exercise reaped a considerable profit for Windfields and helped establish a stallion with an unknown pedigree as a viable outcross for North American mares.

During the final days of Joe's life, Windfields achieved the historic one-two finish at the 1984 Epsom Derby, with Secreto edging El Gran Senor at the finish post. Although the race was on the television at the Thomas home, Joe could not hear or see it. He heard the great cheer from other family members and asked, "How did we do?" Joe had been hoping El Gran Senor would win because of the impending deal to stand the horse at Windfields the following year.

His daughter Leslie said to him, "The Northern Dancers went one-two, Dad."

"Good," said Joe, always keeping the farm's well-being in his heart.

Joe's writing displayed his keen insights on the racing and breeding industry. He was a student of the sport's history and learned from both the failures of the past and the successes. He could see trends forming before most others could and acted accordingly to position Windfields to take advantage. He was as aware of the high end of the breeding world as he was of the lower and modestly budgeted sector, and he was able to provide quality for every breeder.

The racing and breeding world held Thomas in high regard. He worked tirelessly for the sport in general and for Windfields in particular, and he was constantly promoting racing through his writing and public speaking. Charles Taylor said of Joe in 1982, "There is no more creative and ingenious and resourceful person in the industry than Joe Thomas."

Edward Plunket Taylor

"E.P. Taylor was the most dynamic man I ever met." These are the words of George Blackwell, who, as a world-renowned blood-stock agent, would have known many dynamic personalities in his time dealing with people of wealth and power in the racing game. He had dealings with royalty, business moguls and successful Thoroughbred breeders and owners during his life, but he still considered Edward Plunket Taylor the most dynamic.

"Dynamic" may be the most fitting way to describe Taylor in one word. He could command a room with his presence. Though he was clearly a man who was used to, and at ease with, being in charge, he was also adept at making people feel comfortable and was as good a listener as he was a speaker. Taylor possessed a firm handshake, looked at people directly when in conversation, spoke with confidence and displayed a keen sense of humour. He was equally at ease with royalty or the common man. Only a dynamic soul could be as versatile, or as successful.

E.P. Taylor was a deep thinker. He was legendary to all who knew him well as someone who became almost oblivious to outside distraction while he sorted out in his mind whatever he was concerned about. A classic example of this is a story told to the authors by Norma MacDonald, Oshawa farm secretary, about E.P. and a cigarette lighter.

"Mr. Taylor was driving with Winnie and his executive secretary, Mary Binley, and was deep in thought. While in this state, he used the cigarette lighter off the dashboard to light a smoke. He then absent-mindedly tossed the lighter out the window, forgetting it wasn't a regular match. He did this on several occasions."

Another time, Taylor went into Barn Six smoking a pipe and was immediately ushered out by foaling manager Ernie Priestman. Taylor apologized to his employee and left. His employees appreciated the fact that the boss knew he was in the wrong and actually applauded Ernie for his dedication to the safety of the horses.

Late in 1980, this dynamic and well-respected man suffered a debilitating stroke from which he never fully recovered. Since E.P. was the most visible personality of every entourage he was part of, his absence was noted. Gone were the days when he attended the races and yearling sales, held court with the rich and famous, went for a ride on his personal mount, Mudpuddle, or patrolled his farms, talking to horsemen and horsewomen about his stock. With his son, Charles, assuming the helm of the ship, E.P. Taylor spent most of his time at his Lyford Cay residence in New Providence, Bahamas.

In many ways, E.P. Taylor was misunderstood by those who did not know him. He was portrayed by many acerbic press people as an uncaring, greedy business mogul, seeking only power and money. In truth, Edward Plunket Taylor was as far removed from that type of human being as it was possible to be. While he did make a fortune in business, he was always aware of humanitarian concerns and spent his money developing industries to employ average citizens so they could earn and prosper. He funded affordable housing and products for everyday consumption. His Thoroughbred enterprise was his personal passion, and he was able to shape the Canadian industry so it would spread the wealth and encourage the involvement of like-minded enthusiasts, which helped to grow the sport.

E.P. Taylor was also a great philanthropist and donated money and land to the Canadian Centre for Advanced Film Studies, then under the watch of acclaimed filmmaker Norman Jewison. The centre, now known as the Canadian Film Centre, was up and running in 1988 as an advanced film school on Windfields Estate in Toronto. He funded the building of the O'Keefe Centre for the Performing Arts and the Art Gallery of Ontario. Many scholarships in the arts and writing are handed out each year to young university entrants in the Taylor family name.

He treated his employees with respect and dignity. E.P. Taylor set up a pension fund for his Windfields staff that is still supporting many long-serving employees today. In the farming industry, a pension plan is almost unheard of, but Taylor wanted to be sure his farm employees would not be left high and dry when their careers had ended, or if the farm closed.

Those who did know E.P. Taylor remember him as a kind, jovial man with a high degree of intelligence and sincerity. His hearty laugh and firm handshake made all who knew him feel at ease. Taylor knew his standing in the community, but he never lorded it over anyone or flaunted his position. He was fiercely loyal to his friends and colleagues, including his Windfields staff, who in turn were fiercely loyal to him. He did not demand loyalty; he earned it.

As a horseman, E.P. Taylor received the Eclipse Award for outstanding breeder twice and is a member in the Pillars of the Turf category at the National Museum of Racing's Hall of Fame at Saratoga. He is a charter member of the Canadian Racing Hall of Fame and led the breeders' lists in both Canada and the United States longer than any other. Nineteen times, he led the list of winners bred in North America, and nine times was the leading money-winning breeder.

In 1978, two years before his stroke, this great icon of racing had his final grand moment in the winner's circle. Regal

Embrace had just won the Queen's Plate, and the Taylors, E.P. and Winnie, led the colt they had bred in to receive the traditional pouch of fifty sovereigns. It was heartwarming to see the saviour of Canadian racing have another opportunity to be photographed as the winning breeder/owner of the race he coveted so much. Legendary Canadian jockey Sandy Hawley guided Regal Embrace to victory and said, "That win was probably my biggest thrill at Woodbine. It was a real privilege to win the Plate for him."

With all the success E.P. Taylor had in his life, his success as a breeder and patron of the turf was most important to him. His daughter Judith put it eloquently: "I think if my father were here today, he would say that he would like to be remembered as the breeder and owner of Northern Dancer more than anything else he accomplished." Of all the many achievements in his remarkable life, E.P. Taylor drew the greatest pleasure from Northern Dancer and Windfields Farm.

On May 14, 1989, he passed away at his residence in New Providence, Bahamas. Edward Plunket Taylor was a remarkable man and one of the most influential Canadians in history. He was dynamic.

Seen It All

During Windfields Farm's time in Chesapeake City, there were many changes in the breeding industry. For example, when Northern Dancer was syndicated and relocated to the farm in 1968, the syndication agreement consisted of three sheets of paper and a series of handshakes between the syndicate members. By the time The Minstrel and Deputy Minister were syndicated, more than fifty sheets of paper and teams of lawyers were involved.

The stunning rise in importance of the elite yearling sales, led of course by Windfields' offerings, coincided with the Maryland tenure. While, in the end, this may have been the predominant reason for the farm's closure when the bottom fell out of the market, the fact that the Maryland farm held sway during the boom years is significant.

Windfields Maryland was visited by royalty, such as Queen Elizabeth II, Sheikh Mohammed, the Aga Khan IV and Prince Khalid bin Abdullah. The elite breeders of racing came to the farm to inspect the yearlings—both the top Canadian-bred and the Maryland-bred, prepped by Don Coulter and his crack team—who would sell for record prices in the sales arena. Some of the best mares on the planet came to the court of Windfields stallions standing in Maryland.

The farm itself was the envy of the Thoroughbred world, a huge, stunningly beautiful property with sprawling paddocks, a world-class training facility, and handsome, well-maintained homes, all in a serene setting. The prestige of the inhabitants rivalled that of the great farms of Kentucky, Newmarket and other renowned Thoroughbred breeding areas.

For twenty years, the Maryland farm was the home of the greatest stallion of the twentieth century and the birthplace of elite champions worldwide. It brought a proud state back into the spotlight of Thoroughbred racing.

{ 13 }

DISPERSAL AND WINDING DOWN

WITH THE CLOSING of the Maryland farm, the Oshawa farm carried on at a reasonably profitable pace during the early 1990s. However, the steady decline in the yearling market was still felt by breeders hoping to make a profit at the sales. The market seemed to be stabilizing, but the recovery was slow and cautious.

Windfields continued to provide quality stallions and services to breeders and began consigning yearlings as agents for clients beginning in 1986. This service helped to keep the farm in the black on the ledger sheet, and it also gave small breeding outfits a means to have their yearlings come to the sales in top condition by taking advantage of Windfields' decades of experience.

In a situation reminiscent of the demise of the Willowdale farm north of Toronto thirty years earlier, though, the city of Oshawa was expanding north and began to build up around the once serene land of the farm. Durham College, located on Conlin Road, at the southern border of the farm, was planning to expand and become a full-fledged university, and it required additional land.

Starting in 1996, the farm was broken up in distinct parcels of land. The southeast corner, bounded by Simcoe Street and Conlin Road, which contained half of the yearling area, is now the site of upscale housing. Many of the streets in this area are named in honour of famous horses (including Northern Dancer Drive, Iribelle Avenue and Victoria Park Street). What was the entire southern portion of the main farm, stretching along Conlin from Simcoe, is today occupied by Durham College/ University of Ontario Institute of Technology. There are several indoor and outdoor athletic facilities on this land, including the Campus Ice Centre and Vasco Field, as well as the Campus Field-house and the registrar's office.

The Taylor family sold the land at reasonable current rates and also donated additional land to the university. Piece by piece, the 1,240 acres of Windfields Farm dwindled. E.P Taylor had envisioned back in the 1970s that the city would eventually engulf the farm, as it now has. By the 1990s, the family knew an extension of Highway 407 was to be built just north of the farm border along the north side of Winchester Road. This portion of the highway is complete today.

Even during this time of change and urban growth, Windfields continued to provide the racing industry with quality stallions and services. But the end was coming.

Vice Regent

In another echo of the past, the Oshawa farm's long-time stalwart stallion was ageing. Vice Regent's era was coming to a close, casting shadows on the farm's future, just as the end of the tenure of his sire, Northern Dancer, as top stallion at Windfields Maryland spelled trouble for that farm.

Stud manager Alan Kerr was devoted to "Reege" and worked tirelessly to keep him fit for duty and comfortable when he was troubled by sore feet. Vice Regent loved his work, and the farm staff loved Vice Regent. The big, beautiful, chestnut son of Northern Dancer dominated the Canadian sire list and was a constant in the top ten sire rankings of North America throughout his career. He was also an important source of revenue for the Oshawa farm.

On Sunday, June 18, 1995, Vice Regent passed away at the age of twenty-eight. At the time of his death, he had been credited with siring ninety stakes winners and had earned eleven sire titles. He gained two more sire titles posthumously, and when his get finished running, Vice Regent was credited as the sire of 105 stakes winners. On the day he died, his son Glenbarra won the Sir Ivor Stakes at Laurel.

Vice Regent was given a chance to become a stallion due to the stellar race record of his full brother Viceregal and his distinguished pedigree. He flourished in the role and outdid his brother. Vice Regent sired such champions as Bessarabian, Ruling Angel, Regal Intention, Regal Classic, Deputy Minister and Christy's Mount. Also among his get are important stakes winners Trumpet's Blare, Native Regent, Twice The Vice, Excellent Tipper, Hangin On A Star, Regal Embrace and Bounding Away. He remained a breeding stallion right to the end.

Bernard McCormack described Vice Regent as the perfect stallion. "Vice Regent was a much beloved member of the

Windfields family in Canada. He came in, did his job and left without hesitation. He got more than 70 percent of his mares in foal from first covers. His record speaks for itself. He was to Canada what Northern Dancer was to the rest of the world at large. His death is a blow to all of us, and especially to Alan Kerr. Alan was his sole groom for twenty-four years, and they were as close as a horse and human could possibly be."

Looking for an heir to carry on the line, Windfields stood sons of Vice Regent. Deputy Minister was emerging as a hot sire, and although he began at Windfields Maryland, and Windfields had retained shares in the stallion, "The Deputy" now stood in Kentucky at Brookdale Farm. Deputy Minister has carried the line to further generations, with Queen's Plate and Breeders' Cup Classic winner Awesome Again leading the charge. Awesome Again is still the leading money-earning Canadian-bred on the track and has become a world-class stallion, standing at Frank Stronach's Adena Springs farm in Kentucky.

This line is flourishing through Awesome Again's champion son Ghostzapper, who won the Breeders' Cup Classic, as his sire did, and is now the sire of two Queen's Plate winners and several champions. Shaman Ghost and the filly Holy Helena, who also won the Woodbine Oaks, are the Plate winners and are front and centre among Ghostzapper's progeny. Ghostzapper is currently siring above the 10-percent mark for stakes winners. And in 2019, Shaman Ghost is joining his sire and grandsire at Adena Springs in Kentucky for stud duty.

Champion racer Regal Classic seemed to be a viable heir to the throne of his sire, Vice Regent, and had some early success, leading the sire list in Canada twice. He and his former stable-mate Regal Intention (both were bred and raced by Sam-Son Farm), as well as Brave Regent, Regal Embrace and Iskandar Elakbar, were given a chance to carry the Vice Regent line to future generations as Windfields stallions.

Silver Deputy, a handsome stakes-winning son from Deputy Minister's first foal crop, raced under Windfields colours and began a successful career at stud in Oshawa. This grandson of Vice Regent sired the final Windfields-bred winner of the Queen's Plate, Archer's Bay, who took the 139th edition in 1998. However, Silver Deputy's reputation as an emerging top stallion led to his being transferred to Brookdale Farm so he would have access to higher-quality mares and fulfill his potential.

Quality Above All Else

The high quality of the stallions who stood in Oshawa never wavered throughout the farm's existence. Stallions such as French-bred Dom Alaric and Nearctic's son Briartic, a grey son of Graustark named Ruritania, as well as the perennial leading Canadian sire Vice Regent and the groundbreaking patriarch Victoria Park, all sired champions from their Oshawa home. Windfields stood a broad array of bloodlines for breeders to tap into. While the most expensive stallions (Vice Regent being the exception) stood at the Maryland farm due to its location, the stallions standing at the Oshawa farm generally catered to the home market.

Ruritania, for example, had an abbreviated career at stud, but he sired some classy offspring who achieved success both on the track and in the breeding shed. Ruritania won the Manhattan Handicap, finished second in the Belmont and Man O' War Stakes, and kept company with many of the top horses of his generation. He was an honest and game competitor during his racing career. Bred by the famous Greentree Stud in Kentucky, Ruritania stood at the Oshawa Farm and was received enthusiastically by Canadian breeders. He had a nice enough disposition and did what was asked of him when needed, but his outstanding characteristic was a voracious appetite. His favourite occupation was eating. Bruce Clazie told the authors that when Ruritania was turned out, the grey stallion would run to the far corner of his paddock and then eat his way back. Keeping the horse's weight down was a constant battle, and he died of colic at the age of nine.

Dom Alaric was a dark bay son of Sassafras, the conqueror of Nijinsky in the Arc. Dom Alaric raced under Windfields colours after he was purchased by a syndicate led by E.P. Taylor that included Harry Hindmarsh, Jean-Louis Lévesque, Pierre Levesque and Robert Anderson. Coming from a strong German female family, the attractive Dom Alaric also represented the top French breeding on his sire's side. His hallmark was stamina, and he passed on this quality to his get. Dom Alaric was also a very friendly and social horse—so much so that he became a favourite of all who met him.

Briartic did not begin his stallion career at Windfields. He came to the farm after one year at Dr. M.F. Bennett's farm in Sarnia, Ontario, and he made a significant contribution, giving local breeders a son of Nearctic to breed to. Briartic is the sire of Queen's Plate winners Steady Growth and Son Of Briartic, as well as multiple stakes winners Impetuous Gal and Solartic.

Ascot Knight came to Windfields fresh off his successful Group Two–winning race career in Europe. He was a solid stallion and led the Canadian list twice during his tenure.

Northern Answer, Viceregal, Lord Durham, Regal Classic, Silver Deputy, Whiskey Wisdom, Cool Victor and D'Wildcat all sired champions from their home base in Oshawa, continuing the traditions set by Chop Chop, Victoria Park, Menetrier, Bull Page, New Providence, Nearctic, Canadian Champ, Northern Dancer and, of course, the horse named Windfields.

Windfields forged long-time alliances with such breeders as George Strawbridge, Allaire du Pont, Jean-Louis Lévesque, Robert Anderson, Harry Hindmarsh and Bill Beasley. Later, enthusiastic newcomers to the sport like Steve Stavro and

Eugene Melnyk kept their mares at Windfields and bred to the stallions who stood there. There were many stakes winners and champions bred and raised in Oshawa and Maryland for Windfields clients by the expert staff employed in these locations.

Only two horses bred in Canada have won the Kentucky Derby. We know about Northern Dancer, but the other was the 1983 winner, Sunny's Halo. David "Pud" Foster had a few mares and boarded them at the Oshawa farm. He hit the jackpot when he bred his mare Mostly Sunny to Halo while the latter was standing in Maryland in 1979. The following spring, Mostly Sunny produced a chestnut colt on the Oshawa farm. Foster raced the colt and realized a rare accomplishment when Sunny's Halo captured the "Run for the Roses."

Jean-Louis Lévesque bred many of his great champions, such as La Prevoyante, Fanfreluche and L'Enjoleur, on the Oshawa farm as a Windfields client. Steve Stavro and Eugene Melnyk bred many of their champions on this hallowed land. Ernie Samuel's great foundation mare No Class was bred at Windfields by Jack Hood. No Class's family includes the great Dance Smartly, Smart Strike, Sky Classic, Classy 'n Smart and Dance-thruthedawn, Hall of Fame members all. No Class herself is also in the Hall of Fame.

When we say "hallowed ground," we mean the term in every way possible.

Charles P.B. Taylor

Everyone who met or worked with Charles Taylor has the same remembrance of him. The most eloquent statement we heard came from Warren Gibson: "Charles was highly intelligent, had an absolutely infectious laugh and loved a good story. He was smart enough to surround himself with people of integrity and honesty who were each specialists in various areas. Charles would listen to opinions, sometimes dissenting from one another, and invariably would choose the correct path. That in itself tells what a wonderful listener, communicator and simply 'nice person' Charles was. Honest, sincere, great integrity, passionate about his interests and compassionate about the people he worked and lived with. I miss him dearly."

Charles Taylor was diagnosed with cancer in 1986. When his father died three years later, Charles, as one of the trustees of his father's estate, took on the responsibility for the entire Taylor family. Even as racing declined in popularity and in public awareness, as the city of Oshawa engulfed the farm's land, and as he dealt with his own health concerns, Charles continued to work tirelessly to find solutions to keep Windfields operating.

Known as an astute, highly intelligent man, Charles Taylor had carved out a successful career as a journalist and author of contemporary social commentary. He took over the management of Windfields when his father was incapacitated by a stroke. He also became a leader in the promotion of racing and in instituting programs to improve the sport. He did all of this with a warm and social personality, and a sense of humour, that endeared him to all who met him.

As Charles's health declined, it became difficult for him to give the operation his full attention. His wife, Noreen, and sister Judith Mappin tried to help in whatever way they could, but they were not horsepeople and were basically learning as they went. The children of Charles and his sisters had established careers of their own and did not have much interest in the horse-raising business.

The apple did not fall far from the Taylor tree in Charles's case, however, as he had absorbed his father's passion for racing. He made enormous contributions, not only to Windfields but also as a chairman and chief steward of the Jockey Club of Canada. He served as a director of the Canadian Thoroughbred Horse Society, *Blood-Horse* magazine, the Keeneland Association and the Grayson-Jockey Club Research Foundation. His portfolio in racing also included trusteeships with the Thoroughbred Owners and Breeders Association, the National Museum of Racing and the E.P. Taylor Equine Research Fund. Like his father, Charles P.B. Taylor was also a member of the Jockey Club of America.

Charles was a keen supporter of the now enormously successful Breeders' Cup program. In fact, he was a founding director and vice-president of the Breeders' Cup during its launch and early years. One of the ways in which the money for the huge purses was to be raised was from stallion nominations to the program. These nominations would qualify the get of the stallion for the Breeders' Cup races. The cost of nomination was the price of one breeding season to the stallion in the year of conception. Taylor was the head of Windfields, whose stallions were generally expensive—and, in the case of Northern Dancer, out of reach to most breeders. Still, Charles nominated every Windfields stallion to the program, including the great Northern Dancer, and thus set an example to encourage the other elite breeding farms to nominate their top stallions. The fledgling Breeders' Cup gained momentum from this bold initiative and has not looked back since.

To honour Charles's devotion to racing, and to the Breeders' Cup in particular, the 1996 edition of the championship card was held at Woodbine, the only time the Breeders' Cup championship has been held outside the United States. It was a testament to the status of Woodbine, but even more to the devoted enthusiasm Charles Taylor displayed for the Breeders' Cup program. Without his support and encouragement, the Breeders' Cup would never have come to Woodbine.

Unfortunately, Charles could not attend the the Breeders' Cup races at Woodbine. He was waiting in his hospital room with Noreen for another surgery. They watched the races on television.

Charles's declining health led to a refocusing of Windfields' involvement in breeding and racing. By 1996, it was apparent that the demands of running the operation were too much for him. Just as in 1988, when he made the hard decision to scale down the operation, he faced the same choice eight years later with the beloved Oshawa farm. In May, it was announced that Windfields would be selling the broodmare colony and all of their weanlings at Keeneland in a public dispersal.

Heartbreaking

Imagine going through your house, finding cherished mementos such as furniture, clothing, paintings or other artifacts that tell the story of your family, and realizing that, due to circumstances beyond your control, you will be forced to sell all these items. That was the prevailing feeling for everyone in the Windfields family in 1996 when it was announced that Windfields would be dispersing its entire breeding stock.

Windfields had been selling broodmares for a few years before the announcement in order to increase the available stall space for client mares to be boarded in Oshawa while maintaining a reasonable population of their own horses for the yearling sales. In 1996, there were still forty-one Windfields mares on the farm, many descending from equine families that had seen multiple generations in the broodmare colony, along with twenty-nine weanlings born during the year. The entire lot was to be sold.

Many of the mares had been bred to farm stallions and were in foal come sales time in early November. All of the foals born earlier in the year had been weaned from their mothers and were prepped for sale. Bernard McCormack, John Neville, Simon Cassidy, Dave Whitford, Bobby Pearson and Bruce Clazie worked with the junior staff to get each one of the seventy horses ready and shipped to Lexington. They did so professionally and efficiently, but with heavy hearts. This activity was in addition to preparing the yearlings on the farm who were to be sold in September at the CTHS Woodbine sales.

The Keeneland November Breeding Stock Sale was chosen for the dispersal because of Windfields' confidence in, and long-standing association with, the leading sales venue for breeding stock in North America. The week-long event was, and still is, a marathon, where the cream of the broodmares up for sale is auctioned. Many well-bred weanlings are also sold during these sales. This top-of-the-market venue brought out many of the top breeders looking to add quality to their bloodstock.

Among the mares going to the sale were champion La Lorgnette and stakes winners Health Farm, Adorned, Legarto, Linda North, Play All Day, Street Ballet and Starita. Windfields had raced these mares and then kept them for breeding. Of the forty-one mares to be sold, thirteen had already produced stakes winners, while eight did not yet have foals old enough to race. There were seven mares not in foal when consigned to the dispersal. The younger mares came from known stakes-producing families, so they were attractive to buyers. Fourteen mares were descendants of long-term Windfields-developed families. Each mare had a pedigree of substantial merit, in keeping with Windfields' tradition of quality. The weanlings were obviously also well pedigreed.

Twenty-four foals who were in utero at the sale became winners for their new owners. Four became stakes winners, including Group One Dubai Golden Shaheen winner Caller One, out of Baltic Sea. Caller One captured nine stakes races in total and also finished third in the 2001 Breeders' Cup Sprint.

There would be many more stakes winners after the new owners bred these mares. Perhaps the most notable was Hawk Wing, by Woodman, out of La Lorgnette. Hawk Wing was bred by Canadian breeder Hill 'n' Dale Farm at their Kentucky location. Sold to Sue Magnier, daughter of Vincent O'Brien, Hawk Wing was trained by Aidan O'Brien (no relation) and won the National Stallion Stakes and Futurity Stakes at two. He went on to win the Eclipse Stakes and finished second to High Chaparral in the Derby Stakes, to Rock of Gibraltar in the 2000 Guineas and to Grandera in the Irish Champion Stakes at three. Hawk Wing won the Lockinge Stakes the following year before an injury necessitated his retirement from racing.

Another notable dispersal mare was Angelic Song. A full sister to champions Glorious Song and Devil's Bag, as well as leading sire Saint Ballado, Angelic Song was sold to Richard O'Gorman Bloodstock for $240,000 and went to Ireland. After she foaled her stakes-winning daughter Lady Ballade, whom Angelic Song was carrying during the dispersal, her first breeding was to Sadler's Wells. The following year, Angelic Song produced Grade One stakes winner Sligo Bay.

The quality offered in the Windfields dispersal was apparent. Among the twenty-seven weanlings sold (two were removed from the sale due to injury) were Grade One stakes winner Norquestor and Coronation Futurity winner Zaha. There were thirteen winners in all from the weanlings sold, and three of the fillies sold as weanlings went on to become producers of stakes winners.

Horse auctions are one of the last bastions of a bygone era of salesmanship. They still feature the fast-talking, high-energy voice of the auctioneer in a patter only associated with such events. During the 1996 November sales, though, the hustle and bustle were halted when the auctioneers, noting the significance of the day, paid tribute to Windfields Farm for its success in improving the breed and for its dedicated commitment to the big Kentucky sales over the years. The entire audience erupted for a five-minute standing ovation in honour of Windfields.

Watching the remaining horses sell at Keeneland on November 10, 1996, was the saddest day for the entire Windfields family.

Charles Taylor had organized a party at the Marriott Hotel in Lexington following the sale for all the staff in attendance. As John Neville put it so eloquently, "Although it was intended to be a thank-you from Charles in appreciation for our hard work, the party was more like a wake. After seeing all of those wonderful mares go, none of us felt jovial about what had transpired. There weren't many smiles in the room."

Charles could not attend the event due to his advanced illness. He watched the proceedings from home on closed-circuit television set up by the Keeneland Association.

The highest-priced mares in the sale were Play All Day, in foal to Gone West, for $450,000; Secret Truth, in foal to Pleasant Tap, for $370,000; and Adorned, who was barren, for $350,000. Minister's Song, a daughter of The Minstrel, out of Ballade, also sold for $350,000. The highest-priced weanling was Play All Day's chestnut son by Kingmambo, later named Zaha.

The sale netted $7,238,000, and Charles Taylor gave every member of Windfields a pro-rated bonus. He then had Warren Gibson set aside the rest of the money, after taxes and fees were paid, to go toward keeping the farm running. Charles passed away in July 1997.

After the dispersal, the Oshawa farm became a stallion station/sales consignor/boarding farm for various clients. There was not enough revenue in these aspects of the industry to maintain such a large property. To make ends meet, several stallions were sold, as well as parcels of land. Although the farm carried on, the feeling was different. Staff still had pride in their craft and high standards to maintain, and for eleven years, loyal employees stayed on to keep Windfields going. But with the emphasis now on customer mares and foals, and with only a handful of Windfields stock purchased to keep the name going (none of it from the exalted equine families that had carried the torch in the past), the farm's status was diminished. Windfields would no longer be a yearly leader in Thoroughbred breeding.

All Good Things...

The Oshawa farm was a community unto itself. There were two dormitories for single employees, one for men and one for women, with a full-time cook preparing meals. Staff with families lived on the farm in various houses and cottages. Victoria Park Hall was the scene for company darts tournaments and card nights. Children of farm residents were raised on the farm, and many of them later became members of the staff or went on to careers in the racing and breeding industry. Employees working the yearling sales were encouraged to bring their families along, with all expenses paid by Windfields.

There were many galas and Christmas parties held in the large arena for employees and their children. One of the most memorable was the retirement party for Peter Poole in 1986. Everyone we spoke to has said it was one of the most enjoyable non-equine-related events on the farm. Everyone looked out for everyone else in the extended Windfields family, and all had the common goal and passion to make Windfields Farm a continued success in the face of a struggling industry.

But after decades, this community life was coming to an end as construction of a planned general community within the boundaries of a city began, and an educational community was expanded. Over the next few years, piece by piece, the famed Windfields Farm land was sold off. Most of the land has been, or is being, at time of writing, redeveloped into housing subdivisions. The streets in these newer subdivisions are also named in honour of some of the famous horses that once roamed the lush paddocks where these homes now sit.

The hub of the farm—the central core where the stallion barn, arena, Barns Two and Six, veterinarian's residence and main house for the resident farm manger were located—are all the property of the University of Ontario Institute of Technology. The university also controls the area that includes the main cemetery, where Northern Dancer, Vice Regent, Windfields and others have their final resting place. The Trillium Cemetery, where additional horses are buried, such as Lady Angela, Chop Chop and more, is in a wooded area just to the west of this main farm core.

Noreen Taylor and Judy Mappin ran the farm together following the death of Charles Taylor. They could see the writing on the wall, with highways, universities and urban housing surrounding the area. They also were privy to the development plans of the various levels of government. Though the end was clearly in sight, the two women should be credited for keeping the standards of equine care, and the farm in general, up to the high level everyone was accustomed to, right until Windfields' final days. Bernard McCormack summed up their tenure perfectly. "Noreen and Judy did a wonderful job. They guided the old lady out gracefully."

Contrary to popular belief, the addition of a casino at Woodbine, which increased purse money at the track, did not produce an infusion of revenue for breeding farms, not even a trickle down. The consumer appetite for racing was in decline during Windfields' last years, and the Canadian dollar was trading on world markets at a much lower value than in previous decades. The stars did not align to sustain the farm.

The last stakes winner bred under the E.P. Taylor/Windfields banner was a colt of 2005 named Pool Play. His sire was Silver Deputy and his dam was Zuri Ridge, by Metropolitan Handicap winner Cox's Ridge. Windfields had purchased Zuri Ridge a few years after the major dispersal of 1996 and bred her to their best stallion at that time. Pool Play raced until he was an eight-year-old and now stands at T.C. Westmeath Stud in Ontario. Pool Play was the 359th stakes winner bred by Windfields Farm.

In 2008, the farm laid off thirty-five employees. Some had enough time on the books to retire and collect their pension from Windfields, while many had to seek new employment. Windfields helped each laid-off employee find a new place to work and gave them generous severance packages. The retirees are living comfortably and with dignity thanks to the pension plan E.P. Taylor set up. The employees of Windfields were always treated as family.

General manager Simon Cassidy stated, "We're all proud of our time here. It is a sad loss for everyone who has lived and worked here. There is a lot to walk away from and to be proud of."

Judy Mappin said, "Though everybody in the family loved the horses and watching them run, nobody was prepared to run the show after my brother passed away. My father knew that someday the city would grow around the farm. Now that is happening. It makes no sense to have a farm in the middle of a city."

Windfields operated as a private farm in 2009 and then closed its doors for good. On March 6, 2010, the Taylor family held a public auction to liquidate the remaining assets of farm equipment and horse memorabilia. The rest of the farm land had already been sold to developers, and the end of a glorious chapter in Canadian history was upon us.

A handful of mares gave birth on the farm after it was closed, and in October 2009, the remaining mares and weanlings were sold at auction. As this is written, the last horse bred by Windfields still in training is a grey daughter of D'Wildcat, out of Stellar Babe by With Approval. Her name is Strawberry Scarlet and she is the last of her kind.

Top Simon Cassidy (L) and John Neville (R) at Keeneland yearling sales. PHOTO CREDIT: JOHN NEVILLE

Bottom Oshawa stallion Vice Regent in his paddock. PHOTO CREDIT: COLIN NOLTE

Above Dr. Rolph de Gannes DVM. PHOTO CREDIT: MARIANNE DE GANNES-ORTEPI

Facing Top Young foals on the Oshawa farm, circa 1983. PHOTO CREDIT: COLIN NOLTE

Facing Bottom Grave marker for Northern Dancer. His final resting place. PHOTO CREDIT: COLIN NOLTE

NORTHERN DANCER
NEARCTIC — NATALMA
BY NATIVE DANCER
1961   1990

Top Corner of Lady Angela Ave. and South Ocean Drive, located on the land where Windfields Farm Oshawa once stood. PHOTO CREDIT: COLIN NOLTE

Bottom Northern Dancer Public School named in honour of the great Windfields Thoroughbred. The school is within a subdivision built on land once occupied by Windfields Farm. PHOTO CREDIT: COLIN NOLTE

{ 14 }

THE SUPPORTING CAST
(CANADA)

Dr. Howard Aldous

THE FIRST THING people notice about Dr. Howard Aldous is his height. At six foot six, he looked more like a basketball player than the resident veterinarian at the Oshawa farm. People also remember his dedication to his profession and his genial personality. Aldous headed the vet program for fifteen years, through many innovations in horse care, feeding and yearling development. He ran a well-organized foal and mare care program that became the envy of the breeding world. And he oversaw the birth and early development of many legendary Windfields-bred horses.

He was there when Northern Dancer was born in Barn Six. Dr. Aldous also helped to bring into the world the likes of Victoria Park, Flaming Page, Nijinsky, Canebora, Viceregal, Vice Regent, New Providence, Titled Hero, Cool Reception and client foals such as Fanfreluche, La Prevoyante and No Class. All these Thoroughbreds, and many more, went on to become famous.

Dr. Aldous had an uncanny way of dealing with challenges and facing them head-on. In the early 1970s, he decided he wanted a new challenge and went back to his native British Columbia to change his medical practice from horses to humans. He did not leave until a suitable replacement was found, staying until Dr. Rolph de Gannes took over the Windfields veterinary mantle in 1973.

Bert Alexandra

One of the more colourful trainers in Canadian history was British-born A.E. "Bert" Alexandra. He began his Thoroughbred career as a jockey and won his first race at the age of thirteen in Mexico. When his battle to "make weight" (maintain the low weight needed to be a jockey) became too much to overcome, Bert set his sights on training horses in order to stay in the sport he loved. His father had been a trainer in England, and Bert made a very good living in his new profession. He became particularly adept at claiming improving horses and winning with them at higher levels.

Known as "the Claiming King" on the backstretches of the Ontario circuit, Bert was planning to retire when he was contacted by E.P. Taylor in 1936. He stayed with Taylor exclusively for fourteen years before he decided to hang up his bandages and retire for good. While training for the Taylors, Alexandra had his most successful years in the business. He won his first and only King's Plate in 1949, training the Taylor's homebred

Epic to victory. He also conditioned the horse Windfields and had considerable success with Bull Page and the unfortunate Mona Bell. Of course, he was the one who bought the foundation mare Nandi for Taylor as a $1,500 claim.

Alexandra was essentially a blue-collar soul. His forte was the claiming ranks, and the haltering and selling of horses was what he did best. He was not much for stakes races. Although he was never averse to trying an improving horse in such a race, these events were not his priority. In contrast, E.P. Taylor was looking to breed and race for stakes glory.

Bert and the Taylors parted ways, with Bert moving into retirement with a bigger bank account than the one he had before he met E.P. Taylor. The split was amicable. Bert was an integral part of the early successes achieved by first the Cosgrave Stable and then the Windfields Racing Division. E.P. Taylor hired Pete McCann for the next phase in Windfields history, and Bert Alexandra rode off into the sunset.

Mac Benson

Trainer Macdonald "Mac" Benson came to Windfields in Maryland in 1976 and was one of several conditioners employed by the organization. Joe Thomas wanted to consolidate the Canadian racing division under one trainer and offered the job to Mac. The native of Wilmington, Delaware, accepted the position and took over the entire Canadian-based racing stable in 1978. His timing could not have been better. One of the young horses he inherited was Regal Embrace. Mac trained the colt, nicknamed "Moose," to win the Queen's Plate that year. It was a significant victory because Moose was the last Queen's Plate winner E.P. Taylor led into the winner's circle.

Mac trained many of the top horses who raced under the farm's turquoise and gold silks in its later years. The list is impressive: Dom Alaric, Brave Regent, Bridle Path, Bold Agent, La Lorgnette, Silver Deputy, Bounding Away, Choral Group and Health Farm are just a few of his highlight horses for Windfields. When Windfields cut back on its racing involvement in the 1990s, Mac took on clients such as George Strawbridge and Robert Costigan. Multiple Canadian champions Arravale, Deputy Jane West, Santa Amelia and Inish Glora were all conditioned by this exceptional horseman.

Mac learned the ropes as an assistant trainer for Morris Dixon in California. Along the way, the affable and easygoing Benson made many friends, including Kelso's trainer Carl Hanford and long-time trainer Charlie Peoples. Both of these distinguished horsemen recommended Mac to Joe Thomas. Mac trained for a couple of years on the East Coast circuit for Windfields, based out of the Chesapeake City facility, before his promotion to become the trainer for the entire operation in Canada. He was inducted into the Canadian Racing Hall of Fame in 2002.

The move to Canada was rewarding for Mac in other ways. He met rider Barbara Przedrzymirska in 1979, and the two have been a couple ever since. Barbara has been involved in breaking yearlings and exercise riding for many years, and worked closely with Mac with both Windfields horses and the horses Mac trained after Windfields closed its racing stable. Today, Barbara works with young horses for Chiefswood Stable in Canada. Mac retired in 2010. Between them, Barbara and Mac have been involved with many of the top Canadian Thoroughbreds since the late 1970s.

Andre Blaettler

Born in Switzerland, Andre Blaettler came to Windfields in 1951 after moving to Canada from his home country the year before. Andre left Windfields in 1955 to manage Conklin Farm near Brantford, Ontario, but he returned to Windfields to head the yearling division three years later. He remained in this post until his retirement in 1988. His tenure at Windfields was a vital ingredient for the yearling sales successes the farm achieved—an aspect of racing that goes unnoticed by the average racing fan.

Andre was present during the rise of Windfields as a leading breeder and consignor. As the manager of the yearling division, Blaettler handled some of the greatest Thoroughbreds to come out of Windfields. He and his staff prepped Northern Dancer, Nijinsky, Flaming Page, Victoria Park and many more. Andre would also squire the elite bloodstock agents, and often their high-profile clients, around the yearling paddocks to show off the next batch of young horses due to show up at the sales.

As a key member of the Windfields sales team, Andre would have as many as thirty-six employees, part- or full-time, under his management for the prepping and sale of yearlings. This was a vital source of revenue for the organization, perhaps the most important source, and Andre was relied on for twenty-eight years to organize and display the yearlings in top condition so they would fetch as high a price as possible. That the yearlings always came to the sales in top condition was a testament to his craft and skills as a horseman.

Simon Cassidy

Irishman Simon Cassidy was born into a family of horsepeople. He cut his teeth in the industry in his homeland and found a job as a groom at the famed Coolmore Stud in County Tipperary. He spent five years with the organization, doing a stint at Coolmore's Kentucky farm, Ashford Stud. Among the legendary Coolmore horses he rubbed were Windfields-bred champions Storm Bird and El Gran Senor. He left Coolmore to take a position at Cotswold Stud in Gloucestershire, England, and worked in sales.

Simon spent eighteen months with Cotswold and then immigrated to Canada to work for Windfields Farm. He went into the yearling division in 1990 under John Neville. Simon's training in sales became a valuable asset to John and the Windfields consignments. Although he had spent the least amount of time in the management team at the time of the 1996 dispersal, the sense of the historical significance did not escape him. And he agonized over the sale, just as longer-term staff did.

He left Windfields briefly but returned to become the head director of management in 2002, succeeding Bernard McCormack. Simon stayed with Windfields until the doors closed for good in 2009. "The Taylor family are a class act," he said. "There was no pretense. They are honest, caring exceptional people." Simon also said that the pension plan E.P. Taylor set up was unprecedented. "You just don't see it anywhere else in the industry. An amazing gesture by a class family."

Today, Simon Cassidy runs the Chiefswood Stable Farm in Schomberg, Ontario. Chiefswood has become one of the new leaders on the Ontario racing circuit and breeds its own horses as well as buying quality stock at the yearling sales. Simon is an easygoing, approachable man who always has a smile. At the yearling sales, he can be seen casting his experienced eye over the stock, on the lookout for quality runners to compete for Chiefswood. And on the farm, he employs the standards he learned at Windfields.

Bert Chatten

Maintenance of a large-scale farm such as Windfields is crucial to the success of the operation. Not only do the buildings, residences and service roads need constant care, but the paddocks, fields and general appearance also have to be kept in good order. This vital aspect of farm life was managed for forty years by Bert

Chatten, who became the longest-serving member of the Windfields family.

Bert and his team took care of the daily chores beyond the care of horses. His official title was "operations manager," and that is exactly what he did. Bert oversaw the farm as it grew from the original 450 acres purchased in 1950, preparing the new pastures and fields for horse care. He managed all the pastures for both the horses and the rotating herds of cattle, organized the hay fields at harvest time and monitored the stored hay in the steel silos.

His team took care of repairs to all buildings, from barns to houses, as well as the fences around the paddocks. They also made sure the attractive gardens adorning the main core of the farm, the graves that marked the final resting places of cherished Windfields horses, and the signage at the main gate and all other access gates around the sprawling property were kept in impeccable order. Visitors could see the detail and craftsmanship in his work, which made for a pleasant experience while at the farm.

Bert's favourite expression was "We'll get 'er done." He always did.

Bruce Clazie

Bruce began his tenure at Windfields in 1977, after learning the ropes at Paul Johnson's farm in Ontario. In his early years, Bruce served as a veterinary assistant to Dr. de Gannes and Dr. Patrick Hearn, and as a yearling trainer in the fall breaking program when John Neville ran this division. As office administrator and assistant to Bernard McCormack, he was a key contributor to Windfields' entry into the computer age of record storage.

He worked in various divisions on the Oshawa farm, including another stint with John Neville in the yearling division.

Bruce became the breeding shed foreman and then worked with Bobby Pearson and Dave Whitford in the broodmare division. His "jack of all trades" ability was an important aspect to his Windfields career. Following Dave's departure to head Sam-Son Farm, Bruce became the full-time broodmare manager. He stayed in this role until the farm closed and was one of the last people to leave the grounds. He had put in enough time to collect the full pension from Windfields. Bruce has reflected on his time with Windfields and says, "I wouldn't change a thing." He is another of the Windfields family who is held in high regard by those who worked with him.

Gil Darlington

The first manager of what was then known as the National Stud on the Oshawa site, Gil Darlington had previously owned and operated Trafalgar Farm near Milton, Ontario. He stood Chop Chop there on a lease arrangement and had many clients in the Ontario breeding industry. One of his clients was the emerging dynamo E.P. Taylor, with whom he had developed a strong relationship. When Taylor purchased the former Parkwood Stables in Oshawa from Colonel R.S. McLaughlin, the new owner came to Darlington and asked if he would like to run the farm.

Gil accepted Taylor's proposal and sold his own farm to become the manager of both the Oshawa property and the existing Willowdale farm. He worked from the Oshawa base, but since the original Windfields was only thirty miles west, he could commute between the two. Darlington quickly developed both farms into well-run, efficient operations. He was an astute horseman and had exceptional leadership skills.

Darlington was also front and centre for the new, improved feed program developed at Windfields during his time as the farm manager. George Blackwell is on record as stating that one of the biggest causes of the differences between the health of Windfields-raised horses and others of similar breeding was the feed program Gil Darlington initiated at the Oshawa farm.

One of his first hires was a young Peter Poole, and Gil soon decided that the young man should become his protege. Gil could recognize talent when he saw it. He also was adept at stallion promotion, having learned from his days with his own farm, and was instrumental in the promotion of Windfields, Menetrier, Bull Page and, later, the early careers of Victoria Park, Nearctic and Northern Dancer.

Gil Darlington passed away suddenly in 1968. His death was a shock to the Windfields family, but because of his great organizational skill, he left the farm in good hands and on the path to further success. It was sad that he did not live to see the farm attain the global prominence that would come just a few years following his death. Gil had helped establish Windfields and was a huge reason the farm had the foundation to achieve all that would come.

Dr. Rolph de Gannes

Born in Trinidad, Dr. Rolph de Gannes came to Canada on a scholarship to the Ontario Veterinary Collage at Guelph University. There, he met his wife, Sheila, whom he refers to as "the Saint, because she puts up with me." Rolph graduated in 1961, the year after he and Sheila married, and then returned to Trinidad. Rolph practised veterinary medicine, trained and owned Thoroughbreds, and became a father of four children while in Trinidad.

Owen Slocumb, professor emeritus in parasitology at the University of Guelph, was consulting with E.P. Taylor when the Windfields owner mentioned that his resident vet, Dr. Aldous, was planning to leave and pursue human medicine. Slocumb recommended Rolph for the position. De Gannes received a letter from E.P. Taylor in October 1972, asking if he would be interested in relocating to Canada with his family. Rolph and Sheila were very interested. On December 26, 1972, they received a phone call from Peter Poole, who asked how quickly they could move to Canada. Dr. de Gannes and his family arrived in Oshawa on February 25, 1973, and he became the resident vet for the Windfields Oshawa farm. They had a fifth child, Marianne, after they came to Canada.

Dr. de Gannes was one of the first vets to use palpation on a large scale as a way to examine the reproductive tract of a mare for ovulation and to determine the optimum time for breeding. While not a new procedure, Rolph perfected the method so it became standard industry practice. Monitors and sophisticated high-tech sensors are used today, but de Gannes's palpation methods offered increased pregnancy rates before such equipment was invented. He estimates he would perform this exam as many as 8,500 times in a single breeding year.

Like the horses he worked with, Dr. de Gannes was born to be who he is. His father was a vet, his uncle was a vet and his son Greg later became a vet and trainer. Rolph has worked with many of the elite Canadian Thoroughbreds in history, including Northern Dancer, Storm Bird, The Minstrel, Victoria Park (one of his personal favourites), Vice Regent and Viceregal, to name a few at Windfields. After his tenure at the famous farm ended and he opened his public practice in Schomberg, Ontario, he worked with Triple Crown winners With Approval, Izvestia and Wando for clients D.G. Wilmot and Gustav Schickedanz.

Dr. de Gannes was honoured by the Canadian Thoroughbred Horse Society with the Mint Julep Award in 1985 for outstanding service to the Thoroughbred industry. He also was honoured with the Paul Harris Award for his work and service with the Rotary Club. Rolph retired from veterinary practice in 2017 and was again awarded by the CTHS with the lifetime Award of Merit. He received three standing ovations on the night he accepted the award. He deserves no less.

Harry Green

A good stallion manager plays a vital role in any breeding operation where stallions are standing. The manager is responsible for the health and well-being of what is perhaps the most integral part of such a farm. The millions of dollars invested in top-quality stallions place intense focus on these horses. They are viewed and visited by breeders throughout the year. Keeping a stallion fit, happy and handsome is no easy task, especially considering many are headstrong, dominant types. You need to have patience, strong arms and legs, and a high degree of confident horsemanship to handle stallions every day. Harry Green was one such individual.

Harry arrived at Windfields in the late 1940s. He worked on the Willowdale farm before he went to the new National Stud in Oshawa, working in a variety of farm capacities before he became the head stud groom/stallion manager. Harry had a rare ability to be able to understand a horse's needs and moods. This is a gift and cannot be taught. In Chapter Six, we told how Harry was the man dispatched to collect a pregnant Lady Angela and her foal from the ship in Montreal and bring them to Oshawa. This piece of Windfields lore highlights how good a horseman Harry Green was.

Of course, as we now know, the foal Lady Angela was carrying turned out to be Nearctic. Harry and Nearctic became best friends when the great stallion stood in Oshawa. Harry also took care of Northern Dancer while that one stood in Oshawa, as well as Windfields, Bull Page, Victoria Park, Chop Chop, the very volatile Menetrier and all the other top-class stallions residing on the Oshawa farm until his retirement in the 1970s. Every one of his stallions was groomed to perfection and turned out in impeccable order.

At first glance, Harry Green's impact on Windfields success is another of those invisible contributions. But, on consideration, one can see how Harry's innate horse sense was invaluable when it came to establishing Windfields as the place in Canada for top-quality stallions. "Unsung hero" would be the best way to summarize Harry Green's involvement.

Dr. Patrick Hearn

Dr. Patrick Hearn, a member of the Royal College of Veterinary Surgeons, obtained his doctorate of veterinary medicine from Guelph University, Dr. de Gannes's alma mater. Patrick did his internship with Stan Cosgrove in Kildare, Ireland, and then signed on with Windfields in June 1986.

His arrival at Windfields coincided with veterinary medicine's move into the modern age of ultrasound and computer technology. Patrick oversaw Windfields' deployment of the new medical practices at Oshawa, and he worked with Bruce Clazie and Bobby Pearson when he did his rounds on the farm. He also oversaw, with Al Kerr, the constant battle with laminitis waged by valued stallion Vice Regent.

Patrick left Windfields in 2003 to start his own practice in the Hockley Valley with his wife, Elizabeth, also a veterinary doctor. He did not leave the Windfields realm entirely, however, as he assisted Dr. Andre Macko during foaling season for two more years. Today, Patrick and Elizabeth are still at Hockley Valley and have a thriving veterinary practice catering to all kinds of equines.

Alan Kerr

Windfields was blessed with wonderful, talented horsemen. Just as Harry Green was vital during the early years of the farm, Alan Kerr was important for the final decades. Peter Poole appointed him head stud groom/stallion manager after Harry's retirement, and Alan shared all the same qualities as his predecessor, from whom he learned the intricacies of working with stallions. He also had that elusive ability to understand a horse's needs and moods.

Alan was a quiet man who clearly enjoyed his work. He knew his horses inside and out. His respect for the animals was clearly evident, and in return the animals respected him. The stallions always looked fresh and well cared for, which was important for a farm selling its services to prospective clients.

The highlight of Alan's career was being the sole groom to star stallion Vice Regent. Al and "Reege" were best pals, and the human half of this relationship spent many hours dealing with the equine half's specific needs to alleviate constant foot problems. Vice Regent suffered daily from laminitis, but his best buddy kept him as comfortable as possible. Vice Regent never laboured during his work in the breeding shed, a testament to Al's great horsemanship.

Alan stayed with Windfields until it closed its doors for public service in 2008. He retired with a full pension set up by E.P. Taylor, and he is remembered fondly by all who worked with him as a genuinely kind person and expert horseman.

Norma MacDonald

Nova Scotia–born Norma MacDonald arrived in Oshawa in 1965 with secretarial training. She was looking for a job in the area and worked for many firms before learning that the National Stud farm was seeking secretarial help. She met farm manager

Gil Darlington and was hired, beginning May 2, 1966. Norma stayed for twenty-eight years, through the grand years of the farm's breeding achievements, having to retire early when she was stricken with multiple sclerosis.

During her career in the office above Barn Two, Norma came in contact with many of the high rollers in racing and breeding. She describes her time at Windfields as "the best days of my life." Norma is a colourful, upbeat lady full of witty colloquialisms. "As long as I am on the right side of the grass, I'm fine," she says to anyone listening.

Norma's job was a vital part of the operation. She was the one to register the incoming and outgoing mares during the hectic breeding season, and she filed all breeding reports, foaling registrations, health reports, and service and foaling certificates. Norma did this for every horse on the farm, whether Windfields owned or client owned. It was an extensive and never-ending job that took great organizational skill and an exceptional work ethic. Norma not only did all of this efficiently, but she also maintained her folksy charm and genial personality each and every day.

When Norma was diagnosed with MS, she kept working because she enjoyed her life on the farm and the people she worked with. As the disease took a firmer hold, she would work half days. Norma was forced to retire in 1994, but Charles Taylor made sure she received her full salary for the next three years, until her Windfields pension kicked in. Such was her contribution to the farm that the boss took care of her in a way that is generally unheard of in the farming industry. Norma has said, though, that when she comes back, "I will come back as a stallion, not a broodmare."

Gordon "Pete" McCann

Gordon "Pete" McCann was known as "Pete" only at the track or when addressed by fellow horsemen. He was always called Gordon by his family. A quiet, unassuming man of integrity and an unending work ethic, Pete McCann was a very gifted horseman. A former jockey, he had been the leading rider at the meet in Havana, Cuba, in winter 1926. He was also an exceptional boxer in the "flyweight" division.

Before taking over the Windfields stable based at Woodbine, Pete had earned the respect of owners such as E.P. Taylor by winning the 1940 King's Plate with first-time starter Willie The Kid. Pete had taken out his trainer's licence earlier that year and was in his first season as a conditioner. It was an incredible beginning to a Hall of Fame career. After taking over the reins of the Windfields stable in 1951, he won five more King's/Queen's Plates, and two of his winners, New Providence in 1959 and Canebora in 1963, went on to win the Canadian Triple Crown. He also trained six horses who would be named Canadian Horse of the Year, including his favourite, Viceregal. Pete's work with Nearctic might be his greatest training accomplishment, as it was he who understood better than anyone else what that head-strong animal needed to succeed.

Pete regularly exercised the horses in his care himself, which allowed him to determine the fitness and mental state of each horse. His ability to understand every one of his charges was a valuable asset to E.P. Taylor's racing division. Pete's consistent success provided the proof.

McCann went into semi-retirement following the 1971 season, when he was in his eighties. He cut back his involvement and thus relinquished his role as Windfields trainer, but he bought a handful of horses and trained them for himself. He could still be seen riding these horses during training, galloping or breezing a colt or filly. When riding and training horses, Pete was in his element, whether the horse was a top-level stakes winner or a low-rung claimer.

McCann had two passions in his life, his family and his horses. Gordon "Pete" McCann passed away in 2000, having lived his life on his terms. He was a remarkable man.

Bernard McCormack

Norma MacDonald has said she never saw Bernard mad: "He was always smiles and chuckles." When one meets Bernard, one is greeted with a warm handshake and an endearing smile that says "I am pleased to see you." Bernard understands the importance of first contact, as well as renewed contact, and has an uncannily accurate memory. He has been in contact with hundreds, if not thousands, of people involved in the racing industry, from owners, jockeys, trainers and grooms to exercise riders on the backstretch and handlers on farms, and he remembers each of them by name as if he had just seen them a day before.

The son of the successful turf writer Tom McCormack, Bernard wanted to be involved in the Thoroughbred business from an early age. He took the course offered at the Irish National Stud to learn basic horse care and breeding, came to Kentucky in 1979 seeking work and found a job at Walmac, where he groomed horses, including the notoriously bad-tempered Alleged. A year later, he went to work for Windfields in Maryland, moving to the Oshawa farm a year after that. He was noticed by manager Peter Poole, who promoted him within a couple of years to assistant manager.

Upon Poole's retirement, Bernard was promoted to operations manager by Charles Taylor in 1987 and held the position until 2002. Bernard oversaw the stud careers of many of the later Windfields stallions, such as Vice Regent, Ascot Knight, Dom Alaric, Silver Deputy, Regal Classic, Whiskey Wisdom and more. He worked hard to promote the young stallions and fill their books, Silver Deputy being a good example, and was a mentor to many of the young men and women who went on to more prominent roles in the racing industry. He was a member of Charles Taylor's inner circle of pedigree consultants during the meetings to discuss future breeding mates for farm mares.

When Windfields decided to become a consignor for other breeders in the big sales, Bernard was the guiding light who steered the operation to success. He was always available to each and every staff member, and they have told the authors that his leadership helped them through those dark times. Bernard likes to give credit to those who did not jump ship and stayed on, but the staff say that Bernard was the glue that held it all together.

Bernard McCormack is an accomplished horseman and today operates the successful Cara Bloodstock Agency with his wife, Karen. They have consigned a number of stakes winners through the sales auctions. Bernard and Karen are also currently among the leading breeders in Canada. Their Mapleshade Farm in Janetville, Ontario, has been the birthplace of two Canadian classic winners (Sir Dudley Digges and Cool Catomine), as well as many other stakes winners. Bernard and Karen operate their hundred-acre boutique farm in the same way he operated Windfields when he was the general manager, with class and efficient, proven horsemanship. There is an air of serenity when visiting the farm, reminiscent of the atmosphere when one visited Windfields during the glory years.

John Neville

English-born John Neville came to Windfields in 1980. He got his start working with horses back in 1954, becoming an apprentice rider for the famous Park House Stables at Kingsclere training yard in Newbury when Ian Balding was in charge of this historic ground. John rode workouts for Balding and had the privilege of riding the great Mill Reef on the training gallops during that one's storied racing career. John also worked Hot Grove, the determined colt who placed second to The Minstrel in the 1977 Derby.

When John and his family arrived at the Oshawa farm, he began in the yearling breaking division and gradually moved to the yearling sales division, working for Andre Blaettler. Upon Andre's retirement in 1988, John was promoted to yearling manager by Charles Taylor. He had as many as thirty people, mostly students from around the Thoroughbred world, working for him during the sales season.

John Neville is an astute horseman with a keen eye for conformation and pedigrees. He became part of the senior staff that planned mare and stallion pairings for each breeding season. It was John's responsibility to oversee the preparation of each horse offered in the 1996 dispersal sale, which he did with his usual professionalism but also with a heavy heart. He called it the saddest time of his life, seeing all the history of the great families leaving the Windfields domain.

He stayed with Windfields until the farm closed its public breeding operation in 2008. John then retired to a lakeside home his sons built for him and wife Rosalind, which is located in a beautiful, peaceful setting on Balsam Lake. John deserves his quiet life, having been a key member of staff for people like Lord Stanley (a descendant of the 17th Earl of Derby), Ian Balding, E.P. Taylor, Joe Thomas and, of course, Charles Taylor. John earned their respect and is highly regarded by those who worked with him.

Bobby Pearson

One could describe Bobby Pearson as the Swiss army knife of the Oshawa farm. He had his hand in many aspects of the Windfields operation, beginning in 1967 when he was hired by

E.P. Taylor. Bobby brought his family from England, where he had worked as an apprentice rider, starting at age fifteen, and groom for Ron Smythe at Epsom. Taylor had a small stable with Smythe, and Bobby was pointed out by George Blackwell, who noticed his work ethic and horsemanship, so Taylor offered him employment in Canada.

E.P. took care of the immigration papers and passage for Bobby and his family, and when they arrived in Oshawa, they moved into one of the cottages on the farm. Bobby went straight to work in the yearling breaking division, though he experienced a certain amount of culture shock when he noticed Windfields used different methods for breaking than he was accustomed to. He adapted and became a regular fixture on the farm—and distinctly remembers Kennedy Road being a savage during the breaking process.

Bobby Pearson has an infectiously jovial personality and was one of the popular employees on the farm. His skill with horses enabled him to work in all facets of the operation: assisting Dr. de Gannes with worming, mucking stalls, helping out at the yearling sales and assisting head stud groom Alan Kerr in the stallion barn and during stallion covers of mares. He worked with John Neville in the yearling division and with Dick Collins, and later Dave Whitford, in the broodmare division. He was never one to stand still when there was work to be done.

In the early 1990s, Bobby was attacked by farm stallion Secret Claim while turning the horse out into his paddock. Alan Kerr came to his rescue before the animal could inflict irreparable damage. Bobby was laid up for many months but was eager to return to work. He assisted Bruce Clazie after the incident until he retired from the farm with a full pension from the Taylor family. Bobby spent thirty years at Windfields and now lives the quiet life at his lakeside home in the Kawarthas.

Peter Poole

Thirty-six years of service for Windfields Farm was celebrated on October 16, 1986, when Peter Poole retired from the business. Peter had seen it all during his career. His standing in the Thoroughbred community was such that on the night of his retirement gala, held in the large arena on the Oshawa farm, as many as eight hundred racing dignitaries, breeders, owners and farm employees paid tribute to him. Vice Regent even made an appearance to wish him well.

Peter was hired by Gil Darlington back in 1950 when the Oshawa property was purchased by E.P. Taylor from Colonel Sam McLaughlin and transformed into the National Stud. He took over the helm upon the sudden passing of Darlington in 1968, the same year the farm name was changed to Windfields, and he steered the organization through the heady days of the 1970s and '80s. He was the main man at Oshawa and ran the farm with determination, passion, loyalty and tremendous organizational skill. He was a firm but fair leader, and his leadership was a key ingredient for the global success Windfields enjoyed. When Peter spoke, people listened.

Poole saw and worked with all the elite horses bred on the farm such as Nijinsky, The Minstrel and, of course, Northern Dancer. He was in the foaling barn when Northern Dancer was born. Peter is a member of the Oshawa Sports Hall of Fame and received the Mint Julep Cup from the Canadian Thoroughbred Horse Society for his lifetime achievements in the industry.

Peter Poole was one of the most highly respected individuals in the Thoroughbred industry. Upon his retirement, he devoted his energies to another passion, fishing, spending time along the shores of Lake Ontario, casting for salmon and trout, and occasionally coming back to the farm to say hello. Peter passed away on May 9, 2010, at Rouge Valley Hospital in Ajax, Ontario.

Dave Whitford

Dave Whitford came to Windfields from Ireland in March 1987, at the age of twenty-two, on a one-year work visa. He was hired by fellow Irish National Stud grad Bernard McCormack to work in the broodmare division, and he also helped with yearling breaking later in the year. Dave had previously worked internships at Aston Upthorpe Stud in England for Sheikh Mohammed and at Cheltenham during the National Hunt meets. He came from a good base of horsemanship training.

Three years of working at Windfields under renewed visas convinced Dave to stay in Canada, and he filled out his immigration papers to do so. He became chief assistant to John Neville in the yearling division and worked closely with John, learning the ropes of management. Following the dispersal of Windfields' broodmares and younger stock in 1996, with Dave playing a vital role in preparing the horses for the sale, he became the broodmare manager. Dave now oversaw all the clients' mares and the few who were purchased by Windfields during the final phase of the farm's existence.

Dave spent sixteen years with Windfields. Much happened to him during his tenure. He met and married his wife, Stephanie, in 1993—she had worked on the farm during the summer months—and they moved into a house near Barn Eight on the Thornton Road side of the farm. The Whitfords started their own family, which now consists of two sons and one daughter, as Dave moved up through the ranks. In 2003, Dave was offered the position of farm manager at the successful Sam-Son Farm. After much soul searching, Dave and Stephanie decided to accept the offer and moved their young family to Milton, Ontario.

Today, Dave Whitford is the manager of Sam-Son Farm's broodmare and breeding division. He has been an important reason for the continued success of this great Canadian racing outfit after the tragic year of 2008, when the deaths of Tammy

Samuel-Balaz and, two months later, her mother, Liza Samuel, were profound setbacks for this proud and enthusiastic leading family of Canadian racing. This was only eight years after the passing of Sam-Son founder Ernie Samuel.

Today, Sam-Son, under Dave Whitford's management, is one of the few remaining private breeders that raise the foals for their own racing stable. Their red and gold silks have been carried to victory by some of the greatest horses ever bred in Canada.

{ 15 }

THE SUPPORTING CAST
(WORLDWIDE)

Russell Alexander

ORN INTO A family of prominent Kentucky horsemen, Russell Alexander became the manager of E.P. Taylor's Windfields private division in Maryland in 1968. Russ grew up at the famed Greentree Stud in Kentucky. He worked for another famous Kentucky farm, Elmendorf, and then became manager at Live Oak Stud in Florida before coming to Windfields Maryland.

Alexander oversaw the breeding and development of all foals born from the Windfields broodmare colony, as well as the training area and the yearlings who were prepped for sales in the United States. He was there for all the highlights of the farm's glorious run of success. As the head of the private section of the expansive Windfields Maryland operation, Russell was an important ingredient to the farm success and kept the family name in the spotlight of superior horsemen.

Russell Alexander's brothers Robert and Joe became farm mangers at Darby Dan Farm in Kentucky and Keswick Stables in Virginia, respectively. His cousin Perry managed Greentree, the family home, and Russell's son Jimmy managed Bwamazon Farm in Kentucky, and later went to Sunrise Thoroughbred Farm in Florida.

Russell, a Second World War veteran, retired from Windfields in January 1986. He moved back to his Kentucky roots in Winchester and passed away in his home on December 22, 1987.

George Blackwell

George Blackwell came into E.P. Taylor's life in 1952 and made an immediate impression. He was responsible for the purchase of Lady Angela, one of the most important mares in Windfields history, if not in Thoroughbred breeding worldwide. Blackwell, who was then working for the British Bloodstock Agency, continued to find outstanding broodmares and yearlings for Windfields. He also helped secure shares in top-rated stallions in Europe for Windfields to breed to, worked the North American yearling sales for Windfields and became a key figure in the Windfields domain.

Blackwell had a very good eye for conformation and knew pedigrees inside out and backwards. His reputation was such that many in the industry considered him one of the finest bloodstock agents in history. George was an outgoing, personable man, always seen with his pipe between his teeth. He stayed with Windfields as a consultant throughout the glory years, earning respect and friendship from many of the top people in the organization, including Ric Waldman, Bernard McCormack and John Neville. George was as affable as he was brilliant.

Ric Waldman got to know George very well. They shared a passion for golf, and Ric learned much from the long-time Windfields advisor. George Blackwell was also a good friend and advisor to Charles Taylor when the son of the founder became the head of the farm. The passing of Joe Thomas in 1984, early in Charles's tenure as Windfields president, was a devastating blow, and George's friendship and knowledge were invaluable to Charles as the latter navigated the treacherous waters after the sales market crash.

George Blackwell's contributions are stamped throughout Windfields history, and one cannot ignore the great expertise and insight he brought to the success of the entire operation. All of the great imports from Europe were scouted and bought for Windfields by George. One can only imagine how different the story of Windfields Farm would have been without George Blackwell.

Dr. Joseph C. Campbell

Dr. Joseph Campbell was a graduate of the University of Pennsylvania School of Veterinary Medicine. He came to the new Windfields Maryland farm in 1967 following many years in the Thoroughbred world in a private practice. Broodmare reproductive frequency and care were his specialties, which led to his hiring. Campbell was in charge of the veterinary program for both the main farm and the commercial farm until his retirement in 1986.

Along with Dr. de Gannes in Oshawa, Dr. Campbell was an exponent of follicle palpation to determine the optimum time for breeding. This practice became the industry standard until the use of ultrasound and computer technology changed the face of the breeding world.

Paul "Junior" Clevenger

Paul "Junior" Clevenger was born in Paris, Kentucky, not far from fabled Claiborne Farm. His journey to fabled Windfields Farm in Maryland began when he started to work with horses at Clovelly Farms while he was still in school. He moved to Maryland with his family and was hired to work at Allaire du Pont's Woodstock Farm. He supervised the foaling for four years before he signed on with Windfields, just across the road, in 1976.

He went to work in the stallion division and later became a groom for many of the important stallions, including Northern Dancer. His work elevated him to head stud groom/stallion manager. Junior was responsible for the breeding efficiency of the valuable stallions in the Maryland stud barn. He had to handle some very tough, headstrong animals during his tenure, including the volatile Halo, the challenging Snow Knight and the king of the farm, Northern Dancer. He looked after the Dancer in the horse's final years.

Clevenger continued with Windfields until the closing of the Maryland farm. He stayed on as stallion manager when the property became the Northview Stallion Station. His expertise with the remaining stallions, Smarten, Two Punch and Caveat, was a key reason for his remaining.

Don Coulter

Don Coulter became a vital contributor to Windfields' success, especially in the yearling sales. He learned his craft as a teenager, and his practical horsemanship led to his becoming the yearling division manager.

Don came to Windfields in 1971 after apprenticing in the show ring with hunters and jumpers. He worked with all of the elite yearlings, from both Maryland and Canada, that went into the Keeneland and Saratoga sales. He and his team, which included three of his own sons, had every one of the yearlings in prime condition at sales time. The team, known as the "Bumble Bees" because of their yellow Windfields jackets, was an efficient and friendly group, eager to show their prized colts and fillies to clients.

Don Coulter stayed with Windfields until the closing of the Maryland farm. His son Tom became his chief assistant. Charles Taylor said of Don, "We would not have had the success we had at the sales were it not for Don and his talent in preparing the yearlings to look their finest at sales time."

Grover "Buddy" Delp

Buddy Delp was a public trainer and one of the Maryland-based conditioners Windfields employed. Famous as the trainer of the great champion Spectacular Bid (who Delp described as "the greatest horse to ever look through a bridle"), the Maryland native trained sixty-eight stakes winners in total. Many were for Windfields. He won 3,674 races in his distinguished career, which was more than 20 percent of his race entries. Truly Bound, Shake A Leg, Sweet Alliance, Northern Sea and Street Ballet were some of the important fillies Buddy conditioned for Windfields' American racing stable. The colourful, gifted trainer was inducted into the National Museum of Racing Hall of Fame in 2002. He passed away on December 29, 2006.

Warren Gibson

Warren Gibson met E.P. Taylor in 1977 when he was working for the accounting firm of Clarkson Gordon. Warren was at the Bayview Gatehouse Office on Windfields' Willowdale farm, conducting the annual audit for the operation, when Mr. Taylor walked from his office down the corridor and politely introduced himself.

Warren left Clarkson Gordon in 1980 to take a position in Windfields' accounting and finance department. His appointment came shortly after the Windfields founder suffered a debilitating stroke, so Warren worked closely with Charles Taylor. In the seventeen years they worked together, he came to regard Charles as a close friend and had much admiration for how Taylor conducted his business. "From my time when I began to work with Charles until the closing, senior staff only stopped working due to death or retirement. There was no turnover. That in itself tells what a wonderful boss Charles was."

Warren worked on the financial side of the entire Windfields operation, both Canadian and international, but he did have some opportunities to work with Joe Thomas for four brief years and enjoyed the experience thoroughly. He also cites his working relationships with Peter Poole and Bernard McCormack as highlights. Warren loved to be around the horses during the farm's existence. He grew into the role of financial advisor for both Windfields and the Taylor family, and he took on an active and vital role in the Windfields management team. "Wonderful, incisive and astute" is how Noreen Taylor sums up Warren's contributions.

Today, Warren Gibson continues to advise and work for the Taylor and Mappin families. "My relationship with the entire Taylor and Mappin family is something I will always cherish and never forget. It is an overused cliché about 'being part of a family,' but this is the closest family I have outside my own and, in my case, the cliché is more than appropriate."

Joe Hickey

Joe Hickey began working for Windfields on March 1, 1969. He had previously worked as a racing official in West Virginia and Maryland, and he did a tour of duty as public relations director at Pimlico Race Course. His background in administrative work was a key reason Joe Thomas hired him to join the Maryland team. His arrival coincided with the start of Northern Dancer's stud career at the farm.

Well-versed in the business, and well-connected, Joe handled stallion syndicate business and bookings, and oversaw the various Windfields publications, such as stallion brochures and yearling catalogues. Joe also wrote many articles pertaining to the Thoroughbred industry and was a frequent contributor to publications such as *Blood-Horse* magazine and *The Thoroughbred Record.*

Joe became the general manager of Windfields operations in the United States, succeeded by Ric Waldman in 1987. He remained with Windfields until the closing of the Maryland farm. Joe Hickey was a highly regarded man in the industry and a valuable asset to the Windfields success.

Gus Koch

Born in southern Ohio, Gus Koch learned his early lessons in horsemanship at Stoner Creek Stud, a Standardbred facility. Thoroughbreds had been bred on the farm before 1964, including Kentucky Derby winners Reigh Count and his son Count Fleet, who also won the Triple Crown. Gus's father was a writer for the *Daily Racing Form* and *Blood-Horse,* so Gus came from a racing family.

Gus met Joe Thomas at Saratoga in August 1972. Joe was impressed with Gus as a horseman and learned that he was looking to advance his career in the breeding business. Gus was hired by Peter Poole not long after, and he brought his family to the Oshawa farm, where he became principal assistant to Andre Blaettler in the yearling division. Gus worked with the broodmares as well, and he spent five years in Canada.

A year after moving his family to live on the Maryland farm, Gus was offered a position as broodmare manager at historic Claiborne farm in Kentucky. After much deliberation, Gus decided to accept the post, and with the blessings and well wishes of the Taylor family and Joe Thomas, he moved his growing family back to Kentucky. Gus worked with some elite mares, such as Numbered Account and Personal Ensign, and top stallions, such as Nijinsky II and Mr. Prospector, in his career at Claiborne.

When we say Gus had a growing family, we mean it was growing not just by age but also in numbers. Gus and his wife, Teresa, have ten children together, five boys and five girls. His son Matt owns Shawhan Place Farm, located adjacent to his own farm, and breeds and consigns for the major sales in the industry. Son Steve is also in the Thoroughbred business and has served as a vice-president of racing at Woodbine Racetrack in Toronto.

Gus Koch is a warm and engaging man, and as such has kept many friends in racing. He considers his time at Windfields as "an exciting time in my life, and I owe a great debt to those I met and worked with." People who worked with Gus remember him as a go-to person. If you were not sure how to handle certain situations pertaining to horse care, your best bet was to "ask Gus," and he would always be willing to advise. At the time of writing, Gus helps Bernard McCormack's Cara Bloodstock agency prepare yearlings for upcoming sales in Kentucky and Saratoga. So he isn't fully retired.

Horatio Luro

One of the most colourful and memorable trainers in history, Horatio Luro left an indelible mark on Windfields' and horse racing's history. "El Gran Senor" came from a horse-crazy family and emigrated from his native Argentina to seek his fame in America as a Thoroughbred trainer, arriving in 1937.

The suave Luro married Georgia native Frances Weinman Latimer and set up Old Mill Farm in Cartersville, Georgia. Here, he could have a central training base and winter his stable during the off season. Many of his famous charges spent time at this location during their racing careers.

His most famous horse was obviously Northern Dancer, but Luro was a gifted horseman and conditioned many other notables, including Princequillo, Decidedly, One For All, Flaming Page and Victoria Park. He won the Canadian International three times, as well as such important races as the Jockey Club Gold Cup, Kentucky Oaks and more.

Luro trained horses until 1984, a forty-eight-year span. He was inducted into the National Museum of Racing Hall of Fame in 1980 and the Canadian Racing Hall of Fame in 2014. Horatio Luro, horse trainer and architect of Northern Dancer's racing career, died in 1991 at his home in Bal Harbour, Florida, at the age of ninety. Safe to say that, like his "leetle buddy" Northern Dancer, there will never be another quite like El Gran Senor.

Ben Miller

Born in Wilmington, Delaware, Ben Miller began to learn about horse care through his work with show horses and steeplechasers. He mucked stalls and groomed and rubbed horses, and in doing so, he found a vocation he wished to pursue.

Ben later went to Ocala, Florida, and learned about stallion and broodmare care. While there, he met Dr. Dan Hawkins, who had worked with Dr. Joseph Campbell for E.P. Taylor's US racing division. Young Ben must have made an impression on the doctor, because when Taylor decided to turn the Maryland operation into a breeding farm, Dr. Hawkins recommended Ben to Joe Thomas for hire. Ben began his duties at Windfields in September 1968. The farm was located close to the Maryland/Delaware border, so he was not too far from his roots.

In charge of the teasing program, Ben met Dr. Campbell and worked closely with him. Ben eventually became an assistant manager and then the broodmare manager of the stallion division. At the height of the Windfields operation, as many as 650 mares per year were entered into Ben's records. He recalls that Windfields policy was no more than two covers a day for any of the stallions, and he says that Halo had the largest book on record in a single season, sixty mares.

Ben began his service in the stallion division on the day it started, and he later took on responsibility for the entire mare population, both the home mares and those visiting the courts of the stallions. He saw it all and had contact with most of the major foals born on the farm. His position gave him some keen insight into many of the famous equines who called the farm home. He remembers Northern Dancer as "always on the muscle. He never walked; he pranced." Another memory was the day Halo was so eager to get to a mare that the volatile stallion dragged his groom to the breeding shed and then flung him away to do his deed with the mare. A kinder memory for Ben was of the yearling sales, where he was one of the "Bumble Bees" parading the yearlings for clients.

Following the closure of the Maryland farm, Ben Miller continued to work with horses for another twelve years in Florida, until he retired. Ben and his wife, Norma, are now living in their hometown of Wilmington. An accomplished horseman and a very warm, kind man, Ben made contributions to Windfields success that give him a prominent place in the farm's history.

MacKenzie "Mack" Miller

Mack Miller was one of the American trainers for Windfields, as well as for other top stables, such as Cragwood for Charles Engelhard and Rokeby for Paul Mellon. He trained seventy-two stakes winners in his Hall of Fame career and was known as "the Gentleman Trainer."

Miller trained several horses Windfields purchased, such as Tentam and Halo, and guided Snow Knight to Eclipse Award champion grass horse honours. Miller trained the first two for Cragwood before Windfields purchased them as stallion prospects, but both Tentam and Halo captured the important United Nations Handicap in back-to-back years under Windfields colours.

He was adept at handling tough, headstrong horses and could get the best from them on the track. Mack Miller passed away on December 10, 2010, following a stroke.

Bill Reeves

Bill Reeves became one of the longest-serving members of the Windfields family. A former rider who became a trainer, Bill began at the Oshawa farm in March 1954, working with broodmares, stallions and yearlings. In 1959, he became an assistant trainer to Pete McCann and worked with the Woodbine-based stable for twelve years.

In 1971, Bill was offered, and accepted, the job as farm trainer on the Maryland property. He and his family moved from Canada and took up residence in one of the farm houses. He oversaw the farm training facility and worked with the likes of Mac Benson, Buddy Delp, Peter Richards, Roger Laurin, Del Carroll and Mack Miller, many of whom, along with Pete McCann, are now enshrined in either the US or Canadian Hall of Fame.

Bill's son Bill Jr., known to all as Billy, grew up at Windfields. After the retirement of Russell Alexander, he became the broodmare manager to the main farm mares owned by the Taylors. Bill Sr. stayed with the farm until its closure and retired with a full pension. His skill with horses led him to thirty-four years of service to Windfields and the Taylor family.

Ric Waldman

Another horseman key to Windfields success, who was born into the business, is Ric Waldman. Ric's father, Marvin, was a successful breeder and owner and had much success with his partner Lee Eaton. They bred Kentucky Derby and Belmont Stakes winner Bold Forbes. The partnership also owned the great broodmare Courtly Dee and bred from her the stakes winners Ali Oop and Native Courier, as well as Foreign Courier, dam of Group One winner and leading sire Green Desert. Marvin tried to talk his son into not working in the Thoroughbred industry, but Ric was eager to get involved and began his career in 1973.

Ric worked eight years at Fasig-Tipton in Kentucky under Brereton Jones, then branched out with his own bloodstock consulting firm. Along the way, he met George Blackwell, and the two became close friends. This friendship led to Ric working for Windfields as a contract consultant. In 1987, he was appointed vice-president of Thoroughbred Operations for Windfields' us division. Although the farm closed the following year, Ric remained in this position to oversee Windfields' interest in the stallion careers of The Minstrel, Deputy Minister, Imperial Falcon and Silver Deputy when they were moved to Kentucky.

Since he was in charge of the stallion syndicates, Ric was in constant communication with Charles Taylor and the senior staff in Oshawa. When Silver Deputy was syndicated and relocated from Oshawa to Brookdale in Kentucky, Ric did the groundwork to make the deal. He stayed with Windfields until the end of 1996, then returned to his consulting agency with Windfields as one of his key clients.

Ric Waldman is one of the more respected bloodstock experts in the industry. His time with Windfields was, in his words, "a highlight of my career." He adds, "I have great respect and admiration for Charles Taylor, Peter Poole and Bernard McCormack and of course George Blackwell." The life of a bloodstock expert/

consultant/agent is demanding and busy, but Ric Waldman is still at it because, as he says, "When you do what you enjoy to do as a living, then it isn't work."

{ 16 }

LEGACY OF A DYNASTY

———————

THE WORD "FOUNDATION" has been used many times throughout this book. E.P. Taylor is regarded as the founding father of modern Canadian racing. We have touched on the foundation mares and stallions and the foundation of the greatest single sporting enterprise in Canadian history. However, Windfields Farm's greatest legacy is as the foundation of today's elite breeding and racing enterprises.

Consider this: Coolmore, Darley, Juddmonte, Lane's End, Adena Springs, Shadai and Gainesway are all world leaders in breeding and racing. They have achieved their success through astute buying and trading of Windfields-bred and -influenced Thoroughbreds. Using the Windfields-bred horses as building blocks, these leading enterprises have held sway in worldwide Thoroughbred racing. The lists of top runners, stallions and producers are full of the descendants of the horses born at Windfields.

Long-established enterprises, such as Claiborne, Spendthrift, the Aga Khan Studs and the National Studs of England and Ireland have all benefited from Windfields breeding to maintain their lofty places in the Thoroughbred world. Look at the current stallion rosters of any one of these establishments and you will see Windfields breeding in those stallions' pedigrees.

The top stallions in the world today all have Windfields lineage. Galileo is recognized as the world leader at the time of writing. He is a grandson of Northern Dancer via that one's world-leading son Sadler's Wells. Dubawi is by Dubai Millennium, a son of Colorado Dancer by Shareef Dancer. Dubawi also has a second cross of Northern Dancer on his dam's side in her fourth generation. Deep Impact, who is by Sunday Silence, is a grandson of Halo and has a cross of Northern Dancer in his fourth generation through his dam.

Looking further at today's elite stallions, Tapit is out of a granddaughter of Nijinsky II and carries a second cross from this Windfields-bred champion. Giant's Causeway is by Storm Cat, a son of Storm Bird. Giant's Causeway is also the sire of the exceptional stallion Shamardal, who adds a cross of Halo through a granddaughter of Natalma in his pedigree. Medaglia d'Oro and Kitten's Joy are both sired by El Prado, a grandson of Northern Dancer.

Danehill's domination in Australia is another example of Windfields' extended influence. Danehill is inbred to Natalma 3x3, being a grandson of Northern Dancer through Danzig and out of Razyana, a daughter of Windfields-bred Spring Adieu, who in turn is out of Natalma. Danehill sons are everywhere and are consistently occupying the top spots in sire lists in Australia and other racing jurisdictions. Danehill is still the all-time leader in stakes winners sired, but Galileo is closing fast.

Recent US Triple Crown winners American Pharoah and Justify possess strong Windfields influence in their respective pedigrees. The first duplicated name in the pedigree of American Pharoah is Northern Dancer, through Windfields-bred El Gran Senor and Storm Bird. Justify carries six crosses of Northern Dancer in his lineage, four of which come via Nijinsky II, with one each from Vice Regent and Storm Bird, all Windfields-bred champions. This pattern of breeding multiple crosses to Northern Dancer and many of his outstanding sons and daughters, along with other influential Windfields-bred horses, has become significant in today's breeding successes.

Unbeaten wonder horse Frankel is inbred to Northern Dancer 3x4 and carries a third cross of Natalma. Golden Horn carries two crosses of Northern Dancer in the fourth generation of his pedigree and two more in his sixth generation. Champion sprinter Brazen Beau descends in direct female line from foundation mare Windy Answer and has three crosses of Nearctic and two crosses of Windy Answer. Champion juvenile Teofilo descends from Willow Lake and has two crosses of Northern Dancer and a third cross of Natalma within his first five generations. These recent superstars are all embarking on highly anticipated stud careers.

Furthermore, recent Hall of Fame horses such as Awesome Again and his exceptional son Ghostzapper, two-time Horse of the Year Curlin, and the mighty Cigar are all heavily influenced by Windfields breeding. California Chrome's pedigree has three crosses of Northern Dancer. Makybe Diva has three crosses of Northern Dancer in her fourth generation. Black Caviar has two Northern Dancer crosses. Winx has two crosses of Natalma through Windfields-bred offspring. Zenyatta has Windfields-bred Coup De Folie, a granddaughter of Natalma, in the third generation of her pedigree. Rachel Alexandra is inbred to Northern Dancer 4x4. Beholder carries four crosses of Nearctic, three of which are through Northern Dancer. Preakness winner Exaggerator has three crosses of Windfields-bred ancestors in his first five generations. Songbird carries three crosses of Northern Dancer. The list is endless.

In 2018 alone, Australia has seen many descendants of Windfields breeding excelling on the track. Winx, of course, is the darling of the group, but there is also the Golden Slipper winner Estijaab, who is sired by Snitzel, a stallion inbred to Northern Dancer 4x4. New Zealand–bred Grunt won a pair of Group One races, the Australian Guineas and the Makybe Diva Stakes, with three crosses of Northern Dancer and a cross of Halory in his genes. Santa Ana Lane, however, might be the world's leader in the number of Windfields Thoroughbreds in a pedigree. There are no fewer than ten crosses of Windfields ancestors in this fleet gelding's pedigree, with eight descending from Natalma alone. Five of these come through Northern Dancer, two through Raise The Standard and another through Spring Adieu. Flaming Page and Glorious Song also appear in this pedigree.

Cross Counter, 2018 winner of the Melbourne Cup, carries five crosses of Natalma, four of which come through Northern Dancer (the other is from Spring Adieu). Cross Counter has an additional important Windfields connection through his sire Teofilo, due to that one's direct female family descending from foundation mare Compensate.

In Japan, we have witnessed the ascent to greatness of Almond Eye, a beautiful bay filly. She became the fifth filly to capture the Japanese Filly Triple Crown and then took on all comers with style when she won the prestigious Japan Cup against a world-class field of older male and female Thoroughbreds. Almond Eye took her talent to Dubai and again showed her class, and her heels, to a fine field of world-class horses when she won the Group One Dubai Turf in a canter. Not only does Almond Eye carry five crosses of Windfields breeding in her pedigree, but she is also a direct descendant of foundation mare Sex Appeal.

The 2018 Epsom Derby winner Masar carries three crosses of Northern Dancer and is sired by Epsom Derby winner New Approach, a descendant of highlighted mare Lachine. Another notable winner is 2018 Cartier Award champion two-year-old colt Too Darn Hot. This blazingly fast, undefeated colt has three crosses of Northern Dancer and is out of champion mare Dar Re Mi by Singspiel, a son of Glorious Song.

Cracksman added to his 2017 Cartier champion three-year-old season with outstanding wins in the Prix Ganay, Coronation Cup and Champion Stakes (for the second consecutive year) in 2018. Cracksman is full of Northern Dancer blood, as all four sires in his third-generation pedigree are Northern Dancer–line stallions. Another Northern Dancer–line sire, Be My Guest, is the sire of Cracksman's third dam, the 1000 Guineas winner On The House.

The 2018 Cartier Horse of the Year in Europe is the outstanding Roaring Lion, a son of 2018's leading sire Kitten's Joy. Roaring Lion won four major Group One races (the Eclipse, Juddmonte International, Irish International, Queen Elizabeth II Stakes) in an impressive season, displaying his speed and class. This John Gosden–trained champion from the Qatar Racing Stable has three crosses of Northern Dancer through Sadler's Wells, Dixieland Band and Fanfreluche, as well as a further cross from Natalma.

In this decade, we have also seen two superior fillies win Europe's most coveted race, the Prix de l'Arc de Triomphe. Treve and Enable each captured the great Longchamp race twice. Treve was sired by Epsom Derby winner Motivator, and she carries Sadler's Wells, Danzig and Lyphard in her pedigree. Her grandsire Montjeu is also an Arc winner. Enable captured the race in 2017 and 2018. She carries two crosses of Sadler's Wells, a cross of Nijinsky II and a cross of Icecapade, arguably Nearctic's second most important son at stud, in her outstanding pedigree. Enable added further laurels in 2018 when she won the Breeders' Cup Turf as a reigning Arc winner. She is the first to accomplish this feat.

The 2018 Breeders' Cup not only featured Enable's major accomplishment but also saw the emergence of an exceptional filly in Newspaperofrecord. This undefeated, and so far unchallenged, filly has no fewer than nine crosses of Windfields breeding in her blood. Another standout at the 2018 Breeders' Cup was Expert Eye, who carries seven crosses of Windfields excellence. Both of these BC champions are on the Northern Dancer sire line, as is the Juvenile Turf winner of the 2018 Breeders' Cup edition, Line Of Duty. He is by Galileo, Northern Dancer's phenomenal grandson.

The successful Breeders' Cup series of championship races, which was enthusiastically supported by Charles Taylor from the onset, has been led by descendants of Northern Dancer. There have been 332 Breeders' Cup races run at the time of writing. Northern Dancer male line descendants have won 108 of these events (32.5 percent). And note that this is counting only the direct tail male descendants from just one Windfields-bred horse. The Halo-sired Saint Ballado, sire of two BC winners (Saint Liam and Ashado), and Southern Halo, who in turn sired More Than Ready (sire of five BC winners of six BC races), are two more Windfields-bred stallions to beget a male line of Breeders' Cup champions.

There have been many multiple Breeders' Cup winners along the Northern Dancer male line: Goldikova (three BC Mile wins), Miesque (two BC Mile wins), High Chaparral (two BC Turf wins), Beholder (two BC Distaff wins and one Juvenile Fillies win), Ouija Board (two Filly and Mare Turf wins), Lure (two BC Mile wins), Wise Dan (two BC Mile wins), Goldencents (two BC Dirt Mile wins), Stormy Liberal (two BC Turf Sprint wins), Groupie Doll (two BC Filly and Mare Sprint wins), and Stephanie's Kitten (BC Juvenile Fillies Turf and BC Filly and Mare Turf).

We could go on and on, listing today's elite runners and breeding champions from around the world.

But to turn to another of Windfields' major contributions, the breeding industry in Canada prospered during the farm's existence. For five decades in Ontario, and throughout Canada, racing continued to grow in quality and numbers of horses, in part thanks to E.P. Taylor's foresight in bringing foundation stallions and mares to Ontario, making them accessible to Canadian breeders and also offering the Windfields yearlings for sale each year. Windfields was the taproot for quality in the industry infrastructure. The breeding industry in Canada is still reaping the benefits of Taylor's pursuit of high breeding standards at Windfields Farm, long after the farm closed its doors.

As described in Chapter One, Taylor also helped rejuvenate the horse-racing industry in Ontario, consolidating tracks, creating a showplace track at Woodbine, opening the races up for better competition and ensuring more money for purses. For decades, Thoroughbred racing was a popular sport in Canada, with extensive coverage in the press and hundreds of thousands of people visiting the track each year. Capacity crowds were the norm at big events such as the Queen's Plate and Canadian International, or when a famous horse was entered in the featured stakes race on the day's racing card. Woodbine is still acknowledged to be one of the best racing facilities in the world.

Two recent Grade One winners who have come down the generations are Hard Not To Like and Camp Creek. They each descend in direct female line from Iribelle, through Britannia, Myanna, Supper Club and Likeashot to It's A Ruby. The latter is the second dam of both.

The Canadian-bred Hard Not To Like won her first stakes race in Canada at Woodbine in the prestigious Cup and Saucer Stakes against colts on the grass. After placing in the Grade One Ashland Stakes as a three-year-old, Hard Not To Like came back at four to win the Grade Three Marshua's River Stakes. Continuing her career at five, she became a Grade One winner when she took the Jenny Wiley Stakes at Keeneland, and as a six-year-old, she won two Grade One races—the Diana, setting a new course record, and the Gamely Stakes. In the latter race, Hard Not To Like defeated champion Tepin, who of course is inbred to Northern Dancer 4x4 through Storm Bird and Nureyev.

Camp Creek won the third jewel of the Canadian Triple Crown in 2016 when he won the Breeders' Stakes at Woodbine. He finished ahead of that year's Queen's Plate winner Sir Dudley Digges, a colt who is inbred to Northern Dancer 5x5 through Nijinsky II and Storm Bird. Sir Dudley Digges was bred by Bernard and Karen McCormack at their Mapleshade Farm in Ontario. The dam of Sir Dudley Digges was My Pal Lana, trained by long-serving Windfields trainer Mac Benson.

As you can see, the legacy of Windfields Farm is a never-ending story. As long as Thoroughbreds are bred and raced, Windfields' influence will be prevalent. This influence is also seen in the continuing participation of people who made huge contributions to the farm's success when it was operating. Bernard McCormack achieved the thrill of breeding a Queen's Plate winner, just as his esteemed employer did before him. He also bred another Canadian classic winner, Cool Catomine, who captured the 2017 Prince of Wales Stakes.

In no other sport does history have as much influence as it does in horse racing. Breeding dictates that we need the past to build the future, through pedigrees of yesterday's equine stars. The glories of the past spawn the glories of today, which in turn produce the glories of the future. This aspect of racing has been the cornerstone of success since the dawn of the breed and will continue long past our lifetime. Windfields Farm may no longer be in operation, but it remains a major influence in the sport.

There are two constants in the world, time and change. The first marches on relentlessly, while the second brings new wonders and frontiers, but also a chance to look nostalgically at what has been left behind. The heady and glorious run of E.P. Taylor's Windfields Farm may be fading into a distant memory for those who experienced the magic, but because of the nature of Thoroughbred racing, the Windfields legacy continues. There can be no illustration of that legacy more remarkable than seeing the descendants of Windfields breeding remaining at the top of the Thoroughbred world. It is a testament to the fine people who engineered this legacy, and to their exceptional talent at their craft. The result was a truly great Canadian institution from which the world continues to benefit and prosper.

ACKNOWLEDGEMENTS AND RESOURCES

THE WRITERS WOULD like to specially thank Marianne de Gannes-Ortepi. Her enthusiasm, friendship and guidance were our shining light during the research and writing of the book. Without Marianne, much of the book could not have been written.

We would like to thank the following Windfields alumni, who embraced our project with enthusiasm and friendship. The recollections and insight of these people gave us a unique understanding of the Windfields family and key events through history. They made us feel a part of the Windfields family, and we are proud to call each one friend: Bernard McCormack, founder and president of Cara Bloodstock agency; Noreen Taylor, chancellor of the University of Ontario Institute of Technology; and Dr. Rolph de Gannes DVM, John Neville, Ric Waldman, Norma Mac-Donald, Ben Miller, Gus Koch, Bobby Pearson, Leslie Thomas,

McDonald "Mac" Benson, Dave Whitford, Simon Cassidy, Bruce Clazie, Warren Gibson, Dr. Patrick Hearn DVM.

We would like to thank the following people for their insight and enthusiastic support during the research and writing of this project: Kathleen Donnelly, Tom Cosgrove, Lou Cauz, Caitlyn Grguric, Diane Stephen, Cathy Schenk, Roda Ferraro, Karen McCormack, Sheila de Gannes, Barbara Przedrzymirska, Fran Okihiro, Audrey McClellan, Peter Winants Jr.

Research Sources

WINDFIELDS PUBLICATIONS

Annual *Sirelines* stallion handbooks
Annual yearling catalogues
Drummer Boy
Fanfare Newsletter
The Flaming Page
The Maple Leaf
National Stud Newsletter
St. Augustine Post
Windfields Facts

ORGANIZATIONS AND INSTITUTIONS

Australian Racing Hall of Fame
Canadian Racing Hall of Fame (Woodbine)
Canadian Thoroughbred Horse Society (CTHS)
Japan Racing Association (JRA)
Keeneland Association Library
National Horse Racing Hall of Fame Newmarket
National Horseracing Authority South Africa
National Museum of Racing Hall of Fame (Saratoga)
The Jockey Club

BOOKS

Baerlin, Richard. *Nijinsky: Triple Crown Winner*. Pelham Books, 1971.

Barry, Quintin. *Lord Derby and His Horses*. The Red Horse Press, 2012.

Bowen, Edward. *Dynasties*. Blood-Horse Publications/Eclipse Press, 2000.

Bowen, Edward. *Legends of the Turf*, Volume 2. Blood-Horse Publications/Eclipse Press, 2004.

Cauz, Louis E., and Beverly A. Smith. *The Plate: 150 Years of Royal Tradition*. ECW Press, 2009.

Gzowski, Peter. *An Unbroken Line*. McClelland and Stewart, 1983.

Hunter, Avalyn. *The Kingmaker: How Northern Dancer Founded a Racing Dynasty*. Blood-Horse Publications/Eclipse Press, 2008.

Lennox, Muriel. *E.P. Taylor, A Horseman and His Horses*. Burns and MacEachern, 1976.

Magee, Michael, and Pat Bayes. *Champions*. Bryant Press, 1980.

O'Brien, Jacqueline, and Ivor Herbert. *Vincent O'Brien: The Official Biography*. Transworld Publishers/Bantam Press, 2005.

Rohmer, Richard. *E.P. Taylor: The Biography of Edward Plunket Taylor*. McClelland and Stewart, 1978.

Willett, Peter. *The Classic Racehorse*. Stanley Paul and Co., 1981.

MAGAZINES, NEWSPAPERS, AND WEB-SITES

Blood-Horse magazine

Canadian Thoroughbred magazine

CTHS Yearbook (published annually)

CTHS yearling sales catalogues

Daily Racing Form

Fasig-Tipton yearling sales catalogues

Globe and Mail

Keeneland yearling sales catalogues
The Racing Post
The Sporting Post
Thoroughbred Owner and Breeder Magazine
Thoroughbred Racing Ancestry
Thoroughbred Racing Commentary
Thoroughbred Record
Toronto Daily Star
Toronto Sun
Toronto Telegram
Turf and Sport Digest

VIDEOS

The Canadians (Canadian Broadcasting Corporation production)
The Life and Times of Northern Dancer (Canadian Broadcasting Corporation production)
World of Horseracing: Northern Dancer Tribute (Bradford Diamond Productions/TSN)

GLOSSARY OF HORSE RACING TERMS

Allowance Race—A non-claiming race in which the racing secretary imposes conditions, usually varying weights for runners to carry based on their previous purse earnings and/or types of victories.

Backstretch—The straight part of the track opposite the finish line. The same term is used to describe the stable area, which is usually located on the outside of the backstretch portion of the track.

Bay—A term used for a horse body colour that ranges from a light reddish or golden-brown to very dark brown with "black points" (points refer to the mane, tail and lower legs). The main variations are dark bay, which is a very dark red or brown, difficult to distinguish from seal brown (some dark bays look black under certain light conditions); blood bay, a very bright red, which is often considered simply "bay"; and brown, a term used by some breed registries to describe dark bays.

Beyer Speed Figure—A system for rating the performance of Thoroughbred racehorses in North America designed in the early 1970s by Andrew Beyer. First published in book form in 1975, *Daily Racing Form* began incorporating Beyer Speed

Figures in a horse's past performances in 1992, and the system now assigns a Beyer number for each horse race.

Black Type—When a horse wins or places in a stakes race, these results appear bold or black type in a sales catalogue or pedigree chart.

Blinkers—A piece of equipment that takes the form of a hood with cups of varying sizes over the eye holes to limit a horse's peripheral vision; generally used to reduce distraction and help the horse concentrate on running straight. Blinkers are used less frequently in Europe and are commonly referred to there as a "Rogue's Badge."

Blue Hen Mare—A mare who consistently produces high-quality foals.

Bowed Tendon—An inflammation and enlargement of the superficial or deep digital flexor tendon (located behind the cannon bone—the long bone from the knee to the pastern or ankle). The injury usually occurs in the front limbs, and the general cause is severe strain. The bowed appearance is due to inflammation followed by the formation of scar tissue.

Breeders' Cup—Inaugurated in 1984 as a day of seven championship races in North America run for various divisions of gender, distance, track surfaces and age. Usually run in late October or early November, these races carry a high level of prestige to the winners. There are now fourteen Breeders' Cup events, which are run on two consecutive days at one racing facility. This racing festival attracts many of the world's best horses in training.

Breeze—A workout in which a horse runs easily under a hold without encouragement from the rider.

Broodmare—A female horse used for breeding.

Bucked Shins—Inflammation of the tissue covering the front of the cannon bone (the long bone from the knee to the pastern or ankle), which can also extend into the cortex of the bone itself. Most frequently occurs in the front legs of young horses adjusting to the increased workload/concussion of training.

Cartier Award—Europe's horse-racing award system, founded in 1991, and sponsored by Société Cartier, a French producer of luxury goods. The award winners are decided by points earned in European group races plus the votes cast by British racing journalists and readers of the *Racing Post* and *Daily Telegraph* newspapers. There are divisional awards for age, gender and race distances, with the most outstanding horse named Horse of the Year.

Chestnut—A reddish body colour with no black marking. Mane and tail are the same shade or lighter than the body coat. The main colour variations are liver chestnut, which is a dark brownish red coat (sometimes a liver chestnut is simply called "brown"); blond or light chestnut, a seldom-used term for a lighter tan coat with pale mane and tail (see also the "Flaxen" entry); the most common shade of chestnut is a reddish tan to red coat, about the colour of a new penny.

Claiming Race—A race in which each runner has a price and can be purchased by any person who makes a valid claim prior to the running of the race. Claiming races generally draw horses from the lower ranks of racing; they are also the most frequently run races on a daily race card.

Classic Races—Major races consisting of the Triple Crown events in various countries for both colts and fillies. The classic distance is considered to be a mile and a quarter to a mile and a half. The former is the distance of the Kentucky Derby and the Breeders' Cup Classic. A mile and a half is the classic distance outside North America and is used for such races as the Derby Stakes at Epsom and the Prix de l'Arc de Triomphe.

Colic—A term that encompasses all forms of gastrointestinal conditions that cause severe pain. There are a variety of causes of colic, some of which can prove fatal without surgical intervention. Clinical signs of colic generally require veterinary treatment.

Colt—A male horse four years old and under.

Conformation—A horse's build and general physical structure; the way he is put together.

Cover—The act of a stallion breeding a mare.

Dead Heat—The result when two or more horses cross the finish line simultaneously.

Eclipse Awards—Awards for Thoroughbreds racing in North America, sponsored by the National Thoroughbred Racing Association (NTRA), *Daily Racing Form* and the National Turf Writers Association. Similar to the Cartier Awards, but restricted to horses who have raced during the season in North America. These awards have been handed out annually since 1971 and have various divisions for age, gender, racing surface and distance. There is also a Horse of the Year honoured.

Filly—A female horse four years old or under.

Flaxen—A chestnut horse with mane and tail distinctly lighter than the body colour. This is not an official colour designation, but the term is used by horse-racing people to describe an attractive colouring.

Floating (teeth)—The process of filing sharp points off a horse's teeth to make the chewing surface smooth.

Foundation Mare—A broodmare who, through her progeny, has established a high-achieving family of stakes winners, stakes-producing daughters, and/or highly successful stallions.

Furlong—A measure of distance used in racing. A furlong is 220 yards, or one-eighth of a mile, so a 10-furlong race is exactly a mile and a quarter in distance.

Gelding—A male horse who has been castrated. This can be done for a variety of reasons, the most common of which are to curb his boisterousness (temperament) or his growth (if his body is becoming too large for his legs to support him when running).

Get—The progeny of a stallion.

Giving Weight—A term used when a horse carries more weight in a race than other entrants. This occurs in "Weight for Age" races and in handicap races. The theory in handicap races is that putting heavier weights on better horses will equalize the competition for slower horses.

Graded or Group Races—Stakes race that are assigned a grade (one, two or three) based on the importance of the race compared to all other races. Group or Grade One races are the highest level of racing.

Grey—A term used to describe a horse whose coat has a mixture of white and black hair in it. A grey horse's coat will become lighter in hue with age. Greys can also have a sprinkling of brown or red hair in their coat.

Groom—The person who cares for a horse, feeding, brushing, bathing and preparing the horse for workouts or races.

Hand—A unit of measure used to determine a horse's height, which is measured from the ground to the withers (the point of bone at the base of the horse's neck). A hand is four inches, so a horse that stands 16 hands is actually 64 inches tall at the withers. This does not include the height of the horse's head, which is carried above the point of the withers.

Handicap Race—A race for which the racing secretary will assign a different weight to each individual runner based on their previous performances. The aim is to allocate weight so that, in theory, all runners would finish in a dead heat.

Homestretch—The straight section of a track from the final turn to the finish post.

Jockey Club—The governing body for Thoroughbred racing and breeding.

Laminitis—A painful, potentially crippling disease that affects the feet of a horse. In laminitis, blood flow to tissues in the hoof is affected, resulting in inflammation and swelling of the laminae, layers of cells that cushion the bones of the hoof and act as shock absorbers. If treatment is ineffective, the horse may have to be humanely euthanized to prevent suffering.

Lunging—A form of exercise in which a long tether is used to trot a horse around in a circle without a rider. Lunging is used when a horse is recuperating from an injury or another ailment that prohibits full training with a rider.

Maiden—A racehorse who has not won a race.

Maiden Race—A race specifically for non-winning horses.

Mare—A female horse five years or older.

National Hunt Racing—A racing series popular in the UK and Ireland in which horses race longer distances and are required to jump over fences and other obstacles.

Nick—Breeding crosses (usually of a sire over a mare from a certain broodmare sire) that show an above-average record for producing stakes winners.

Outcross—A breeding term used for a Thoroughbred who has no duplicated names within the first four generations of their pedigree. If a stallion or mare is present more than once within the first four generations, then that Thoroughbred is considered "Inbred" to the duplicated anscestor.

Palpation—A examination, performed by a veterinarian, to check ovarian size and consistency, follicle size and consistency, uterine tone, cervical relaxation and pelvic structure when preparing a broodmare for breeding to a stallion.

Quarter Crack—A crack in the wall of the hoof between the toe and heel, usually extending into the coronary band (the junction between the hair and the hoof).

Rating—A term used when a jockey restrains his mount early in a race so the horse will save energy for a faster run later in the race.

Roan—A coat colour similar to grey, but the coat hue does not lighten with age.

Rubbing Horses—Common description of a horse groom's duties.

Sovereign Awards—Similar to Cartier and Eclipse Awards, but for horses who have made a least three race starts in Canada during a single calendar year. Awards for various divisions of gender, age, race distance and racing surface, as well as Horse of the Year, have been awarded by the Jockey Club of Canada since 1975.

Stakes Races—The upper echelon of horseracing. Many stakes races are graded (known as Group races outside North America)—see the "Graded/Group Races" entry. Ungraded stakes races can be for restricted entrants, such as horses bred in a specific state or province, etc., or are known as "Listed" stakes. Owners pay a predetermined fee to enter a horse in a stakes race, which may become part of the prize money.

Stakes-Placed Winner—A horse who has won a non-stakes race and has additionally placed second or third in a stakes race.

Stallion—A male horse used for breeding.

Stallion or Stud Groom—The man or woman appointed to tend to a stallion's needs and well-being.

Stayer—A stout-hearted Thoroughbred who can win long-distance races through their stamina.

Stud—A farm at which breeding horses takes place. Also used to describe a breeding stallion.

Syndication—A process in which a group, or syndicate, purchases a stallion, with equal shares for breeding rights distributed to the syndicate members.

Tail Female Line—The line of mares along the bottom of a horse's pedigree chart, flowing from the horse's dam back through the generations.

Tail Male Line—Similar to the above, but follows the top line of stallions in a pedigree chart.

Teasing—A method used by a breeding farm to determine if a mare is ready to be bred. A "teaser" stallion will be put into a paddock adjacent to the mare. If she appears interested in him, the mare will be taken to the breeding shed to be bred to the stallion she has been booked to meet.

Walking Hots—The activity of walking horses after workouts or races to cool them off, avoid muscle stiffness and allow their body temperature, pulse and respiration to return to normal.

Win Going Away—Phrase used to describe how a Thorough-bred won a race by extending their lead to a greater margin of victory at the finish post.

LIST OF STALLIONS WITH AT LEAST ONE STUD SEASON AT WINDFIELDS FARM

THE FOLLOWING LIST is an alphabetical account of every stallion who stood a minimum of one breeding season at Windfields Farm. This list includes stallions who stood at either the Willowdale location, Oshawa or Maryland. This list does not include stallions in whom Windfields held a share or multiple shares within a syndicate but who stood at other stud farms.

STALLION NAME	YEAR OF BIRTH	SIRE – DAM – SIRE OF DAM
Ace Admiral	Ch. C. 1945	Heliopolis-War Flower by Man O' War
Ace Marine	Ch. C. 1952	Ace Admiral-Mazarine by Sweepster
Admirals Mate	Db./Br. C. 1947	War Admiral-Fantine by Whichone
Akureyri	B. C. 1978	Buckpasser-Royal Statute by Northern Dancer
Alydeed	Db./Br. C. 1989	Shadeed-Bialy by Alydar
Archer's Bay	B. C. 1995	Silver Deputy-Adorned by Val de l'Orne
Ascot Knight	B. C. 1984	Danzig-Bambee T.T. by Better Bee
Assert	B. C. 1979	Be My Guest-Irish Bird by Sea-Bird II
Best Of The Bests	Ch. C. 1997	Machiavellian-Sueboog by Darshaan
Bold Agent	B. C. 1976	Bold Bidder-Reagent by Rasper II
Brave Regent	Db./Br. C. 1979	Vice Regent-Buh Buh Buh Bold by Bold Monarch
Briartic	Ch. C. 1968	Nearctic-Sweet Lady Briar by Round Table
Bridle Path	Db./Br. C. 1976	Kennedy Road-Roman Gun by Roman
Bull Page	B. C. 1940	Bull Lea-Our Page by Blue Larkspur
Canadian Champ	B. C. 1953	Windfields-Bolesteo by Filesteo
Canebora	Db./Br. C. 1960	Canadian Champ-Menebora by Menetrier

STALLION NAME	YEAR OF BIRTH	SIRE - DAM - SIRE OF DAM
Captor	Ch. C. 1952	Djeddah-Little Sphinx by Challenger II
Castleton	B. C. 1949	Windsor Slipper-Clandon by Hyperion
Cat's At Home	B. C. 1997	Tabasco Cat-Homewrecker by Buckaroo
Caucasus	B. C. 1972	Nijinsky II-Quill by Princequillo
Caveat	Db./Br. C. 1980	Cannonade-Cold Hearted by The Axe II
Censor	Db./Br. C. 1953	Bull Page-Compensate by Reaping Reward
Chain Reaction	Db./Br. C. 1950	Chop Chop-Erstwhile by Helter Skelter
Champlain	B. C. 1962	Nearctic-Canadiana by Windfields
Chop Chop	B. C. 1940	Flares-Sceptical by Buchan
Chopavane	B. C. 1956	Chop Chop-La Pavane by Rodosto
Choperion	Db./Br. C. 1959	Chop Chop-Lady Angela by Hyperion
Commemorate	B. C. 1981	Exclusive Native-Reminiscing by Never Bend
Cool Victor	Db./Br. C. 1975	Tentam-Polar Victress by Nearctic
Country Light	B. C. 1983	Majestic Prince-Harbor Flag by Hoist The Flag
Dancing Champ	B. C. 1972	Nijinsky II-Mrs. Peterkin by Tom Fool
Dancing Count	B. C. 1968	Northern Dancer-Snow Court by King's Bench

STALLION NAME	YEAR OF BIRTH	SIRE – DAM – SIRE OF DAM
Dauphin Fabuleux	Ch. C. 1982	Le Fabuleux-Jansum Regal by Viceregal
Deputy Minister	Db./Br. C. 1979	Vice Regent-Mint Copy by Bunty's Flight
Devil Begone	Db./Br. C. 1990	Devil's Bag-Endear by Alydar
Dom Alaric	Db./Br. C. 1974	Sassafras-Ordenstreue by Orsini II
Double Edge Sword	Ch. C. 1970	Sword Dancer-Jeanelou by Discovery
D'Wildcat	Ch. C. 1998	Forest Wildcat-D'Enough by D'Accord
El Gran Senor	B. C. 1981	Northern Dancer-Sex Appeal by Buckpasser
Epic	Db./Br. C. 1946	Bunty Lawless-Fairy Imp by Gino
Espalier	B. C. 1949	Borealis-Garden Path by Fairway
Eurasian	Ch. C. 1962	Swaps-Manihiki by Polynesian
Fabuleux Dancer	Ch. C. 1980	Nijinsky II-Fabuleux Jane by Le Fabuleux
Fairaris	Ch. C. 1939	Fair Trial-Nunnery by Friar Marcus
Fenelon	B. C. 1937	Sir Gallahad III-Filante by Sardanapale
Firethorn	Db./Br. C. 1932	Sun Briar-Baton Rouge by Man O' War
Granacus	B. C. 1985	Sweet Candy-Lucinda Light by Laser Light

STALLION NAME	YEAR OF BIRTH	SIRE - DAM - SIRE OF DAM
Gregorian	Db./Br. C. 1976	Graustark-Natashka by Dedicate
Grey Monarch	Gr. C. 1955	Grey Sovereign-White Lodge by Casanova
Hail To Victory	Db./Br. C. 1964	Hail To Reason-New Peace by Olympia
Halo	Db./Br. C. 1969	Hail To Reason-Cosmah by Cosmic Bomb
Idyll	Db./Br. C. 1977	Riva Ridge-Arrangement by Intentionally
Illuminable	Ch. C. 1946	Sun Again-Flaming Top by Omaha
Imperial Falcon	Db./Br. C. 1983	Northern Dancer-Ballade by Herbager
Impressive	Db./Br. C. 1963	Court Martial-High Voltage by Ambiorix
Iskandar Elakbar	Ch. C. 1987	Vice Regent-Honest Gal by Honest Pleasure
Kamaraan II	B. C. 1971	Tanerko-Diamond Drop by Charlottesville
King Emperor	B. C. 1966	Bold Ruler-Irish Jay by Double Jay
King's Bishop	B. C. 1969	Round Table-Spearfish by Fleet Nasrullah
Limbo Dancer	B. C. 1986	Northern Dancer-South Ocean by New Providence
Lord Durham	Ch. C. 1971	Damascus-Solar Princess by Summer Tan
Master Willie	Ch. C. 1977	High Line-Fair Winter by Set Fair

STALLION NAME	YEAR OF BIRTH	SIRE – DAM – SIRE OF DAM
Medaille d'Or	Ch. C. 1976	Secretariat-Fanfreluche by Northern Dancer
Megas Vukefalos	Db./Br. C. 1988	Cool Victor-Bold Debra by Dom Alaric
Mobil	B. C. 2000	Langfuhr-Kinetical by Naksra
Nail	Gr. C. 1953	Nirgal-No Strings by Occupation
Navy Page	Ch. C. 1950	War Admiral-Our Page by Blue Larkspur
Nearctic	Db./Br. C. 1954	Nearco-Lady Angela by Hyperion
Nentego	Ch. C. 1962	Never Say Die-Tideless by Persian Gulf
Northern Answer	B. C. 1966	Northern Dancer-Windy Answer by Windfields
Northern Dancer	B. C. 1961	Nearctic-Natalma by Native Dancer
Northern Fling	B. C. 1970	Northern Dancer-Impetuous Lady by Hasty Road
Northern Native	Db./Br. C. 1966	Nearctic-Natalma by Native Dancer
Oh Say	B. C. 1978	Hoist The Flag-Light Hearted by Cyane
Presidial	B. C. 1969	Psidium-Rose Of North by Nearctic
Protanto	B. C. 1967	Native Dancer-Foolish One by Tom Fool
Queen's Own	Ch. C. 1951	War Jeep-Sea Reigh by Reigh Count

STALLION NAME	YEAR OF BIRTH	SIRE – DAM – SIRE OF DAM
Racing Room	B. C. 1964	Restless Wind-Crowding In by Mister Gus
Rambunctious	B. C. 1960	Rasper II-Danae II by The Solicitor II
Regal Classic	Ch. C. 1985	Vice Regent-No Class by Nodouble
Regal Embrace	B. C. 1975	Vice Regent-Close Embrace by Nentego
Regal Intention	Db./Br. C. 1985	Vice Regent-Tiffany Tam by Tentam
Right Combination	Db./Br. C. 1966	Round Table-Oak Cluster by Nasrullah
Robellino	B. C. 1978	Roberto-Isobelline by Pronto
Royal Orbit	Ch. C. 1956	Royal Charger-Admiral's Belle by War Admiral
Ruritania	Gr. C. 1969	Graustark-Aiming High II by Djebe
San Romano	Db./Br. C. 1989	Cool Victor-Bye The Bye by Balzac
Schossberg	Db./Br. C. 1990	Broad Brush-Bye The Bye by Balzac
Search For Gold	B. C. 1969	Raise A Native-Gold Digger by Nashua
Secret Claim	B. C. 1985	Mr. Prospector-Secrettame by Secretariat
Sevastopol	B. C. 1973	Nijinsky II-South Ocean by New Providence
Silver Deputy	B. C. 1985	Deputy Minister-Silver Valley by Mr. Prospector

STALLION NAME	YEAR OF BIRTH	SIRE – DAM – SIRE OF DAM
Smarten	Db./Br. C. 1976	Cyane-Smartaire by Quibu
Snow Knight	Ch. C. 1971	Firestreak-Snow Blossom by Flush Royal
Stratus	Ch. C. 1956	Nimbus-Straight Offer by Straight Deal
T.V. Commercial	Ch. C. 1965	T.V. Lark-Your Hostess by Alibhai
Teddy Wrack	B. C. 1938	Bull Dog-Decree by Wrack
Tentam	Db./Br. C. 1969	Intentionally-Tamarett by Tim Tam
Tethra	B. C. 1992	Cure The Blues-Ada Prospect by New Prospect
The Minstrel	Ch. C. 1974	Northern Dancer-Fleur by Victoria Park
Tournoi	B. C. 1945	Tourbillon-Eroica by Banstar
Two Punch	Gr. C. 1983	Mr. Prospector-Heavenly Clause by Grey Dawn II
Val de l'Orne	B. C. 1972	Val de Loir-Aglae by Armistice
Vice Regent	Ch. C. 1967	Northern Dancer-Victoria Regina by Menetrier
Viceregal	Ch. C. 1966	Northern Dancer-Victoria Regina by Menetrier
Victoria Park	B. C. 1957	Chop Chop-Victoriana by Windfields
Victorian Era	B. C. 1962	Victoria Park-Ivy by Nasrullah
War Deputy	Db./Br. C. 1991	Deputy Minister-Sweet Alliance by Sir Ivor

STALLION NAME	YEAR OF BIRTH	SIRE – DAM – SIRE OF DAM
Weather Warning	B. C. 2004	Storm Cat-City Band by Carson City
Whiskey Wisdom	Db./Br. C. 1993	Wild Again-Primarily by Lord At War
Windfields	Db./Br. C. 1943	Bunty Lawless-Nandi by Stimulus

WINDFIELDS FOUNDATION MARES FAMILY TREES

THE FOLLOWING CHARTS contain the direct tail female line descendants emanating from Windfields' foundation mares, highlighted in the narrative of this book. The charts lead to the stakes winners descending from the foundation mare along the line. Stakes winners are highlighted in bold/ black type. Descendants who are not stakes winners but who lead to future stakes winners are in regular type.

In a few circumstances, a descent line leads to a non–stakes winner. These horses have been included because they became important stallions of stakes winners and champions. Since these charts deal only with the tail female line, the progeny of stallions is not included. Only the ancestors of stakes winners, and the few important non–stakes-winning stallions, are featured.

The charts are accurate to January 1, 2019. For information beyond January 1, you can visit the website Northernerdancing (mfdarmstrong.wordpress.com). Co-author Michael Armstrong will continue to track stakes winners and notable winners on this website to keep you up to date.

NANDI B. F. 1932 by Stimulus–Golden Feast by Golden Sun

Windfields Db./Br. C. 1943 (by Bunty Lawless)

Nandina B. F. 1953 (by Bull Page)

Milton Man Ch. C. 1958 (by Menetrier)

Cut Flower B. F. 1960 (by Chop Chop)

Chilly B. F. 1966 (by Nearctic)

Impressive Lady Db./Br. F. 1970 (by Impressive)

Impressive Prince Db./Br. C. 1977 (by Kamaraan II)

Supertam Db./Br. F. 1979 (by Tentam)

Caucasienne Ch. F. 1980 (by Caucasus)

Adorned B. F. 1987 (by Val de l'Orne)

Acadia B. F. 1994 (by Silver Deputy)

Strike Oil B. C. 2008 (by Forest Wildcat)

Archer's Bay B. C. 1995 (by Silver Deputy)

Foregone Db./Br. C. 1999 (by Gone West)

Nashinda Db./Br. F. 2001 (by Silver Deputy)

Silver Mission Gr. C. 2014 (by Mission Impazible)

Celebrate Ch. F. 2003 (by Rahy)

Occasional View Db./Br. C. 2008 (by Silver Deputy)

Lucky Lindy B. C. 2012 (by Harlan's Holiday)

Chilly Hostess Db./Br. F. 1982 (by Vice Regent)

Neat Dish B. F. 1987 (by Stalwart)

Neat Shilling B. F. 1996 (by Bob Back)

Farthing B. F. 2002 (by Mujadil)

Frutireu Ch. C. 2015 (by Casamento)

Staceymac Ch. F. 2003 (by Elnadim)

Easton Angel Gr. F. 2013 (by Dark Angel)

Kalahari Gold Ch. C. 2005 (by Trans Island)

Riddlesdown Ch. C. 1997 (by Common Grounds)

Tanks For Lunch B. F. 1990 (by Tank's Prospect)

Polish Hostess B. F. 1998 (by Polish Numbers)

Western Winter Db./Br. C. 1992 (by Gone West) *Leading sire in South Africa*

No Huggy No Kissy B. F. 1994 (by Gone West)

No Small Wonder Db./Br. F. 1999 (by Capote)

Wonderful Luck Ch. F. 2006 (by Trust N Luck)

Rockshaw Ch. C. 2014 (by MacLean's Music)

Kapen Cat Db./Br. F. 2004 (by Lion Hearted)

Bulleting Home Ch. C. 2011 (by Western Winter)

Great Hostess B. F. 2007 (by Great Notion)

Greatbullsoffire B. C. 2014 (by Bullsbay)

Imperial Colony Db./Br. C. 1985 (by Pleasant Colony)

Assert Lady Db./Br. F. 1988 (by Assert)

Unbridled Lady B. F. 1996 (by Unbridled)

Cool Combo Db./Br. F. 1971 (by Right Combination)

Seven Stones B. F. 1980 (by Habitony)

Cool Ted Db./Br. C. 1973 (by New Providence)

Right Chilly Db./Br. F. 1975 (by Right Combination)

Darcia Db./Br. F. 1988 (by Travelling Victor)

Stage Queen Gr. F. 1976 (by Ruritania)

Stage Flite Ch. F. 1983 (by Lord Durham)

Cozzene's Flite Gr. F. 1989 (by Cozzene)

Cozzene'saffair Gr. F. 1996 (by Black Tie Affair)

Duke Of Flite B. C. 1993 (by Alleged)

Bold Ruritana B. F. 1990 (by Bold Ruckus)

Preemptive Attack B. F. 1999 (by Smart Strike)

Sky Treasure Ch. F. 2010 (by Sky Mesa)

Surgical Strike Ch. C. 2013 (by Red Giant)

Hanto Yo Db./Br. F. 1991 (by Deputy Minister)

High Speed Travel Db./Br. C. 1997 (by Bold Ruckus)

Snake Pit Db./Br. C. 2000 (by Kiridashi)

Decew Falls Db./Br. C. 2002 (by Kiridashi)

Fleet Run B. F. 1967 (by Northern Dancer)

Fleet Image B. F. 1971 (by Dancer's Image)

Tremor B. F. 1982 (by Tromos)

Falling Sky Db./Br. C. 1987 (by Star de Naskra)

Move Ch. F. 1994 (by Forty Niner)

Dither Ch. F. 1995 (by Housebuster)

Swither B. F. 2002 (by Anees)

How Bout No B. F. 2003 (by Precise End)

Reforest B. F. 2001 (by Forestry)

Our Nanny Ch. F. 1969 (by Victorian Era)

Mythical Ruler Gr. C. 1978 (by Ruritania)

IRIBELLE B. F. 1942 by Osiris II–Belmona by King James

Bennington Db./Br. C. 1947 (by Boswell)

Britannia Db./Br. F. 1948 (by Bunty Lawless)

Myanna Db./Br. F. 1954 (by Chop Chop)

Nearanna Blk. F. 1964 (by Nearctic)

Faribole Db./Br. F. 1969 (by Princegret)

Mean Little Queen B. F. 1976 (by Handsome Kid)

Rey Cantor Db./Br. C. 1989 (by Get The Axe)

Elegent Kid Db./Br. C. 1977 (by Handsome Kid)

Honored Princess Db./Br. F. 1984 (by Well Decorated)

Keep Dealing Ch. F. 1991 (by Explosive Bid)

Keepondealing Db./Br. F. 1998 (by Friendly Lover)

La Bourrasque Db./Br. F. 1972 (by Victoria Park)

Le Grand Seigneur Db./Br. C. 1978 (by Snow Knight)

Feu d'Enfer Db./Br. C. 1980 (by Tentam)

Ben Fab Db./Br. C. 1977 (by Le Fabuleux)

Supper Club Db./Br. F. 1965 (by New Providence)

Avant Coureur B. F. 1974 (by Barachois)

Likeashot Db./Br. F. 1975 (by Gun Shot)

Out Of A Cannon Db./Br. F. 1980 (by Raise A Bid)

No Hot Shot Ch. C. 1992 (by It's Freezing)

Human Missile Ch. C. 1993 (by Saratoga Six)

Caveat's Shot Ch. F. 1995 (by Caveat)

Senor Verde B. C. 1982 (by Medieval Man)

Firery Ensign Gr. C. 1985 (by Blue Ensign)

Kimberlight B. F. 1987 (by Diamond Prospect)

Likeashotabrandi B. F. 1989 (by Stalwart)

Jilted Gr. F. 1999 (by Runaway Groom)

Run Away And Hide B. C. 2006 (by City Zip)

Afreeta Db./Br. F. 1992 (by Afleet)

Davide Umbro B. C. 1997 (by In The Wings)

It's a Ruby Ch. F. 1997 (by Rubiano)

Go Go Neigh Ch. F. 2002 (by Storm Boot)

Camp Creek Gr. C. 2013 (by Dunkirk)

Like A Gem Gr. F. 2003 (by Tactical Cat)

Hard Not To Like Gr. F. 2009 (by Hard Spun)

Win And Reign Db./Br. C. 2006 (by Tomahawk)

Kamakura B. C. 1967 (by Pago Pago)

Canadiana B. F. 1950 (by Chop Chop)

All Canadian B. C. 1957 (by Windfields)

Cailey Jane B. F. 1970 (by Right Combination)

Glenorum B. C. 1977 (by Prove Out)

Torrie Ann B. F. 1981 (by Blushing Groom)

Via Lactea B. F. 1993 (by Capote)

Medalha Milagrosa B. F. 1998 (by Miner's Mark)

Smart Tiffany Db./Br. F. 2006 (by Smart Strike)

Grand Martini Ch. C. 2013 (by Melon Martini)

Lots O' Lex Db./Br. F. 2011 (by Kitalpha)

Victoriana B. F. 1952 (by Windfields)

Bull Vic B. C. 1956 (by Bull Page)

Victoria Park B. C. 1957 (by Chop Chop)

Victoria Regina Ch. F. 1958 (by Menetrier)

Viceregal Ch. C. 1966 (by Northern Dancer)

Vice Regent Ch. C. 1967 (by Northern Dancer) *13 times leading sire*

Northern Queen Db./Br. F. 1962 (by Nearctic)

Buckstopper Ch. C. 1969 (by Buckpasser)

Against All Flags Db./Br. F. 1973 (by Hoist The Flag)

Pass All Flags Ch. F. 1978 (by Buckpasser)

Pass All Hope B. F. 1982 (by Damascus)

Green Passer B. F. 1991 (by Vice Regent)

Hatano Adonis B. C. 1996 (by Adjudicating)

Jodi's Sweetie Ch. C. 1988 (by Time For A Change)

Dewan's Flag B. F. 1980 (by Dewan)

Recoup The Cash B. C. 1990 (by Copelan)

Pause To Pray Ch. F. 1992 (by Timeless Moment)

Praise From Dixie B. C. 1996 (by Dixie Brass)

Up With The Flag B. C. 1994 (by Time For A Change)

Summer Exhibition B. F. 2001 (by Royal Academy)

Summer Applause B. F. 2009 (by Harlan's Holiday)

My Native Flag Ch. F. 1982 (by Raise A Native)

Bandeira Nativa Ch. F. 1993 (by Elmaamul)

Dixieland Dancer B. F. 2001 (by Dixieland Band)

Miss Dixie Dancer B. F. 2006 (by Olmodavor)

Dixie Beat B. C. 2011 (by Minister Eric)

Victorian Dancer B. F. 1966 (by Northern Dancer)

Imperial March Ch. C. 1972 (by Forli)

Victorian Heiress B. F. 1968 (by Northern Dancer)

Elegant Victress Ch. F. 1975 (by Sir Ivor)

Sharply Elegant Ch. F. 1982 (by Sharpen Up)

Very Elegant Ch. F. 1989 (by Flying Paster)

Elegant Fellow B. C. 1997 (by Memo)

Sharp Victor Ch. C. 1984 (by Sharpen Up)

Flying Victor Ch. C. 1985 (by Flying Paster)

Desert Victress Ch. F. 1988 (by Desert Wine)

Desert Digger Ch. F. 1994 (by Mining)

Sirmione Db./Br. F. 2004 (by Cozzene)

Paved Db./Br. F. 2015 (by Quality Road)

Vying Victor B. C. 1989 (by Flying Paster)

Explicit Ch. C. 1997 (by Distant View)

Northern Blossom Ch. F. 1980 (by Snow Knight)

Jape B. C. 1989 (by Alleged)

Generous Lady Ch. F. 1993 (by Generous)

High Accolade B. C. 2000 (by Mark Of Esteem)

Mango Lady Gr. F. 2005 (by Dalakhani)

Mix And Mingle Ch. F. 2013 (by Exceed And Excel)

LADY ANGELA Ch. F. 1944 by Hyperion-Sister Sarah by Abbot's Trace

Mary Martin Ch. F. 1950 (by Nearco)

Make Merry Ch. F. 1955 (by Chanteur)

Taut Ship Ch. C. 1960 (by Correlation)

Nearctic Db./Br. C. 1954 (by Nearco)

Countess Angela B. F. 1957 (by Bull Page)

Titled Hero Blk. C. 1963 (by Canadian Champ)

Titled Heroine Ch. F. 1964 (by Canadian Champ)

Titled B. F. 1976 (by Impressive)

Stolen Title Ch. F. 1981 (by Nasty And Bold)

Stolen Skates Ch. F. 1986 (by Overskate)

Miz United States Db./Br. F. 1997 (by Valid Appeal)

Exaggerated Db./Br. F. 2012 (by Blame)

Stolen Prayer Ch. F. 2003 (by Songandaprayer)

Fit For A Queen Ch. F. 1986 (by Fit To Fight)

Gold Rush Queen Ch. F. 1994 (by Seeking The Gold)

On A Roll Ch. F. 2006 (by A.P. Indy)

Doctor Mounty B. C. 2013 (by Street Sense)

Dabster Ch. C. 2014 (by Curlin)

Ender's Shadow B. C. 2000 (by A.P. Indy)

Ender's Sister B. F. 2001 (by A.P. Indy)

A.P. Indian B. C. 2010 (by Indian Charlie)

Tiz Shea D B. C. 2012 (by Tiznow)

Birthright Db./Br. F. 1995 (by Belong To Me)

Embellished Db./Br. F. 2008 (by Bellamy Road)

Hungria Ch. F. 1978 (by Nodouble)

Choperion Db./Br. C. 1959 (by Chop Chop)

Lady Victoria B. F. 1962 (by Victoria Park)

Canadian Victory B. C. 1968 (by Canadian Champ)

Northern Taste Ch. C. 1971 (by Northern Dancer) *10 times leading sire in Japan*

Tanzor B. C. 1972 (by Nijinsky II)

COMPENSATE B. F. 1945 by Reaping Reward–Niblick by Fairway

Dress Circle Db./Br. F. 1949 (by Boswell)

Censor Db./Br. C. 1953 (by Bull Page)

Willow Lake Db./Br. F. 1955 (by Windfields)

Miss Snow Goose B. F. 1964 (by Nearctic)

Willowfield B. F. 1965 (by Stratus)

Victorian Queen B. F. 1971 (by Victoria Park)

Judge Angelucci Ch. C. 1983 (by Honest Pleasure)

War B. C. 1984 (by Majestic Light)

Peace B. C. 1985 (by Naskra)

Saviour B. F. 1987 (by Majestic Light)

Graduated B. C. 1992 (by Royal Academy)

Elida B. F. 1994 (by Royal Academy)

Bring Back Matron B. F. 2004 (by Rock Of Gibraltar)

Dubai Sand Ch. C. 2014 (by Teofilo)

Maria Lee B. F. 2007 (by Rock Of Gibraltar)

Glamorous Approach Ch. F. 2013 (by New Approach)

Speirbhean B. F. 1998 (by Danehill)

Teofilo B. C. 2004 (by Galileo)

Bean Feasa B. F. 2014 (by Dubawi)

Poetic Charm B. F. 2015 (by Dubawi)

Extraterrestral B. F. 1993 (by Storm Bird)

Alienated Db./Br. F. 1999 (by Gone West)

Rally Cry Db./Br. C. 2013 (by Uncle Mo)

Exhaust Note Db./Br. C. 2002 (by A.P. Indy)

Radharcnafarraige B. F. 2008 (by Distorted Humor)

Lady Sylvie B. F. 1976 (by Victoria Park)

Motel Lady Db./Br. F. 1985 (by Bates Motel)

Roy's Trigger B. C. 2000 (by Roy)

Fly Bye Dancer B. F. 1993 (by Fire Dancer)

Asi Asi B. F. 2005 (by Yes It's True)

Dundrum Dancer B. F. 1980 (by Caucasus)

Northern Willow B. F. 1968 (by Northern Dancer)

May Combination B. C. 1972 (by Right Combination)

L'Alezane Ch. F. 1975 (by Dr. Fager)

Bay Willow B. F. 1985 (by Fappiano)

Aragen B. F. 1991 (by Rory's Jester)

Northern Lake B. F. 1969 (by Northern Dancer)

Southern Arrow Db./Br. C. 1981 (by Smarten)

Tintaburra B. F. 1983 (by Bold Agent)

Tinted Ivory B. F. 1990 (by Sir Ivor)

Mr. Fixed Income Db./Br. C. 2001 (by Sahm)

Woolloomooloo Ch. F. 1992 (by Regal Intention)

Affirmed Dancer Ch. F. 1999 (by Affirmed)

La Gran Bailadora B. F. 2007 (by Afleet Alex)

Sir Winston Ch. C. 2016 (by Awesome Again)

Gudai Might B. C. 1995 (by Seattle Dancer)

Matilda Dancer B. F. 1997 (by Green Dancer)

Diamond Lucy B. F. 2010 (by Lewis Michael)

Masake B. F. 1988 (by Master Willie)

Victorian Prince Db./Br. C. 1970 (by Victorian Era)

Windlesham Db./Br. F. 1961 (by Windfields)

Setting Sun B. F. 1970 (by Sunny)

Regent Bird B. C. 1974 (by Vice Regent)

Fuel To Burn Db./Br. F. 1973 (by Northern Native)

Flaming Emperor Ch. C. 1986 (by Hail Emperor)

Prospector's Fuel B. F. 1992 (by Allen's Prospect)

FLARING TOP Ch. F. 1947 by Menow-Flaming Top by Omaha

Gleam Ch. F. 1952 (by Tournoi)

Evening Bag Ch. F. 1965 (by Bagdad)

Coz O'Nijinsky Ch. F. 1969 (by Involvement)

My Niche Ch. F. 1973 (by Fiddle Isle)

    Utmost Celerity Ch. F. 1977 (by Timeless Moment)

        Non Perjorative B. F. 1987 (by Two Davids)

            Melted Cheese B. F. 1992 (by Sovereign Don)

    Fairmont Express B. F. 1978 (by Our Michael)

        Stanley's Girl B. F. 1985 (by Deputy Minister)

            Vanna Go Db./Br. F. 1995 (by Private Terms)

            Tannersmyman B. C. 1998 (by Lord Carson)

    Thunder Runner B. C. 1979 (by Full Out)

Royal Ski Ch. C. 1974 (by Raja Baba)

Blushet Ch. F. 1981 (by Blushing Groom)

    Hokuto Gleam Ch. F. 1988 (by Time For A Change)

        Hokuto Robin B. F. 1994 (by Blanco)

Cuz's Star Ch. F. 1983 (by Galaxy Libra)

    Stella Cielo Ch. F. 1991 (by Conquistador Cielo)

        Rucielo Ch. F. 1997 (by Rubiano)

            Appealing Stella Ch. F. 2008 (by Closing Argument)

Top Tourn Ch. C. 1953 (by Tournoi)

Flaming Wind B. F. 1955 (by Windfields)

    Flaming Issue Ch. F. 1960 (by Ace Marine)

    Dobbinton B. F. 1966 (by New Providence)

        Dobbinee Gr. F. 1976 (by Ruritania)

            Rosedon Gr. F. 1983 (by Vice Regent)

                Areydne B. F. 1988 (by Silent Sceen)

                    Nabatina B. F. 1995 (by Time For A Change)

                        Schooner Bay B. F. 2001 (by Archer's Bay)

                            Indian Pond Db./Br. F. 2008 (by Speightstown)

                Benburb Gr. C. 1989 (by Dr. Carter)

                Lady Aloma Gr. F. 1990 (by Cozzene)

                    Karra Kul Gr. C. 1995 (by Stawberry Road)

                    Chopinina Gr. F. 1998 (by Lear Fan)

                    Despite The Odds Gr. C. 2006 (by Speightstown)

                Amynteon Gr. F. 1991 (by Rahy)

My Girl Lisa Gr. F. 1998 (by With Approval)

Rosekris Gr. F. 1995 (by Kris S)

Bountempo Gr. F. 2003 (by Cape Town)

Cash Bonus B. C. 2013 (by Corinthian)

Elusive Rose Gr. F. 1997 (by Cozzene)

Royal Flush Db./Br. F. 2001 (by Smart Strike)

Legacy Db./Br. F. 2010 (by Sightseeing)

Ferdeleh Ch. F. 1974 (by Viceregal)

Ferd d'Ferh B. F. 1986 (by Heron Bay)

Strubinger Db./Br. C. 1996 (by York Minster)

New Regent Ch. C. 1977 (by Vice Regent)

Flamme d'Or B. F. 1969 (by Champlain)

Holiday Isle Db./Br. F. 1970 (by New Providence)

Sandy Isle Ch. F. 1975 (by Viceregal)

Barrier Reef B. F. 1980 (by Lord Durham)

Chapdelaine Ch. F. 1984 (by Vice Regent)

Countess Delainea Ch. F. 1991 (by Geiger Counter)

Daddy Warbucks B. C. 2004 (by Valid Expectations)

Celeberty Dancer B. F. 1974 (by Northern Dancer)

Jordy's Baba B. F. 1979 (by Raja Baba)

Our Pavlova Db./Br. F. 1988 (by Vanlandingham)

Prima Neenya Db./Br. F. 1995 (by Spend A Buck)

Lovely Cool Db./Br. F. 2005 (by Indian Charlie)

Lulu Wong B. F. 2009 (by Badge Of Silver)

Dancelikethedevil B. F. 1992 (by Devil's Bag)

Bon Fearless B. F. 1998 (by Mighty Magee)

French Wind B. F. 1961 (by Menetrier)

Merry And Bright Ch. F. 1956 (by Menetrier)

Fanfaron B. C. 1966 (by Victoria Park)

Quintain B. C. 1957 (by Tournoi)

Flashing Top Ch. F. 1958 (by Menetrier)

Flaming Page B. F. 1959 (by Bull Page)

Fleur B. F. 1964 (by Victoria Park)

Far North B. C. 1973 (by Northern Dancer)

The Minstrel Ch. C. 1974 (by Northern Dancer)

Flower Princess Db./Br. F. 1975 (by Majestic Prince)

Dance Flower B. F. 1981 (by Northern Dancer)

Pilgrim B. C. 1979 (by Northern Dancer)

Nijinsky B. C. 1967 (by Northern Dancer) *English Triple Crown winner*

Minsky Ch. C. 1968 (by Northern Dancer)

Flaming Victress B. F. 1963 (by Victoria Park)

Juana Del Mar Ch. F. 1968 (by Fortino II)

Rumpole Db./Br. C. 1982 (by Golden Reserve)

Kalispera B. F. 1987 (by Golden Reserve)

Senita Lane Db./Br. F. 1994 (by Ascot Knight)

Latin Lynx Db./Br. F. 1999 (by Forest Wildcat)

Sean Avery B. C. 2006 (by Cherokee Run)

Stayclassysandiego Gr. F. 2009 (by Rockport Harbor)

Pretty And Cool Gr. F. 2013 (by Scat Daddy)

Teniente Coronel B. C. 2011 (by Colonel John)

Flaming Tam B. F. 1975 (by Tentam)

Phoenix Factor B. F. 1985 (by Briartic)

Hillsburgh Rumors B. F. 1992 (by Bold Ruckus)

Winter Garden B. F. 2000 (by Roy)

Title Contender Db./Br. C. 2010 (by Pulpit)

Moonlit Garden B. F. 2014 (by Malibu Moon)

Midnightontheoasis B. F. 1994 (by Gulch)

Tejano's Oasis B. F. 2004 (by Tejano Run)

All For Victory B. C. 1976 (by One For All)

Friendly Relations Ch. F. 1966 (by Nearctic)

Timely Affair Db./Br. F. 1971 (by Bold Hour)

Icy Time Db./Br. F. 1980 (by Icecapde)

Be Cool B. F. 1988 (by Tank's Prospect)

Cool Dixie B. F. 1995 (by Dixieland Band)

Blue Begonia Db./Br. F. 1993 (by Seeking The Gold)

Alpha Angel B. F. 2000 (by Alphabet Soup)

Tree Pose B. F. 2008 (by Old Forester)

Biding Time Db./Br. F. 1994 (by Seeking The Gold)

Kindheartedness Ch. F. 1977 (by Exclusive Native)

Endow B. C. 1986 (by Flying Paster)

Viendra Ch. F. 1978 (by Raise A Native)

Irish Forever Ch. F. 1991 (by Irish River)

Elzevir B. F. 1984 (by Elocutionist)

Bellzevir Db./Br. C. 1990 (by Bellotto)

You Sun Polish B. F. 1997 (by El Senor)

Super Hornet B. C. 2003 (by Rodrigo De Triano)

STALINA B. F. 1949 by Stalino-Boscabell by Fairford

Sunday Sail B. C. 1956 (by Alycidon)

Cut Steel B. C. 1958 (by Chop Chop)

Grand Garcon B. C. 1961 (by Censor)

Speediness Ch. F. 1963 (by Nearctic)

Speedy Zephyr Ch. C. 1968 (by Restless Wind)

Drama School Ch. F. 1966 (by Northern Dancer)

Stagetime Ch. F. 1971 (by Victorian Era)

Tamworth B. F. 1979 (by Tentam)

Far Too Loud Ch. F. 1990 (by No Louder)

Lady Tamworth Db./Br. F. 1995 (by No Louder)

Norcliffe Db./Br. C. 1973 (by Buckpasser)

Vaguely Dramatic B. F. 1978 (by Vaguely Noble)

Dam Dramatic Ch. F. 1986 (by Damascus)

El Sultan Gr. C. 1991 (by Morning Bob)

Madrama Ch. F. 1983 (by Master Willie)

Cheeky Rockette B. F. 1989 (by Temperence Hill)

Cut A Check B. F. 1996 (by Polish Numbers)

Admiral's War Chest B. C. 2011 (by Elusive Charlie)

Smartalma Db./Br. F. 1984 (by Smarten)

Satan's Sequel B. F. 1993 (by Rubiton)

Money Exchange Db./Br. C. 2001 (by Magic Of Money)

L'Insatiable B. F. 1985 (by Caveat)

Lodge Hill Ch. C. 1997 (by Cozzene)

Dontellmichelle Ch. F. 1998 (by Regal Classic)

Hightap Gr. F. 2006 (by Tapit)

FAIR COLLEEN Ch. F. 1950 by Preciptic-Fairvale by Fairford

New Providence B. C. 1956 (by Bull Page) *Canadian Triple Crown winner*

Maid O'North Db./Br. F. 1958 (by Bull Page)

Own Colleen Ch. F. 1959 (by Queen's Own)

Ice Palace Ch. C. 1966 (by Nearctic)

Winlord Ch. C. 1968 (by Canebora)

Royal Colleen Ch. F. 1973 (by Viceregal)

Beau Genius Ch. C. 1985 (by Bold Ruckus)

Kathie's Colleen Ch. F. 1992 (by Woodman)

Wando Ch. C. 2000 (by Langfuhr) *Canadian Triple Crown winner*

Six Sexy Sisters B. F. 2001 (by Langfuhr)

Go Bro B. C. 2011 (by Proud Citizen)

EVENSONG Db./Br. F. 1950 by The Phoenix-Angelus by Blandford

Song Of Even Db./Br. F. 1958 (by Vimy)

Queen's Song Db./Br. F. 1959 (by Queen's Own)

Backstretch B. C. 1971 (by Northern Answer)

Song Of Victory B. F. 1962 (by Victoria Park)

New Tune B. F. 1968 (by New Providence)

Sound Reason B. C. 1974 (by Bold Reason)

Northern Empress B. F. 1975 (by Northern Answer)

Northern Dominion Db./Br. F. 1981 (by Dom Alaric)

Snow County Honey Db./Br. F. 1991 (by Foolish Pleasure)

Country Humor Db./Br. C. 2004 (by Distorted Humor)

Breezy Stories B. F. 1978 (by Damascus)

Nakiska Wind Ch. F. 1986 (by Lyphard)

The Exeter Man B. C. 1992 (by Capote)

Icy Wind Ch. F. 1997 (by Clackson)

Quick Wind B. C. 2005 (by Public Purse)

Desert Stormer B. F. 1990 (by Storm Cat)

Sahara Gold B. F. 1997 (by Seeking The Gold)

Enrichment B. F. 2008 (by Ghostzapper)

Libreta B. F. 2013 (by Girolamo)

Forest City Girl B. F. 2002 (by Deputy Minister)

Outskirt Lady B. F. 2007 (by Purge)

Sahara Heat Db./Br. C. 2004 (by A.P. Indy)

Better Lucky B. F. 2009 (by Ghostzapper)

Ensenada Db./Br. F. 2001 (by Seeking The Gold)

Casino Host Db./Br. C. 2008 (by Dynaformer)

Desert Stormette B. F. 1991 (by Storm Cat)

Desert Gold Ch. F. 1999 (by Seeking The Gold)

Conchita Gr. F. 2005 (by Cozzene)

Chiquita Picosa Ch. F. 2009 (by Congaree)

Homerique Gr. F. 2015 (by Exchange Rate)

White Moonstone B. F. 2008 (by Dynaformer)

Albasharah B. F. 2009 (by Arch)

Kalahari Cat Db./Br. F. 2000 (by Cape Town)

Francois Db./Br. C. 2009 (by Smarty Jones)

Black Onyx Blk. C. 2010 (by Rock Hard Ten)

Nesselrode Ch. F. 2003 (by Lemon Drop Kid)

Street Gem Ch. F. 2010 (by Street Boss)

Tune Writer B. F. 1983 (by Master Willie)

Herat's Tune B. F. 1990 (by Herat)

Sea Mist Db./Br. F. 1998 (by Mecke)

Robyn's Tune B. F. 1995 (by Robyn Dancer)

United Db./Br. C. 2002 (by Dixie Union)

Arctic Song B. F. 1962 (by Nearctic)

Victoria Song B. C. 1969 (by Victoria Park)

REPLY B. F. 1951 by Teddy Wrack-Alaris by Alsab

Windy Answer B. F. 1955 (by Windfields)

Breezy Answer Db./Br. F. 1960 (by Bull Page)

Arctic Blizzard Db./Br. C. 1965 (by Nearctic)

Ciboulette B. F. 1961 (by Chop Chop)

Fanfreluche B. F. 1967 (by Northern Dancer)

L'Enjoleur B. C. 1972 (by Buckpasser)

L'Extravagante B. F. 1973 (by Le Fabuleux)

Montelimar B. C. 1981 (by Alleged)

Royal Extravagance B. F. 1983 (by Secretariat)

Dhion Ch. F. 1996 (by Royal Danzig)

Medici Db./Br. C. 2005 (by Sir Cat)

L'Extra Honor Ch. F. 1987 (by Hero's Honor)

Majestic Roi Ch. F. 2004 (by Street Cry)

Noor Al Hawa Ch. C. 2013 (by Makfi)

Black Spirit B. C. 2007 (by Black Minnaloushe)

Exigent Ch. F. 1992 (by Miswaki)

Taletobetold Db./Br. F. 2004 (by Tale Of The Cat)

Ballet d'Amour B. F. 2005 (by Stravinsky)

Russian Revolution B. C. 2013 (by Snitzel)

Grand Luxe Ch. F. 1974 (by Sir Ivor)

Islands Ch. F. 1981 (by Forli)

Forli's Secret Ch. F. 1986 (by Secretariat)

Bold Caleb Db./Br. C. 1996 (by Kris S)

Secret Launch Gr. C. 1997 (by Relaunch)

Unbridled Secret Ch. F. 2001 (by Unbridled)

Unbridled Courage Ch. F. 2012 (by Leroidesanimaux)

Fit To Lead Db./Br. F. 1990 (by Fit To Fight)

Leading The Way B. F. 1996 (by Septieme Ciel)

Dance Lead B. F. 2000 (by Nureyev)

Trust Or Bust Db./Br. C. 2005 (by Trust N Luck)

Honoris Causa Ch. F. 1991 (by Miswaki)

Historia Ch. F. 1999 (by French Deputy)

Hinz Ch. C. 2008 (by Pure Prize)

Hi Happy Ch. C. 2012 (by Pure Prize)

Hispanidad Ch. F. 2013 (by Pure Prize)

A.P. Indy's Lady B. F. 1995 (by A.P. Indy)

Unbridled Echo B. F. 2001 (by Unbridled's Song)

Honey Hues Ch. F. 2009 (by Henny Hughes)

Categorical Ch. F. 1999 (by Hennessy)

Krupt Ch. C. 2005 (by Flying Spur)

Anevay Ch. F. 2008 (by Exceed And Excel)

Salvora Ch. F. 1982 (by Spectacular Bid)

Special Gallery B. F. 1989 (by Tate Gallery)

Aube Indienne Ch. F. 1990 (by Bluebird)

Maruka Hannibal Db./Br. C. 2004 (by Special Week)

Spenderella Ch. F. 1992 (by Common Grounds)

Common World Ch. C. 1999 (by Spinning World)

Star Band B. F. 2001 (by Dixieland Band)

I Am A Star B. F. 2013 (by I Am Invincible)

Speciale B. F. 2002 (by War Chant)

Raisonnable B. F. 1993 (by Common Grounds)

Sensible B. C. 1998 (by Sadler's Wells)

Mare Nostrum B. F. 1998 (by Caerleon)

Marie De Medici Ch. F. 2007 (by Medicean)

Local Time B. F. 2012 (by Invincible Spirit)

Erupt B. C. 2012 (by Dubawi)

Rolls Ch. F. 1984 (by Mr. Prospector)

Shoal Creek Ch. F. 1988 (by Star Way)

Encosta De Lago B. C. 1993 (by Fairy King) *Leading sire in Australia*

Ballincrea Lady Db./Br. F. 1990 (by Bletchingly)

Ballybleue B. F. 2001 (by Peintre Celebre)

Think Bleue Db./Br. F. 2014 (by So You Think)

Flying Spur B. C. 1992 (by Danehill) *Leading sire in Australia*

Smackover Creek B. C. 1986 (by Mr. Prospector)

Nice Dancing Ch. F. 1990 (by Bering)

Musidora Ch. F. 2004 (by Rock Of Gibraltar)

Sacred Eye B. F. 2012 (by High Chaparral)

Tulip B. F. 2014 (by Pierro)

La Voyageuse Db./Br. F. 1975 (by Tentam)

Society Lady Ch. F. 1990 (by Mr. Prospector)

Bint Allayl B. F. 1996 (by Green Desert)

Nasmatt B. F. 1998 (by Danehill)

Emmrooz B. C. 2005 (by Red Ransom)

Khelyef Db./Br. C. 2001 (by Green Desert)

Laa Rayb B. C. 2004 (by Storm Cat)

French Shoes Db./Br. F. 1992 (by Fast Play)

French Braid B. F. 1997 (by Flying Spur)

Innovative Ch. C. 1993 (by Time For A Change)

Time Bandit Ch. C. 1996 (by Time For A Change)

Medaille d'Or Ch. C. 1976 (by Secretariat)

D'Accord Ch. C. 1979 (by Secretariat)

La Pepite Db./Br. F. 1985 (by Mr. Prospector)

Soldera B. F. 2000 (by Polish Numbers)

Exhi B. C. 2007 (by Maria's Mon)

Soldata B. F. 2008 (by Maria's Mon)

Alignement B. C. 2013 (by Pivotal)

L'On Vite B. F. 1986 (by Secretariat)

Heart Of Oak Ch. C. 1992 (by Woodman)

Eishin Maysville Ch. F. 1995 (by Jade Hunter)

Zelsnitz B. F. 2007 (by Snitzel)

Big Viking Db./Br. C. 1996 (by Theatrical)

Milanova B. F. 1999 (by Danehill)

Pretty Perfect B. F. 2013 (by Galileo)

Holy Roman Emperor B. C. 2004 (by Danehill)

Slew And Easy B. F. 1987 (by Slew O' Gold)

Scads Ch. F. 1993 (by Forty Niner)

Plenty Ch. F. 2001 (by Boundary)

Plethora Ch. F. 2009 (by First Samurai)

Border Dispute B. F. 2002 (by Boundary)

Long Lashes B. F. 2007 (by Rock Hard Ten)

Conserve B. C. 1996 (by Boundary)

Coco La Terreur B. C. 1968 (by Nearctic)

Barachois Ch. C. 1969 (by Northern Dancer)

Silk Lilly Db./Br. F. 1976 (by Never Bend)

Silky Pleasure Db./Br. F. 1981 (by Honest Pleasure)

Genial B. C. 1989 (by Gate Dancer)

Lilly's Pleasure Db./Br. F. 1983 (by What A Pleasure)

Lillycut Db./Br. C. 1988 (by Cutlass)

Sovereign Lilly Db./Br. F. 1985 (by Sovereign Dancer)

Valid Fixation B. F. 1989 (by Valid Appeal)

Dynaspice Db./Br. F. 2000 (by Dynaformer)

Benwill Db./Br. C. 2009 (by Leestown)

The Pickett Factor Db./Br. C. 2012 (by Gold Tribute)

Glinka Blk. F. 2006 (by Devil His Due)

Rouge B. F. 2011 (by Privately Held)

Silken Moment Ch. F. 1989 (by Timeless Moment)

Beau Gentleman Ch. C. 1996 (by Beau Genius)

Make Contact Ch. F. 1997 (by Time To Explode)

Irish Day Dancer Db./Br. F. 2005 (by Vicar)

Go For Guinness Db./Br. C. 2010 (by Rosberg)

Cut Class Leanne B. F. 1990 (by Cutlass)

Chapel Royal Db./Br. C. 2001 (by Montbrook)

Crusading Lil B. F. 1993 (by Crusader Sword)

Motspur Ch. C. 2002 (by Flying Spur)

Silky Sweep Ch. C. 1996 (by End Sweep)

Silk Ending Db./Br. F. 1997 (by End Sweep)

Gypsy Tucker Db./Br. F. 2004 (by Zabeel)

Gypsy Diamond B. F. 2010 (by Not A Single Doubt)

Somfas Db./Br. F. 1978 (by What A Pleasure)

Russian Bond B. C. 1986 (by Danzig)

Snaadee B. C. 1987 (by Danzig)

Cristofori Db./Br. C. 1989 (by Fappiano)

Sombreffe B. F. 1992 (by Polish Precedent)

Ransom O' War B. C. 2000 (by Red Ransom)

Machera B. F. 1993 (by Machiavellian)

L'Enjoleuse B. F. 2002 (by Montjeu)

Charm Spirit B. C. 2011 (by Invincible Spirit)

Sonata B. F. 1995 (by Polish Precedent)

Regal Solo B. C. 2005 (by Louis Quatorze)

Crossover B. F. 2002 (by Cape Cross)

Night Shift B. C. 1980 (by Northern Dancer) *Sire of Grade/Group One winners*

Icy Reply Ch. F. 1963 (by Nearctic)

Diademata B. F. 1971 (by Ribocco)

Talc Shaker Blk. F. 1979 (by Talc)

Geraldine Db./Br. F. 1986 (by Deputy Minister)

Sandpile B. C. 1995 (by Cure The Blues)

Carr Shaker B. F. 1987 (by Carr de Naskra)

Dewars Rocks Db./Br. F. 1994 (by Big Mukora)

Honour Shaker B. F. 2001 (by Honor And Glory)

Molly's Honour Db./Br. F. 2010 (by Etesaal)

Shaky Canyon B. F. 2004 (by Gulch)

Prospector's Blues Db./Br. C. 2012 (by Benton Creek)

Fortified Effort Db./Br. C. 2015 (by EZ Effort)

She's A Shaker Db./Br. F. 1988 (by Carr de Naskra)

Shake Loose B. C. 1997 (by Son Of Briartic)

Mt. Airy Lass B. F. 1990 (by Carr de Naskra)

Tin Smithen B. C. 1997 (by The Names Jimmy)

Victory Road Db./Br. F. 1999 (by Ikari)

Noisy Feet B. F. 2006 (by Tapit)

Touching Beauty B. F. 2007 (by Tapit)

Cool Reception Ch. C. 1964 (by Nearctic)

Prize Answer Db./Br. F. 1965 (by Choperion)

Noble Answer B. C. 1971 (by Viceregal)

Nearctic Answer Db./Br. F. 1973 (by Nearctic)

Majestic Answer Db./Br. C. 1979 (by Majestic Light)

Sansapa Blk. F. 1988 (by Bletchingly)

Sansadee Blk. F. 2000 (by Snaadee)

Brazen Beau Db./Br. C. 2011 (by I Am Invincible)

Regal Response B. F. 1975 (by Viceregal)

Hear Music Ch. F. 1983 (by Master Willie)

Dance On The Green B. F. 1990 (by Green Dancer)

Gold Pirate B. C. 1996 (by Goldwater)

Formal Miss B. F. 2000 (by Formal Dinner)

Blue Twisted Steel B. C. 2016 (by Caleb's Posse)

Northern Answer B. C. 1966 (by Northern Dancer) *Sire of Grade/Group One winners*

Windy Response B. F. 1960 (by Windfields)

Canadian Jerry B. C. 1967 (by New Providence)

Respond B. F. 1968 (by Canadian Champ)

Cold Reply Ch. F. 1972 (by Northern Dancer)

Question d'Argent B. F. 1977 (by Tentam)

Croupier Lady Db./Br. F. 1982 (by What Luck)

Genuine Blk. C. 1992 (by Sunday Silence)

Croupier Star Ch. F. 1996 (by Sunday Silence)

Asakusa Kings B. C. 2004 (by White Muzzle)

Question N Answer Ch. F. 1984 (by Dust Commander)

Gold Answer Ch. F. 1990 (by Gold Alert)

Mayano Starlight Ch. F. 2000 (by Jade Robbery)

Kurino Star O Blk. C. 2010 (by Admire Boss)

Premier Answer Ch. F. 1992 (by Premiership)

Marrakech Gold Ch. F. 1999 (by Native Regent)

San Onofre B. C. 2010 (by Surf Cat)

Argent Question Ch. F. 1985 (by Critique)

Lady Question B. F. 1997 (by Alleging)

Great Destroyer B. C. 1998 (by Macau)

Nonez B. C. 2001 (by Italian Danzig)

Premier Question B. F. 1987 (by Premiership)

Aly's Question B. F. 1992 (by Alysheba)

Kissin Ty B. C. 2001 (by Kissin Kris)

Deloram Ch. F. 1978 (by Lord Durham)

Smart Lord B. C. 1985 (by Smarten)

Halo Reply Ch. F. 1980 (by Halo)

Prayer Wheel Ch. F. 1986 (by Conquistador Cielo)

Strategic Maneuver B. F. 1991 (by Cryptoclearance)

Ishiguru B. C. 1997 (by Danzig)

Cat Fighter Db./Br. F. 2000 (by Storm Cat)

Tacticmove B. F. 2001 (by Deputy Minister)

Good Luck Gus B. C. 2012 (by Lookin At Lucky)

Wile Cat B. F. 2003 (by Storm Cat)

Shumoos Ch. F. 2009 (by Distorted Humor)

Lynnette B. F. 2008 (by Johannesburg)

Jennifer Lynnette B. F. 2013 (by Elusive Quality)

Secret Psalm B. F. 1992 (by Cryptoclearance)

One Twenty One B. F. 1997 (by Devil's Bag)

Stole One B. F. 2001 (by Pembroke)

Delovientos Db./Br. C. 2003 (by Siphon)

Heart's Song Db./Br. F. 2012 (by Desert Party)

Ashford Castle B. F. 1994 (by Bates Motel)

Aspasias Tizzy Db./Br. F. 2003 (by Tiznow)

Above The Rest B. C. 2011 (by Excellent Art)

Missionary Ch. C. 1995 (by Deputy Minister)

Fornalina B. F. 1996 (by Capote)

Daiwa Zoom Ch. F. 2009 (by Heart's Cry)

Heaven For Bid Gr. F. 1987 (by Spectacular Bid)

Berriesfromheaven Ch. F. 1993 (by Strawberry Road)

Berriestoheaven B. F. 2004 (by Smoke Glacken)

Talverna Ch. F. 2003 (by Gilded Time)

Wanda's Dream Ch. F. 1988 (by Miswaki)

Dehere's Dream Ch. F. 1998 (by Dehere)

Chit Chat Pam Db./Br. F. 2003 (by Valid Expectations)

Favorable Ruling Ch. C. 1993 (by Woodman)

Halory Ch. F. 1984 (by Halo)

Speak Halory B. F. 1989 (by Verbatim)

Sashay Away Db./Br. F. 1997 (by Farma Way)

New Edition Ch. F. 2004 (by Stormy Atlantic)

Shamaal Nibras B. C. 2009 (by First Samurai)

Red Sashay Ch. F. 2012 (by Big Brown)

Parlez B. F. 1999 (by French Deputy)

Fools In Love B. F. 2006 (by Not For Love)

Seahenge B. C. 2015 (by Scat Daddy)

D C Dancer Db./Br. C. 2010 (by Not For Love)

International Star B. C. 2012 (by Fusaichi Pegasus)

Raven Quiver B. F. 2002 (by Old Trieste)

Karun B. C. 2007 (by Arch)

Prory B. C. 1992 (by Procida)

Key Lory Ch. C. 1994 (by Key To The Mint)

Halory Hunter Ch. C. 1995 (by Jade Hunter)

Brushed Halory B. F. 1996 (by Broad Brush)

Sly Storm B. F. 2005 (by Storm Cat)

Brushed Strokes B. F. 2008 (by Bluegrass Cat)

Bellamy V B. F. 2014 (by Bellamy Road)

Miss Halory Ch. F. 1999 (by Mr. Prospector)

Stormalory B. C. 2006 (by Storm Cat)

Gyllen Db./Br. C. 2015 (by Medaglia d'Oro)

Van Nistelrooy Ch. C. 2000 (by Storm Cat)

Antrim Solina B. F. 1990 (by Country Light)

Rodeo Springs Gr. F. 1998 (by Wekiva Springs)

High Voltage Sport Gr. F. 1976 (by High Echelon)

Exploding High B. F. 1983 (by Explodent)

Premier Explosion B. C. 1990 (by Premiership)

Shocking Sport B. F. 1986 (by Lypheor)

Gala Knockout B. C. 1992 (by Two Punch)

Shock Value Db./Br. C. 1995 (by Private Terms)

Misty Ocean B. F. 2005 (by Stormy Atlantic)

Maverick Wave Ch. C. 2011 (by Elusive Quality)

Devinette B. F. 1980 (by Secretariat)

Provinette B. F. 1986 (by Private Account)

Hazel's Honor B. F. 1995 (by Honor Grades)

Time Honored B. F. 2000 (by Gilded Time)

West Side Bernie Db./Br. C. 2006 (by Bernstein)

Gypsy Cab Company Ch. F. 2006 (by Malibu Moon)

Ole's Miss B. F. 2011 (by Officer)

My Sweet Country B. F. 1989 (by Bold Ruckus)

Patriot Love Gr. C. 1995 (by With Approval)

My Canada Ch. F. 1997 (by With Approval)

Romantic Hideaway Ch. F. 2007 (by City Zip)

Disposablepleasure Gr. F. 2009 (by Giacomo)

Deputy Country B. C. 1998 (by Silver Deputy)

Riley Tucker Db./Br. C. 2005 (by Harlan's Holiday)

Hey Hazel B. F. 1990 (by Ascot Knight)

Bal Boree B. F. 1998 (by Seattle Slew)

Nakayama Jeune Db./Br. F. 2006 (by Petionville)

Phantom Trip Db./Br. C. 2013 (by Summer Bird)

Secret World B. F. 1993 (by Careafolie)

Secret Ridge B. C. 2001 (by Choctaw Ridge)

Pura Classe B. F. 2007 (by Grand Slam)

Zuzu Bem B. F. 2014 (by First American)

Archregent B. C. 1981 (by Vice Regent)

Coqueluche B. F. 1970 (by Victorian Era)

Archmillionaire B. F. 1981 (by Medaille d'Or)

Uanme Ch. F. 1995 (by Marquetry)

Mikrokosmos B. F. 2009 (by Neo Universe)

Cosmic Force B. C. 2015 (by King Kamehameha)

Laluche B. F. 1984 (by Alleged)

Lala Musa B. F. 1991 (by Kris)

Stella Irlandese Ch. F. 1998 (by Ashkalani)

Miss Bikini Ch. F. 2003 (by Titus Livius)

Holy Waters B. C. 2014 (by Falco)

Miss Moon B. F. 2016 (by Elusive City)

SOLAR DISPLAY Ch. F. 1951 by Sun Again-Dark Display by Display

Dr. Em Jay B. C. 1955 (by Chop Chop)

Men At Play Ch. C. 1957 (by Menetrier)

Solar Day B. F. 1958 (by Menetrier)

Victoria Day B. F. 1964 (by Victoria Park)

Hatch Cover B. C. 1974 (by Ship Leave)

Brave Today B. F. 1979 (by Bravest Roman)

Royal Scot B. C. 1969 (by George Royal)

Combat Day B. C. 1970 (by Bold and Brave)

Solarism B. F. 1959 (by Menetrier)

Champ de Soleil B. F. 1968 (by Champlain)

Deep Meadow Db./Br. F. 1973 (by Right Combination)

Every Effort Db./Br. F. 1980 (by Full Out)

Complete Endeavor B. C. 1987 (by Fiddle Dancer Boy)

Valiant Jewel Ch. F. 1990 (by Buckley Boy)

Abba Gold Ch. F. 1998 (by Devil's Bag)

Kathmanblu B. F. 2008 (by Bluegrass Cat)

Kathballu Ch. F. 2012 (by Bluegrass Cat)

Friendly Michelle Ch. F. 2001 (by Artax)

Bonita Bianca Ch. F. 2014 (by Curlin)

Superfine City Ch. F. 2002 (by Carson City)

Someplace Else B. F. 2008 (by Harlan's Holiday)

Ms Tenacious Ch. F. 1991 (by Buckley Boy)

Trebbiano Ch. C. 1999 (by Mystery Storm)

Albarino Ch. C. 2001 (by Langfuhr)

Freisa B. F. 2002 (by Lil's Lad)

Trincadeiro B. F. 2007 (by Pollard's Vision)

Adventcia B. F. 2006 (by Petionville)

Sioux City Db./Br. F. 1995 (by Carson City)

Santerra B. F. 2000 (by Tejabo)

Whisper Number Ch. F. 2008 (by First Samurai)

Ms Locust Point Ch. F. 2014 (by Dialed In)

Celestial Day Db./Br. F. 1960 (by Censor)

Naughty Celeste Gr. F. 1969 (by Yusuf)

> **Naughty Jimmy** B. C. 1977 (by Roanoke Island)

> **Celestial Ballet** Gr. F. 1980 (by Dancing Count)

Sherzad Db./Br. C. 1970 (by Yusuf)

Shining Sun B. F. 1962 (by Chop Chop)

South Ocean B. F. 1967 (by New Providence)

> **Northernette** B. F. 1974 (by Northern Dancer)

>> **Gold Crest** Db./Br. C. 1982 (by Mr. Prospector)

>> **Scoot** Db./Br. F. 1983 (by Mr. Prospector)

>>> Individual Spirit Db./Br. F. 1989 (by Seattle Slew)

>>>> **Individual Dance** B. F. 2006 (by Dance Brightly)

>>> Bring Me Joy B. F. 1994 (by Deputy Minister)

>>>> **Joyful Ballad** Db./Br. F. 2000 (by Saint Ballado)

>> Wyndalia B. F. 1987 (by Seattle Slew)

>>> Pim Pam Pum B. F. 1992 (by Thatching)

>>>> Qualibet B. F. 2002 (by Burooj)

>>>>> **Didimo** B. C. 2008 (by Nedawi)

>>>>> **La Vie En Rose** B. F. 2013 (by Nedawi)

>>> Windy Gulch B. F. 1995 (by Gulch)

>>>> **Windya** Gr. F. 2002 (by Linamix)

>>>>> **Mr. Satchmo** Gr. C. 2015 (by Mr. Sidney)

>>>> **Sendingmylovetorose** B. F. 2010 (by Bahamian Bounty)

>> Fextal Db./Br. F. 1989 (by Alleged)

>>> Eubee B. F. 1994 (by Common Grounds)

>>>> **Lenatareese** B. F. 2001 (by Broad Brush)

>>>>> **Miss Chatelaine** Ch. F. 2012 (by Pulpit)

>>>>> **Big Bend** B. C. 2014 (by Union Rags)

>> Midnight Oasis Ch. F. 1993 (by Java Gold)

>>> **Tosho Knight** Ch. C. 2001 (by Timber Country)

>> Limbo B. F. 1996 (by A.P. Indy)

>>> **Gentleman Chester** Db./Br. C. 2004 (by Chester House)

>>> **Back Forty** B. C. 2008 (by Speightstown)

> **Ocean's Answer** B. F. 1976 (by Northern Answer)

Soundings B. F. 1983 (by Mr. Prospector)

Didyme B. F. 1990 (by Dixieland Band)

Green Tune Ch. C. 1991 (by Green Dancer)

Ecoute B. F. 1993 (by Manila)

Ecoutila B. F. 2001 (by Rahy)

Enticement B. F. 2006 (by Montjeu)

Diploma B. F. 2015 (by Dubawi)

Surfrider B. C. 2008 (by Dansili)

Listen A.P. B. F. 2004 (by A.P. Indy)

Silentio Db./Br. C. 2009 (by Silent Name)

Pas de Reponse B. F. 1994 (by Danzig)

Sunday Doubt Db./Br. C. 2001 (by Sunday Silence)

Saying B. F. 2007 (by Giant's Causeway)

Dicton B. C. 2013 (by Lawman)

Sonnerie B. F. 2012 (by More Than Ready)

Oceanique B. F. 2005 (by Forest Wildcat)

Snowday Db./Br. C. 2010 (by Falco)

Okana B. F. 2013 (by Zamindar)

Tiramisu Ch. F. 1984 (by Roberto)

Lac Dessert Ch. F. 1993 (by Lac Ouimet)

Devil's Oceanette Ch. F. 1986 (by Devil's Bag)

Miss Oceanette Ch. F. 1992 (by Miswaki)

Royal Corona Gr. F. 1998 (by Holy Bull)

Smooth Brandy Gr. F. 2003 (by Awesome Again)

Bella Paella Db./Br. F. 2012 (by Bellamy Road)

Dr. Zic Ch. F. 2006 (by Milwaukee Brew)

Tidal Treasure B. F. 1992 (by Crafty Prospector)

Igman B. C. 1997 (by Mt. Livermore)

Call Me Fleet B. F. 1993 (by Afleet)

Warrior Queen B. F. 1997 (by Quiet American)

A.P. Warrior Db./Br. C. 2003 (by A.P. Indy)

Egyptian Queen Db./Br. F. 2004 (by Storm Cat)

Global View Db./Br. C. 2011 (by Galileo)

Call Me Pretty B. F. 1998 (by Peaks and Valleys)

Born To Rock B. F. 2007 (by Fastnet Rock)

Prettyhappyaboutit B. F. 2009 (by Magnus)

Tiger's Rock B. C. 2006 (by Giant's Causeway)

Speak Softly To Me B. F. 1994 (by Ogygian)

High Maintenance B. F. 1999 (by Danehill)

Master Merion B. C. 2014 (by Quality Road)

Artful Whisper Db./Br. F. 2002 (by Machiavellian)

Whispering Brook Db./Br. F. 2013 (by Hinchinbrook)

Let's Go South B. C. 1977 (by One For All)

Storm Bird B. C. 1978 (by Northern Dancer)

South Sea Dancer B. F. 1981 (by Northern Dancer)

Island Wedding B. F. 1987 (by Blushing Groom)

Winter Romance Ch. C. 1993 (by Cadeaux Genereux)

Signal Tap B. C. 1991 (by Fappiano)

Longue Vue B. F. 1994 (by Miswaki)

Youllbeinmyheart Db./Br. F. 1999 (by Broad Brush)

Destiny Calls Gr. F. 2000 (by With Approval)

Nowandforevermore Ch. C. 2003 (by Sky Classic)

Coral Sea Gr. F. 1995 (by Rubiano)

Coral Genius B. F. 2000 (by Smart Strike)

Desert Power Ch. C. 2006 (by Newfoundland)

Kathleen's Reel B. F. 2004 (by Lemon Drop Kid)

Cool Coal Man B. C. 2005 (by Mineshaft)

Oceana B. F. 1983 (by Northern Dancer)

Water Angel B. F. 1988 (by Halo)

Exponent Db./Br. F. 1995 (by Exbourne)

Drayton Db./Br. C. 2004 (by Danetime)

West Indies B. F. 1991 (by Gone West)

Indian Halo B. F. 1995 (by Halo)

Megan's Halo B. F. 2000 (by Jules)

Indian Ocean B. C. 2002 (by Stormy Atlantic)

Colony Bay B. F. 1992 (by Pleasant Colony)

Lindsay Jean B. F. 1998 (by Saint Ballado)

Crozet B. F. 2001 (by Charismatic)

Honour Colony B. F. 2002 (by Honor and Glory)

Biwa Shinseiki B. C. 1998 (by Forty Niner)

Silky Craft Ch. F. 2004 (by Crafty Prospector)

T O Energy Ch. C. 2015 (by Kane Hekili)

Stormette B. F. 1984 (by Assert)

Marillette B. F. 1990 (by Diesis)

Khamsin Db./Br. F. 1991 (by Mr. Prospector)

Subeen B. F. 1996 (by Caerleon)

Stupendous Miss Db./Br. F. 2001 (by Dynaformer)

Do It All Db./Br. C. 2007 (by Distorted Humor)

Tales Of Grimm B. C. 2009 (by Distorted Humor)

Closing Range Db./Br. F. 2009 (by After Market)

Storm Trooper B. C. 1993 (by Diesis)

Forest Storm B. F. 1994 (by Woodman)

Fann B. F. 2003 (by Diesis)

Black Arrow Blk. C. 2009 (by Teofilo)

Barometer Db./Br. F. 2005 (by Point Given)

Giada Vegas Db./Br. F. 2013 (by Scat Daddy)

Solar Park B. F. 1963 (by Victoria Park)

Rome Frolic Db./Br. F. 1970 (by Roman Line)

Solar Path B. F. 1971 (by Prince D'Amour)

Maple Grove B. C. 1975 (by Forward Pass)

Solar Command B. F. 1978 (by Bold Commander)

Solometeor B. F. 1965 (by Victoria Park)

Victoria Star Ch. F. 1972 (by Northern Dancer)

Bucksplasher Ch. C. 1977 (by Buckpasser) *Sire of Grade/Group One winners*

Starstruck Gal Ch. F. 1981 (by Stage Door Johnny)

Glitzy Gal Ch. F. 1986 (by Commemorate)

Almost Sma Ch. F. 1995 (by Cure The Blues)

Rolling Sea Ch. F. 2003 (by Sefapiano)

Starry Val B. F. 1989 (by Val de l'Orne)

Such Charisma Ch. C. 1994 (by Zilzal)

Stellaria Ch. F. 1986 (by Roberto)

En Garde Ch. F. 1996 (by Irish River)

Rebel Soldier Ch. C. 2007 (by Danehill Dancer)

Observatory Ch. C. 1997 (by Distant View)

High Praise B. F. 2000 (by Quest For Fame)

Vistaria Ch. F. 2004 (by Distant View)

Mount Logan Ch. C. 2011 (by New Approach)

Meteor Dancer B. F. 1974 (by Northern Dancer)

Xwoni Xwoni B. C. 1992 (by Track Barron)

Solartic Ch. F. 1977 (by Briartic)

Solo Native Ch. C. 1982 (by Exclusive Native)

Scierpan Ch. F. 1984 (by Sharpen Up)

Princess Victoria B. F. 1997 (by Deploy)

Lucky Game B. F. 2005 (by Montjeu)

Music Lover B. F. 2014 (by Palace Episode)

Tralos B. C. 1985 (by Roberto)

Polemic Ch. F. 1988 (by Roberto)

Cyrillic Ch. F. 1995 (by Irish River)

ORCHESTRA Db./Br. F. 1953 by Menetrier-Abondance by Maurepas

Allegro B. F. 1960 (by Chop Chop)

Icy Note B. C. 1965 (by Nearctic)

Swinging Apache B. C. 1967 (by Northern Dancer)

Dance In Time B. C. 1974 (by Northern Dancer)

Dancing Regent B. F. 1979 (by Vice Regent)

Sandsprite Ch. F. 1987 (by Coastal)

Arenosa Ch. F. 1997 (by Olympio)

Primero Nieto Ch. C. 2004 (by Alezan Dancer)

Orchestrina Db./Br. F. 1961 (by Nearctic)

New Pro Escar Db./Br. C. 1968 (by New Providence)

Chou Fleur B. F. 1969 (by Victoria Park)

Bon Debarras B. F. 1975 (by Ruritania)

Eternal Search Db./Br. F. 1978 (by Northern Answer)

Vigorous Search Db./Br. F. 1987 (by Vigors)

Misty Rain Gr. F. 1996 (by Rubiano)

Delta Weekend Gr. F. 2005 (by Jump Start)

Altamura B. F. 2015 (by Artie Schiller)

Lunar Mist Gr. F. 2007 (by Malibu Moon)

South Andros Gr. F. 2010 (by Sky Mesa)

Setareh Db./Br. F. 1997 (by Sky Classic)

Kentucky Whisper Db./Br. F. 2001 (by Southern Halo)

Love To Tell Ch. F. 2005 (by Stage Colony)

Volcat Db./Br. F. 2009 (by After Market)

Young Brodie Db./Br. F. 1990 (by Broad Brush)

Jiggs Coz Gr. C. 2004 (by Cozzene)

Sieze The Queen B. F. 1993 (by Afleet)

Alta Aire Db./Br. F. 2001 (by Slew City Slew)

Tiny Giant Db./Br. C. 2007 (by Lost Canyon)

Destroy Db./Br. F. 1997 (by Housebuster)

Smokey Fire Gr. C. 2005 (by Smoke Glacken)

Utterly Cool Gr. C. 2006 (by Smoke Glacken)

Ghost Fleet Db./Br. C. 2007 (by Arch)

Flame Mingo Db./Br. F. 2015 (by Blame)

Eternal Legend Db./Br. F. 2001 (by Gold Legend)

Frumious Db./Br. C. 2006 (by Grindstone)

Randie's Legend Db./Br. F. 2007 (by Benchmark)

Daddy Is A Legend Db./Br. F. 2015 (by Scat Daddy)

Eternal Rule Db./Br. C. 2008 (by Tribal Rule)

Finally Found B. F. 1979 (by Lord Durham)

Stolen Beauty Db./Br. F. 1989 (by Deputy Minister)

Moonlightandbeauty Db./Br. F. 1999 (by Capote)

Giant Moon B. C. 2005 (by Giant's Causeway)

Moonlight Song Db./Br. C. 2007 (by Unbridled's Song)

Heaven's Gate Ch. F. 1992 (by Septieme Ciel)

Tap Dancer Ch. C. 2001 (by Sword Dance)

This Ones For Phil Ch. C. 2006 (by Untuttable)

Finality Ch. C. 1999 (by Dehere)

Gone To Royalty Db./Br. C. 1980 (by Royal Chocolate)

Vevila B. F. 1984 (by The Minstrel)

Embur Sunshine Db./Br. F. 1993 (by Bold Ruckus)

Ten Flat B. C. 1998 (by Meadowlake)

Dawn Raid Db./Br. F. 2005 (by Vindication)

Exaggerator Db./Br. C. 2013 (by Curlin)

Embur's Song B. F. 2007 (by Unbridled's Song)

Raslaan B. C. 1985 (by Shareef Dancer)

Savethelastdance Db./Br. F. 1988 (by Nureyev)

Sue's Last Dance Db./Br. F. 1995 (by Forty Niner)

Island Sand Db./Br. F. 2001 (by Tabasco Cat)

Niigon Db./Br. C. 2001 (by Unbridled)

Gay Prelude B. F. 1972 (by Dr. Fager)

Funny Tammy B. F. 1977 (by Tentam)

Tammy Jean B. F. 1983 (by Fabulous Bid)

Tammy Two Gr. F. 1989 (by Two Punch)

She Two Gr. F. 2003 (by Stormy Atlantic)

It's Me Mom Ch. F. 2008 (by Put It Back)

Platinum Punch Ch. F. 1991 (by Two Punch)

Slew O' Platinum B. F. 2004 (by Stephen Got Even)

Joe's Tammie Db./Br. F. 1985 (by Zoning)

Knock Twice Db./Br. F. 1999 (by Two Punch)

Silver Knockers B. F. 2004 (by Silver Deputy)

Victory Chant B. F. 1962 (by Victoria Park)

Theme Song B. F. 1967 (by Nearctic)

Durham's Theme B. F. 1977 (by Lord Durham)

Soprano Miss Gr. F. 1978 (by Ruritania)

Galway Song B. F. 1985 (by Irish Tower)

Why Not Willie B. F. 1983 (by Master Willie)

Bunbeg Ch. F. 1992 (by Mining)

Vila Vella Ch. F. 1999 (by Iskandar Elakbar)

Megavella Ch. F. 2006 (by Megas Vukefalos)

Cindervella B. F. 2014 (by Silent Name)

Eseni Ch. F. 1993 (by Granacus)

Alezzandro Db./Br. C. 2004 (by High Yield)

Talk Back Db./Br. F. 1997 (by Talkin Man)

City Talk Db./Br. F. 2004 (by Carson City)

Art I Awesome Ch. C. 2010 (by Equality)

Fastestwhogetspaid B. C. 2009 (by Henny Hughes)

Victory Songster B. F. 1968 (by Stratus)

Northern Songster B. F. 1972 (by Northern Answer)

Certainly Super Ch. F. 1982 (by Bold Ruckus)

Certain Exchange Ch. F. 1991 (by Time For A Change)

Certainly Regal Ch. F. 2001 (by Regal Remark)

Wise Strategy Ch. C. 1988 (by Strategic Command)

Golden Answer B. F. 1973 (by Northern Answer)

King Midas B. C. 1980 (by King Pellinore)

Do's Melody B. F. 1974 (by Right Combination)

Do's Gent B. F. 1981 (by Vice Regent)

Dos And Donts B. C. 1988 (by Commemorate)

Gentleman Beau B. C. 1992 (by Beau Genius)

Plus Beau B. F. 1993 (by Beau Genius)

Dundalk Dust Db./Br. F. 2007 (by Military)

Luv Bandit B. C. 2009 (by Yonaguska)

Gen Corp Purposes B. F. 1995 (by Beau Genius)

Beau Dare B. F. 2003 (by Military)

Turfiste Db./Br. C. 2006 (by Military)

Andrea Ruckus B. F. 1986 (by Bold Ruckus)

Gold Star Deputy Ch. C. 1994 (by Silver Deputy)

Eastern Ruckus B. F. 1996 (by Eastern Echo)

Ladyecho B. F. 2000 (by Alphabet Soup)

Queen Del Valle Ch. F. 2014 (by Baryshnikov)

Whatdreamsrmadeof Ch. F. 2004 (by Graeme Hall)

Curalina Ch. F. 2012 (by Curlin)

Captivating B. F. 2002 (by Arch)

Dancing Raven B. F. 2007 (by Tomahawk)

Uncaptured Db./Br. C. 2010 (by Lion Heart)

Regent's Rhythm Ch. F. 1980 (by Vice Regent)

Legal Rhythm B. F. 1987 (by Drone)

Moonshine Justice Db./Br. C. 2002 (by Whiskey Wisdom)

Muskoka Command B. F. 1987 (by Top Command)

Bahamian Knight Db./Br. C. 1993 (by Ascot Knight)

Palace Songster B. F. 1988 (by Palace Music)

Dynashore B. F. 1994 (by Dynaformer)

Bobadieu Ch. C. 2003 (by Silver Deputy)

Sensible Girl B. F. 2010 (by Street Sense)

Shades Of Victory Gr. C. 2014 (by Thorn Song)

Boldly Victorious B. F. 1997 (by Bold Executive)

Bold Jubilation B. F. 2001 (by Smoke Glacken)

Stormin The Jewels B. C. 2013 (by Attila's Storm)

New Chant Db./Br. F. 1969 (by New Providence)

Casual Gr. F. 1979 (by Caro)

Pamela Peach Gr. F. 1986 (by Habitat)

Marl Ch. F. 1993 (by Lycius)

Meadow B. F. 2001 (by Green Desert)

Danehill Kodiac B. C. 2013 (by Kodiac)

Medley Ch. F. 2004 (by Danehill Dancer)

Light Music B. F. 2013 (by Elusive Quality)

Rowaasi Gr. F. 1997 (by Green Desert)

Nightlong Gr. F. 1987 (by Night Shift)

Yukon Pete Gr. C. 1995 (by Peteski)

Quick Blue B. F. 1998 (by Cure The Blues)

Azul Leon B. C. 2006 (by Lion Heart)

Dawson Place Db./Br. C. 1988 (by Green Desert)

Miller's Creek Db./Br. F. 1982 (by Star De Naskra)

Pure Misk B. F. 1990 (by Rainbow Quest)

Shfoug B. F. 1995 (by Sheikh Albadou)

Creeking B. F. 1993 (by Persian Bold)

Coconut Squeak B. F. 2002 (by Bahamian Bounty)

Angels Will Fall B. F. 2009 (by Acclamation)

South Cove B. F. 1985 (by Forli)

Jet Freighter Gr. C. 1991 (by Cozzene)

Spanish Harbor Db./Br. F. 1994 (by Corporate Report)

Desirae's My Candy B. F. 1998 (by Candy Stripes)

Double Harbor Db./Br. F. 2009 (by Rockport Harbor)

Sky Writer Db./Br. C. 2015 (by Sky Mesa)

Sierra Star B. C. 1986 (by Mill Reef)

Malvado Db./Br. C. 1972 (by Nearctic) *Multiple times leading sire in India*

Giboulee B. C. 1974 (by Northern Dancer)

Victorious Answer Db./Br. F. 1976 (by Northern Answer)

Vicky's Orient Db./Br. F. 1983 (by Far Out East)

Northern Sky B. C. 1992 (by Conquistador Cielo)

Eastern Answer Db./Br. C. 1995 (by Bold Ruckus)

Victorious Trick Db./Br. F. 1986 (by Clever Trick)

Oriental Answer B. F. 1987 (by Far Out East)

Young Turk B. C. 1994 (by El Prado)

Papa Fuse Ch. C. 2001 (by Lite The Fuse)

Little Star Vicky Db./Br. F. 1988 (by Bold Ruckus)

Clever Response Db./Br. C. 1995 (by Clever Trick)

Morning Star Db./Br. F. 1996 (by Shotiche)

Hudson Landing Ch. C. 2007 (by Maria's Mon)

Starbeau Db./Br. C. 1998 (by Barbeau)

Star Flicker Db./Br. F. 1999 (by Woodman)

Symphony Db./Br. F. 2008 (by Eagle Eyed)

Perfect Warrior Blk. C. 2010 (by Perfect Storm)

Starstruck Vicky B. F. 2004 (by Langfuhr)

Bolita Boyz B. C. 2011 (by Act Of Duty)

Vickey's Echo Db./Br. F. 1989 (by Clever Trick)

French Braids Db./Br. F. 1995 (by Personal Flag)

Donegal Db./Br. C. 2005 (by Menifee)

Our Liebling Db./Br. F. 1995 (by Clever Trick)

Miss Kipling Db./Br. F. 2008 (by Kipling)

Victory Trick Db./Br. F. 1998 (by Clever Trick)

Camp Victory Db./Br. C. 2007 (by Forest Camp)

Last Answer B. C. 2000 (by Langfuhr)

QUEEN'S STATUTE B. F. 1954 by Le Lavandou-Statute by Son-In-Law

Epic Queen Ch. F. 1958 (by Epic)

Court Royal B. F. 1959 (by Chop Chop)

Menedict B. F. 1960 (by Menetrier)

Bye Bye Mercedes Db./Br. F. 1980 (by Roman Line)

Mercedes Won B. C. 1986 (by Air Forbes Won)

Queen's Law Db./Br. F. 1961 (by Queen's Own)

Queen's Splendour B. C. 1970 (by Impressive)

Victorian Order B. F. 1963 (by Victoria Park)

Complete Order B. F. 1979 (by Princely Native)

Lisa Lide Ch. F. 1989 (by Bel Bolide)

My Desert Lady B. F. 2002 (by Desert God)

Runnin Red B. C. 2006 (by Desert God)

Cross Chris Run Db./Br. C. 2007 (by Desert God)

Lisa's Pride Db./Br. F. 2008 (by Desert God)

Hute Db./Br. C. 2014 (by Western Gambler)

Dance Act Ch. C. 1966 (by Northern Dancer)

Royal Statute B. F. 1969 (by Northern Dancer)

Konafa B. F. 1973 (by Damascus)

Proskona B. F. 1981 (by Mr. Prospector)

Noesis Gr. F. 1986 (by Persepolis)

Summer Sonnet Gr. F. 1991 (by Baillamont)

Summer Solstice B. F. 1997 (by Caerleon)

Adirondack Summer Ch. C. 2008 (by Thunder Gulch)

Summer Breezing B. C. 2009 (by Langfuhr)

Act One Gr. C. 1999 (by In The Wings)

Ibuki Perceive Gr. F. 1993 (by Caerleon)

Laca Gr. F. 2005 (by Cherokee Run)

Chief Kitten Gr. C. 2012 (by Kitten's Joy)

Space Ritual B. F. 1988 (by Top Ville)

Space Time B. F. 1995 (by Bering)

Cosmodrome B. F. 2004 (by Bahri)

Splashdown Ch. F. 2006 (by Falbrav)

Kapuchka B. F. 1990 (by Soviet Star)

Kentucky Rose Ch. F. 1998 (by Hernando)

Calista B. F. 1998 (by Caerleon)

Epitome B. F. 1999 (by Nashwan)

Synopsis Ch. F. 2004 (by In The Wings)

Ultra Ch. C. 2013 (by Manduro)

Korveya Ch. F. 1982 (by Riverman)

Hector Protector Ch. C. 1988 (by Woodman)

Shanghai B. C. 1989 (by Procida)

Gioconda Ch. F. 1990 (by Nijinsky II)

Lirio Ch. F. 1995 (by Forty Niner)

Trailblazer B. C. 2007 (by Zenno Rob Roy)

Ciro Ch. C. 1997 (by Woodman)

Bosra Sham Ch. F. 1993 (by Woodman)

Rosberg Db./Br. C. 2001 (by A.P. Indy)

Reve de Ville Db./Br. F. 2005 (by Storm Cat)

Reve Enchante Db./Br. F. 2010 (by Medaglia d'Oro)

Dream It Is B. F. 2015 (by Shackleford)

Maria Isabella Ch. F. 1995 (by Kris)

Utrecht Ch. F. 2004 (by Rock Of Gibraltar)

Tapatina Ch. F. 2001 (by Seeking The Gold)

Internallyflawless Ch. F. 2006 (by Giant's Causeway)

Internal Bourbon Ch. F. 2012 (by Not Bourbon)

Billy's Star B. C. 2012 (by Perfect Soul)

Reflective Ch. F. 2003 (by Seeking The Gold)

Biographer B. C. 2009 (by Montjeu)

Truant Db./Br. F. 2005 (by Gone West)

Dream Kirari Blk. C. 2012 (by Giant's Causeway)

Carnet Solaire B. F. 1983 (by Sharpen Up)

Symeterie B. F. 1988 (by Seattle Song)

Caterina Sforza Ch. F. 1995 (by Machiavellian)

Riario B. C. 2004 (by Beat Hollow)

Beyond The Sun B. F. 1996 (by Kingmambo)

Carnera Db./Br. C. 2003 (by Old Trieste)

Red Giant Ch. C. 2004 (by Giant's Causeway)

Wyomia Db./Br. F. 2008 (by Vindication)

Carousel Girl B. F. 1997 (by Gulch)

Caucasienne B. F. 2003 (by Galileo)

Chopin B. C. 2010 (by Santiago)

Calantha Gr. F. 2013 (by Literato)

Talon d'Aiguille B. F. 1985 (by Big Spruce)

Decant B. F. 1991 (by Rousillon)

Gruntled B. C. 1999 (by Blushing Flame)

Leo's Lucky Lady B. F. 1987 (by Seattle Slew)

Seattle's Wood B. F. 1997 (by Woodman)

O'Keefe B. F. 2009 (by Peintre Celebre)

O'Juke Ch. C. 2015 (by Jukebox Jury)

Falconet Db./Br. C. 2010 (by Falco)

It's Our Time Db./Br. F. 2000 (by Seeking The Gold)

On My Way Ch. F. 2006 (by Giant's Causeway)

King Zachary Ch. C. 2015 (by Curlin)

Leo's Pegasus B. F. 2003 (by Fusaichi Pegasus)

Battle Force B. C. 2009 (by Giant's Causeway)

Gaudeamus B. F. 2004 (by Distorted Humor)

Cloelia B. F. 1990 (by Lyphard)

Passinetti B. C. 1997 (by Slew O' Gold)

Keos Db./Br. C. 1994 (by Riverman)

Kamaina Ch. F. 1995 (by Mr. Prospector)

Kalpita Ch. F. 2000 (by Spinning World)

California Memory Gr. C. 2006 (by Highest Honor)

      Mouro Ch. C. 2009 (by Grand Slam)

Royal Stance B. F. 1977 (by Dr. Fager)

    Majuscule B. C. 1981 (by Majestic Light)

    Royal Cielo B. F. 1984 (by Conquistador Cielo)

      Royal Di Ch. F. 1997 (by Diesis)

        King Of Sale Ch. C. 2004 (by Not For Sale)

    Luhuk Ch. C. 1991 (by Forty Niner)

    Edie Cox B. F. 1992 (by Seeking The Gold)

      Hail Holy Queen B. F. 1997 (by Mt. Livermore)

Akureyri B. C. 1978 (by Buckpasser)

Awaasif B. F. 1979 (by Snow Knight)

    Snow Bride Ch. F. 1986 (by Blushing Groom)

      Lammtarra Ch. C. 1992 (by Nijinsky II)

      Kammtarra Ch. C. 1993 (by Zilzal)

      Saytarra B. F. 1996 (by Seeking The Gold)

      Abhisheka B. F. 2003 (by Sadler's Wells)

        Aesop's Fables B. C. 2009 (by Distorted Humor)

      Snow Ballerina B. F. 2004 (by Sadler's Wells)

        Powder Snow Ch. F. 2013 (by Dubawi)

      Concordia Ch. F. 2006 (by Pivotal)

        Polarisation B. C. 2012 (by Echo Of Light)

    Ibn Al Haitham B. C. 1999 (by Zafonic)

Royal Lorna B. F. 1981 (by Val de l'Orne)

    Forlorna B. F. 1995 (by Nashwan)

    Lycitus B. C. 1997 (by Lycius)

    Liscune B. F. 2002 (by King's Best)

      Ektihaam B. C. 2009 (by Invincible Spirit)

      Music Box B. F. 2014 (by Invincible Spirit)

Victoress B. F. 1984 (by Conquistador Cielo)

    Gwynn B. F. 1997 (by Darshaan)

      Gagnoa B. F. 2005 (by Sadler's Wells)

      Pour Moi B. C. 2008 (by Montjeu)

Down North B. C. 1970 (by Victoria Park)

North Of The Law Ch. C. 1972 (by Northern Dancer)

Falafel B. F. 1973 (by Northern Dancer)

Fiscal Fun B. F. 1980 (by Foolish Pleasure)

Fiscal Gold B. F. 1990 (by Slew O' Gold)

Fiscal Year Db./Br. F. 1995 (by Half A Year)

Yearly Report B. F. 2001 (by General Meeting)

Condo Commando Db./Br. F. 2012 (by Tiz Wonderful)

Again Tomorrow B. C. 1982 (by Honest Pleasure)

Brief Truce B. C. 1989 (by Irish River)

LA BELLE ROSE B. F. 1954 by Le Lavandou–Missy Suntan by Tai-Yang

Floral Victory B. F. 1962 (by Victoria Park)

Victego B. C. 1968 (by Nentego)

Happy Victory B. F. 1969 (by New Providence)

Victory Kingdom B. F. 1975 (by Viceregal)

Blushing All Over B. F. 1982 (by Blushing Groom)

Nausica Ch. F. 1996 (by Diesis)

Memory B. F. 2008 (by Danehill Dancer)

Recorder Ch. C. 2013 (by Galileo)

Call To Mind B. C. 2014 (by Galileo)

Come On Rossi B. F. 1987 (by Valivar)

Bin Rosie B. C. 1992 (by Distant Relative)

Generous Rosi B. C. 1995 (by Generous)

Victania B. F. 1977 (by Ruritania)

Jenny D B. F. 1987 (by Regal Embrace)

Bragadocious B. F. 1993 (by Salem Drive)

Cashmere Miss Ch. F. 2000 (by Kokand)

Stonehouse B. C. 2004 (by Chester House)

Northern Ballerina B. F. 1974 (by Northern Dancer)

Nonparrell B. C. 1976 (by Hoist The Flag)

Crimean Rose B. F. 1979 (by Sevastopol)

Whistling Maid B. F. 1990 (by Bold N' Flashy)

Pennywhistle Db./Br. F. 2007 (by Grand Reward)

King And His Court Db./Br. C. 2014 (by Court Vision)

Athena Rose Ch. F. 2008 (by Mutakddim)

Snow Blossom B. F. 1981 (by The Minstrel)

Color Me Beautiful B. F. 1983 (by Vice Regent)

Colors Inthe Storm B. F. 1989 (by Relaunch)

Easy Lover B. F. 1994 (by Alwasmi)

Rise Line B. C. 2011 (by Screen Hero)

Princesscassandra B. F. 2000 (by Valid Expectations)

Carenage Ch. F. 1990 (by Bold Ruckus)

Legs O'Neal Db./Br. F. 2000 (by Nelson)

Voodoo Gold Db./Br. C. 2003 (by Gold Tribute)

Sweet Ruston Ch. F. 2008 (by Lydgate)

Floral Dancer B. C. 1987 (by Limbo Dancer)

Rose Of North Db./Br. F. 1963 (by Nearctic)

Presidial B. C. 1969 (by Psidium)

HELIOSTRINGS B. F. (twin) 1955 by Heliopolis-No Strings by Occupation

Greek Victress B. F. 1965 (by Victoria Park)

Grecian Victress B. F. 1969 (by Nearctic)

Greek Nixy Db./Br. F. 1979 (by Snow Knight)

Grecian Pass Gr. F. 1987 (by Pass The Tab)

Midi Skirt Db./Br. F. 1970 (by Canebora)

Queen Riviera Ch. F. 1973 (by Vice Regent)

Tao Mina Ch. F. 1979 (by Ivy's Prince)

Impulsive Desire B. F. 1977 (by Vice Regent)

Grumble And Grunt Db./Br. F. 1984 (by Brave Shot)

Ptarmigan Hunting Db./Br. F. 1999 (by Tejano Run)

Inuit Fisher Ch. C. 2004 (by Mutakddim)

Water Spider Ch. F. 1980 (by Briartic)

Renee's Reflection Ch. F. 1984 (by Bold Ruckus)

Al Renee Ch. C. 1991 (by Al Mamoon)

Avid Affection Ch. C. 1989 (by Lord Avie)

Spider Wire Ch. C. 1993 (by Bold Ruckus)

Barbed Wire Ch. F. 1994 (by Affirmed)

Tearfull Moment Ch. F. 1997 (by Schossberg)

Field Commission Ch. C. 2005 (by Service Stripe)

Futurette B. F. 1981 (by Sevastopol)

Linda's Secret Ch. F. 1986 (by Nijinsky's Secret)

Secret Of Mecca B. F. 1998 (by Mecke)

Secret Action B. F. 2012 (by Tiz Wonderful)

Dance Skirt Ch. F. 1987 (by Caucasus)

Daisy Dukes Db./Br. F. 1998 (by Ghazi)

Surplus Singer B. C. 2004 (by Songandaprayer)

Legendary King B. C. 2008 (by Brahms)

Greek Answer Db./Br. C. 1972 (by Northern Answer)

Grecian Victory B. F. 1976 (by Dr. Fager)

Vicky Dearest B. F. 1982 (by Affirmed)

Make The Cut B. F. 1988 (by Cutlass)

The Count Db./Br. C. 1986 (by Halo)

Valid Victress B. F. 1990 (by Valid Appeal)

Perfect Sting B. F. 1996 (by Red Ransom)

Smart Sting B. F. 2008 (by Smart Strike)

Reggae Queen Db./Br. F. 1997 (by Dynaformer)

Reggae Rose Db./Br. F. 2006 (by Touch Gold)

Shakhimat Db./Br. C. 2013 (by Lonhro)

Celtic New Year B. C. 2007 (by North Light)

Lawmaker B. C. 1978 (by Round Table)

Greek Sky B. C. 1981 (by Nijinsky II)

NATALMA B. F. 1957 by Native Dancer-Almahmoud by Mahmoud

Northern Dancer B. C. 1961 (by Nearctic)

Native Victor Db./Br. C. 1962 (by Victoria Park)

Arctic Dancer B. F. 1963 (by Nearctic)

La Prevoyante B. F. 1970 (by Buckpasser)

Quat'Sous B. F. 1971 (by Buckpasser)

L'Anse Au Griffon B. F. 1980 (by Prove Out)

Northern Lance B. C. 1991 (by Sovereign Dancer)

Excitations Db./Br. F. 1994 (by Jolie's Halo)

Bond James Bond B. C. 2008 (by Old Topper)

Danseuse Etoile B. F. 1974 (by Buckpasser)

Danseur de Corde B. C. 1980 (by Foolish Pleasure)

Dauphine Gr. F. 1983 (by Spectacular Bid)

Irish Boss B. C. 1993 (by Waajib)

Drapeau Tricolore B. C. 1985 (by Irish River)

Danse Bleu Ciel B. F. 1987 (by Green Forest)

Donatio B. F. 1992 (by Royal Academy)

Dancing Shuffle B. F. 2010 (by Big Shuffle)

Dampierre B. C. 1988 (by Lear Fan)

Drums Of Freedom B. F. 1990 (by Green Forest)

Proud Citizen B. C. 1999 (by Gone West)

Regal Dancer Gr. C. 1964 (by Grey Monarch)

Native Era Db./Br. F. 1969 (by Victorian Era)

Eranos B. F. 1973 (by Arts And Letters)

Godsrun B. F. 1980 (by Godswalk)

Thanksgiving B. F. 1990 (by Riyahi)

Marathon Db./Br. F. 1986 (by Runnit)

Northern Sister B. F. 1982 (by Gregorian)

Sky Trist B. F. 1994 (by Sir Tristram)

Barzana Gr. F. 1984 (by Icecapade)

Gray Not Bay Gr. C. 1990 (by Procida)

Spring Adieu B. F. 1974 (by Buckpasser)

You're My Lady B. F. 1980 (by Roberto)

Gabbing Gloria B. F. 1986 (by Desert Wine)

Diatribe B. C. 1996 (by Brief Truce)

My Lady's Key Db./Br. F. 1987 (by Key To The Mint)

Al Samer B. C. 2002 (by Redoute's Choice)

Youthful Legs Blk. C. 1991 (by Explodent)

Lady's Delight B. F. 1992 (by Local Talent)

Sunday Service Db./Br. F. 1999 (by Sunday Silence)

Come Sunday B. F. 2006 (by Redoute's Choice)

Ace High Blk. C. 2014 (by High Chaparral)

Kneeling Db./Br. F. 2008 (by Encosta De Lago)

That's A Good Idea B. C. 2009 (by Flying Spur)

Express Power Db./Br. F. 2009 (by Snitzel)

Daphne Donnelly Ch. F. 1994 (by Golden Touch)

Queen's Bay B. F. 2005 (by Fort Wood)

Announce Ch. C. 1997 (by National Assembly)

Razyana B. F. 1981 (by His Majesty)

Danehill B. C. 1986 (by Danzig) *13 times leading sire*

Euphonic Ch. F. 1989 (by The Minstrel)

Phone West B. F. 1996 (by Gone West)

Payphone B. F. 2001 (by Anabaa)

Newsletter B. F. 2012 (by Sir Percy)

Conference Call B. F. 2005 (by Anabaa)

Teletext B. C. 2011 (by Empire Maker)

Eagle Eyed B. C. 1991 (by Danzig)

Anziyan B. C. 1993 (by Danzig)

Harpia B. F. 1994 (by Danzig)

Shibboleth B. C. 1997 (by Danzig)

Family B. F. 1999 (by Danzig)

Dundonnell B. C. 2010 (by First Defense)

Final Farewell Ch. F. 1989 (by Proud Truth)

Rain Dancer B. F. 1998 (by Sadler's Wells)

Boca Dancer B. F. 2004 (by Indian Ridge)

Raise The Standard B. F. 1978 (by Hoist The Flag)

Coup De Folie B. F. 1982 (by Halo)

Machiavellian Db./Br. C. 1987 (by Mr. Prospector)

Exit To Nowhere B. C. 1988 (by Irish River)

Hydro Calido Db./Br. F. 1989 (by Nureyev)

Heraklia Db./Br. F. 1994 (by Irish River)

Fifty Oner Db./Br. C. 2002 (by Fusaichi Pegasus)

Esperero Db./Br. C. 1995 (by Forty Niner)

Shinko Calido Ch. C. 1998 (by Silver Hawk)

Lady Succeed Blk. F. 2000 (by Brian's Time)

   Supido Db./Br. C. 2011 (by Sebring)

Salchow B. F. 1990 (by Nijinsky II)

Way Of Light Db./Br. C. 1996 (by Woodman)

Simadartha B. F. 1997 (by Gone West)

   Big Sink Star Ch. F. 2005 (by A.P. Indy)

      Calgary Cat Ch. C. 2010 (by Cowtown Cat)

   Waltzing Matilda B. F. 2011 (by Danehill Dancer)

Coup De Genie B. F. 1991 (by Mr. Prospector)

Moonlight's Box B. F. 1996 (by Nureyev)

   Bago Db./Br. C. 2001 (by Nashwan)

   Beta B. F. 2004 (by Selkirk)

   Maxios Db./Br. C. 2008 (by Monsun)

Snake Mountain Ch. C. 1998 (by A.P. Indy)

Glia B. F. 1999 (by A.P. Indy)

Soothing Touch B. F. 2004 (by Touch Gold)

   Emollient B. F. 2010 (by Empire Maker)

   Courtier B. C. 2012 (by Pioneerof The Nile)

   Hofburg Ch. C. 2015 (by Tapit)

Dream Of Genie B. F. 2008 (by Pivotal)

   Fan Dii Na Db./Br. F. 2014 (by Deep Impact)

Loving Kindness Db./Br. F. 2000 (by Seattle Slew)

   Peace Camp Db./Br. F. 2006 (by Storm Cat)

Denebola Db./Br. F. 2001 (by Storm Cat)

Beta Leo Db./Br. F. 2007 (by A.P. Indy)

   Bolting B. C. 2013 (by War Front)

   Senga B. F. 2014 (by Blame)

Rafina Db./Br. F. 1994 (by Mr. Prospector)

   Admiralofthefleet Db./Br. C. 2004 (by Danehill)

Houdini's Honey Ch. F. 1996 (by Mr. Prospector)

   Awesome Act Ch. C. 2007 (by Awesome Again)

   Fastest Magician Ch. C. 2008 (by Johannesburg)

Ocean Of Wisdom B. C. 1997 (by Mr. Prospector)

Bonita Francita B. F. 1987 (by Devil's Bag)

Black Penny B. F. 1992 (by Private Account)

Bluemamba B. F. 1997 (by Kingmambo)

Indigo Cat Ch. C. 2002 (by Storm Cat)

Etterby Park B. C. 1993 (by Silver Hawk)

Jules B. C. 1994 (by Forty Niner)

Esther Rose Db./Br. F. 1995 (by Seeking The Gold)

Record Holder Db./Br. C. 2006 (by Giant's Causeway)

Great Warrior B. C. 2008 (by Leroidesanimaux)

Orpen B. C. 1996 (by Lure)

Welcometotheworld B. F. 1997 (by Woodman)

Free World Db./Br. C. 2010 (by Stormy Atlantic)

Madam North B. F. 1988 (by Halo)

Birdsong Db./Br. F. 1992 (by Irish River)

Pineyville Db./Br. F. 1998 (by Pine Bluff)

Call Me Wild B. C. 2003 (by Caller I.D.)

Rubicon Db./Br. F. 1997 (by Irish River)

River Crossing B. C. 2008 (by Caesour)

Relight My Fire B. F. 1993 (by Blushing John)

Relight's Best B. F. 2003 (by Grand Lodge)

Racemate B. F. 2008 (by Hurricane Run)

Nutcase B. F. 1999 (by Forest Wildcat)

Nutello B. C. 2009 (by Lemon Drop Kid)

Born A Lady B. F. 1981 (by Tentam)

Deviltante Db./Br. F. 1986 (by Devil's Bag)

Granny Kelly Ch. F. 1994 (by Irish River)

Six Hitter Ch. C. 1999 (by Boundary)

Tilli of Strafford B. F. 1995 (by Deputy Minister)

Asukano Himiko B. F. 2003 (by Tabasco Cat)

Asukano Roman Ch. C. 2011 (by Agnes Digital)

Arrowtown Db./Br. C. 1988 (by Mr. Prospector)

Natalma's Dream B. F. 1989 (by Alydar)

Stormy Dream B. F. 1993 (by Storm Cat)

  Newscaster Ch. F. 2000 (by Marscay)

    Swing Dance Ch. F. 2005 (by Danehill Dancer)

      Rapper Dragon Ch. C. 2012 (by Street Boss)

    Turf Express Ch. C. 2006 (by Danehill Damcer)

    Amanpour Ch. F. 2010 (by Northern Meteor)

    Sports Edition Ch. C. 2011 (by Northern Meteor)

Lambada Lady Db./Br. F. 1990 (by Seattle Slew)

  Lyre Melody Db./Br. F. 2003 (by Admire Vega)

    Tagano Azaghal Db./Br. C. 2012 (by Bago)

Timber Nymph Db./Br. F. 1993 (by Woodman)

  Theorie B. F. 1998 (by Anabaa)

    Theoricienne Gr. F. 2006 (by Kendor)

      Tour To Paris B. C. 2015 (by Fuisse)

    Blacktype Db./Br. C. 2011 (by Dunkerque)

Lady Bonanza Ch. F. 1995 (by Seeking The Gold)

Little Arrow B. F. 1998 (by Kingmambo)

  Antonio Barows Db./Br. C. 2006 (by Manhattan Café)

MIDINETTE II B. F. 1958 by Tantieme-Milonga by Arco

Buena Notte B. F. 1964 (by Victoria Park)

  Come Near B. F. 1969 (by Nearctic)

    Come Lucky Chance Db./Br. F. 1976 (by Jammed Lucky)

      Pick Ten Db./Br. F. 1992 (by Ten Gold Pots)

        Keg Of Dynamite Db./Br. C. 1996 (by Bold Executive)

        Top Ten List Db./Br. F. 2002 (by Bold Executive)

        Tenjectory Db./Br. F. 2005 (by Trajectory)

    Regal Stafford B. C. 1978 (by Vice Regent)

    Cuddle Up Closer B. F. 1979 (by Vice Regent)

      Cryptocloser B. C. 1994 (by Cryptoclearance)

    Johnandjo B. F. 1984 (by Well Decorated)

      Quest Of Fate Db./Br. C. 1998 (by Norquestor)

  Beau Arctic B. F. 1970 (by Champlain)

Sageata B. C. 1977 (by Dangblastit)

Pot Of Gold B. F. 1974 (by Search For Gold)

Ten Gold Pots Db./Br. C. 1981 (by Tentam)

Romantic Story B. F. 1985 (by Quadratic)

Anet Db./Br. C. 1994 (by Clever Trick)

Atul B. C. 2003 (by Clever Trick)

Shake Shake Shake B. C. 1975 (by Dancing Count)

El Hamo B. F. 1976 (by Search For Gold)

Exquisite Mistress B. F. 1986 (by Nasty And Bold)

Go Scotty Ch. C. 1994 (by Bold Ruckus)

Guilty Pleasure B. F. 1997 (by Pine Bluff)

Ready To Please Db./Br. F. 2003 (by More Than Ready)

Nac Venus Db./Br. F. 2013 (by Daiwa Major)

Chief Officer B. F. 2004 (by Officer)

Ready's Gal Ch. F. 2002 (by More Than Ready)

Machen Ch. C. 2008 (by Distorted Humor)

Adrina Ch. F. 2009 (by A.P. Indy)

Secular Nation Ch. C. 2015 (by Distorted Humor)

Count On Bonnie B. F. 1981 (by Dancing Count)

Hansel B. C. 1988 (by Woodman)

Lahint B. C. 1991 (by Woodman)

Military Bearing B. C. 1973 (by Vice Regent)

LACHINE B. F. 1960 by Grey Sovereign-Loved One by Vigorous

Lachute Ch. F. 1965 (by Match II)

Victorianette B. F. 1970 (by Victoria Park)

Matcher Br. F. 1966 (by Match II)

Myra's Best Ch. F. 1980 (by Pampapaul)

Waky Na Ch. F. 1988 (by Ahonoora)

Waky Nao B. C. 1993 (by Alzao)

Wakytara Ch. F. 1999 (by Danehill)

Wamika B. F. 2010 (by Shirocco)

Whispering Angel B. F. 2016 (by Soldier Hollow)

Wai Key Star B. C. 2013 (by Soldier Hollow)

Wing And A Prayer B. C. 1981 (by Oats)

Park Express Db./Br. F. 1983 (by Ahonoora)

Park Heiress B. F. 1991 (by Sadler's Wells)

Silent Heir Db./Br. F. 1999 (by Sunday Silence)

Young Pretender B. C. 2005 (by Oasis Dream)

Quiet Oasis B. F. 2008 (by Oasis Dream)

Castlethorpe B. C. 2007 (by Not A Single Doubt)

Shinko Forest Db./Br. C. 1993 (by Green Desert)

Dazzling Park Db./Br. F. 1996 (by Warning)

Glinting Desert B. F. 2002 (by Desert Prince)

Alfred Nobel B. C. 2007 (by Danehill Dancer)

Alluring Park Db./Br. F. 1999 (by Green Desert)

Janood B. C. 2008 (by Medicean)

Was B. F. 2009 (by Galileo)

Douglas MacArthur B. C. 2014 (by Galileo)

New Approach Ch. C. 2005 (by Galileo)

Grand Lachine B. C. 1969 (by Northern Dancer)

Quick Selection Ch. F. 1972 (by Viceregal)

Charge My Account Ch. F. 1979 (by Majestic Prince)

Miss Audimar B. F. 1981 (by Mr. Leader)

Rosy Sunset B. F. 1989 (by Red Sunset)

Evening Promise B. F. 1996 (by Aragon)

Gaily Eagle Ch. C. 1993 (by Mujtahid)

Bandari B. C. 1999 (by Alhaarth)

IMPETUOUS LADY Ch. F. 1965 by Hasty Road-Escocesa by Nigromante

Hasty Gal Ch. F. 1969 (by Maribeau)

Once Upon A Dream Ch. F. 1974 (by Protanto)

Dreamhawk B. C. 1980 (by Groshawk)

No. One Bundles Ch. F. 1978 (by Vice Regent)

Double Bundles Ch. F. 1983 (by Nodouble)

Bundle Bits Ch. F. 1987 (by Nodouble)

Northern Fling B. C. 1970 (by Northern Dancer)

Regal Gal Ch. F. 1973 (by Viceregal)

    Honest Gal B. F. 1980 (by Honest Pleasure)

        Memories of Spring Ch. F. 1988 (by Commemorate)

            Corisco Ch. C. 1998 (by Burkaan)

    Malagra B. C. 1986 (by Majestic Light)

    Holy Mountain Db./Br. C. 1991 (by Devil's Bag)

    Bacall Ch. F. 1993 (by Alysheba)

        Silver Seven Ch. F. 2002 (by Silver Deputy)

            Silver Baubles Ch. C. 2009 (by Gilded Time)

    Relaxing Rhythm Ch. F. 1994 (by Easy Goer)

        Spring Waltz Gr. F. 2003 (by Silver Charm)

Impetuous Gal Ch. F. 1975 (by Briartic)

    First Guess Ch. C. 1982 (by Mr. Prospector)

    Banker's Lady Ch. F. 1985 (by Nijinsky II)

        Banker's Gold Ch. C. 1994 (by Forty Niner)

        Society Column B. F. 1996 (by Seeking The Gold)

            Latest Scoop B. F. 2005 (by Tiznow)

                Personal Diary Ch. F. 2011 (by City Zip)

        Lucrative Ch. F. 1998 (by Seeking The Gold)

            Bank Merger Ch. C. 2007 (by Consolidator)

        Sweet Charity Ch. F. 1999 (by A.P. Indy)

            Spicer Boy Ch. C. 2005 (by Lemon Drop Kid)

            Charity Belle B. F. 2006 (by Empire Maker)

                Hallie Belle B. F. 2014 (by Medaglia d'Oro)

    Idabel B. C. 1986 (by Mr. Propector)

    Devil's Dispute Ch. F. 1989 (by Devil's Bag)

        Patent Pending B. C. 1994 (by Conquistador Cielo)

        Carson City Girl Ch. F. 1998 (by Carson City)

            Dublin Girl Ch. F. 2014 (by Dublin)

        Daisy Devine B. F. 2008 (by Kafwain)

    Daring Danzig B. F. 1990 (by Danzig)

        Ecton Park Ch. C. 1996 (by Forty Niner)

Pit Fighter B. C. 1999 (by Pulpit)

Daring Heart Ch. F. 2002 (by Sunday Silence)

Niner's Gal Ch. F. 1992 (by Forty Niner)

Illusive Note B. F. 1996 (by Dixieland Band)

Noble Maz Db./Br. F. 2006 (by Storm Boot)

Noble Indy B. C. 2015 (by Take Charge Indy)

Countess North Ch. F. 1976 (by Northern Dancer)

Westheimer Ch. C. 1981 (by Blushing Groom)

Countess Aura Ch. F. 1985 (by Halo)

Count To Six B. F. 1990 (by Saratoga Six)

Knox Ch. C. 2001 (by Menifee)

Meribel Db./Br. F. 2003 (by Peaks And Valleys)

Palangana B. F. 1993 (by His Majesty)

Informed Decision Gr. F. 2005 (by Monarchos)

NANGELA B. F. 1965 by Nearctic-Angela's Niece by Tim Tam

Square Angel B. F. 1970 (by Quadrangle)

Kamar B. F. 1976 (by Key To The Mint)

Key To The Moon Db./Br. C. 1981 (by Wajima)

Forli's Key Db./Br. F. 1982 (by Forli)

Clever Return Db./Br. C. 1986 (by Clever Trick)

Scipio B. F. 1987 (by Danzig)

Sister Girl Db./Br. F. 1992 (by Conquistador Cielo)

Sister Girl Blues B. F. 1999 (by Hold For Gold)

Firing Line B. C. 2012 (by Line Of David)

Mint Lane B. C. 2005 (by Maria's Mon)

So Sharp Db./Br. F. 2007 (by Saint Liam)

Sharp Azteca Db./Br. C. 2013 (by Freud)

Remembered Db./Br. F. 2010 (by Sky Mesa)

Bowie's Hero B. C. 2014 (by Artie Schiller)

Secret Sip B. F. 1997 (by Secret Hello)

Hiaam Ch. F. 1984 (by Alydar)

Maftool Ch. C. 1990 (by Shadeed)

Munnaya Ch. F. 1991 (by Nijinsky II)

Mystic Melody B. F. 2000 (by Seattle Slew)

Alpha B. C. 2009 (by Bernardini)

Sheer Reason B. F. 1994 (by Danzig)

I'm Right B. F. 2004 (by Rahy)

Fauguernon B. C. 2014 (by Martaline)

Mall Queen B. F. 1997 (by Sheikh Albadou)

Don't Rush B. F. 1985 (by Alleged)

Reine de Neige B. F. 1990 (by Kris)

Reine Galante B. F. 2002 (by Danehill)

Reine Heureuse B. F. 2007 (by Big Shuffle)

La Zona B. F. 2006 (by Singspiel)

Gorgeous B. F. 1986 (by Slew O' Gold)

Dreamboat B. F. 1992 (by Mr. Prospector)

Misty Waters Db./Br. F. 1998 (by Caerleon)

Gardening Leave B. C. 2007 (by Selkirk)

Music Show B. F. 2007 (by Noverre)

Glamorous B. F. 1993 (by Danzig)

Glamorous One Db./Br. F. 2001 (by Gone West)

Galan De Sine Db./Br. C. 2008 (by Successful Appeal)

Sweetheart Db./Br. F. 1994 (by Mr. Prospector)

Sweet Maple Db./Br. F. 2010 (by Big Brown)

Americium Db./Br. F. 2014 (by Brilliant Speed)

Fabulous Ch. F. 1995 (by Seeking The Gold)

Bonay Db./Br. F. 2000 (by Wild Again)

R U Watchingbud Db./Br. C. 2012 (by Kentucky Bear)

Roger's Sue Db./Br. F. 2001 (by Forestry)

Turbulent Descent B. F. 2008 (by Congrats)

Spanish Steps B. C. 2014 (by Galileo)

Couturier Gr. F. 2006 (by El Prado)

Minks Aprise B. F. 2012 (by Northern Afleet)

Glasgow's Gold B. F. 1996 (by Seeking The Gold)

Croisiere B. F. 2002 (by Capote)

Masham Star B. C. 2014 (by Lawman)

Swift Temper Ch. F. 2004 (by Giant's Causeway)

Stunning B. F. 1998 (by Nureyev)

Attagal Db./Br. F. 1999 (by Atticus)

Rock Flower Db./Br. F. 2004 (by Thunder Gulch)

King White Gr. C. 2009 (by Giacomo)

La Alpujarra Blk. F. 2011 (by Pioneerof The Nile)

Eximius Ch. F. 2001 (by Atticus)

Sarach Db./Br. F. 2010 (by Arch)

All Included Ch. C. 2011 (by Include)

Seaside Attraction B. F. 1987 (by Seattle Slew)

Red Carnival B. F. 1992 (by Mr. Prospector)

Carnival Dancer B. C. 1998 (by Sadler's Wells)

Funfair B. C. 1999 (by Singspiel)

Desert Lord B. C. 2000 (by Green Desert)

Golden Attraction B. F. 1993 (by Mr. Prospector)

Gold Trader B. C. 1998 (by Storm Cat)

Return To Grace Ch. F. 2012 (by English Channel)

Cape Town B. C. 1995 (by Seeking The Gold)

Cape Canaveral Db./Br. C. 1996 (by Mr. Prospector)

Wilayif B. F. 1988 (by Danzig)

Morning Pride B. F. 1997 (by Machiavellian)

Flashing Ch. F. 2006 (by A.P. Indy)

Floodlight B.C. 2013 (by Medaglia d'Oro)

Jood B. F. 1989 (by Nijinsky II)

Wanice B. F. 1995 (by Mr. Prospector)

Zembu B. F. 1999 (by Fuji Kiseki)

Your Song Db./Br. C. 2009 (by Fastnet Rock)

Anees B. C. 2014 (by Harlan's Holiday)

Fantastic Light B. C. 1996 (by Rahy)

Hi Dubai Ch. F. 2000 (by Rahy)

Daanet Al Dunya Ch. F. 2003 (by Rahy)

Tarquin B. C. 2012 (by Hard Spun)

Stellarette B. F. 1978 (by Tentam)

  Graphite Db./Br. F. 1984 (by Mr. Prospector)

    Clovis Point B. F. 1991 (by Kris)

      Temple Of Peace B. F. 1998 (by Carnegie)

        Whobegotyou Ch. C. 2005 (by Street Cry)

    Columbite Db./Br. F. 1996 (by Caerleon)

      Mejiro Nicolas Db./Br. C. 2001 (by Sunday Silence)

    Rose Quartz B. F. 1997 (by Lammtarra)

      Rosawa Gr. F. 2002 (by Linamix)

        Rosanara Gr. F. 2007 (by Sinndar)

      Rajsaman Gr. C. 2007 (by Linamix)

      Radanpour B. C. 2012 (by Sea The Stars)

  Nuryette B. F. 1986 (by Nureyev)

    Boss Soss B. C. 1990 (by Sauce Boat)

    Northern Afleet B. C. 1993 (by Afleet)

    Cravatte Noir Gr. F. 1994 (by Black Tie Affair)

      Hamriya B. C. 2001 (by Alzao)

    Tap To Music B. F. 1995 (by Pleasant Tap)

      Bear's Kid B. C. 2003 (by Lemon Drop Kid)

  Cuddles B. F. 1988 (by Mr. Prospector)

    Efficiently B. F. 1993 (by Seattle Slew)

      Dondoca B. F. 2002 (by Cat Thief)

        Machisa Db./Br. C. 2008 (by Safado)

      Driving Rain Db./Br. F. 2005 (by Storm Cat)

        The Absolute One Db./Br. C. 2010 (by Songandaprayer)

    Imaginary Cat B. F. 1995 (by Storm Cat)

      Cause To Believe Gr. C. 2003 (by Maria's Mon)

      Imaginary Sailor Gr. C. 2005 (by Mizzen Mast)

    Katz Me If You Can Db./Br. F. 1997 (by Storm Cat)

      Unkatzable Db./Br. F. 2003 (by A.P. Indy)

        Comfort B. C. 2012 (by Indian Charlie)

    Country Romance Db./Br. F. 2000 (by Saint Ballado)

      Greenwich Db./Br. F. 2009 (by Forestry)

Lord Vancouver Db./Br. C. 2013 (by Teide)

Augusta Springs B. F. 1990 (by Nijinsky II)

Clearwater B. F. 1997 (by Seeking The Gold)

Clear Distinction Db./Br. F. 2003 (by Storm Cat)

Aireofdistinction Db./Br. F. 2010 (by Songandaprayer)

Buffythecenterfold B. F. 2000 (by Capote)

Love Smitten B. F. 1981 (by Key To The Mint)

Alamosa Db./Br. F. 1988 (by Alydar)

Trafalger B. C. 1994 (by Storm Cat)

Etizaaz B. F. 1996 (by Diesis)

Munadaam Ch. C. 2002 (by Aljabr)

Santolina B. F. 1998 (by Boundary)

Swain Db./Br. C. 1992 (by Nashwan)

Water Poet Db./Br. C. 1993 (by Sadler's Wells) *Leading sire in South America*

Thief Of Hearts B. C. 1995 (by In The Wings)

Dancing On A Cloud B. F. 1983 (by Nijinsky II)

Hearts And Clouds B. F. 1989 (by Blushing Groom)

Qualatative Db./Br. F. 1995 (by Woodman)

Rich In Spirit Db./Br. F. 2002 (by Repriced)

Wishing Gate B. F. 2010 (by Indian Charlie)

Summering B. F. 2016 (by War Front)

Dancing On A Slew Db./Br. F. 1992 (by Seattle Slew)

How About Dattt B. F. 2001 (by Souvenir Copy)

City Of Weston Gr. C. 2010 (by Holy Bull)

Hadley B. F. 1995 (by Kingmambo)

Mountain Mambo Ch. F. 2002 (by Mt. Livermore)

Antitrust B. C. 1996 (by Affirmed)

Aerial Ballet B. F. 1997 (by Kingmambo)

Life In Fiction B. F. 2000 (by Whiskey Wisdom)

Shadowless Db./Br. C. 2006 (by Stormy Atlantic)

Miss Nanith B. F. 1971 (by Victoria Park)

Loose Wire Gr. F. 1978 (by Ruritania)

Lucy Scott Gr. F. 1982 (by Duns Scotus)

Scott The Great Gr. C. 1986 (by Great Neck)

Scottish Monk Db./Br. C. 1983 (by Duns Scotus)

Greatly Shocked Gr. F. 1985 (by Great Neck)

Excitabull Trick Db./Br. F. 1998 (by Clever Trick)

Corredor Del Oro Db./Br. C. 2004 (by El Corredor)

Tastetheteardrops B. F. 1989 (by What Luck)

Septem Ch. F. 1994 (by Septieme Ciel)

Demay Ch. F. 2008 (by Dehere)

William And Mary Ch. C. 2015 (by Windsor Castle)

September Charmer B. F. 1995 (by Septieme Ciel)

Five Star Daydream B. F. 2004 (by Five Star Day)

Gas Station Sushi B. F. 2015 (by Into Mischief)

Whitaker B. F. 1998 (by Torrential)

Beacon Falls Db./Br. F. 2004 (by Benton Creek)

Taste Of Paradise Db./Br. C. 1999 (by Conquistador Cielo)

Crafty Tears Db./Br. F. 2001 (by Crafty Friend)

This Cats on Fire Db./Br. F. 2008 (by Fire Blitz)

Taste Sis B. F. 2005 (by Marquetry)

Wire Me Collect Db./Br. C. 1993 (by Clever Trick)

Electric Shock Gr. F. 1996 (by Cure The Blues)

Treetop Shock Gr. F. 2006 (by Forestry)

Shock Hazard B. C. 2011 (by Dunkirk)

Queen of the Empire Gr. F. 2008 (by Empire Maker)

True Emperor Ch. C. 2014 (by Yes It's True)

Fish Trappe Road Gr. C. 2013 (by Trappe Shot)

Clever Electrician B. C. 1999 (by Clever Trick)

Spell Victory Db./Br. F. 1980 (by Dance Spell)

What A Spell Db./Br. C. 1988 (by What Luck)

Susan Powter B. F. 1990 (by Native Prospector)

Miss Lawless B. F. 1994 (by Present Value)

Joey Franco Db./Br. C. 1999 (by Avenue Of Flags)

Maitlin B. F. 1991 (by Cutlass Reality)

Molly's Prospector Db./Br. F. 1994 (by Native Prospector)

Bob Black Jack Db./Br. C. 2005 (by Stormy Jack)

Speed Dial B. C. 1996 (by Phone Trick)

Mimi Baker B. F. 1981 (by What Luck)

Miss Femme Fatale Db./Br. F. 1989 (by Slew O' Gold)

Fatale Attraction B. F. 1994 (by Carson City)

Dancing Angela Gr. F. 1973 (by Dancer's Image)

Bejilla Gr. C. 1977 (by Quadrangle)

Blue Angel's Image Gr. F. 1978 (by Ruritania)

Flyaway Bride Gr. F. 1983 (by Blushing Groom)

Chickaree Gr. F. 1989 (by Sadler's Wells)

Ars Blanca Gr. C. 1999 (by Last Tycoon)

Deep Summer Gr. C. 2002 (by Taiki Shuttle)

Marlene's Days Gr. F. 1985 (by Olden Times)

Devil's Tail Gr. F. 1993 (by Devil's Bag)

Quinian Tiller Gr. C. 2003 (by Dodge)

Blue Daisy Gr. F. 1988 (by Shahrastani)

Bravada Gr. F. 1991 (by Rahy)

Western Brave Db./Br. F. 1997 (by West By West)

Brave Cherokee Db./Br. C. 2002 (by Fabulous Frolic)

Le Danseur B. C. 1979 (by Lord Durham)

Retinue B. F. 1982 (by Vice Regent)

Kirby Meadow B. F. 1991 (by Meadowlake)

Phantom Light Gr. C. 1999 (by Alphabet Soup)

Regal Angela Gr. F. 1995 (by Regal Intention)

Bigger Is Bettor Gr. C. 2008 (by Grand Reward)

Happy Vixen B. F. 1974 (by Quadrangle)

Minutes Away B. C. 1982 (by Just In Time)

Velveteen Db./Br. F. 1983 (by Pirateer)

Warren's Whistle Gr. F. 1998 (by Wolf Power)

GAY MEETING B. F. 1967 by Sir Gaylord-Secret Meeting by Alibhai

Passing Look B. F. 1971 (by Buckpasser)

Look North B. F. 1976 (by Northern Dancer)

Raja's Revenge B. C. 1983 (by Raja Baba)

Shepherd's Moon B. F. 1992 (by Silver Hawk)

Deed I Do Db./Br. F. 1997 (by Alydeed)

War Dancer Db./Br. C. 2010 (by War Front)

Glance Ch. F. 1980 (by Briartic)

I's Right Ch. F. 1987 (by Deputy Minister)

Corporate Vision Ch. F. 1994 (by Corporate Report)

Media Play Ch. C. 2004 (by Alphabet Soup)

National Pride Ch. C. 2005 (by Macho Uno)

Vision In Gold Db./Br. F. 2007 (by Medaglia d'Oro)

Rosie Dooley Ch. F. 1997 (by Trempolino)

Devil's Bag Copy B. C. 2005 (by Devil's Bag)

In My Cap Ch. F. 1982 (by Vice Regent)

In On The Secret Ch. F. 1988 (by Secretariat)

Ask Me No Secrets B. F. 1998 (by Seattle Slew)

Bright Feather B. F. 1989 (by Fappiano)

Watch The Bird B. C. 1995 (by Rahy)

Sheer Bliss B. F. 1996 (by Relaunch)

Albert The Great B. C. 1997 (by Go For Gin)

Sean Bright B. F. 2001 (by Silver Charm)

Utesa B. F. 2008 (by Eddington)

Mo Money Db./Br. C. 2015 (by Caiman)

Marie J B. F. 1995 (by Mr. Prospector)

Autumnal Ch. F. 2003 (by Forestry)

Homecoming Dance Db./Br. F. 2008 (by Vindication)

Empire Line Db./Br. C. 2016 (by Morning Line)

Milam B. F. 2011 (by Street Sense)

Rushing Fall B. F. 2015 (by More Than Ready)

Marie's Rights Db./Br. F. 2005 (by Vindication)

Marie d'Argent B. F. 2014 (by Kendargent)

Alleynedale Ch. F. 1998 (by Unbridled)

James Street B. C. 2007 (by El Prado)

Favorite Feather Db./Br. F. 1999 (by Capote)

Feather Bed Ch. F. 2004 (by Smart Strike)

Dynamic Impact B. C. 2011 (by Tiznow)

Grandma G Ch. F. 1986 (by Vice Regent)

Freecielo Ch. F. 1997 (by Conquistador Cielo)

Lake Secret B. C. 2002 (by Greenwood Lake)

Trumpets Blare B. F. 1987 (by Vice Regent)

Passing Vice B. F. 1990 (by Vice Regent)

Gay Jitterbug B. C. 1973 (by Northern Dancer)

DECEIT Db./Br. F. 1968 by Prince John–Double Agent by Double Jay

Slight Deception Ch. F. 1973 (by Northern Dancer)

Halo Dancer Ch. F. 1978 (by Halo)

Madame Treasurer B. F. 1983 (by Key To The Mint)

Negano Ch. F. 1996 (by Miswaki)

Dasher Go Go B. C. 2007 (by Sakura Bakushin O)

Dasher One Ch. C. 2008 (by French Deputy)

Smart Halo B. F. 1984 (by Smarten)

My Jean Ch. F. 1989 (by Time For A Change)

Term Sheet Db./Br. C. 1998 (by Concern)

Classiest Carat Db./Br. F. 1995 (by Pleasant Colony)

Classiest Gem Db./Br. F. 2000 (by Dehere)

Malagacy Ch. C. 2014 (by Shackleford)

Impossible Time B. F. 2005 (by Not Impossible)

Arctic Mirage Ch. F. 1981 (by Snow Knight)

Kirathimo Db./Br. F. 1987 (by Lear Fan)

Arctic Blossom Db./Br. F. 1993 (by Full Partner)

Kelly's Guest Ch. F. 2001 (by Weekend Guest)

Cool Halo Db./Br. C. 1983 (by Halo)

Emily's Charm B. F. 1984 (by Dom Alaric)

Little Emily Ch. F. 2008 (by Castledale)

Dancing In Seattle Db./Br. F. 1993 (by Seattle Song)

Miss Grindstone Db./Br. F. 1999 (by Grindstone)

Accomplice B. C. 1976 (by Graustark)

Lady Hamilton Ch. F. 1979 (by The Minstrel)

> **Lord Nelson** Db./Br. C. 1997 (by Maudlin)

Nagurski B. C. 1981 (by Nijinsky II)

Deceit Dancer Ch. F. 1982 (by Vice Regent)

Diana Dance Ch. F. 1986 (by Northern Dancer)

Diana's Quest Ch. F. 1992 (by Rainbow Quest)

Duke d'Alba Ch. C. 1997 (by Monsun)

Deva Ch. F. 1999 (by Platini)

Devastar B. C. 2012 (by Areion)

Dragon Fly Ch. C. 2002 (by Acatenango)

Divya Ch. F. 2006 (by Platini)

Dschingis Secret B. C. 2013 (by Soldier Hollow)

Destino B. C. 2015 (by Soldier Hollow)

Deceit Princess B. F. 1990 (by Vice Regent)

Comanche Star Ch. F. 2001 (by Saint Ballado)

Canonize Db./Br. C. 2006 (by Aldebaran)

Declan's Warrior Ch. C. 2010 (by Majestic Warrior)

LOVER'S WALK B. F. 1969 by Never Bend-Honey Lake by Spy Song

Lover's Answer Db./Br. C. 1976 (by Northern Answer)

Lovely Briar B. F. 1977 (by Briartic)

Lovely Dancer Db./Br. F. 1986 (by Mambo)

Mo Faster B. C. 2004 (by Moro Oro)

Our Dani Db./Br. F. 1993 (by Homebuilder)

You Db./Br. F. 1999 (by You And I)

You And I Forever B. C. 2005 (by A.P. Indy)

Causeway's Kin Ch. C. 2006 (by Giant's Causeway)

Saravati Db./Br. F. 2006 (by Giant's Causeway)

Mask Zorro Db./Br. C. 2011 (by Roman Ruler)

Le Promeneur B. C. 1978 (by Tentam)

Greatest Dancer Ch. F. 1980 (by Sevastopol)

Go For Roses Ch. F. 1989 (by Brave Shot)

Regent's Walk Ch. F. 1981 (by Vice Regent)

Marquetry Ch. C. 1987 (by Conquistador Cielo)

Reggie V Ch. F. 1990 (by Vanlandingham)

Margay Ch. F. 1995 (by Conquistador Cielo)

High Finance Ch. C. 2003 (by Talk Is Money)

Five Star Day Ch. C. 1996 (by Carson City)

Rendezvous Point Ch. F. 2001 (by Kingmambo)

Kitten's Point Ch. F. 2010 (by Kitten's Joy)

Spain Lane B. F. 1991 (by Seeking The Gold)

Lover's Talk B. F. 1984 (by Vice Regent)

Lovermore B. F. 1988 (by Commemorate)

Love Call B. F. 2000 (by Don't Forget Me)

Love Grows B. C. 1992 (by Steady Growth)

Barley Talk B. C. 1993 (by Charlie Barley)

Whispered Wishes Gr. F. 1994 (by With Approval)

Starlight Wishes Gr. F. 2000 (by Carson City)

Addy Annie B. F. 2007 (by Posse)

Tin Badge B. C. 2015 (by The Deputy)

Quiet Action Gr. F. 2004 (by Forest Wildcat)

Torrid Affair Db./Br. F. 1997 (by Alydeed)

Seductively B. F. 2003 (by Thunder Gulch)

Wild Whiskey Db./Br. C. 1999 (by Whiskey Wisdom)

SHAKE A LEG B. F. 1970 by Raise A Native-Fleeting Doll by Fleet Nasrullah

Vaguely Modest B. F. 1976 (by Vaguely Noble)

Danarani B. F. 1991 (by Danehill)

Zahani B. F. 2001 (by Zabeel)

Galizani B. F. 2006 (by Galileo)

Danzatore B. C. 1980 (by Northern Dancer)

Nadia Nerina B. F. 1981 (by Northern Dancer)

Zorina B. F. 1991 (by Shirley Heights)

Zaza Top Ch. F. 1998 (by Lomitas)

Zazou B. C. 2007 (by Shamardal)

SEX APPEAL Ch. F. 1970 by Buckpasser-Best In Show by Traffic Judge

  Try My Best B. C. 1975 (by Northern Dancer)

  Solar Ch. F. 1976 (by Halo)

    Solariat Ch. F. 1980 (by Secretariat)

      Alex Nureyev B. C. 1983 (by Nureyev)

      Angelina Ballerina Ch. F. 1985 (by Nureyev)

        Angelina Carolina Ch. F. 1986 (by Kris)

        Alamagna B. F. 2005 (by Anabaa)

          Way Back B. C. 2015 (by Motivator)

      Sexy Slew B. F. 1986 (by Slew O' Gold)

        Main Edition Ch. F. 1992 (by Nureyev)

          Platinum Ballet Gr. F. 2001 (by Skip Away)

      Margot Ch. F. 1991 (by Nijinsky II)

        Queen Mambo B. F. 1995 (by Kingmambo)

          Queen Tango Ch. F. 2000 (by Lode)

            Que Felicidad B. F. 2004 (by Bernstein)

              Quiet Brazilian B. C. 2014 (by Catcher In The Rye)

            Que Vida Buena B. C. 2005 (by Bernstein)

            Que Clase B. F. 2008 (by Bernstein)

            Que Bella Noche Ch. F. 2010 (by Giant's Causeway)

          Queen Of Time Db./Br. F. 2007 (by Orpen)

          Quick Mambo Ch. C. 2010 (by Giant's Causeway)

    Energie Solaire B. F. 1982 (by Alleged)

      Sea Exhibition B. F. 1990 (by Tate Gallery)

        Mar Hondo B. C. 2000 (by Hussonet)

    Love From The Air Ch. F. 1986 (by Deputy Minister)

      Takeawakatlove Ch. C. 1991 (by Miswaki)

      Westwood Ch. F. 1992 (by Storm Bird)

        Clapton Ch. C. 1996 (by Fly So Free)

    Shining Through Ch. F. 1989 (by Deputy Minister)

      Bahamian Pirate Ch. C. 1995 (by Housebuster)

      Strong Hope B. C. 2000 (by Grand Slam)

      Fondness B. F. 2006 (by Elusive Quality)

Discreetness B. C. 2013 (by Discreet Cat)

Fayrooz B. F. 1991 (by Gulch)

Beryl Ch. F. 1996 (by Bering)

Vauquelin B. C. 2004 (by Xaar)

Classic Colori Ch. C. 2007 (by Le Vie Dei Colori)

Apex Princess Db./Br. F. 1995 (by Deputy Minister)

Oklawaha B. F. 2001 (by Carson City)

Steel Cut Db./Br. F. 2011 (by Cactus Ridge)

Waha Wild Db./Br. C. 2012 (by Offlee Wild)

Northern Guest B. C. 1977 (by Northern Dancer) *13 times leading sire in South Africa*

Carillon Miss Ch. F. 1979 (by The Minstrel)

Try My Segnor B. C. 1993 (by Tirol)

Blu Carillon Ch. C. 1995 (by Love The Groom)

Blu Air Force B. C. 1997 (by Sri Pekan)

Blu Air Gun Ch. C. 1998 (by Spectrum)

Northern Prancer B. F. 1980 (by Northern Dancer)

Chisme Db./Br. F. 1984 (by Secretariat)

Iniki Ch. F. 1990 (by Miswaki)

Entepreneur B. C. 1997 (by Cure The Blues)

Cartagena Db./Br. F. 1987 (by Secretariat)

Cartakris Db./Br. F. 1992 (by Kris)

Roman Romance Ch. F. 1998 (by San Romano)

Sensational Slam Ch. C. 2008 (by Grand Slam)

Tandra Gee Db./Br. F. 1988 (by Commemorate)

Biru Lang B. F. 1996 (by Pine Bluff)

Joku Br. C. 2004 (by Xaar)

Tijuana Tango Ch. F. 1993 (by Tejano)

Jarama Ch. F. 2000 (by Hector Protector)

Chinchon B. C. 2005 (by Marju)

El Gran Senor B. C. 1981 (by Northern Dancer)

Golden Oriole Ch. F. 1983 (by Northern Dancer)

Sunny Morning B. F. 1987 (by Law Society)

Shirokita Cross B. C. 1993 (by Tamano Cross)

Castle Gandolfo Ch. C. 1999 (by Gone West)

Ailesbury Hill Ch. F. 1993 (by Woodman)

Sultry Girl Blk. F. 2003 (by Special Week)

Rhein Ruf Ch. C. 2012 (by French Deputy)

Dance Fever Db./Br. F. 2002 (by Fusaichi Pegasus)

Estrela Monarchos Gr. F. 2010 (by Monarchos)

Sense Of Class Db./Br. F. 2003 (by Fusaichi Pegasus)

The Sense Angel Db./Br. F. 2008 (by Mineshaft)

Analyze The Odds Ch. C. 2015 (by Overanalyze)

Bella Senora B. F. 1984 (by Northern Dancer)

Darros B. C. 1989 (by Baillamont)

Napoli B. F. 1991 (by Baillamont)

Domedriver Db./Br. C. 1998 (by Indian Ridge)

Tau Ceti B. C. 1999 (by Hernando)

Russian Ballet Ch. F. 1988 (by Nijinsky II)

Dr. Johnson Ch. C. 1994 (by Woodman)

Ballette Ch. F. 2002 (by Giant's Causeway)

Cerro Ch. C. 2010 (by Mr. Greeley)

Lotta Lace Ch. F. 1992 (by Nureyev)

Fusaichi Pandora Ch. F. 2003 (by Sunday Silence)

Almond Eye B. F. 2015 (by Lord Kanaloa)

NOBLE FANCY B. F. 1971 by Vaguely Noble-Amerigo's Fancy by Amerigo

Katsura Ch. F. 1977 (by Northern Dancer)

Rambushka B. F. 1986 (by Roberto)

Tugela Db./Br. F. 1995 (by Riverman)

Makybe Diva B. F. 1999 (by Desert King)

Valkyrie Diva Db./Br. F. 2001 (by Jade Robbery)

Wales B. C. 2009 (by Redoute's Choice)

Musket B. C. 2003 (by Redoute's Choice)

La Amistad B. F. 2009 (by Redoute's Choice)

Ranales B. F. 1990 (by Majestic Light)

Fame At Last Db./Br. F. 1997 (by Quest For Fame)

Famous Name B. C. 2005 (by Dansili)

Renown Ch. C. 2011 (by Champs Elysees)

Discipline B. F. 2013 (by Dansili)

Regent's Fancy B. F. 1987 (by Vice Regent)

Pete's Fancy B. F. 1995 (by Peteski)

Tres Borrachos B. C. 2005 (by Ecton Park)

Chinglish Db./Br. C. 2008 (by War Front)

Byzantine B. F. 1996 (by Quiet American)

Roses 'N' Wine Ch. F. 2005 (by Broken Vow)

Hampton Court B. C. 2011 (by Redoute's Choice)

BALLADE Db./Br. F. 1972 by Herbager-Miss Swapsco by Cohoes

Glorious Song B. F. 1976 (by Halo)

Rahy Ch. C. 1985 (by Blushing Groom)

Rakeen B. C. 1987 (by Northern Dancer)

Morn Of Song B. F. 1988 (by Blushing Groom)

Halwa Song Ch. F. 1996 (by Nureyev)

Halwa Sweet Ch. F. 2001 (by Machiavellian)

Verxina Blk. F. 2009 (by Deep Impact)

Cheval Grand Ch. C. 2012 (by Heart's Cry)

Vivlos Blk. F. 2013 (by Deep Impact)

Frere Jacques B. C. 2008 (by Deep Impact)

Martinborough Db./Br. C. 2009 (by Deep Impact)

Mezzo Soprano B. F. 2000 (by Darshaan)

Claremont B. C. 2006 (by Sadler's Wells)

Perfect Note B. F. 2007 (by Shamardal)

Strathspey B. F. 2014 (by New Approach)

Emirates To Dubai Ch. C. 2003 (by Storm Cat)

Singspiel B. C. 1992 (by In The Wings)

Ring Of Music B. F. 1993 (by Sadler's Wells)

Dubai Soprano B. F. 1999 (by Zafonic)

Isobel Baillie Ch. F. 2003 (by Lomitas)

Alaura Michele Db./Br. F. 2009 (by Arch)

Isabella Sings Ch. F. 2012 (by Eskendereya)

Tobacco Road B. C. 2016 (by Quality Road)

Marine Winner Ch. F. 2005 (by Fuji Kiseki)

White Fugue Gr. F. 2012 (by Kirofune)

Armilla B. F. 2000 (by Rainbow Quest)

Paeroa B. F. 2006 (by Dubai Destination)

Ability B. C. 2012 (by Reward For Effort)

Well Rounded Db./Br. F. 2006 (by Reset)

Peace Bell B. F. 2004 (by Kingmambo)

One Fine Day B. F. 2011 (by Trippi)

Campanologist B. C. 2005 (by Kingmambo)

Devil's Bag Db./Br. C. 1981 (by Halo)

Thaidah B. F. 1985 (by Vice Regent)

Tawaaded Ch. F. 1993 (by Nashwan)

Shakis B. C. 2000 (by Machiavellian)

Irtifa Ch. F. 1994 (by Lahib)

Sayuri B. F. 1999 (by Sadler's Wells)

Ocean And Beyond B. C. 2007 (by Kingsala)

With Certainty Db./Br. F. 2000 (by Broad Brush)

Certainly Special B. F. 2005 (by Distorted Humor)

Crysta's Court B. F. 2010 (by Silent Name)

Coltimus Prime Db./Br. C. 2011 (by Milwaukee Brew)

Andrea Dora Ch. F. 1998 (by Lion Cavern)

Countess Andora Ch. F. 2002 (by Count Dubois)

Pacific Breeze B. F. 2008 (by Lithuanian)

Nosferatu Ch. C. 1986 (by Vice Regent) *9 times leading sire in Barbados*

Angelic Song B. F. 1988 (by Halo)

Divorce Testimony Ch. F. 1992 (by Vice Regent)

Fusaichi Seven B. C. 2006 (by Fusaichi Pegasus)

Macarena Macarena B. F. 1994 (by Gone West)

Yuzuru B. F. 2010 (by Medaglia d'Oro)

Geriba Db./Br. F. 1995 (by Gone West)

Grand Rousse Gr. F. 2004 (by Act One)

Light In Paris B. F. 2012 (by Aussie Rules)

Lady Ballade Db./Br. F. 1997 (by Unbridled)

    Danon Ballade Db./Br. C. 2008 (by Deep Impact)

Sligo Bay B. C. 1998 (by Sadler's Wells)

Wolf Tone B. C. 2001 (by Sadler's Wells)

Millennium Wing B. C. 2003 (by Sadler's Wells)

Ydillique B. F. 2005 (by Sadler's Wells)

    Tristesse B. F. 2011 (by Broken Vow)

Saint Ballado Blk./Br. C. 1989 (by Halo) *Leading sire in North America*

THE TEMPTRESS B. F. 1973 by Nijinsky II–La Sevillana by Court Harwell

Sword Ballet B. F. 1979 (by Damascus)

    Bayonet B. C. 1996 (by Wallenda)

La Lorgnette B. F. 1982 (by Val de l'Orne)

    Alexandrina B. F. 1987 (by Conquistador Cielo)

        Alexandrovna B. F. 1993 (by Lear Fan)

            Caucus B. F. 2000 (by General Meeting)

                Lady Candidate Ch. F. 2009 (by Bob And John)

        Thornfield Ch. C. 1994 (by Sky Classic)

        Pantaccaria Ch. F. 1998 (by San Romano)

            Nicki Knew B. F. 2005 (by Tethra)

                Imperial Dream Db./Br. C. 2012 (by Stormy Atlantic)

Halo My Darlin Ch. F. 1989 (by Halo)

    Oakley's Song B. F. 1999 (by Bertrando)

        Nechako Db./Br. C. 2004 (by Vying Victor)

        Chela Ch. F. 2005 (by Vying Victor)

Hawk Wing B. C. 1999 (by Woodman)

Race For The Stars B. F. 2003 (by Fusaichi Pegasus)

    Sir John Lavery B. C. 2014 (by Galileo)

Schonbrunn B. F. 1989 (by Val de l'Orne)

    La Habitant Time Ch. F. 1994 (by Iskandar Elakbar)

    Nymphenburg B. F. 1996 (by San Romano)

    Marie Louise B. F. 2007 (by Theatrical)

        Star Galcia B. F. 2015 (by Jimmy Creed)

PACIFIC PRINCESS B. F. 1973 by Damascus-Fiji by Acropolis

Pacificus B. F. 1981 (by Northern Dancer)

Biwa Hayahide Gr. C. 1990 (by Sharood)

Narita Brian Db./Br. C. 1991 (by Brian's Time)

Biwa Takahide B. C. 1995 (by Brian's Time)

Superior Pearl B. F. 1998 (by Timber Country)

Last Impact Db./Br. C. 2010 (by Deep Impact)

Catequil B. F. 1990 (by Storm Cat)

Phalaenopsis Db./Br. F. 1995 (by Brian's Time)

Sunday Break B. C. 1999 (by Forty Niner)

Kizuna Blk. C. 2010 (by Deep Impact)

NORTHERN SEA B. F. 1974 by Northern Dancer-Sea Saga by Sea-Bird

Southern Halo B. C. 1983 (by Halo) *10 times leading sire in South America*

Excellent Lady Db./Br. F. 1986 (by Smarten)

General Challenge Ch. C. 1996 (by General Meeting)

Jeweled Lady B. F. 1997 (by General Meeting)

Jewel Of The Night Ch. F. 2002 (by Giant's Causeway)

Evening Jewel B. F. 2007 (by Northern Afleet)

Maggie McGowan Db./Br. F. 2008 (by Salt Lake)

Denman's Call Ch. C. 2013 (by Northern Afleet)

Black Valentine Blk. F. 2009 (by Cindago)

Roos Valentine Db./Br. F. 2013 (by Vronsky)

Deep Jewelry B. F. 2012 (by Deep Impact)

Petition The Lady Ch. F. 2005 (by Petionville)

Saucy Evening Ch. F. 2006 (by More Than Ready)

Notable Career Db./Br. F. 1998 (by Avenue Of Flags)

Western Hemisphere Ch. F. 2001 (by General Meeting)

Galactic Princess Db./Br. F. 2014 (by Ready's Image)

Northern Pageant Ro. F. 1987 (by Spectacular Bid)

Pageant Princess B. F. 1992 (by Silver Deputy)

Panacea B. F. 2001 (by Luhuk)

Panegirico B. C. 2007 (by Russian Blue)

Snow Dance Gr. F. 1998 (by Forest Wildcat)

From Scratch Db./Br. F. 2005 (by Grand Slam)

Wish Happiness Db./Br. F. 2011 (by Gold Allure)

Most Remakable Gr. F. 1999 (by Marquetry)

Remarkable Remy Db./Br. F. 2005 (by Hennessy)

Keiai Leone Gr. C. 2010 (by Henny Hughes)

Elsie Jay Gr. F. 2003 (by Giant's Causeway)

Northern Eclipse Db./Br. F. 2012 (by Northern Afleet)

SWEET ALLIANCE B. F. 1974 by Sir Ivor-Mrs. Peterkin by Tom Fool

Shareef Dancer B. C. 1980 (by Northern Dancer)

War Deputy Db./Br. C. 1991 (by Deputy Minister)

COUNTRY ROMANCE Ch. F. 1976 by Halo-Sweet Romance by Gun Bow

Firey Affair Ch. F. 1984 (by Explodent)

Swearingen B. F. 1994 (by Deposit Ticket)

Prettyatthetable B. F. 2003 (by Point Given)

Pomeroy's Pistol B. F. 2008 (by Pomeroy)

I'm Classic Quality B. F. 2004 (by Elusive Quality)

Toowindytohaulrox B. C. 2011 (by Harlan's Holiday)

Sugah B. F. 1995 (by Procida)

Obi Wan Kenobi Db./Br. C. 2003 (by Skywalker)

Romanticat Gr. F. 1987 (by Gato Del Sol)

Things Change Gr. F. 1996 (by Stalwart)

Dinner Break Db./Br. F. 2004 (by Tale Of The Cat)

Harlan Db./Br. C. 1989 (by Storm Cat)

BETTY'S SECRET Ch. F. 1977 by Secretariat-Betty Loraine by Prince John

Secreto B. C. 1981 (by Northern Dancer)

Catopetl B. F. 1982 (by Northern Dancer)

Newton's Law Db./Br. C. 1990 (by Law Society)

Close Conflict B. C. 1991 (by High Estate)

From Sea To Sea Db./Br. F. 1983 (by Gregorian)

Cape Fire Gr. F. 1990 (by Relaunch)

Border Fire Gr. F. 1997 (by Boundary)

Takin The Bullet Gr. C. 2005 (by Red Bullet)

Dancing Viking B. F. 1991 (by Nureyev)

Clever Cloggs Ch. F. 2000 (by Woodman)

Carbonel B. C. 2006 (by Black Minnaloushe)

Sealaunch Gr. C. 1993 (by Relaunch)

Fluid Move B. F. 1994 (by Nureyev)

Catch The Moment B. F. 2001 (by Unbridled)

Smooth Roller B. C. 2011 (by Hard Spun)

Hear The Sea B. F. 1995 (by Dixieland Band)

Absolute Nectar Ch. F. 2001 (by Carson City)

California Nectar B. F. 2009 (by Stormy Atlantic)

Redstart B. F. 2012 (by Blame)

Interrex Ch. C. 1984 (by Vice Regent)

Istabraq B. C. 1992 (by Sadler's Wells)

STREET BALLET B. F. 1977 by Nijinsky II–Street Dancer by Native Dancer

Arbela Db./Br. F. 1985 (by Conquistador Cielo)

Apelia Db./Br. F. 1989 (by Cool Victor)

Saoirse B. F. 1996 (by Cure The Blues)

Hide And Chic B. F. 2002 (by Seeking The Gold)

Autobahn Girl Ch. F. 2004 (by A.P. Indy)

More Happy Db./Br. F. 2005 (by Vindication)

Camlan B. F. 1991 (by Brave Shot)

Slabovia Db./Br. F. 1995 (by Cool Victor)

Explicitly Db./Br. F. 2001 (by Exploit)

Gallant Son Db./Br. C. 2006 (by Malabar Gold)

Street Rebel B. C. 1988 (by Robellino)

Ponche Gr. C. 1989 (by Two Punch)

Come Dancing Gr. F. 1991 (by Two Punch)

Brush Hour Db./Br. F. 2000 (by Broad Brush)

Thethiefatmidnight B. F. 2005 (by Cat Thief)

Brushed By A Star B. F. 2008 (by Eddington)

Street Tapin B. F. 1995 (by Housebuster)

Bossanova Db./Br. C. 2000 (by Pine Bluff)

Fleetstreet Dancer Db./Br. C. 1998 (by Smart Strike)

TRULY BOUND B. F. 1978 by In Reality-Natashka by Dedicate

Bound To Dance B. F. 1986 (by Northern Dancer)

Silk Prima Donna B. F. 1997 (by Brian's Time)

Grand Prix Blood B. C. 2009 (by Deep Impact)

Flamme de Gloire Ch. C. 2010 (by Daiwa Major)

Moere Admiral Ch. C. 2002 (by Brain's Time)

Secret Truth Ch. F. 1989 (by Secretariat)

Pleasant Secret Ch. C. 1997 (by Pleasant Tap)

Secret Cause Ch. F. 2003 (by Giant's Causeway)

Escado B. C. 2009 (by Casino Prince)

Se Sauver B. F. 2010 (by Bel Esprit)

Housebound B. C. 1991 (by Pancho Villa)

Shell Ginger Ch. F. 1994 (by Woodman)

Clarins Ch. F. 2001 (by Storm Cat)

Pumpkin Rumble Ch. C. 2011 (by English Channel)

Yeoman's Point B. C. 1996 (by Sadler's Wells)

VADSA B. F. 1979 by Halo-Rainbow's Edge by Crème DeLa Crème

Vadlava Db./Br. F. 1984 (by Bikala)

Vadlawys Db./Br. C. 1991 (by Always Fair)

Vadlamixa Gr. F. 1992 (by Linamix)

Vadaza B. F. 1997 (by Zafonic)

Vadawina B. F. 2002 (by Unfuwain)

Vadamar Gr. C. 2008 (by Dalakhani)

Vedouma B. F. 2012 (by Dalakhani)

The Pentagon B.C. 2015 (by Galileo)

Vadapolina Ch. F. 2004 (by Trempolino)

Vadsalina Db./Br. F. 2005 (by Sagacity)

Vazira Db./Br. F. 2011 (by Sea The Stars)

Valixir B. C. 2001 (by Trempolino)

Celebre Vadala B. F. 2003 (by Peintre Celebre)

Celenza B. F. 2008 (by Dansili)

Tornibush B. C. 2014 (by Dream Ahead)

Vadamos B. C. 2011 (by Monsun)

Vadlawysa B. F. 1995 (by Always Fair)

Valima Gr. F. 2002 (by Linamix)

Valasyra B. F. 2007 (by Sinndar)

Valiyr B. C. 2008 (by Alhaarth)

Valyra B. F. 2009 (by Azamour)

Valirann B. C. 2010 (by Nayef)

Val Royal B. C. 1996 (by Royal Academy)

Grand Vadla B. F. 2003 (by Grand Lodge)

Vagrancy B. C. 1987 (by Bikala)

Vadsagreya Gr. F. 1992 (by Linamix)

Spinamix Gr. F. 1999 (by Spinning World)

San Sicharia Ch. F. 2005 (by Daggers Drawn)

Spin Cycle B. C. 2006 (by Exceed And Excel)

Tucuman B. C. 2008 (by Hawk Wing)

Spinacre Gr. F. 2010 (by Verglas)

Vadsa Honor Gr. F. 1993 (by Highest Honor)

Vahorimix Gr. C. 1998 (by Linamix)

Kiddy Sing Gr. C. 2000 (by Linamix)

Vadorga B. F. 2002 (by Grand Lodge)

Voleuse de Coeurs B. F. 2009 (by Teofilo)

ABOUT THE AUTHORS

COLIN NOLTE IS a writer and lifelong follower of Thorough-bred racing and breeding. He currently owns and operates his successful website "Thoroughbred Racing Ancestry," which contains hundreds of articles about many of the great racehorses and breed-shaping Thoroughbreds in the long history of the sport. Colin has also contributed writing and research material for Woodbine Racetrack and Thoroughbred Racing Commentary websites, and he is well known as a Thoroughbred pedigree expert and racing historian.

MICHAEL ARMSTRONG IS also a lifelong Thoroughbred fan and has his own website "Northernerdancing," in which he tracks the latest descendants of Windfields breeding found within the pedigrees of today's rising stars in racing. Michael has published a personal book titled *Stable in Bedlam* and is recognized for his knowledge pertaining to Windfields Farm breeding. He has been identified as the "Archivist of Windfields" by many of the surviving Windfields alumni due to his enthusiastic knowledge of the farm's breeding achievements.

www.ingramcontent.com/pod-product-compliance
Lightning Source LLC
Chambersburg PA
CBHW020857060726
47591CB00004B/985